THE NEOCONSERVATIVE
THREAT TO WORLD ORDER

THE
NEOCONSERVATIVE
THREAT
TO
WORLD ORDER

WASHINGTON'S PERILOUS WAR
FOR HEGEMONY

PAUL CRAIG ROBERTS

CLARITY PRESS, INC.

In-house editor: Diana G. Collier
Cover: R. Jordan P. Santos

Library of Congress Cataloging-in-Publication Data

Roberts, Paul Craig.
  The neoconservative threat to world order : America's perilous war for
hegemony / by Paul Craig Roberts.
     pages cm
  Includes bibliographical references and index.
   ISBN 978-0-9860769-9-2 (alk. paper) -- ISBN 978-0-9860853-0-7
(Ebook)
1. United States--Foreign relations--2009- 2. Hegemony--United
States. 3. Conservatism--United States. 4. United States--Foreign
relations--Ukraine. 5. Ukraine--Foreign relations--United States.
6. United States--Foreign relations--Russia (Federation) 7. Russia
(Federation)--Foreign relations--United States. I. Title.

  E895.R625 2015
  327.73009'05--dc23

                                    2015022018

Clarity Press, Inc.
2625 Piedmont Rd. NE, Suite 56
Atlanta, GA. 30324
http://www.claritypress.com

TABLE OF CONTENTS

To my readers

To my readers

FOREWORD

This book deals with events from February, 2014 through the summer of 2015. This period encompasses the Obama regime's overthrow of the democratically elected government in Ukraine and establishment of a vassal state. Events have developed as I expected. Russia has been alienated from the West and declared to be a threat. Ukraine has undergone dismemberment and economic chaos. Washington's European vassals have suffered from the sanctions that Washington forced Europe to impose on Russia. The compliance of Europe with Washington's will is being tested as ·Europeans realize that Washington has forced Europe into conflict with Russia.

Washington's recklessly aggressive actions toward Russia have made China realize that China faces the same threat from American hegemony. Consequently, China and Russia have formed an economic and military alliance that is altering the correlation of forces. Washington's credibility and that of the presstitute media diminishes as Washington increasingly relies on lies to cloak its agenda and to cover up its mistakes. The events during this period are leading the world to war or to the breakup of Washington's empire.

Among its contributions this book comprises an important historical record of the development of events in Ukraine in view of the propagandistic misreporting by the Western media. In pursuit of its hegemonic agenda, Washington has poisoned American-Russian relations and European-Russian relations and perhaps in the end American-European relations. Washington can purchase European politicians but not the European peoples who will be among those who suffer from the ruined relationship with Russia. Sooner or later every population on earth, if not the purchased politicians, will realize that Washington's agenda is diametrically opposed to their interests.

It is an irony of history that the collapse of the Soviet Union has increased the likelihood of nuclear war.

The Soviet collapse in 1991 gave rise to the neoconservative doctrine of US world hegemony. This doctrine became the basis for US foreign and military policy. The doctrine proclaims "the end of history," by which is meant that there is no viable alternative to "American democratic capitalism." In effect, History has chosen American capitalists, and not the proletariat.

The neoconservative doctrine has many implications. It defines the United States as the "indispensable, exceptional" country above all others with the right to exercise hegemony over the world in order to bring the world into line with History's choice of American democratic capitalism as the final socio-economic political system. American superiority is also superiority over, or immunity to, international law as there can be no constraints on Washington's unilateral action as History's chosen Uni-power.

To guard against History having second thoughts, the neo-conservatives established the "first objective" of US foreign and military policy to be "to prevent the re-emergence of a new rival, either on the territory of the former Soviet Union or elsewhere, that poses a threat [to US unilateral action] on the order of that posed formerly by the Soviet Union. This is a dominant consideration underlying the new regional defense strategy and requires that we endeavor to prevent any hostile power from dominating a region whose resources would, under consolidated control, be sufficient to generate global power." A "hostile power" is a country sufficiently strong to have a foreign policy independent from Washington's.

This doctrine is known as the Wolfowitz Doctrine. It was written in 1992 by Undersecretary of Defense Paul Wolfowitz. As the language reeked of American imperialism, the document was rewritten in more diplomatic terms but without changing the content.

Once in place the Wolfowitz Doctrine resulted in the Clinton regime abandoning the guarantees that the George H. W. Bush administration had given to Gorbachev that NATO would not move one inch to the East. In violation of the US government's word, former Warsaw Bloc countries were incorporated into NATO. Then NATO was used to attack Yugoslavia and Serbia. Then the George W. Bush regime withdrew the US from the Anti-Ballistic Missile Treaty and began locating anti-ballistic missile bases on Russia's borders. Washington orchestrated "color revolutions" in the former Russian provinces of Georgia and Ukraine. When the Orange Revolution failed to deliver Ukraine into Washington's hands, Washington spent $5 billion cultivating Ukrainian politicians and creating pro-American Non-Governmental Organizations (NGOs) that were used in Washington's 2014 overthrow of the elected government of Ukraine.

Washington has used the coup it orchestrated to damage Europe's economic and political relationships with Russia. By forcing its EU vassal states to go along with sanctions against Russia based on lies that Russia invaded Ukraine, Washington has forced Europe into a conflict situation with Russia.

Moreover, Washington's plans to incorporate Ukraine into NATO and to establish US/NATO military bases in Ukraine are unacceptable to the Russian government. From all indications, Washington intends further "color revolutions" in Armenia, Kyrgyzstan, and, perhaps, Belarus. These are hostile actions against Russia, the purpose of which is to increase the difficulties that Russia faces, leaving it too distracted to interfere with Washington's unilateralism.

It is irresponsible to threaten a well-armed nuclear power such as Russia, and even more irresponsible when Russia is allied with China, another nuclear power. During the long Cold War every effort was made to contain and limit the use of nuclear weapons, which were assigned the role of retaliation in the event of a nuclear attack. The doctrine, Mutually Assured Destruction, gave nuclear weapons only a retaliatory role. The George W. Bush regime changed this and introduced the wild card of pre-emptive nuclear attack. The Bush regime rewrote US war doctrine and elevated nuclear weapons to a pre-emptive first-strike role. This irresponsible action has cost Washington very little in terms of protests by any country other than Russia.

By accepting and participating in Washington's 21st century aggressions—war crimes under international law—in the Middle East and Africa, Europeans have made war with Russia more likely. By endorsing Washington's lawlessness, Europeans have helped the neoconservative warmongers create a monster that is capable of launching nuclear Armageddon as a way of securing Washington's hegemony.

In order to save the face of Washington's European, Canadian, Australian, and Japanese vassals, Washington calls its vassals "allies," which implies an independence that these countries do not have. If the world is to be saved from Washington's aggression and nuclear war, the vassals must transform themselves into allies, serve their own peoples with a peaceful policy, not Washington with a war policy, and confront Washington with opposition to yet more war and more dangerous war. The hope for mankind is that Europeans cease to aid and abet American aggression.

NATO needs to be disbanded. NATO's original purpose no longer exists. NATO should have disappeared with the Soviet Union and the Warsaw Pact. Instead, NATO has been turned into a cover for Washington's aggression that, if undertaken alone, would be denounced as a war crime, but when undertaken in consort with other countries can be misrepresented as a "war on terror" or justified as "bringing democracy" to a country by overthrowing a dictator. The cowardice of European politicians has made Europe complicit in Washington's crimes against humanity and resurrected the specter of nuclear war.

Possibly NATO's demise might result from the EU policy of looting its own member states, such as Ireland, Greece, Italy, and Spain. Greece cannot pay the full value of its debt. The austerity imposed on Greece has driven the economy down, thus making it even more impossible to pay the debts. Instead of helping Greece, the EU is helping Wall Street and speculators, who have bought up the Greek debt at pennies on the dollar, seeking to make enormous profits by forcing Greece to pay the full face value of its bonds, not to creditors but to speculators.

If the Greek government has courage and vision, the government will default on the bonds and turn, debt free, to Russia for financing. This would begin the stampede to do likewise, as Italy and Spain are in the same fix as Greece and face being looted and driven into poverty for the sake of the profits of Wall Street and the banks.

Unless European politicians wake up and realize that the real threat that they face is war with Russia, not the impaired balance sheets of the German and Netherlands banks, they are going to be driven to their destruction by the crazed American neoconservatives.

In the process of editing these essays, the decision was made to accept some repetition. The repetition might annoy those who read this collection as a book. To these readers I apologize for the repetition. On the other hand, the repetition serves to preserve the independence of each essay, thus enabling other readers to use the book as a collection of essays on the topic of the neoconservative threat to international order.

WASHINGTON
DESTABILIZES UKRAINE

February 6, 2014

The control freaks in Washington think that only the decisions that Washington makes and imposes on other sovereign countries are democratic. No other country on earth is capable of making a democratic decision.

The world has witnessed this American self-righteousness for eons as Washington overthrows one democratic government after the other and imposes its puppets, as Washington did in Iran in 1953 when the CIA, as it now admits, and as Ervand Abrahamian proves in his book *The Coup* (The New Press, 2013), overthrew the elected government of Mossadeq, and more recently the elected government of Honduras and many governments in between.

Currently Washington is working overtime to overthrow the governments of Syria, Iran (again), and Ukraine. Washington has also targeted Venezuela, Bolivia, Ecuador, Argentina, and Brazil, and in its wildest dreams, the governments of Russia and China.

On January 26 Syrian government advisor Bouthaina Shaaban asked Wolf Blitzer, a propagandist for Washington and the Israel Lobby, on mainstream US TV why the US government, speaking through Secretary of State John Kerry, has the right to decide who is to be the government of Syria instead of the Syrian people. [Polls show that Syrian president Assad's approval ratings exceed those of every Western leader.] Even the slimy Blitzer wasn't slimy enough to answer, "Because we are the exceptional, indispensable people." But that's what Washington thinks.

Washington will soon be back at work destabilizing the government of Iran, a habit I suppose, but for the moment Washington is focused on destabilizing Ukraine.

Ukraine has a democratically elected government, but Washington doesn't like it because Washington didn't pick it. The Ukraine, or the western part of it, is full of Washington-funded NGOs whose purpose is to deliver Ukraine into the clutches of the EU where US and European banks can loot the country, as they looted, for example, Latvia, and simultaneously weaken Russia by stealing a large part of traditional Russia and converting it into US/ NATO military bases against Russia.

Perhaps Putin, an athlete, is distracted by the Olympic Games in Russia. Otherwise, it is something of a puzzle why Russia hasn't put its nuclear missiles on high alert and occupied the western Ukraine with troops in order to prevent Ukraine's overthrow by Washington's money. Every country has citizens that will sell out their country for money, and western Ukraine is overflowing with such traitors.

As we have seen for decades, Washington can find Arabs and Muslims who will sell out their people for Western money: they depose or kill the others. So it will be with western Ukrainians. The NGOs financed by Washington are committed to delivering Ukraine into Washington's hands to become American serfs and this integral part of Russia can become a staging ground for the US military.

Of all the violent protests that we have witnessed, the Ukrainian one is the most orchestrated.

On February 6, *Zero Hedge*, one of the intelligent and informed Internet sites, posted a leaked recording from the despicable Victoria Nuland, an Assistant Secretary of State in the Obama Regime. Nuland is caught discussing with the US envoy to Ukraine, Geoffrey Pyatt, Washington's choice for who will head the next Ukrainian government.

Nuland is incensed that the European Union has not joined Washington in imposing sanctions on the Ukrainian government in order to complete Washington's takeover of Ukraine. Nuland speaks as if she is God with the God-given right to select the government of Ukraine, which she proceeds to do.

The EU, as corrupted as it is by Washington's money, nevertheless understands being made rich by Washington is no protection against Russian nuclear missiles. Nuland's response to Europe's hesitancy to risk its existence for the benefit of US hegemony is: "Fuck the EU."

So much for Washington's attitude toward its captive allies and the peoples of the world.

WASHINGTON ORCHESTRATES PROTESTS IN UKRAINE

February 12, 2014

The protests in the western Ukraine are organized by the CIA, the US State Department, and by Washington- and EU-financed Non-Governmental Organizations (NGOs) that work in conjunction with the CIA and State Department. The purpose of the protests is to overturn the decision by the independent government of Ukraine not to join the EU.

The US and EU were initially cooperating in the effort to destroy the independence of Ukraine and make it a subservient entity to the EU government in Brussels. For the EU government, the goal is to expand the EU. For Washington the purposes are to make Ukraine available for looting by US banks and corporations and to bring Ukraine into NATO so that Washington can gain more military bases on Russia's frontier. There are three countries in the world that are in the way of Washington's hegemony over the world–Russia, China, and Iran. Each of these countries is targeted by Washington for overthrow or for their sovereignty to be degraded by propaganda and US military bases that leave the countries vulnerable to attack, thus coercing them into accepting Washington's will.

The problem that has arisen between the US and EU with regard to Ukraine is that Europeans are concerned that the takeover of Ukraine is a direct threat to Russia, which can cut Europe off from oil and natural gas, and if there is war, can completely destroy Europe. Consequently, the EU is having second thoughts about provoking the Ukraine protests.

The response of the neoconservative, Victoria Nuland, appointed Assistant Secretary of State by the duplicitous Obama, was "fuck the EU." She proceeded to name the members of the Ukraine government that Washington imposed on a people so unaware as to believe that they are achieving independence by rushing into Washington's arms. I once thought that no population could be as unaware as the US population. But I was wrong. Western Ukrainians are more unaware than Americans.

The orchestration of the "crisis" in Ukraine is easy. The neoconservative Assistant Secretary of State Victoria Nuland told the National Press Club in Washington on December 13, 2013, that the US has "invested" $5 billion in agitation in Ukraine.[1]

The crisis essentially resides in western Ukraine where romantic ideas about Russian oppression are strong and the population is less Russian than in the eastern Ukraine.

The hatred of Russia in western Ukraine creates such dysfunction that the duped protesters are unaware that joining the EU means the end of Ukraine independence and rule by the EU bureaucrats in Brussels, the European Central Bank, and US corporations. Perhaps Ukraine is two countries. The western half could be given to the EU and US corporations, and the eastern half could be reincorporated as part of Russia, where the entire Ukraine resided for as long as the US has existed.

The disaffection from Russia that exists in western Ukraine makes it easy for the US to cause trouble.

Those in Washington and Europe who wish to destroy Ukraine's independence portray an independent Ukraine as a hostage of Russia, while a Ukraine in the EU is allegedly under the protection of the US and Europe. The large sums of money that Washington funnels into NGOs in Ukraine propagate this idea and work the population into a mindless frenzy. I have never in my life witnessed people as mindless as the Ukrainian protesters who are destroying the independence of their country.

The US- and EU-financed NGOs are fifth columns designed to destroy the independence of the countries in which they operate. Some pretend to be "human rights organizations." Others indoctrinate people under cover of "education programs" and "building democracy." Others, especially those run by the CIA, specialize in provocations such as "Pussy Riot." Few if any of these NGOs are legitimate. But they are arrogant. The head of one of the NGOs announced prior to the Iranian elections in which Mousavi was Washington and the CIA's candidate that the election would result in a Green Revolution. He knew this in advance, because he had helped to finance it with US taxpayer dollars. I wrote about it at the time. I wrote about it at the time,[2] and in my book, *How America Was Lost*.

The Ukrainian "protesters" have been violent, but the police have been restrained. Washington has a vested interest in keeping the protests going in the hopes of turning the protests into revolt so that Washington can grab Ukraine. This week the US House of Representatives passed a resolution threatening sanctions should the violent protests be put down by the police.

In other words, if the Ukrainian police behave toward violent protesters in the way that US police behave toward peaceful protesters, it is reason for Washington to interfere in the internal affairs of Ukraine.

Washington is using the protests to destroy the independence of Ukraine and has ready the list of puppets that Washington intends to install as Ukraine's next government.

RUSSIA
UNDER ATTACK

February 14, 2014

As I have often explained, the Soviet Union served as a constraint on US power. The Soviet collapse unleashed the neoconservative drive for US world hegemony. Russia under Putin, China, and Iran are the only constraints on that neoconservative agenda.

Russia's nuclear missiles and military technology make Russia the strongest military obstacle to US hegemony. To neutralize Russia, Washington broke the Reagan-Gorbachev agreements, expanded NATO into former constituent parts of the Soviet Empire and now intends to bring former constituent parts of Russia herself—Georgia and Ukraine—into NATO. Washington withdrew from the treaty that banned anti-ballistic missiles and has established anti-ballistic missile bases on Russia's frontier. Washington changed its nuclear war doctrine to permit nuclear first strike.

All of this is aimed at degrading Russia's deterrent, thereby reducing the ability of Russia to resist Washington's will.

The Russian government (and also the government of Ukraine) foolishly permitted large numbers of US funded NGOs to operate as Washington's agents under cover of "human rights organizations," "building democracy," etc. The "pussy riot" event was an operation designed to put Putin and Russia in a bad light. (The women were useful dupes.) The Western media attacks on the Sochi Olympics are part of the ridiculing and demonizing of Putin and Russia. Washington is determined that Putin and Russia will not be permitted any appearance of success in any area, whether diplomacy, sports, or human rights.

The American media is a Ministry of Propaganda for the government and the corporations, and helps Washington paint Russia in bad colors. Stephen F. Cohen accurately describes US media coverage of Russia as a "tsunami of shamefully unprofessional and politically inflammatory articles."[3]

As a holdover from the Cold War, the US media retains the image of a free press that can be trusted. In truth, there is no free press in America (except for Internet sites).[4] During the later years of the Clinton regime, the US government permitted 6 large conglomerates to concentrate the varied, dispersed and somewhat independent media. The value of these large mega-companies depends on their federal broadcast licenses. Therefore, the media dares not go against the government on any important issue. In addition, the media conglomerates are no longer run by journalists but by corporate advertising executives and former government officials, with an eye not on facts but on advertising revenues and access to government "sources."

Washington is using the media to prepare the American people for confrontation with Russia and to influence Russians and other peoples in the world against Putin. Washington would love to see a weaker or more pliable Russian leader than Putin.

Many Russians are gullible. Having experienced communist rule and the chaos from collapse, they naively believe that America is the best place, the example for the world, the "white hat" that can be trusted and believed. This idiotic belief, which we see manifested in western Ukraine as the US destabilizes the country in preparation for taking it over, is an important weapon that the US uses to destabilize Russia.

Some Russians make apologies for Washington by explaining the anti-Russian rhetoric as simply a carryover from old stereotypes from the Cold War. "Old stereotypes" is a red herring, a misleading distraction. Washington is gunning for Russia. Russia is under attack, and if Russians do not realize this, they are history.

Many Russians are asleep at the switch, but the Izborsk Club is trying to wake them up. In an article (February 12) in the Russian weekly *Zavtra*, strategic and military experts warned that the Western use of protests to overturn the decision of the Ukraine government not to join the European Union had produceda situation in which a coup by fascist elements was a possibility. Such a coup would result in a fratricidal war in Ukraine and would constitute a serious "strategic threat to the Russian Federation."

The experts concluded that should such a coup succeed, the consequences for Russia would be:

- Loss of Sevastopol as the base of the Russian Federation's Black Sea Fleet;
- Purges of Russians in eastern and southern Ukraine, producing a flood of refugees;
- Loss of manufacturing capacities in Kiev, Dnepropetrovsk, Kharkov where contract work is done for the Russian military;
- Suppression of the Russian speaking population by forcible Ukrainianization;
- The establishment of US and NATO military bases in Ukraine, including in Crimea, and the establishment of training centers for terrorists who would be unleashed upon the Caucasus, the Volga

Basin, and perhaps Siberia.
- Spread of the orchestrated Kiev protests into non-Russian ethnicities in cities of the Russian Federation.

The Russian strategists conclude that they "consider the situation taking shape in Ukraine to be catastrophic for the future of Russia."

What is to be done? Here the strategic experts, who have correctly analyzed the situation, fall down. They call for a national media campaign to expose the nature of the takeover that is underway and for the government of the Russian Federation to invoke the Budapest Memorandum of 1994 in order to convene a conference of representatives of the governments of Russia, Ukraine, the USA, and Great Britain to deal with the threats to the Ukraine. In the event that the Budapest Memorandum governing the sovereignty of Ukraine is set aside by one or more of the parties, the experts propose that the Russian government, using the precedent of the Kennedy-Khrushchev negotiations that settled the 1962 Cuban Missile Crisis, negotiate directly with Washington a settlement of the developing crisis in Ukraine.

This is a pipe dream. The experts are indulging in self-deception. Washington is the perpetrator of the crisis in Ukraine and intends to take over Ukraine for the precise reasons that the experts list. It is a perfect plan for destabilizing Russia and for negating Putin's successful diplomacy in preventing a US military attack on Syria and Iran.

Essentially, if Washington succeeds in Ukraine, Russia would be eliminated as a constraint on US world hegemony. Only China would remain.

I suspected that Ukraine would come to a boiling point when Putin and Russia were preoccupied with the Sochi Olympics, leaving Russia unprepared. There is little doubt that Russia is faced with a major strategic threat. What are Russia's real options? Certainly the options do not include any good will from Washington.

If Russia were to operate from the American script, Russia could use drones like Washington does, and use them to assassinate the leaders of the Washington-sponsored protests. Or send in Special Forces teams to eliminate the agents who are operating against Russia. If the EU continues to support the destabilization of Ukraine, Russia could cut off oil and gas supplies to Washington's European puppet states.

Alternatively, the Russian Army could occupy western Ukraine while arrangements are made to partition Ukraine, which until recently was part of Russia for 200 years. It is certain that the majority of residents in eastern Ukraine prefer Russia to the EU. It is even possible that the brainwashed elements in the western half might stop foaming at the mouth long enough to comprehend that being in US/EU hands means being looted as per Latvia and Greece.

I am outlining the least dangerous responses to the crisis that Washington and its stupid European puppet states have created, not making recommendations to Russia. The worst outcome is a dangerous war. If the Russians sit on their hands, the situation will become unbearable for them. As Ukraine moves toward NATO membership and suppression of the Russian population, the Russian government will ultimately have to attack Ukraine and overthrow the foreign regime or surrender to the Americans. The likely outcome of the audacious strategic threat with which Washington is confronting Russia would be nuclear war.

The neoconservative Victoria Nuland sits in her State Department office, happily choosing the members of the next Ukrainian government. Is this US official oblivious to the risk that Washington's meddling in the internal affairs of Ukraine and Russia could be triggering nuclear war? Are President Obama and Congress aware that there is an Assistant Secretary of State who is provoking Armageddon?

Insouciant Americans are paying no attention and have no idea that a handful of neoconservative ideologues are pushing the world toward destruction.

US AND EU ARE PAYING UKRAINIAN RIOTERS AND PROTESTERS

February 17, 2014

A number of confirmations have come in from readers that Washington is fueling the violent protests in Ukraine with our taxpayer dollars. Washington has no money for food stamps or to prevent home foreclosures, but it has plenty of money with which to subvert Ukraine.

One reader wrote: "My wife, who is of Ukrainian nationality, has weekly contact to her parents and friends in Zhytomyr [NW Ukraine]. According to them, most protesters get an average payment of 200-300 grivna, corresponding to about 15-25 euro. As I additionally heard, one of the most active agencies and 'payment outlets' on EU side is the German 'Konrad Adenauer Stiftung', being closely connected to the CDU, i.e. Mrs. Merkel's party."

Johannes Loew of the Internet site elynitthria.net/ writes: "I am just back from Ukraine (I live in Munich/ Germany) and I was a lot at the Maidan. Most of those people get only 100 grivna. 300 is for Students."

Assistant Secretary of State Victoria Nuland, a rabid Russophobe and neoconservative warmonger, told the National Press Club last December that the US has "invested" $5 billion in organizing a network to achieve US goals in Ukraine in order to give "Ukraine the future it deserves."[5] Nuland is the Obama regime official who was caught red-handed naming the members of the Ukrainian government Washington intends to impose on the Ukrainian people once the paid protesters have unseated the current elected and independent government.

What Nuland means by Ukraine's future under EU overlordship is for Ukraine to be looted like Greece and to be used by Washington as a staging ground for US missile bases against Russia.

From the responses I received to my request for confirmations of the information sent to me from Moldova, there is enough evidence that Washington fomented the violent riots for western newspapers and TV channels to investigate. But they haven't. As we know, the presstitutes are enablers of Washington's crimes and duplicities. However, the US media *has* reported that the Ukrainian government is paying Ukrainians to counter rally in favor of the Yanukovych government.[6] The Ukrainian government will have a hard time matching Washington's $5 billion.

As Karl Marx wrote, money turns everything into a commodity that is bought and sold. I wouldn't be surprised if some protesters are working both sides of the street.

Of course, not all of the protesters are paid. There are plenty of gullible dupes in the streets who think they are protesting Ukraine government corruption. I have heard from several. There is little doubt that the Ukraine government is corrupt. What government isn't? Government corruption is universal, but it is easy to go from the frying pan into the fire. Ukrainian protesters seem to think that they can escape corruption by joining the EU. Obviously, these gullible dupes are unfamiliar with the report on EU corruption issued February 3 by the EU Commissioner for Home Affairs. The report says that a business political nexus of corruption affects all 28 EU member countries and costs the EU economies $162.2 billion per annum.[7] According to the World Bank, the economic cost of EU corruption is almost as large as the size of Ukrainian GDP.[8] Clearly, Ukrainians will not escape corruption by joining the EU. Indeed, Ukrainians will suffer worse corruption.

I have no objection to Ukrainians protesting government corruption. Indeed, such gullible people could benefit from the lesson they would learn once their country is in the hands of corrupt Brussels and Washington. What I object to is the lack of awareness on the part of the protesters that by permitting themselves to be manipulated by Washington, they are pushing the world toward a dangerous war. I would be surprised if Russia is content to have US military and missile bases in Ukraine.

It was fools like Nuland playing the great game that gave us World War I. World War III would be the last war. Washington's drive to exploit every opportunity to establish its hegemony over the world is driving us all toward nuclear war. Like Nuland, a significant percentage of the population of western Ukraine is Russophobic. I know the case for Ukrainian dislike of Russia, but Ukrainian emotions fueled with Washington's money should not direct the course of history. No historians will be left to document how gullible and witless Ukrainians set the world up for destruction.

IS UKRAINE DRIFTING TOWARD CIVIL WAR AND GREAT POWER CONFRONTATION?

February 20, 2014

People ask for solutions, but no solutions are possible in a disinformed world. Populations almost everywhere are dissatisfied, but few have any comprehension of the real situation. Before there can be solutions, people must know the truth about the problems. For those few inclined to be messengers, it is largely a thankless task.

The assumption that man is a rational animal is incorrect. He and she are emotional creatures, not Mr. Spock of Star Trek. Humans are brainwashed by enculturation and indoctrination. Patriots respond with hostility toward criticisms of their governments, their countries, their hopes and their delusions. Their emotions throttle facts, should any reach them. Aspirations and delusions prevail over truth. Most people want to be told what they want to hear. Consequently, they are always gullible and their illusions and self delusions make them easy victims of propaganda. This is true of all levels of societies and of the leaders themselves.

We are witnessing this today in western Ukraine where a mixture of witless university students, pawns in Washington's drive for world hegemony, together with paid protesters and fascistic elements among ultranationalists, are bringing great troubles upon Ukraine and perhaps a deadly war upon the world.

Many of the protesters are just the unemployed collecting easy money. It is the witless idealistic types that are destroying the independence of their country. Victoria Nuland, the American neoconservative Assistant Secretary of State, whose agenda is US world hegemony, told the Ukrainians what was in store for them last December 13, but the protesters were too delusional to hear.

In an eight minute, 46 second speech at the National Press Club sponsored by the US-Ukraine Foundation, Chevron, and Ukraine-in-

Washington Lobby Group, Nuland boasted that Washington has spent $5 billion to foment agitation to bring Ukraine into the EU. Once captured by the EU, Ukraine will be "helped" by the West acting through the IMF. Nuland, of course, presented the IMF as Ukraine's rescuer, not as the iron hand of the West that will squeeze all life out of Ukraine's struggling economy.

Nuland's audience consisted of all the people who will be enriched by the looting and by connections to a Washington-appointed Ukrainian government. Just look at the large Chevron sign next to which Nuland speaks, and you will know what it is all about.[9]

Nuland's speech failed to alert the Ukraine protesters. The unintended consequence of their protest will destroy the independence of Ukraine and place their country in the hands of the IMF so that it can be looted like Greece and every country that ever had an IMF structural adjustment program. All the monies that protesters are paid by the US and EU will soon be given back manifold as Ukraine is "adjusted" by Western looting.

In her short speech the neoconservative agitator Nuland alleged that the protesters whom Washington has spent $5 billion cultivating were protesting "peacefully with enormous restraint" against a brutal government.

According to RT, which has much more credibility than the US State Department (remember Secretary of State Colin Powell's address to the UN setting up the US invasion of Iraq with his "evidence" of Iraqi weapons of mass destruction, a speech Powell later disavowed as Bush regime disinformation), Ukrainian rioters have seized 1,500 guns, 100,000 rounds of ammunition, 3 machine guns, and grenades from military armories.

The human-rights trained Ukrainian police have permitted the violence to get out of hand. A number of police have been burned by Molotov cocktails. The latest report is that 108 police have been shot. A number are dead and 63 are in critical condition.[10] These casualties are the products of Nuland's "peacefully protesting protesters acting with enormous restraint."

Perhaps the Russophobic western Ukrainians deserve the IMF, and perhaps the EU deserves the extreme nationalists who are trying to topple the Ukraine government. Once Ukrainians experience being looted by the West, they will be on their knees begging Russia to rescue them. The only certain thing is that it is unlikely that the Russian part of Ukraine will remain part of Ukraine.

During the Soviet era, parts of Russia herself, such as the Crimea, were placed into the Ukrainian Soviet Socialist Republic, perhaps in order to increase the Russian population in Ukraine. In other words, a large part of today's Ukraine—the eastern and southern provinces—are traditionally Russian territory, not part of historical Ukraine. Indeed, until the Soviet collapse, Ukraine had been part of Russia since the 18th century.

Until Russia granted Ukraine independence in the early 1990s,

Ukraine had experienced scant independence since the 14th century and had been a part of Russia for 200 years. The problem with the granting of independence is that much of Ukraine is not Ukrainian. It is Russian.

As I have reported previously, Russia regards the prospect of Ukraine as a member of the EU and NATO with US bases on Russia's frontier as a "strategic threat." It is unlikely that the Russian government and the Russian territories in Ukraine will accept Washington's plan for Ukraine. Whatever their intention, Secretary of State John Kerry's provocative statements are raising tensions and fomenting war. The vast bulk of the American and Western populations have no idea of what the real situation is, because all they hear from the "free press" is the neoconservative propaganda line.

Washington's lies are destroying not only civil liberties at home and countries abroad, but are raising dangerous alarms in Russia about the country's security. If Washington succeeds in overthrowing the Ukrainian government, the eastern and southern provinces are likely to secede. If secession becomes a civil war instead of a peaceful divorce, Russia would not be able to sit on the sidelines. As the Washington warmongers would be backing western Ukraine, the two nuclear powers would be thrown into military conflict.

The Ukrainian and Russian governments allowed this dangerous situation to develop, because for many years they naively permitted billions of US dollars to flow into their countries where the money was used to create fifth columns under the guise of educational and human rights organizations, the real purpose of which is to destabilize both countries. The consequence of the trust Ukrainians and Russians placed in the West is the prospect of civil and wider war.

UPDATE: Reading the collection of foreign news dispatches provided by Richard Rozoff about the situation in Ukraine[11] reminded me of histories about how the pointless and destructive First World War began. In their blind desire to overthrow the democratically elected government of Ukraine and impose an EU puppet state in its place, the American, British, and French governments are lying through their teeth and provoking a situation that is headed toward armed conflict.

Unless the Russian government and people are willing to accept Washington's hegemony over Russia, Russia cannot tolerate the coup that the West is preparing in Ukraine. As it is unlikely that Western forces would be a match for the Russian army in its own backyard, or that self-righteous, hubristic Washington could accept defeat, the conflict toward which the corrupt Western governments are driving is likely to turn nuclear.

As worldwide polls consistently show, Washington is regarded as the greatest threat to world peace. As I have often written, Washington is not merely a threat to peace. Washington and its despicable European puppet states are a threat to the existence of life on the planet. Essentially, Washington is insane, and European "leaders" are paid to provide cover for Washington's insanity.

The world could end before the unpayable Western debts come due.

SLEEPWALKING AGAIN

On the 100th Anniversary of World War I, the Western powers are again sleepwalking into destructive conflict. Hegemonic ambition has Washington interfering in the internal affairs of Ukraine, but developments seem to be moving beyond Washington's control.

Regime change in Ukraine for a mere $5 billion dollars would be a bargain compared to the massive sums squandered in Iraq ($3,000 billion), Afghanistan ($3,000 billion), Somalia, and Libya, or the money Washington is wasting murdering people with drones in Pakistan and Yemen, or the money Washington has spent supporting al Qaeda in Syria, or the massive sums Washington has wasted surrounding Iran with 40 military bases and several fleets in the Persian Gulf in an effort to terrorize Iran into submission.

So far, in Washington's attempt at regime change in Ukraine, large numbers of Americans are not being killed and maimed. Only Ukrainians are dying, all the better for Washington, as the deaths are blamed on the Ukrainian government that the US has targeted for overthrow.

The problem with Washington's plot to overthrow the elected government of Ukraine and install its minions is twofold: The chosen US puppets have lost control of the protests to armed radical elements with historical links to Nazism, and Russia regards an EU/NATO takeover of Ukraine as a strategic threat to Russian independence.

Washington overlooked that the financially viable part of today's Ukraine consists of the historically Russian provinces in the east and south that the Soviet leadership merged into Ukraine in order to dilute the fascist elements in western Ukraine that fought for Adolf Hitler against the Soviet Union. It is these ultra-nationalist elements with Nazi roots, not Washington's chosen puppets, who are now in charge of the armed rebellion in Western Ukraine.

If the democratically elected Ukraine government is overthrown, the eastern and southern parts would rejoin Russia. The western part would be looted by Western bankers and corporations, and the NATO Ukraine bases would be targeted by Russian Iskander missiles.

It would be a defeat for Washington and their gullible Ukrainian dupes to see half of the country return to Russia. To save face, Washington might provoke a great power confrontation, which could be the end of all of us.

My series of articles on the situation in Ukraine resulted in a number of interviews from Canada to Russia, with more scheduled. It also produced emotional rants from people of Ukrainian descent whose delusions are impenetrable by facts. Deranged Russophobes dismissed as propaganda the easily verifiable report of Assistant Secretary of State Nuland's public address last December, in which she boasted that Washington had spent $5 billion preparing Ukraine to be aligned with Washington's interests. Protest sympathizers claim that the intercepted telephone call between Nuland and the US Ambassador in Ukraine, in which the two US officials chose the government that would be installed following the coup, is a fake.

One person actually suggested that my position should be aligned with the "sincerity of the Kiev students," not with the facts.

Some Trekkers and Trekkies were more concerned that I used an improper title for Spock than they were with the prospect of great power confrontation. The point of my article flew off into space and missed planet Earth.

Spock's mental powers were the best weapon that Starship Enterprise had. Among my graduate school friends, Spock was known as Dr. Spock, because he was the cool, calm, and unemotional member of the crew who could diagnose the problem and save the situation.

There are no Spocks in the US or any Western government and certainly not among the Ukrainian protesters.

I have often wondered if Spock's Vulcan ancestry was Gene Roddenberry's way of underlining by contrast the fragility of human reason. In the context of modern military technology, is it possible for life to survive humanity's penchant for emotion to trump reason and for self-delusion to prevail over factual reality?

DEMOCRACY MURDERED BY PROTEST: UKRAINE FALLS TO INTRIGUE AND VIOLENCE

February 23, 2014

Who's in charge? Certainly not the bought-and-paid-for-moderates that Washington and the EU hoped to install as the new government of Ukraine. The agreement that the Washington and EU-supported opposition concluded with President Yanukovich to end the crisis did not last an hour. Even the former boxing champion, Vitaly Klitschko, who was riding high as an opposition leader until a few hours ago, has been booed by the rioters and shoved aside. The newly appointed president by what is perhaps an irrelevant parliament, Oleksandr Turchynov, has no support base among those who overthrew the government. The BBC reports, "like all of the mainstream opposition politicians, Mr. Turchynov is not entirely trusted or respected by the protesters in Kiev's Independence Square."

In western Ukraine the only organized and armed force is the ultra-nationalist Right Sector. From the way this group's leaders speak, they assume that they are in charge. One of the group's leaders, Aleksandr Muzychko, has pledged to fight against "Jews and Russians until I die." Asserting the Right Sector's authority over the situation, Muzychko declared that now that the democratically elected government has been overthrown, "there will be order and discipline" or "Right Sector squads will shoot the bastards on the spot."

The bastards are any protesters who dare to protest the Right Sector's control.

Muzychko declared, "The next president of Ukraine will be from Right Sector."

Another Right Sector leader, Dmitry Yarosh, declared: "the Right Sector will not lay down its arms." He declared the deal made between the opposition and the President to be "unacceptable" and demanded the liquidation of President Yanukovich's political party.

The Right Sector's roots go back to the Ukrainians who fought for

Adolf Hitler against the Soviet Union during World War II. It was the Right Sector that introduced armed fighters and turned the tide of the protests in Kiev from peaceful protests in favor of joining the EU to violent attacks on police with the view to overthrowing the democratically elected government, which the Right Sector succeeded in doing.

There is a tendency to discount the Right Sector as a small fringe group, but the Right Sector not only took control of the protests away from the Western supported moderates, as moderate leaders themselves admitted, but also the Right Sector had enough public support to destroy the national monument to the Red Army soldiers who died liberating Ukraine from Nazi Germany.

Unlike the US orchestrated toppling of the statue of Saddam Hussein, which was a PR event for the presstitutes in which Iraqis themselves were not involved, Ukrainian rightists' destruction of the monument commemorating the Red Army's liberation of the Ukraine had public support. If the Right Sector hates Russians for defeating the Nazis, the Right Sector also hates the US, France, and England for the same reason. The Right Sector is an unlikely political party to take Ukraine into the EU.

The Russian parts of Ukraine clearly understand that the Right Sector's destruction of the monument commemorating the stand of the Red Army against the German troops is a threat against the Russian population of Ukraine. Provincial governments in eastern and southern Ukraine that formerly were part of Russia are organizing militias against the ultra-nationalist threat unleashed by Washington's stupidity and incompetence and by the naive and gullible Kiev protesters.

Having interfered in Ukraine's internal affairs and lost control, Washington is now issuing ultimatums to Russia not to interfere in Ukraine. Does the idiot Susan Rice, Obama's neoconservative National Security Advisor, think Putin is going to pay any attention to her ultimatums or to any instruction from a government so militarily incompetent that it was unable to successfully occupy Baghdad after 8 years or to defeat a few thousand lightly armed Taliban after 12 years? It only took a few hours for Russian troops to destroy the American and Israeli trained and armed Georgian army that Washington sent to invade South Ossetia.

Where does Obama find morons like Susan Rice and Victoria Nuland? These two belong in a kindergarten for mentally handicapped children, not in the government of a superpower where their ignorance and arrogance can start World War III.

Ukraine is far more important to Russia than it is to the US or EU. If the situation in Ukraine spirals out of control and right-wing extremists seize control, Russian intervention is certain. The arrogant and stupid Obama regime has carelessly and recklessly created a direct strategic threat to the existence of Russia.

According to the *Moscow Times*, this is what a senior Russian official has to say: "If Ukraine breaks apart, it will trigger a war." Ukraine "will lose Crimea first," because Russia "will go in just as we did in Georgia." Another Russian official said: "We will not allow Europe and the US to take Ukraine from us. The states of the former Soviet Union, we are one family. They think Russia is still as weak as in the early 1990s but we are not."

The Ukrainian right-wing is in a stronger position than Washington's paid Ukrainian puppets, essentially weak and irrelevant persons who sold out their country for Washington's money. The Right Sector is organized. It is armed. It is indigenous. It is not dependent on money funneled in from Washington and EU-financed NGOs. It has an ideology, and it is focused. The Right Sector doesn't have to pay its protesters to take to the streets like Washington had to do.

Most importantly, well-meaning but stupid protesters—especially the Kiev students—and a Ukrainian parliament playing to the protesters destroyed Ukrainian democracy. The opposition controlled parliament removed an elected president from office without an election, an obviously illegal and undemocratic action. The opposition controlled parliament issued illegal arrest warrants for members of the president's government. The opposition controlled parliament illegally released criminals from prison. As the opposition has created a regime of illegality in place of law and constitutional procedures, the field is wide open for the Right Sector. Expect everything the opposition did to Yanukovich to be done to the opposition controlled parliament by the Right Sector. By their own illegal and unconstitutional actions, the opposition has set the precedent for their own demise.

Just as the February 1917 revolution against the Russian Tsar set the stage for the October 1917 Bolshevik Revolution, surprising the stupid "reformers," the overthrow of the Ukrainian political order has set the stage for the Right Sector. We can only hope that the Right Sector blows its chance.

The American media is a useless news source. It serves as a Ministry for Government Lies. The corrupt propagandists are portraying the undemocratic removal of Yanukovich as a victory for freedom and democracy. When it begins to leak out that everything has gone wrong, the presstitutes will blame it all on Russia and Putin. The Western media is a plague upon humanity.

Americans have no idea that the neoconservative regime is leading them into a Great Power Confrontation that could end in destruction of life on earth.

Ironic, isn't it. America's "first black president," the person liberals thought would restore justice, morality, and reason to Western civilization, is instead now positioned as the person who will have to accept humiliating defeat or risk the destruction of life on earth.[12]

THE CRISIS
IN UKRAINE

February 25, 2014

In 2004 Hungary joined the EU, expecting streets of gold. Instead, four years later in 2008 Hungary became indebted to the IMF. The rock video by the Hungarian group, Mouksa Underground, sums up the result in Hungary today of falling into the hands of the EU and IMF.[13]

The song is about the disappointing results of leaving socialism for capitalism, and in Hungary the results are certainly not encouraging. The title is "Disappointment with the System Change." Here are the lyrics:

> Over twenty some years now
> We've been waiting for the good life
> For the average citizen
> Instead of wealth we have poverty
> Unrestrained exploitation
> So this is the big system change
> So this is what you waited for
> No housing No food No work
> But that's what was assured wouldn't happen
> Those on top
> Prey upon us
> The poor suffer every day
> So this is the big system change
> So this is what you waited for
> (Repeat)
> When will real change occur?
> When will there be a livable world
> The ultimate solution will arise
> When this economic system is forever abandoned
> So this is the big system change
> So this is what you waited for
> (Repeat)
> There is no solution but revolution

Perhaps if the Kiev students had listened to the Hungarian rock group instead of to Washington's NGOs, they would understand what it means to be looted by the West, and Ukraine would not be in turmoil and headed toward destruction.

As Assistant Secretary of State Victoria Nuland made clear in her speech last December and in the leaked recording of her telephone conversation with the US ambassador in Kiev, Washington spent $5 billion of US taxpayer dollars engineering a coup in Ukraine that overthrew the elected democratic government.

That it was a coup is also underlined by the obvious public lies that Obama has told about the situation, blaming, of course, the overthrown government, and by the total misrepresentation of Ukrainian developments by the US and European presstitute media. The only reason to misrepresent the events is to support the coup and to cover up Washington's hand.

There is no doubt whatsoever that the coup is a strategic move by Washington to weaken Russia.

Washington tried to capture Ukraine in 2004 with the Washington-funded "Orange Revolution," but failed. Ukraine was part of Russia for 200 years prior to being granted independence in the 1990s. The eastern and southern provinces of Ukraine are Russian areas. Crimea was part of Russia until 1954 when Khrushchev attached it to the Ukrainian Soviet Socialist Republic.

The loss of Ukraine to the EU and NATO would mean the loss of Russia's naval base on the Black Sea and the loss of many military industries. If Russia were to accept such strategic defeat, it would mean that Russia had submitted to Washington's hegemony.

Whatever course the Russian government takes, the Russian population of eastern and southern Ukraine will not accept oppression by Ukrainian ultra-nationalists and neo-Nazis.

The hostility already shown toward the Russian population can be seen in the destruction by Ukrainians of the monument to the Russian troops that drove Hitler's divisions out of Ukraine during World War II and the destruction of the monument to Russian General Kutuzov, whose tactics destroyed Napoleon's Grand Army and resulted in the fall of Napoleon.

The question at the moment is whether Washington miscalculated and lost control of the coup to the neo-Nazi elements who seem to have taken control from the Washington-paid moderates in Kiev, or whether the Washington neocons have been working with the neo-Nazis for years. Max Blumenthal says the latter.[14] The moderates have certainly lost control. They cannot protect public monuments, and they are forced to try to pre-empt the neo-Nazis by legislating the neo-Nazi program. The captive Ukrainian parliament has introduced measures to ban any official use of the Russian language. This, of course, is unacceptable to the Russian provinces.

As I previously noted, the Ukrainian parliament itself is responsible for the destruction of democracy in Ukraine. Its unconstitutional and undemocratic actions have paved the way for the neo-Nazis who now have the precedent to treat the moderates the same way that the moderates treated the elected government, and to cover up their illegality with accusations of crimes and arrest warrants. Today the illegally deposed President Yanukovich is on the run. Tomorrow will the current president, Oleksander Turchinov, put in office by the moderates, not by the people, be on the run? If a democratic election did not convey legitimacy to President Yanukovich, how does selection by a rump parliament convey legitimacy to Turchinov? What can Turchinov answer if the neo-Nazis put to him Lenin's question to Kerensky: "Who chose you?"

If Washington has lost control of the coup and is unable to restore control to the moderates whom it has aligned with the EU and NATO, war would seem to be unavoidable. There is no doubt that the Russian provinces would seek and be granted Russia's protection. Whether Russia would go further and overthrow the neo-Nazis in western Ukraine is unknown. Whether Washington, which seems to have positioned military forces in the region, would provide the military might for the moderates to defeat the neo-Nazis is also an open question, as is Russia's response.

Previously, I described the situation as "Sleepwalking Again," an analogy to how miscalculations resulted in World War I.

The entire world should be alarmed at the reckless and irresponsible interference by Washington in Ukraine. By bringing a direct strategic threat to Russia, the crazed Washington hegemon has engineered a Great Power confrontation and created the risk of world destruction.

UKRAINIAN NEO-NAZIS: "POWER COMES FROM BARRELS OF OUR GUNS"

February 26, 2014

Reality on the ground in Ukraine contradicts the Obama regime's portrait of Ukrainian democracy on the march.

To the extent that government exists in post-coup Ukraine, it is based on laws dictated by gun and threat wielding thugs of the neo-Nazi, Russophobic, ultra-nationalist, right-wing parties. Watch the video of the armed thug, Aleksandr Muzychko, who boosts of killing Russian soldiers in Chechnya, dictating to the Rovno regional parliament a grant of apartments to families of protesters.[15]

Read about the neo-Nazis intimidating the Central Election Commission in order to secure rule and personnel changes in order to favor the ultra-right in the forthcoming elections. Thug Aleksandr Shevchenko informed the CEC that armed activists will remain in CEC offices in order to make certain that the election is not rigged against the neo-Nazis.

Members of President Yanukovich's ruling party, the Party of Regions, have been shot, had arrest warrants issued for them, have experienced home invasions and physical threats, and are resigning in droves in hopes of saving their lives and the lives of their families. The prosecutor's office in the Volyn region (western Ukraine) has been ordered by ultra-nationalists to resign en masse.

Jewish synagogues and Eastern Orthodox Christian churches are being attacked.

I predicted that Washington's organization of pro-EU Ukrainian politicians into a coup against the elected government of Ukraine would destroy democracy and establish the precedent that force prevails over elections, thereby empowering the organized and armed extreme right-wing. The conversation between Nuland and Pyatt in which the two Americans chose the Ukrainian government is available on youtube.[16]

Only Obama, Susan Rice, Victoria Nuland, Washington's European puppets, and the Western prostitute media can describe the brutal reality of post-coup Ukraine as "the forward march of democracy."

The West now faces a real mess, and so does Russia. The presstitutes will keep the American public from ever knowing what has happened, and the Obama regime will never admit it. It is not always clear that even the Russians want to admit it. The intelligent, reasonable, and humane Russian Foreign Minister, a person 100 cuts above John Kerry, keeps speaking as if this is all a mistake and appealing to the Western governments to stand behind the agreement that they pressured President Yanukovich to sign.

The destabilization of Ukraine can lead to war. Only Putin's diplomatic skills could prevent it. However, Putin has been demonized by Washington and the whores who comprise the US print and TV media. European and British politicians would have their Washington paychecks cut off if they aligned with Putin.

There are a number of reasons why the situation is likely to develop in a very bad way. One is that most people are unable to deal with reality even when reality directly confronts them. Reality is simply too much for mentally and emotionally weak people who are capable of holding on to their delusions in the face of all evidence to the contrary. The masses of deluded people and the total inability of Washington, wallowing it its hubris, to admit a mistake, mean that Washington's destabilization of Ukraine is a problem for us all.

RT reports that "Russian President Vladimir Putin has ordered an urgent military drill to test combat readiness of the armed forces across western and central Russia." According to Russia's Defense Minister, the surprise drill tested ground troops, Air Force, airborne troops and aerospace defense.[17]

The Defense Minister said: "The drills are not connected with events in Ukraine at all."

Yes, of course. The Defense Minister says this, because Putin still hopes that the EU will come to its senses. In my opinion, and I hope I am wrong, the European "leaders" are too corrupted by Washington's money to have any sense. They are bought and paid for. Nothing is important to them but money.

Ask yourself, why does Russia need at this time an *urgent* readiness test unrelated to Ukraine? Anyone familiar with geography knows that western and central Russia sit atop Ukraine.

Let us all cross our fingers that another war is not the consequence of the insouciant American public, the craven cowardice of the presstitute media, Washington's corrupt European puppets, and the utter mendacity of the criminals who rule in Washington.

WASHINGTON'S ARROGANCE CAUSED THE RETURN OF CRIMEA TO RUSSIA

March 3, 2014

In some quarters public awareness is catching up with Stephen Lendman, Michel Chossudovsky, Rick Rozoff, myself and a few others in realizing the grave danger in the crisis that Washington has created in Ukraine.

The puppet politicians who Washington intended to put in charge of Ukraine have lost control to organized and armed neo-Nazis, who are attacking Jews, Russians, and intimidating Ukrainian politicians. The government of Crimea, a Russian province that Khrushchev transferred to the Ukraine Soviet Republic in 1954, has disavowed the illegitimate government that illegally seized power in Kiev and requested Russian protection. The Ukrainian military forces in Crimea have gone over to Russia.

As Aleksandr Solzhenitsyn pointed out, it was folly for the Communist Party of the Soviet Union to transfer Russian provinces into Ukraine. At the time it seemed to the Soviet leadership like a good thing to do. Ukraine was part of the Soviet Union and had been ruled by Russia since the 18th century. Adding Russian territory to Ukraine served to water down the Nazi elements in western Ukraine that had fought for Hitler during World War II. Perhaps another factor in the enlargement of Ukraine was the fact of Khrushchev's Ukrainian heritage.

Regardless, it did not matter until the Soviet Union and then the former Russian empire itself fell apart.

Under Washington's pressure, Ukraine became a separate country retaining the Russian territory. In exchange Russia was given a lease to its Black Sea naval base in Crimea.

Washington tried, but failed, to take Ukraine in 2004 with the Washington-financed "Orange Revolution."

EU membership would open Ukraine to looting by Western bankers and corporations, but Washington's main goal is to establish US missile bases on Russia's border with Ukraine and to deprive Russia of its Black Sea naval base and military industries in eastern Ukraine. EU membership for Ukraine means NATO membership.

Washington wants missile bases in Ukraine in order to degrade Russia's nuclear deterrent, thus reducing Russia's ability to resist US hegemony. Only three countries stand in the way of Washington's hegemony over the world, Russia, China, and Iran.

Iran is surrounded by US military bases and has US fleets off its coast. The "Pivot to Asia" announced by the Obama regime is ringing China with air and naval bases. And Washington is surrounding Russia with US missile and NATO bases. The corrupt Polish and Czech governments were paid to accept US missile and radar bases, which makes the Polish and Czech puppet states prime targets for nuclear annihilation.

Washington has acquired the former Russian and Soviet province of Georgia, birthplace of Joseph Stalin, as a vassal state and hopes to put this former Russian territory into NATO.

These highly provocative moves are a direct strategic threat to Russia.

Russia has been slow to react to the many years of Washington's provocations, hoping for some sign of good sense and good will to emerge in the West. Instead, Russia has experienced rising demonization from Washington and European capitals and foaming at the mouth vicious denunciations by the West's presstitutes. The bulk of the American and European populations are being brainwashed to see the problem that Washington's meddling has caused in Ukraine as Russia's fault. On National Public Radio a presstitute from the *New Republic* described Putin as the problem.

The ignorance, absence of integrity, and lack of independence of the US media enhances the prospect for war. The picture being drawn for insouciant Americans is totally false. An informed people would have burst out laughing when US Secretary of State John Kerry denounced Russia for "invading Ukraine" in "violation of international law." Kerry is the foreign minister of a country that has illegally invaded Iraq, Afghanistan, Somalia, organized the overthrow of the government in Libya and Ukraine, tried to overthrow the government in Syria, attacks the civilian populations of Pakistan and Yemen with drones and missiles, constantly threatens Iran with attack, unleashed the US and Israeli-trained Georgian army on the Russian population of South Ossetia, and now threatens Russia with sanctions for standing up for Russians and Russian strategic interests. The Russian government noted that Kerry has raised hypocrisy to a new level.

Kerry has no answer to the question: "Since when does the United States government genuinely subscribe and defend the concept of sovereignty and territorial integrity?"

Kerry, as is always the case, is lying. Russia hasn't invaded Ukraine. Russia sent a few more troops to join those already at its Black Sea base in view of the violent anti-Russian statements and actions emanating from Kiev. As the Ukrainian military in Crimea defected to Russia, the additional Russian troops were hardly necessary.

Kerry, wallowing in his arrogance, has issued direct threats to Russia. The Russian foreign minister has dismissed Kerry's threats as "unacceptable." The stage is set for war.

Note the absurdity of the situation. Kiev has been taken over by ultra-nationalist neo-Nazis. A band of ultra-nationalist thugs is the last thing the European Union wants or needs as a member state. The EU is centralizing power and suppressing the sovereignty of the member states. Note also the alignment of the neoconservative Obama regime with anti-semitic Ukrainian neo-Nazis. The neoconservative clique that has dominated the US government since the Clinton regime is heavily Jewish, and they have brought to power neo-Nazis who preach "death to the Jews"!

The Israeli newspaper *Ha'aretz* reported on February 24 that Ukrainian Rabbi Moshe Reuven Azman advised "Kiev's Jews to leave the city and even the country." Edward Dolinsky, head of an umbrella organization of Ukrainian Jews, described the situation for Ukrainian Jews as "dire" and requested Israel's help.

This is the situation that Washington created and defends, while accusing Russia of stifling Ukrainian democracy. An elected democracy is what Ukraine had before Washington overthrew it.

At this time there is no legitimate Ukrainian government.

Everyone needs to understand that Washington is lying about Ukraine just as Washington lied about Saddam Hussein and weapons of mass destruction in Iraq, just as Washington lied about Iranian nukes, just as Washington lied about Syrian president Assad using chemical weapons, just as Washington lied about Afghanistan, Libya, NSA spying, torture. What hasn't Washington lied about?

Washington is comprised of three elements: Arrogance, Hubris, and Evil. There is nothing else there.

THE LOOTING OF UKRAINE HAS BEGUN

March 6, 2014

According to a report in Kommersant-Ukraine, the finance ministry of Washington's stooges in Kiev who are pretending to be a government has prepared an economic austerity plan that will cut Ukrainian pensions from $160 to $80 so that Western bankers who lent money to Ukraine can be repaid at the expense of Ukraine's poor.[18] It is Greece all over again.

Before anything approaching stability and legitimacy has been obtained for the puppet government put in power by the Washington orchestrated coup against the legitimate, elected Ukraine government, the Western looters are already at work. Naive protesters who believed the propaganda that EU membership offered a better life are due to lose half of their pension by April. But this is only the beginning.

The corrupt Western media describes loans as "aid." However, the 11 billion euros that the EU is offering Kiev is not aid. It is a loan. Moreover, it comes with many strings, including Kiev's acceptance of an IMF austerity plan.

Remember, gullible Ukrainians participated in the protests that were used to overthrow their elected government, because they believed the lies told to them by Washington-financed NGOs that once they joined the EU they would have streets paved with gold. Instead they are getting cuts in their pensions and an IMF austerity plan.

The austerity plan will cut social services, funds for education, layoff government workers, devalue the currency, thus raising the prices of imports which include Russian gas, thus electricity, and open Ukrainian assets to takeover by Western corporations.

Ukraine's agriculture lands will pass into the hands of American agribusiness.

One part of the Washington/EU plan for Ukraine, or that part of Ukraine that doesn't defect to Russia, has succeeded. What remains of the country will be thoroughly looted by the West.

The other part hasn't worked as well. Washington's Ukrainian stooges lost control of the protests to organized and armed ultra-nationalists. These groups, whose roots go back to those who fought for Hitler during World War II, engaged in words and deeds that sent southern and eastern Ukraine clamoring to become part of Russia.

At this time of writing it looks like Crimea has seceded from Ukraine. The people in eastern Ukraine are in the streets demanding separation from the unelected government that Washington's coup has imposed in Kiev. Washington, realizing that its incompetence has lost Crimea, had its Kiev stooges appoint Ukrainian oligarchs, against whom the Maiden protests were partly directed, to governing positions in eastern Ukraine cities. These oligarchs have their own private militias in addition to the police and any Ukrainian military units that are still functioning. The leaders of the protesting Russians are being arrested and disappeared. Washington and its EU puppets, who proclaim their support for self-determination, are only for self-determination when it can be orchestrated in their favor. Therefore, Washington is busy at work suppressing self-determination in eastern Ukraine.

This is a dilemma for Putin. His low-key approach has allowed Washington to seize the initiative in eastern Ukraine. The oligarchs Taruta and Kolomoyskiy have been put in power in Donetsk and Dnipropetrovsk, and are carrying out arrests of Russians and committing unspeakable crimes, but you will never hear of it from the US presstitutes. Washington's strategy is to arrest and deep-six the leaders of the secessionists so that there are no authorities to request Putin's intervention.

If Washington perceives Russian weakness, Washington will push harder and likely provoke a war.

OBAMA COMES
OUT AGAINST
SELF-DETERMINATION

March 7, 2014

Obama has repeatedly, erroneously and foolishly declared that it is "against international law" for Crimea to exercise self-determination. Self-determination, as used by Washington, is a propaganda term that serves Washington's empire but is not permissible for real people to exercise. On March 6 Obama telephoned Putin to tell the Russian President again that only Washington has the right to interfere in Ukraine and to insist against all logic that only the "government" in Kiev installed by the Washington-organized coup is "legitimate" and "democratic."

In other words, the elected government in Crimea pushed by the people in Crimea to give them a vote on their future is "undemocratic" and "illegitimate," but a non-elected government in Kiev imposed by Washington is the voice of self-determination and legitimacy.

Washington is so arrogant that it never occurs to the hubris-infected fools to take into consideration what others think of Washington's blatant hypocrisy.

Since the Clinton regime, Washington has done nothing but violate international law—Serbia, Kosovo, Afghanistan, Iraq, Libya, Syria, Iran, Pakistan, Yemen, Somalia, Honduras, Venezuela, Ecuador, Bolivia.

Does Russia have an Africa Command? No, but Washington does.

Is Russia surrounding the US with military bases? No, but Washington has used the NATO organization, whose purpose disappeared 23 years ago, to organize western, eastern, and southern Europe into an empire army with forward bases on Russia's borders. Washington is determined to extend the boundaries of a North Atlantic Treaty Organization to Georgia in central Asia and to Ukraine on the Black Sea. Both Georgia and Ukraine are former constituent parts of both Russia and the Soviet Union.

Washington is doing the same thing to China and Iran. Washington is working to establish new air and naval bases in Philippines, South Korea, Vietnam, Thailand, Australia, with which to block the flow of oil and other resources into China. Iran is surrounded by some 40 US military bases and has US fleets standing off its coastline.

In Washington's propaganda, this rank militarism is presented as "defending democracy."

The Russian government continues to act as though Washington's thrusts at Russia's independence and strategic interests can be defused with good sense and good will.

But Washington has neither.

Since the Clinton regime, Washington has been in the hands of a collection of ideologues who are convinced that the US is "the exceptional indispensable country" with the right to world hegemony.

Everything that Washington has done in the 21st century is in pursuit of this goal.

Washington intends to break up the Russian Federation itself. Washington funnels huge sums of money into NGOs inside Russia that serve as Washington Fifth Columns and work hand-in-hand with Washington to discredit Russian free elections, to demonize Putin and the Russian government, to spread anti-Russian propaganda and agitation. It is amazing that some Russians actually believe the Western propaganda.

Washington is also working to isolate China with the Trans-Pacific-Partnership, but at this time is primarily focused on destabilizing and isolating Russia. Washington is desperate to break up the BRICS, the emerging organization of Brazil, Russia, India, China, and South Africa. With the largest countries and half of the world's population, the BRICS organization is emerging as a political and economic power, especially with the organization's plan to cease using the US dollar as reserve currency. Ringing Russia with US missile bases on Russia's borders impairs Russian sovereignty and independence and thus weakens the BRICS as a countervailing power to Washington.

Many have been deceived by Washington's propaganda. The world is slowly waking up, but is it in time?

The US media and much of Europe's speak with one voice parroting Washington's propaganda, demonizing Washington's targets, and preparing insouciant Western populations for more war. The Western media, like Western governments, is devoid of integrity. Liars and whores rule.

PUTIN
SPEAKS

On March 4 President Putin of Russia answered questions from the press about the overthrow of the Ukrainian government. Americans have not experienced political leadership or an independent media for such a long time that they will be amazed at the straightforward answers from the Russian President.

Americans will also be struck by how greatly the facts of the Ukraine situation diverge from the constant stream of lies that flow from Washington, its European puppets, and presstitute media.

Putin's calm leadership, the absence of provocative statements and threats, and his insistence on legality and the will of the people stand in stark contrast to the West's threats and support for violent overthrow of a democratically elected government. It is astonishing that the only leadership the world has comes from Russia, China, and three or four countries in South America. The Western world no longer has diplomatic capability. Instead, the Western world relies on propaganda, threats, force, and schemes to overthrow governments that it first demonizes.

Notice that Putin repeatedly asks why the West created the crisis in Ukraine. He makes the important point that in post-Soviet countries, legality and democracy are fragile. Democracy and legality are not furthered by overthrowing democracy before it has taken root and placing in office an unelected government by force and illegality. It is impossible to argue with this point. Why, indeed, did the West murder democracy and constitutional order in Ukraine?

The fact that Putin asks the question does not mean he does not know the answer. He does not give the answer, because he is a diplomat and still has some hope for common sense and good will to prevail. He knows that the West supported the overthrow of the Ukrainian government as part of its strategic thrust against the sovereignty and independence of Russia. Aligning Ukraine with NATO means US missile bases in Ukraine. Remember how terrified Americans were of Soviet missile bases in Cuba?

Putin knows that in pursuit of world hegemony Washington is

driving the world to a dangerous war in which neither side can accept defeat. Thus, nuclear weapons would be unleashed. Putin knows that the reason Washington withdrew from the anti-ballistic missile treaty and installed anti-ballistic missiles in Poland is to degrade Russia's nuclear deterrent. Putin knows that the reason Washington changed its war doctrine to permit preemptive nuclear attack is to be able to threaten to carry out a first strike against Russia and indeed, to do so.

Putin also knows that only Europe can prevent this final devastation. Therefore, Putin does not make provocative statements or take strong actions. He hopes that Europe will notice his reasonable behavior in contrast with the reckless behavior of Washington and realize that Europe and NATO must cease enabling Washington's pursuit of hegemony, a pursuit that is driving the world to its destruction. Putin hopes that Europeans' sense of self-preservation will prevail over their lust for Washington's money and invitations to dinner at the White House.

By taking this humane and rational approach, Putin has established himself as the true leader of the world.

Washington counters Putin's leadership with demonization. Putin's leadership frustrates Washington and makes Putin a candidate for assassination.

An English translation of Vladimir Putin's March 4 press conference is available online.[19]

US ABANDONED INTERNATIONAL LAW, FOLLOWS THE LAW OF THE JUNGLE

March 11, 2014

Willy Wimmer was state secretary at the German Defense Ministry and vice president of the Organization for Security and Co-operation in Europe (OSCE). What this well-informed member of the European Establishment told RT is available online.[20] The translation is not very good, but the message comes through.

Western powers are following an agenda to partition the map of the European region under which a portion of the Black Sea territory will be under US domination, Wimmer, told RT.

The veteran German politician, who served as a Defense Ministry state secretary, reminded us that no Western government is talking about the extreme right element of the government in Kiev.

RT: More than a decade ago, you told your country's leadership of a disturbing connection between NATO's bombing of Yugoslavia and plans for the alliance's expansion. We have some extracts from the letter you wrote to then-Chancellor Gerhard Schröder after a conference organized by the US State Department. You raised concerns over some of the conclusions reached, such as: "It would be good, during NATO's current enlargement, to restore the territorial situation in the area between the Baltic Sea and Anatolia (modern-day Turkey) such as existed during the Roman Empire…" Do you think these plans still exist? And, if so, could the Ukrainian crisis be playing a role?

Willy Wimmer: I think what I thought of Gerhard Schröder is similar to Angela Merkel in May 2000—is exactly what is going on in these days. During the conference in Bratislava which was high ranking with state presidents, prime ministers, defense, and foreign ministers, and organized by the top leadership of the US State Department, they made a proposal to draw a line between Riga on the Baltic Sea, Odessa on the Black Sea, and Diyarbakir. All the territories west of this line should be under US domination, and the territories east of this line—they might be the Russian Federation or somebody else. That was the proposal—and when we see developments since then, I think it's like a schedule which had been presented to the conference participants; everything happens exactly as it was on the timetable in Bratislava.

RT: Let's take a look at another passage from your letter: "In all processes, peoples' rights to self-determination should be favored over all other provisions or rules of international law." That seemed to be agreed upon by high-profile Western diplomats taking part in that conference— why such staunch opposition to Crimea holding a similar referendum on its status now?

WW: Because they didn't make it. What we saw since the middle of the '90s—I think caused all these problems we have here today. Until the mid-90s, all major powers agreed in international law, and in cooperation. But in the middle of the 90s, the US changed habits, changed attitudes. They no longer pursed international law, they proposed the law of the jungle. At the beginning was the war against Yugoslavia, and since then, Afghanistan, Iraq, Syria, Libya, everything is going because of these developments, and they no longer stick to international law and to cooperation. They make use of military might and this creates the trouble and the fear we have in Europe.

RT: Some argue that a referendum cannot be considered legitimate if it's not recognized by the interim authorities in Kiev. Let me ask you this—is the current government in Ukraine legitimate?

WW: I think it was a putsch, a coup d'état, what happened in Kiev. And what we heard in the news before—OSCE and other international bodies are doing what they can to create a legal framework for a government which is not legal at all. The problem with this government is that they are not only not legal, they are working together with people who will be forbidden sooner or later by the Supreme Court here in Germany: right wing people, Nazis, fascists. It is interesting and outstanding that no western government is talking about these people who already created—once last century—disaster, terror, and wars in Europe, and now these people come back...

RT: Why is the legality then not being questioned and indeed the nationalist, the extremist element within the Kiev government?

WW: Because these new Nazis are our 'good Nazis' now and this is disastrous for all of Europe.

RT: Are they a real threat? Because some people are exaggerating this nationalist element within the Kiev government. Russia is really concerned and indeed those people in Crimea and the east of the country. Do they have fears that are justified?

WW: It's not only the people in Ukraine or Crimea or in Russia; the fear is in Dusseldorf, Cologne, Paris, and London as well. We did not create this modern Europe to have these people back again.

RT: So what do you think the next step should be in this stalemate? The West is calling on Russia to revoke its support for the referendum in Crimea—do you believe that's what Moscow should do?

WW: I live here in Germany and next Thursday, the federal Chancellor Dr. Merkel will give a speech to the Bundestag about Ukraine and I expect—I'm not referring to Crimea or to Moscow or to Kiev, I expect here in Berlin—that she will address this Nazi question, that she will address the massacre on Maidan Square. If this happened in China, there would be an uproar in Western countries. Everybody is quiet here. Why doesn't the Council of Europe take into

consideration to make an inquiry as well as the OSCE? I
expect Merkel to address these issues. And we had a major
party conference of our Bavarian brothers some days ago
and the main speaker addressed the audience with an
appeal not to forget the friendship with the Russian people.

More information is available at globalresearch.ca.[21]

OBAMA REGIME'S HYPOCRISY SETS NEW WORLD RECORD

March 12, 2014

From the moment that Washington launched its orchestrated coup in Kiev, Washington has been accusing Russia of "intervening in Ukraine." This propaganda ploy succeeded. The Western presstitute media reported (nonexistent) Russian intervention to the exclusion of coverage of Washington's obvious intervention.

Having falsely accused Russia of invading Crimea, the Obama regime now demands that Russia interfere in Crimea and prevent the referendum set for next Sunday. Unless Russia uses force to prevent the people of Crimea from exercising their right of self-determination, John Kerry declared, the Obama regime will not discuss the Ukrainian situation with Russia.

So, Kerry has given Russia the green light to send in troops to prevent Crimean self-determination.

The presstitute Western media has not noticed that out of one corner of his mouth Kerry denounces Russia for intervening and out of the other corner of his mouth Kerry demands that Russia intervene in behalf of Washington's interest and suppress Crimean self-determination.

What is the point of such an absurd demand on Russia?

The Obama regime claims that the Crimean vote is not legal, because all of Ukraine is not voting on Crimea's future. When Washington stole Kosovo from Serbia, Washington did not allow Serbia to vote on Kosovo secession. In the upcoming Scottish vote on whether to secede from the UK, only the Scottish are voting, not the British population. But these normal processes established in international law cannot be permitted to Crimeans, because the vote will not support Washington's agenda.

Clearly, the Obama regime has no shame.

The neoconservative warmongers who control the Obama regime are boasting that unless Russia prevents Crimean self-determination, Washington will use sanctions to "badly damage the Russian economy."

Sanctions are likely to backfire. Sanctions would damage economies of Washington's NATO puppet states, making them think again about providing cover for Washington's aggressive words and deeds. It is Europe that will pay for Washington's aggressive actions.

Sanctions are likely to speed up the implementation of the BRICS negotiations to leave the dollar system and settle their international accounts in their own currencies. All countries with financial and economic links to the West can be intimidated, punished, and destabilized by Washington. National sovereignty is inconsistent with being part of the US dollar system.

From Washington's standpoint, the importance of sanctions is not in any economic effects.

The importance is the propaganda advantage of portraying Russia as an offending party who is punished by Washington. Not only does this propaganda put Russia in the wrong, it also portrays Russia as subservient to Washington.

The Crimean government is actually elected, whereas the Washington-installed government in Kiev is not. GlobalResearch reports on the "democrats" who comprise the unelected government in Kiev.[22]

During the Clinton, George W. Bush, and Obama regimes, Washington has established that whatever serves Washington's agenda is legal. Laws inconsistent with Washington's agenda are simply not applicable. They are dead letter laws. Therefore, it comes as no surprise that in violation of US law that prohibits giving financial assistance to governments whose leaders come to power via coup or other illegal means, Washington is offering its stooges in Kiev $1 billion to help the coup government get up and running.

THE FAILURE OF
GERMAN LEADERSHIP

March 13, 2014

Washington, enabled by its compliant but stupid NATO puppets, is pushing the Ukrainian situation closer to war.

German Chancellor Merkel has failed her country, Europe, and world peace. Germany is the strength of the EU and NATO. Had Merkel said "No" to sanctions on Russia, that would have been the end of the crisis that Washington is brewing, a crisis unlikely to be ended short of war.

But Merkel has signed away the sovereignty of the German nation and accepted the fate of Germany to be a province in the American Empire. Thus has Merkel and the weak German leadership consigned the world to war. Already blamed for World War I and World War II, now Germany will be blamed for World War III.

Washington's Ukrainian coup is resulting in the dismemberment of Ukraine. Crimea, which Washington wanted most of all in order to deprive Russia of its warm water naval base on the Black Sea, has been lost and the Russian cities of eastern Ukraine will follow. Like Crimea, eastern Ukraine is more Russian than Ukrainian.

In what is clearly a fruitless and pointless effort to get Crimea back, Washington is demanding that Russia interfere in Crimea to prevent Crimea from seceding from Ukraine. If the Russian government refuses to follow Washington's orders, Washington has announced that it will inflict "damaging sanctions" on Russia. Initially, EU countries expressed an unwillingness to go along with Washington, but with bribes and threats, Washington has conquered Merkel and has its European puppets lined up following orders.

Washington understands that economic sanctions are a far lesser threat to Russia than the loss of its Black Sea naval base. Washington also understands that Putin cannot possibly abandon the millions of Russians in eastern and southern Ukraine to the mercy of the anti-Russian and unelected government imposed by Washington in Kiev. As Washington knows that its threat of sanctions is empty, why did Washington make it?

The answer is in order to drive the crisis to war. Washington's neoconservative Nazis have been agitating for war with Russia for a long time. They want to remove one of the three remaining restraints (Russia, China, Iran) on Washington's world hegemony. Washington wants to break up the BRICS (Brazil, Russia, India, China, South Africa) before these countries form a separate currency bloc and avoid the use of the US dollar.

Russia will respond in kind to Washington's sanctions. European peoples and Western banks and corporations will suffer losses. It would be three years before Washington could have in place a means of delivering US natural gas achieved by fracking and contamination of US water supplies to Europe to take the place of a Russian cutoff of energy to Europe.

The Western presstitute media will dramatize the Russian response to sanctions and demonize Russia, while ignoring who started the fight, thereby helping Washington prepare Americans for war.

All of this is perfectly clear, just as was the obvious conclusion of the march of events leading up to World War I. Now, like then, the people who see the outcome are powerless to stop it. Delusion rules.

Arrogance and hubris overflow. Statements and actions become ever more reckless, and then there is hell to pay.

Americans and Europeans, if they had any awareness at all, would be in the streets violently protesting the coming war toward which the insane criminals in Washington are driving the world.

Instead, the German chancellor, the French president, the British prime minister and the Western presstitute media continue to lie: It was legitimate for the West to steal Kosovo from Serbia and to steal the Ukrainian government, but it is not legitimate for the Russian population of Crimea to exercise self-determination and return to Russia. Washington and its EU puppets even have the audacity to declare falsely, after overthrowing an elected government in Ukraine and installing an unelected one, that Crimean self-determination violates the Ukrainian constitution, which no longer exists because Washington destroyed it.

The criminally insane government in Washington is trying to push the Russian bear into a corner. The bear is not going to surrender.

WASHINGTON PREFERS CONFLICT TO CRIMEAN SELF-DETERMINATION

March 16, 2014

Why is Washington so opposed to Crimean self-determination? The answer is that one of the main purposes of Washington's coup in Kiev was to have the new puppet government evict Russia from its Black Sea naval base in Crimea. Washington cannot use the government Washington has installed in Ukraine for that purpose if Crimea is no longer part of Ukraine.

What Washington has made completely obvious is that "self-determination" is a weapon used by Washington in behalf of its agenda. If self-determination advances Washington's agenda, Washington is for it. If self-determination does not advance Washington's agenda, Washington is against it.

The Washington-initiated UN Security Council resolution, vetoed by Russia, falsely declares that the referendum in Crimea, a referendum demanded by the people, "can have no validity, and cannot form the basis for any alteration of the status of Crimea; and calls upon all States, international organizations and specialized agencies not to recognize any alteration of the status of Crimea on the basis of this referendum and to refrain from any action or dealing that might be interpreted as recognizing any such altered status."

Washington could not make it any clearer that Washington totally opposes self-determination by Crimeans.

Washington claims, falsely, that the referendum cannot be valid unless the entire population of Ukraine votes and agrees with the decision by Crimeans. Note that when Washington stole Kosovo from Serbia, Washington did not let Serbians vote.

But overlook Washington's rank hypocrisy and self-serving double-standards. Let's apply Washington's argument that in order to be valid any change in Crimea's status requires a vote on the part of the population of the country that it departs. If this is the case, then Crimea has never been a part of Ukraine.

Under Washington's interpretation of international law, Ukraine is still a part of Russia. When Khrushchev transferred Crimea (but not Sevastopol, the Black Sea base) to Ukraine, Russians did not get to vote. Therefore, according to Washington's own logic it is invalid to recognize Crimea as part of Ukraine in the first place. That also goes for other parts of Russia that Lenin transferred to Ukraine. Under the logic of Washington's UN resolution, large parts of Ukraine are not legitimately part of Ukraine. They have remained parts of Russia, because Russians were not allowed to vote on their transfer to Ukraine.

Thus, there is no issue about "Russia annexing Crimea," because, according to Washington's logic, Crimea is still a part of Russia.

Do you need any more proof that the Ukrainian crisis is made up out of thin air by schemers in Washington who created the entire crisis for one purpose—to weaken Russia militarily?

No one was surprised that *The New York Times* published on March 14 the warmongering rant, written by neoconservatives for John McCain, which described Washington's aggression in Ukraine as Russia's aggression. The US government overthrows an elected democratic Ukrainian government and then accuses Russia of "invading and annexing Crimea" in order to divert attention from Washington's overthrow of Ukrainian democracy. There is no elected government in Kiev. The stooges acting as a government in Kiev were put in office by Washington. Who else chose them?

What surprised some was Rand Paul joining the hysteria. Rand Paul or his handlers wrote his propagandistic rant against Russia for *Time*. Rand Paul claims, falsely, that Putin has invaded Crimea and that it is an affront to "the international community." First of all, the decision of Crimea to leave Ukraine is a decision of the Crimean population and its elected government, not a decision by Russia. But, for the sake of argument, let's take Rand Paul's lie as the truth: Is "Vladimir Putin's invasion of Ukraine a gross violation of that nation's sovereignty and an affront to the international community" like Washington's invasions of Iraq and Afghanistan, and Washington-sponsored invasions of Libya and Syria, and Washington's ongoing slaughter of Pakistanis and Yemenis with drones, and Washington's violation of Iran's sovereignty with illegal sanctions, and Washington's violation of Ukrainian sovereignty by overthrowing the elected government and imposing Washington's stooges?

Even if Putin were behaving as Rand Paul ignorantly asserts, he would just be following the precedents established by Clinton in Serbia, by Bush in Afghanistan and Iraq, and by Obama in Afghanistan, Libya, Syria, and Ukraine. Washington's argument is reduced to: "We, the exceptional and indispensable nation can behave this way, but no other country can."

As some Americans have misplaced hopes in Rand Paul, it is just as well that he revealed in *Time* that he is just another politician prostituting himself for the neoconservative warmongers and the military/security complex. If Rand Paul is the hope for America, then clearly there is no hope.

The propaganda and lies issuing from Washington, its European puppets, *The New York Times*, *Time*, and the entirety of the Western media are repeating the path to war that led to World War I. It is happening right before our eyes.

OBAMA DECLARES CRIMEAN SELF-DETERMINATION A THREAT TO US NATIONAL SECURITY

March 16, 2014

In his March 6 Executive Order, "Blocking Property of Certain Persons Contributing to the Situation in Ukraine," Obama declares that support for Crimean self-determination constitutes "an unusual and extraordinary threat to the national security and foreign policy of the United States, and I hereby declare a national emergency to deal with that threat."[23]

Obama and the lawyers who drafted his executive order did not notice that the way the order is drafted it applies to Obama, to the unelected coup government in Kiev, and to the Washington and EU regimes. The order says that any person "responsible for or complicit in, or to have engaged in, directly or indirectly . . . actions or policies that undermine democratic processes or institutions in Ukraine" is subject to having his assets frozen.

Washington and the EU are the only two governments whose personnel have undermined democratic processes and institutions in Ukraine by overthrowing the elected government and imposing an unelected one.

Obama worshippers—yes there are still people that stupid—object when I call Obama the White House Fool. Yet, here is Obama or his lawyers proving that he is a fool by issuing an executive order that requires the property of Obama, Victoria Nuland, Samantha Powers, Susan Rice, the UK prime minister, the German chancellor, the French president, the EU Commission and any number of associated persons to be frozen by the US government.

Of course, Obama's executive order will not be applied to those to whom it is applicable. It will be applied to those to whom it is not applicable— authorities who permitted the Crimean population to exercise democratic processes in order to determine their own fate.

Washington has stood democracy on its head. Overthrowing Ukraine's democratic government and installing a puppet regime does not undermine democratic processes or institutions in Ukraine, but anything that allows self-determination to go forward in Crimea does undermine democratic processes.

The rejection of democracy by the West could not be made any clearer.

97% OF CRIMEANS
GIVE THE FINGER TO
THE WHITE HOUSE
TYRANT

March 16, 2014

In an unprecedented turnout unmatched by any Western election, Crimeans voted 97% to join Russia.

While Crimeans celebrate in the streets and international observers declare the referendum to be totally fair and free of all interference and threat, the White House declared that "we don't recognize no stinking vote." The moronic White House spokesperson said that the White House and "the international community"—Washington in its arrogance thinks that it is the voice of "the international community"—do not recognize the results of democracy in action.

Democracy is not acceptable to Washington, or to the two-bit punk American puppets who rule for Washington in Germany, UK, and France, when democracy does not serve Washington's agenda of hegemony over the entire world. The White House spokesperson lied through his teeth when he claimed that the referendum, which has been declared by international observers to have been completely free, was "administered under threats of violence and intimidation."

This statement, which the entire world now knows to be false, marks the government in Washington, and its subservient media, as the worst and most dangerous liars the world has ever experienced. All Washington is capable of is lies: Saddam Hussein has weapons of mass destruction and al Qaeda connections, Syrian President Assad used chemical weapons against his own citizens, Iran has a nuclear weapons program, Gaddafi gave his soldiers viagra so they could better rape Libyan women, Russia invaded Crimea, Osama bin Laden was the mastermind of 9/11. I could continue with hundreds of incidences of Washington's lies. Indeed, among aware people the word Washington has become synonymous with serial liar.

52

When will the world sanction the criminal enterprise that pretends to be a government of the United States?

When will the War Crimes Tribunal and the International Criminal Court issue arrest warrants for Obama and his entire criminal regime as well as the criminal regimes of Bush and Clinton?

When will the assets of the US government and its criminal members be seized?

How long will the world tolerate Washington's incessant destruction of countries and peoples from Somalia to Afghanistan to Iraq to Libya to Pakistan to Yemen to Syria to Ukraine, with Russia, Iran, and China waiting in the wings?

The United States government is the worst criminal enterprise in the history of the world. Not a single member of the government has told the truth about anything in the entire 21st century. The executive branch lies consistently to Congress, and Congress pretends it is hearing the truth. Congress is so useless it might as well be abolished. But "we have freedom and democracy and representative government."

The truth is that the evil of the universe is concentrated in Washington. It is this evil that is destroying millions of lives, and it is this evil that will destroy the world.

THE BBC: WASHINGTON'S MOUTHPIECE

March 16, 2014

Once upon a time the BBC was a news organization, but that was before the organization sold out to Washington. Today the BBC is a liar for Washington. Indeed, the BBC has become a despicable organization that believes that "exceptional, indispensable" Washington has the right to determine the fate of other peoples.

The proof is everywhere.[24]

The BBC says that the referendum in Crimea is disputed. But by whom? Not by the people voting. The dispute comes from the anti-democratic forces that are not voting–the Obama regime and its puppet UK government and puppet BBC ministry of propaganda.

How far the BBC has fallen! Look as these BBC lies:

Lie: "Many Crimeans loyal to Kiev boycotted the referendum...."

Fact: More than 83% voted and the vote was 97% against Washington. So who precisely boycotted the vote, and how could it have made any difference? The BBC doesn't care. The BBC's job is to lie for Washington. Let's assume that the 17% of voters who did not turn out would all have voted against rejoining Russia. That 17% together with the 3% who did vote not to rejoin Russia would give a vote of 20% against and 80% for. So, despite the BBC's utterly dishonest attempt to suggest that it wasn't a majority vote, it would have made no difference whatsoever if the voter turnout had been 100% instead of 80%.

Lie: "Pro-Russian forces took control of Crimea in February."

Fact: Anyone who would repeat this Washington lie at this stage is totally devoid of all integrity.

Crimeans took control of their destiny. Crimeans refused to let Washington and its corrupt British puppet take control of Crimea's destiny. Crimeans stood up to the lies and intimidation coming out of Washington and its two-bit punk NATO puppets. Crimeans gave the finger to the corrupt West.

The BBC has totally discredited itself as a news organization and revealed itself as an organ of Washington's Ministry of Propaganda. The BBC has made itself totally unreliable. No informed person will ever again believe a BBC report.

It is extraordinary that the BBC is so biased and careless in its reporting that the BBC did not notice that the BBC itself reported that 58% of the citizens of Crimea are Russian; yet more than 83% of the population voted and 97% voted to return to Russia where Crimea existed until Khrushchev put Crimea, without a vote, into Ukraine. Clearly, not merely the Russian population voted for a return to Russia.

The BBC might as well be abolished. Who needs the BBC when you can tune into the lies issuing directly from the White House?

TWO STEPS FORWARD, ONE STEP BACK

March 17, 2014

Washington's plan to evict Russia from its Black Sea naval base has fallen apart. But to turn around Lenin's quote, "two steps forward, one step back.

Do you remember the threats coming from John Kerry, the White House, Hillary Clinton, and the lickspittle Merkel about the harsh sanctions that would "badly damage" the Russian economy unless Russia prevented the referendum vote in Crimea? Threats, not diplomacy, is Washington's way. As the Russians kept reminding the Europeans, sanctions on Russia would hurt European economies.

Having made threats, something that Washington's presstitute media could hype as sanctions had to be imposed, so Washington came up with sanctions, not on Russia, but on eleven individuals: the deposed Ukrainian president, an advisor to the deposed president, 2 Crimean officials, and 7 Russians.

The choice of the officials is an utter mystery. The seven Russians are a Putin aid, a Putin adviser, four members of the Russian parliament (Duma) and a deputy prime minister. What any of these people had to do with the referendum in Crimea, no one knows.

Moreover, the sanctions only apply to foreign bank accounts that these 11 individuals might have outside Russia, and the deposed Ukrainian president is the only one likely to have a foreign bank account. Other reports say that the sanctions are only for the next six months.

If the Washington and EU criminals steal any money from these persons, the Russian central bank can replenish their stolen accounts.

The people who decided that Crimea would disassociate from Ukraine and return to Russia were the people themselves. Under the wording of Obama's silly sanctions, his sanctions should apply to the Crimean people who voted to disassociate from the US stooge government in Kiev.

Additionally, Obama's sanctions apply to himself and to his regime and to its NATO puppets as it was the West that overthrew the elected government of Ukraine, not Russia or Crimea. Washington, of course, never applies law to itself.

In other words, the sanctions are meaningless, but the White House covered the shortfall by declaring: "If Russia continues to interfere in Ukraine, we stand ready to impose further sanctions." Perhaps Russia should have imposed sanctions by cutting off natural gas deliveries to Europe.

Obama's hypocrisy is hard to take. It is the White House that is interfering in Ukraine. It was Washington that financed and organized the overthrow of the elected Ukraine government, using well organized and well armed neo-Nazis to intimidate the unarmed police and ruling party, thus clearing the way for Washington to set up an unelected government of its well-paid stooges.

What the White House overlooked is that southern and eastern Ukraine are Russian, not Ukrainian, so the neocons' coup has caused Crimea to depart and is causing widespread protests in eastern Ukraine against Washington's stooge unelected government in Kiev. Washington's stooge Kiev government has appointed unelected Ukrainian multibillionaire oligarchs, who have their own private security forces, as mayors of the Russian cities to put down the protests. If the oligarchs use violence against the Russian people, the likely result will be revolt in southern and eastern Ukraine, which in every essential way is Russian.

If eastern Ukraine returns to Russia, Washington will be left with the ultra-nationalists of western Ukraine, people who fought for Hitler during World War II. The EU doesn't want ultra-nationalists as the EU is busy stamping out nationalism and the sovereignty of European countries. Nevertheless, Washington will have gained a strategic advantage over Moscow, as Washington can place anti-ballistic missile and other military bases on western Ukraine's border with Russia, thus completing Washington's encirclement of Russia with hostile military and missile bases.

Russia will neutralize the US bases by targeting them with Iskander missiles, which cannot be intercepted by ABMs.

All that the neocons will have achieved is to further make clear to Russia, and to China, that Washington has both on its target list, because both are in the way of Washington's world hegemony.

One can only wonder why Putin doesn't preempt the coming US military attack on Russia by destroying NATO economically without firing a shot. All Putin needs to do is to cut Europe off from energy. It would take Washington three years to create the capability to deliver US natural gas, achieved by fracking's destruction of US water supplies, to Europe. By that time NATO governments would likely have been overthrown by mass unemployment and economic suffering. Putin could also seize all foreign assets in Russia and rapidly complete the arrangements with China, India,

Brazil, and South Africa to abandon the use of the US dollar in international settlements.

The US dollar as world reserve currency is the source of American imperialism. The five countries that comprise the BRICS have half of the world's population. They can conduct their economic affairs without the dollar.

The world needs to understand that the neoconservative US government is the Third Reich on steroids. It is a malevolent force with no sense of justice or respect for truth, law, or human life. Just ask the residents of Iraq, Afghanistan, Libya, Syria, Palestine, Pakistan, Yemen, Somalia, Lebanon, Honduras, Venezuela, Cuba, Iran. Even the deluded western Ukrainians will soon catch on.

Obama himself declared that the US is "the exceptional nation." This is the neoconservatives' version of Hitler's declaration that the German nation was exceptional and, therefore, above all others. The only difference between Washington and National Socialist Germany is that Washington has a far more powerful police state and nuclear weapons.

The hubris and arrogance that arises from Washington's belief that it is the government of the "indispensable and exceptional nation" means Washington has no respect for any other country, nor for law whether its own or international. Washington can invade countries without cause, a war crime.

Washington can kidnap and torture people, a crime under US and International law. Washington can ignore the self-determination of peoples, such as Crimeans. Who are mere Crimeans to vote on their own future without Washington's consent, without Washington determining the outcome? Washington declares the Crimean people's self-determination "illegitimate and illegal," and refuses to recognize self-determination, while pretending to be the home of "freedom and democracy."

No government in human history can come close to the hypocrisy and malevolence of Washington.

Armed with nuclear weapons and a military doctrine of pre-emptive nuclear first strike, Washington alone stands as the threat to life on earth.

HOW MUCH WAR DOES WASHINGTON WANT?

March 26, 2014

"America does not at the moment have a functioning democracy."
Former US President Jimmy Carter

I doubt that the Ukraine crisis precipitated by Washington's overthrow of the democratic government is over. Washington has won the propaganda war everywhere outside of Russia and Ukraine itself. Within Ukraine people are aware that the coup has made them worse off. The Crimea has already separated from the US puppet government in Kiev and rejoined Russia. Other parts of Russian Ukraine could follow.

In Kiev itself where the unelected, imposed-by-Washington dictatorial government resides, extreme rightwing Ukrainian nationalists, whose roots go back to fighting for National Socialist Germany, are at work intimidating public prosecutors, media editors, and the US imposed "government" itself. There is an abundance of videos available on the Internet, some made by the extreme nationalists themselves, that clearly reveal the intimidation of the imposed and unelected government installed by Washington.

In Kiev US bribes contend with naked neo-Nazi force. Which will prevail?

The murder of ultra-nationalist Right Sector militant leader Oleksandr Muzychko by police of the acting Interior Minister of the American stooge government in Ukraine on March 25 has resulted in another Right Sector leader, Dmitry Yarosh, demanding the resignation of Arsen Avakov, the acting Interior Minister, and the arrest of the police who killed Muzychko. Yarosh declared: "We cannot watch silently as the Interior Ministry works to undermine the revolution." Right Sector organizer Roman Koval in Rovno, Ukraine, warned: "We will take revenge on Avakov for the death of our brother."

How this will play out is uncertain at this time. The violence provided by the Right Sector and other ultranationalist groups was essential to the success of the Washington-backed coup in overthrowing the elected democratic government. But the Right Sector has emerged as both an embarrassment and a threat to the unelected coup government and to its Washington sponsors who are selling the Washington-installed puppet government as a progressive exercise in democracy. This sell is difficult when ultra-nationalist thugs are beating up the imposed government.

Could civil war break out in Kiev between the Right Sector and the government installed by Washington?

We know that the Right Sector was sufficiently organized and disciplined to take over the protests. We don't know how well organized is the Washington puppet government or what force this group has at its disposal. We don't know whether Washington has provided mercenaries to protect the government Washington has installed. It is not clear at this time where the power balance lies between the Right Sector and the US stooge government.

Washington's intervention in Ukraine has unleashed dark forces. Yulia Tymoshenko, the criminal Ukrainian oligarch, who braids her hair or hair piece over her head like a crown, was released from prison by Washington's stooges and has not stopped putting her foot, or both feet, in her mouth. Her latest in her intercepted and leaked telephone conversation is her declaration that "it's about time we grab our guns and go kill those damn Russians together with their leader." She declared that not even scorched earth should be left where Russia stands.[25] Tymoshenko was sentenced to prison by Ukrainians, not by Russians. Contrast her extreme language and Russophobia with the calm measured tones of Putin, who reaffirms Russia's interest to continue good relations with Ukraine.

On March 23 Tymoshenko was interviewed by the German newspaper, *Bild*, a mouthpiece for Washington. The crazed Tymoshenko declared that Putin was even more dangerous than Hitler. This year 2014 is the 100th anniversary of World War I. As my Oxford professor, Michael Polanyi, said, this was the war that destroyed Europe. He meant culturally and morally as well as physically. As John Maynard Keynes made clear in his prediction, the propagandistic way in which World War I was blamed on Germany and the "peace" that was imposed on Germany set up World War II.

We are witnesses today to the same kind of propagandistic lies with regard to Russia that caused World War I. In *The Genesis of the World War*, Harry Elmer Barnes quotes the French chief editor of a French history of the organization of propaganda in France during World War I. The French built a massive building called La Maison de la Presse. In this building images of people were created with hands cut off, tongues torn out, eyes gouged out, and skulls crushed with brains laid bare. These images were then photographed and "sent as unassailable evidence of German atrocities to all parts of the globe, where they did not fail to produce the desired effect." Also provided were "fictitious photographs of bombarded French and Belgian churches, violated graves and monuments and scenes of ruins and desolation. The staging and painting of these scenes were done by the best scene-painters of the Paris Grand Opera."

This vicious propaganda against Germany meant that Germany could be blamed for the war and that all of President Woodrow Wilson's guarantees to Germany of no reparations and no territorial loss if Germany agreed to an armistice could be violated. The propaganda success guaranteed that the peace settlement would be so one-sided as to set up the Second World War.

Russia has observed Washington's strategic moves against Russian national interests and Russian sovereignty for two decades. What does Putin think when he hears the vicious anti-Russian propaganda based 100% in lies?

This is what Putin thinks: The Americans promised Gorbachev that they would not take NATO into Eastern Europe, but the Americans did. The Americans withdrew from the ABM Treaty, which prohibited escalating the arms race with anti-ballistic missile systems. The Americans arranged with Poland to deploy anti-ballistic missile bases on Poland's border with Russia. The Americans tell us the fantastic lie that the purpose of American missile bases in Poland is to protect Europe from non-existent Iranian ICBMs. The Americans change their war doctrine to elevate nuclear weapons from a retaliatory deterrent to a pre-emptive first strike force. The Americans pretend that this change in war doctrine is directed at terrorists, but we know it is directed at Russia. The Americans have financed "color revolutions" in Georgia and Ukraine and hope to do so in the Russian Federation itself. The Americans support the terrorists in Chechnya. The Americans trained and equipped the Georgian military and gave it the green light to attack our peacekeepers in South Ossetia. The Americans have financed the overthrow of the elected government in Ukraine and blame me for the anxiety this caused among Crimeans who on their own volition fled Ukraine and returned to Russia from whence they came. Even Gorbachev said that Khrushchev should never have put Crimea into Ukraine. Solzhenitsyn said that Lenin should not have put Russian provinces into eastern and southern Ukraine. Now I have these Russian provinces agitating to return to Russia, and the Americans are blaming me for the consequences of their own reckless and irresponsible actions.

The Americans say I want to rebuild the Soviet Empire. Yet, the Americans witnessed me depart from Georgia when I had this former Russian province in my hands, thanks to the short-lived war instigated by the Americans.

There is no end to the American lies. I have done everything possible to respond to provocations in a lowkey reasonable manner, offering to work things out diplomatically, as has my Foreign Minister, Lavrov.

But the Americans continue to provoke and to hide their provocations behind lies. The Americans brazenly bring to me a strategic threat in Ukraine. They intend to put Ukraine into NATO, the purpose of which expired with the Soviet collapse. They intend to put more missile bases on Russia's borders, and they intended to evict Russia from its Black Sea naval base, its warm water port. Americans have no intention of working anything out. They intend to subjugate Russia. Washington wants Russia powerless, surrounded with ABM bases that degrade our strategic deterrent to uselessness.

These Americans will not work with me. They will not listen to me or to Russia's Foreign Minister. They only hear their own call for American hegemony over the world. My only alternative is to prepare for war.

The government of China, having read Washington's war plans for war against China and being fully aware of Washington's "pivot to Asia," in which the "indispensable nation" announced its "safe-guarding of peace" by surrounding China with naval and air bases, understands that it has the same Washington enemy as does Russia.

What the entire world faces, every country, every individual regardless of their political orientation, is a Washington-engineered confrontation with Russia and China. This confrontation is enabled by Washington's bought-and-paid-for European and UK puppet states. Without the cover provided by Europe, Washington's acts of aggression would result in war crimes charges against the government in Washington. The world would not be able to enforce these charges without war, but Washington would be isolated.

The European, Canadian, Australian, New Zealand, and UK governments have betrayed not only their own peoples but also the peoples of the entire world by lending the support of Western Civilization to Washington's lawlessness.

NOTE: RT provides insight into the type of Ukrainian violence against the Russian population in Ukraine that could end in Russian occupation of the Russian provinces of Ukraine.[26]

PUSHING TOWARD
THE FINAL WAR

March 28, 2014

Does Obama realize that he is leading the US and its puppet states to war with Russia and China, or is Obama being manipulated into this disaster by his neoconservative speech writers and government officials? World War I (and World War II) was the result of the ambitions and mistakes of a very small number of people. Only one head of state was actually involved—the President of France.

In *The Genesis of the World War*, Harry Elmer Barnes shows that World War I was the product of 4 or 5 people. Three stand out: Raymond Poincaré, President of France; Sergei Sazonov, Russian Foreign Minister; and Alexander Izvolski, Russian Ambassador to France. Poincaré wanted Alsace-Lorraine from Germany, and the Russians wanted Istanbul and the Bosphorus Strait, which connects the Black Sea to the Mediterranean. They realized that their ambitions required a general European war and worked to produce the desired war.

A Franco-Russian Alliance was formed. This alliance became the vehicle for orchestrating the war. The British government, thanks to the incompetence, stupidity, or whatever of its Foreign Minister, Sir Edward Grey, was pulled into the Franco-Russian Alliance. The war was started by Russia's mobilization.

The German Kaiser, Wilhelm II, was blamed for the war despite the fact that he did everything possible to avoid it.

Barnes' book was published in 1926. His reward for confronting the corrupt court historians with the truth was to be accused of being paid by Germany to write his history. Eighty-six years later historian Christopher Clark in his book, *The Sleepwalkers*, comes to essentially the same conclusion as Barnes.

In the history I was taught the war was blamed on Germany for challenging British naval supremacy by building too many battleships. The court historians who gave us this tale helped to set up World War II.

We are again on the road to World War. One hundred years ago the creation of a world war by a few had to be done under the cover of deception.

Germany had to be caught off guard. The British had to be manipulated and, of course, people in all the countries involved had to be propagandized and brainwashed.

Today the drive to war is blatantly obvious. The lies are obvious, and the entire West is participating, both media and governments.

The American puppet, Canadian Prime Minister Stephen Harper, openly lied on Canadian TV that Russian President Putin had invaded Crimea, threatened Ukraine, and was restarting the Cold War. The host of the TV program sat and nodded his head in agreement with these bald-faced lies. The link to the interview has since been removed. The script that Washington handed to its Canadian puppet has been handed to all of Washington's puppets, and everywhere in the West the message is the same. "Putin invaded and annexed Crimea, Putin is determined to rebuild the Soviet Empire, Putin must be stopped."

I hear from many Canadians who are outraged that their elected government represents Washington and not Canadians, but as bad as Harper is, Obama and Fox "News" are worse.

On March 26 I managed to catch a bit of Fox "news." Murdoch's propaganda organ was reporting that Putin was restoring the Soviet era practice of physical exercise. Fox "news" made this a threatening and dangerous gesture toward the West. Fox produced an "expert," who declared that Putin was creating "the Hitler youth," with a view toward rebuilding the Soviet empire.

The extraordinary transparent lie that Russia sent an army into Ukraine and annexed Crimea is now accepted as fact everywhere in the West, even among critics of US policy toward Russia.

Obama, or his handlers and programmers, are relying on the total historical ignorance of Western peoples.

The ignorance and gullibility of Western peoples allows the American neoconservatives to fashion "news" that controls their minds.

Obama recently declared that Washington's destruction of Iraq—up to one million killed, four million displaced, infrastructure in ruins, sectarian violence exploding, a country in total ruins—is nowhere near as bad as Russia's acceptance of Crimean self-determination. US Secretary of State John Kerry actually ordered Putin to prevent the referendum and stop Crimeans from exercising self-determination.

Obama's speech on March 26 at the Palace of Fine Arts in Brussels is surreal. It is beyond hypocrisy.

Obama says that Western ideals are challenged by self-determination in Crimea. Russia, Obama says, must be punished by the West for permitting Crimeans to exercise self-determination. The return of a Russian province on its own volition to its mother country where it existed for 200 years is presented by Obama as a dictatorial, anti-democratic act of tyranny.[27] Here was Obama, who has shredded the US Constitution, speaking of "individual rights and rule of law."

Where is this rule of law? Habeas corpus, due process, the right to open trials and determination of guilt by independent jurors prior to imprisonment and execution, the right to privacy have all been overturned by the Bush/Obama regimes. Torture is against US and international law; yet Washington set up torture prisons all over the globe.

How is it possible that the representative of the war criminal US government can stand before an European audience and speak of "rule of law," "individual rights," "human dignity," "self-determination," "freedom," without the audience breaking out in laughter?

No one applauded Obama's nonsensical speech. But for Europe to accept such blatant lies from a liar without protest empowers the momentum toward war that Washington is pushing.

Obama demands more NATO troops to be stationed in Eastern Europe to contain Russia.[28] Obama said that a buildup of military forces on Russia's borders would reassure Poland and the Baltic states that, as NATO members, they will be protected from Russian aggression. This nonsense is voiced by Obama despite the fact that no one expects Russia to invade Poland or the Baltic countries.

Obama doesn't say what effect the US/NATO military buildup and numerous war games on Russia's border will have on Russia. Will the Russian government conclude that Russia is about to be attacked and strike first? The reckless carelessness of Obama is the way wars start.

Declaring that "freedom isn't free," Obama is putting pressure on Western Europe to pony up more money for a military buildup to confront Russia.[29]

As the delusion takes hold in Washington that the US represents idealism standing firmly against Russian aggression, delusion enabled by the presstitute media, the UN General Assembly vote, and Washington's string of puppet states, self-righteousness rises in Washington's breast.

With rising self-righteousness will come more demands for punishing Russia, more demonization of Russia and Putin, more lies echoed by the presstitutes and puppets. Ukrainian violence against Russian residents is likely to intensify with the anti-Russian propaganda. Putin could be forced to send in Russian troops to defend Russians.

Why are people so blind that they do not see Obama driving the world to its final war?

Just as Obama dresses up his aggression toward Russia as idealism resisting selfish territorial ambitions, the English, French, and Americans presented their World War I "victory" as the triumph of idealism over

German and Austrian imperialism and territorial ambitions. But the Tsar's government failed to gain the Straits and instead lost the country to Lenin. At the Versailles Conference, the Bolsheviks

> revealed the existence of the notorious Secret Treaties embodying as sordid a program of territorial pilfering as can be found in the history of diplomacy. It appears that the chief actual motives of the Entente in the World War were the seizure of Constantinople and the Straits for Russia; not only the return of Alsace-Lorraine to France, but the securing of the west bank of the Rhine, which would have involved the seizure of territory historically far longer connected with Germany than Alsace-Lorraine had ever been with France; the rewarding of Italian entry into the War by extensive territory grabbed away from Austria and the Jugo-Slavs; and the sequestering of the German imperial possessions, the acquisition of the German merchant marine and the destruction of the German navy in the interest of increasing the strength of the British Empire.[30]

The American share of the loot was seized German and Austrian investments in the US.

The secret British, Russian, and French aims of the war were hidden from the public, which was whipped up with fabricated propaganda to support a war whose outcomes were far different from the intentions of those who caused the war. People seem unable to learn from history. We are now witnessing the world again being led down the garden path by lies and propaganda, this time in behalf of American world hegemony.

WESTERN
LOOTING
OF UKRAINE

March 29, 2014

It is now apparent that the "Maiden protests" in Kiev were in actuality a Washington organized coup against the elected democratic government. The purpose of the coup is to put NATO military bases on Ukraine's border with Russia and to impose an IMF austerity program that serves as cover for Western financial interests to loot the country. The sincere idealistic protesters who took to the streets were the gullible dupes of the plot to destroy their country.

Politically Ukraine is an untenable aggregation of Ukrainian and Russian territory, because traditional Russian territories were stuck into the borders of the Ukraine Soviet Republic by Lenin and Khrushchev.

The Crimea, stuck into Ukraine by Khrushchev, has already departed and rejoined Russia. Unless some autonomy is granted to them, Russian areas in eastern and southern Ukraine might also depart and return to Russia. If the animosity displayed toward the Russian speaking population by the stooge government in Kiev continues, more defections to Russia are likely.

The Washington-imposed coup faces other possible difficulties from what seems to be a growing conflict between the well-organized Right Sector and the Washington-imposed stooges. If armed conflict between these two groups were to occur, Washington might conclude that it needs to send help to its stooges. The appearance of US/NATO troops in Ukraine would create pressure on Putin to occupy the remaining Russian speaking parts of Ukraine.

Before the political and geographical issues are settled, the Western looting of Ukraine has already begun.

The Western media, doesn't tell any more truth about IMF "rescue packages" than it does about anything else. The media reports, and many Ukrainians believe, that the IMF is going to rescue Ukraine financially by giving the country billions of dollars.

Ukraine will never see one dollar of the IMF money. What the IMF is going to do is to substitute Ukrainian indebtedness to the IMF for Ukrainian indebtedness to Western banks. The IMF will hand over the money to the Western banks, and the Western banks will reduce Ukraine's indebtedness by the amount of IMF money. Instead of being indebted to the banks, Ukraine will now be indebted to the IMF.

Now the looting can begin. The IMF loan brings new conditions and imposes austerity on the Ukrainian people so that the Ukraine government can gather up the money with which to repay the IMF. The IMF conditions that will be imposed on the struggling Ukraine population will consist of severe reductions in old-age pensions, in government services, in government employment, and in subsidies for basic consumer purchases such as natural gas. Already low living standards will plummet. In addition, Ukrainian public assets and Ukrainian owned private industries will have to be sold off to Western purchasers.

Additionally, Ukraine will have to float its currency. In a futile effort to protect its currency's value from being driven very low (and consequently import prices very high) by speculators ganging up on the currency and short-selling it, Ukraine will borrow more money with which to support its currency in the foreign exchange market. Of course, the currency speculators will end up with the borrowed money, leaving Ukraine much deeper in debt than currently.

The corruption involved is legendary, so the direct result of the gullible Maiden protesters will be lower Ukrainian living standards, more corruption, loss of sovereignty over the country's economic policy, and the transfer of Ukrainian public and private property to Western interests.

If Ukraine falls into NATO's clutches, Ukraine will also find itself in a military alliance against Russia and find itself targeted by Russian missiles. This will be a tragedy for Ukraine and Russia as Ukrainians have relatives in Russia and Russians have relatives in Ukraine. The two countries have essentially been one for 200 years. To have them torn apart by Western looting and Washington's drive for world hegemony is a terrible shame and a great crime.

The gullible dupes who participated in the orchestrated Maiden protests will rue it for the rest of their lives.

When the protests began, I described what the consequences would be and said that I would explain the looting process. It is not necessary for me to do so. Professor Michel Chossudovsky has explained the IMF looting process along with much history.[31]

One final word. Despite unequivocal evidence of one country after another being looted by the West, governments of indebted countries continue to sign up for IMF programs. Why do governments of countries continue to agree to the foreign looting of their populations? The only answer is that they are paid. The corruption that is descending upon Ukraine will make the former regime look honest.

OBAMA ISSUES
THREATS TO RUSSIA
AND NATO

April 6, 2014

The Obama regime has issued simultaneous threats to the enemy it is making out of Russia and to its European NATO allies on which Washington is relying to support sanctions on Russia. This cannot end well.

As even Americans living in a controlled media environment are aware, Europeans, South Americans, and Chinese are infuriated that the National Stasi Agency is spying on their communications. NSA's affront to legality, the US Constitution, and international diplomatic norms is unprecedented. Yet, the spying continues, while Congress sits sucking its thumb and betraying its oath to defend the Constitution of the United States.

In Washington mumbo-jumbo from the executive branch about "national security" suffices to negate statutory law and Constitutional requirements. Western Europe, seeing that the White House, Congress and the Federal Courts are impotent and unable to rein-in the Stasi Police State, has decided to create a European communication system that excludes US companies in order to protect the privacy of European citizens and government communications from the Washington Stasi.

The Obama regime, desperate that no individual and no country escape its spy net, denounced Western Europe's intention to protect the privacy of its communications as "a violation of trade laws."

Obama's US Trade Representative, who has been negotiating secret "trade agreements" in Europe and Asia that give US corporations immunity to the laws of all countries that sign the agreements, has threatened WTO penalties if Europe's communications network excludes the US companies that serve as spies for NSA. Washington in all its arrogance has told its most necessary allies that if you don't let us spy on you, we will use WTO to penalize you.

So there you have it. The rest of the world now has the best possible reason to exit the WTO and to avoid the Trans-Pacific and Trans-Atlantic "trade agreements." The agreements are not about trade. The purpose of

69

these "trade agreements" is to establish the hegemony of Washington and US corporations over other countries.

In an arrogant demonstration of Washington's power over Europe, the US Trade Representative warned Washington's NATO allies: "US Trade Representative will be carefully monitoring the development of any such proposals" to create a separate European communication network.[32] Washington is relying on the Chancellor of Germany, the President of France, and the Prime Minister of the UK to place service to Washington above their countries' communications privacy.

It has dawned on the Russian government that being a part of the American dollar system means that Russia is open to being looted by Western banks and corporations or by individuals financed by them, that the ruble is vulnerable to being driven down by speculators in the foreign exchange market and by capital outflows, and that dependence on the American international payments system exposes Russia to arbitrary sanctions imposed by the "exceptional and indispensable country."

Why it took the Russian government so long to realize that the dollar payments system puts countries under Washington's thumb is puzzling. Perhaps the answer is the success of US Cold War propaganda.

Cold War propaganda portrayed America as the shining light, the great observer of human rights, opponent of torture, upholder of liberty, defender of the downtrodden, lover of peace, and benefactor of the world. This image survived even as the US government prevented the rise of any representative governments in Latin America and while Washington has bombed half a dozen countries into rubble.

Russians emerging from communism naturally aligned with the propaganda image of "American freedom." That the US and Europe were corrupt and had blood on their hands was overlooked.

During the years of anti-Soviet propaganda, Washington was murdering European women and children and blaming communists. The truth came out when President of Italy Francesco Cossiga publicly revealed Operation Gladio, a false flag terrorist scheme run by the CIA and Italian Intelligence during the 1960s, 1970s, and 1980s that targeted European women and children with bombs in order to blame the communists and thereby prevent European communist parties from making electoral gains. This is one of the best known false flag events in history, resulting in extraordinary confessions by Italian intelligence.

Now that the Russian government understands that Russia must depart the dollar system in order to protect Russian sovereignty, President Putin has entered into barter/ruble oil deals with China and Iran.

However, Washington objects to Russia abandoning the dollar international payment system. Zero Hedge, a more reliable news source than the US print and TV media, reports that Washington has conveyed to both Russia and Iran that a non-dollar oil deal would trigger US sanctions.[33]

Washington's objection to the Russian/Iranian deal made it clear to all governments that Washington uses the dollar-based international payments system as a means of control. Why should countries accept an international payments system that infringes their sovereignty? What would happen if instead of passively accepting the dollar as the means of international payment, countries simply left the dollar system? The value of the dollar would fall and so would Washington's power. Without the power that the dollar's role as world reserve currency gives the US to pay its bills by printing money, the US could not maintain its aggressive military posture or its payoffs to foreign governments to do its bidding.

Washington would be just another failed empire, whose population can barely make ends meet, while the One Percent who comprise the mega-rich compete with 200-foot yachts and $750,000 fountain pens.

Aristocracy and serfs. is what America has become, a throwback to the feudal era.

It is only a matter of time before it is universally recognized that the US is a failed state. Let's pray this recognition occurs before the arrogant inhabitants of Washington blow up the world in pursuit of hegemony over others.

Washington's provocative military moves against Russia are reckless and dangerous. The buildup of NATO air, ground, and naval forces on Russia's borders in violation of the 1997 NATO-Russian treaty and the Montreux Convention naturally strike the Russian government as suspicious, especially as the buildups are justified on the basis of lies that Russia is about to invade Poland, the Baltic States, and Moldova in addition to Ukraine.

These lies are transparent. The Russian Foreign Minister Sergey Lavrov has asked NATO for an explanation, stating: "We are not only expecting answers, but answers that will be based fully on respect for the rules we agreed on."[34]

Anders Fogh Rasmussen, Washington's puppet installed as NATO figurehead who is no more in charge of NATO than I am, responded in a way guaranteed to raise Russian anxieties. Rasmussen dismissed the Russian Foreign Minister's request for explanation as "propaganda and disinformation."

Clearly, what we are experiencing is rising tensions caused by Washington and NATO. These tensions are in addition to the tensions arising from Washington's coup in Ukraine.

Little did the protesters in Kiev, called into the streets by Washington's NGOs, realize that their foolishness was setting the world on a path to Armageddon.

WASHINGTON'S CREDIBILITY TAKES HITS

April 9, 2014

Russia and China have had enough of Washington's abuse of the dollar's world currency role and are taking steps to disconnect their international trade from the dollar. Eventually, this means a drop in the demand for US dollars and a corresponding drop in the dollar's exchange value.

As John Williams (shadowstats.com) has made clear, the US economy has not recovered from the downturn in 2008 and has weakened further. The vast majority of the US population is hard pressed from the lack of income growth for years. As the US is now an import-dependent economy, a drop in the dollar's value would raise US prices and push living standards lower.

Washington misjudged the reaction in Ukraine to its overthrow of the elected democratic government and imposition of a stooge government. Crimea quickly departed Ukraine and rejoined Russia. Other former Russian territories in Ukraine might soon follow. Protesters in Luhansk, Donetsk, and Kharkov are demanding their own referendums. Separatists have declared the Donetsk and Luhansk republics.

Washington's stooge government in Kiev has threatened to put the protests down with violence.[35] Washington claims that the protests are organized by Russia, but no informed persons believes Washington, not even Washington's Ukrainian stooges.

Russian news reports have identified US mercenaries among the Kiev force that has been sent to put down the separatists in eastern Ukraine. A member of the right-wing, neo-Nazi Fatherland Party in the Kiev parliament has called for shooting the protesters dead.

With Washington out on a limb issuing threats hand over fist, Washington is pushing Europe into two highly undesirable confrontations. Europeans do not want a war with Russia over Washington's coup in Kiev, and Europeans understand that any real sanctions on Russia, if observed, would do more damage to Europeans. Within the EU, growing economic inequality among the countries, high unemployment, and stringent economic austerity imposed on poorer members have produced enormous strains. Europeans are in no mood to bear the brunt of a Washington-orchestrated conflict with Russia. While Washington presents Europe with war and sacrifice, Russia and China offer trade and friendship. Washington will do its best to keep European politicians bought-and-paid-for and in line with Washington's policies, but the downside for Europe of going along with Washington is now much greater.

Across many fronts, Washington is emerging in the world's eye as duplicitous, untrustworthy, and totally corrupt. A Securities and Exchange Commission prosecuting attorney, James Kidney, used the occasion of his retirement to reveal that higher ups had squelched his prosecutions of Goldman Sachs and other "banks too big to fail," because his SEC bosses were not focused on justice but "on getting high-paying jobs after their government service" by protecting the banks from prosecution for their illegal actions.[36]

The US Agency for International Development has been caught trying to use social media to overthrow the government of Cuba.[37]

This audacious recklessness comes on top of Washington's overthrow of the Ukrainian government, the NSA spying scandal, Seymour Hersh's investigative report that the Sarin gas attack in Syria was a false flag event arranged by NATO member Turkey in order to justify a US military attack on Syria,

Washington's forcing down Bolivian President Evo Morales' presidential plane to be searched, the misuse of the Libyan no-fly resolution for military attack, Saddam Hussein's "weapons of mass destruction," and on and on. Essentially, Washington has so badly damaged other countries' confidence in the judgment and integrity of the US government that belief in US leadership is decling. Washington relies on threats and bribes and increasingly presents itself as a bully.

The self-inflicted hammer blows to Washington's credibility have taken a toll. The most serious blow of all is the dawning realization everywhere that Washington's crackpot conspiracy theory of 9/11 is false.

Large numbers of independent experts as well as more than one hundred first responders have contradicted every aspect of Washington's absurd conspiracy theory. No aware person believes that a few Saudi Arabians, who could not fly airplanes, operating without help from any intelligence agency, outwitted the entire National Security State, not only all 16 US intelligence agencies but also all intelligence agencies of NATO and Israel as well.

Nothing worked on 9/11. Airport security failed four times in one hour, more failures in one hour than have occurred during the preceding

116,232 hours of the 21st century combined. For the first time in history the US Air Force could not get interceptor fighters off the ground and into the sky. For the first time in history Air Traffic Control lost airliners for up to one hour and did not report it. For the first time in history low temperature, short-lived fires on a few floors caused massive steel structures to weaken and collapse at essentially free fall acceleration.

Two-thirds of Americans fell for this crackpot story. The left-wing fell for it because they saw the story as the oppressed striking back at America's evil empire. The right-wing fell for the story because they saw it as the demonized Muslims striking out at American goodness. President George W. Bush expressed the right-wing view very well: "They hate us for our freedom and democracy."

But no one else believed it, least of all the Italians. Italians had been informed some years previously about government false flag events when their President revealed the truth about secret Operation Gladio.

Operation Gladio was an operation run by the CIA and Italian intelligence during the second half of the 20th century to set off bombs that would kill European women and children in order to blame communists and, thereby, erode support for European communist parties.

Italians were among the first to make video presentations challenging Washington's crackpot story of 9/11. An example is the 1 hour and 45 minute film, "Zero." You can watch it on youtube.[38]

Zero was produced as a film investigating 9/11 by the Italian company Telemaco. Many prominent people appear in the film along with independent experts. Together, they disprove every assertion made by the US government regarding its explanation of 9/11.

The film was shown to the European parliament.

It is impossible for anyone who watches this film to believe one word of the official explanation of 9/11.

The conclusion is increasingly difficult to avoid that elements of the US government blew up three New York skyscrapers in order to destroy Iraq, Afghanistan, Libya, Somalia, Syria, Iran, and Hezbollah and to launch the US on the neoconservatives' agenda of US world hegemony.

China and Russia protested but accepted Libya's destruction even though it was to their own detriment.

But Iran became a red line. Washington was blocked, so Washington decided to cause major problems for Russia in Ukraine in order to distract Russia from Washington's agenda elsewhere.

China has been uncertain about the trade-offs between its trade surpluses with the US and Washington's growing encirclement of China with naval and air bases. China has come to the conclusion that China has the same enemy as Russia has—Washington.

The course seems set for one of two things: Either the US dollar will be abandoned and collapse in value, thus ending Washington's superpower status and Washington's threat to world peace, or Washington will lead its puppets into military conflict with Russia and China. The outcome of such a war would be far more devastating than the collapse of the US dollar.

WASHINGTON IS HUMANITY'S WORST ENEMY

April 13, 2014

How does Washington get away with the claim that the country it rules is a democracy and has freedom?

This absurd claim ranks as one of the most unsubstantiated claims in history.

There is no democracy whatsoever. Voting is a mask for rule by a few powerful interest groups. In two 21st century rulings (*Citizens United* and *McCutcheon*), the US Supreme Court has ruled that the purchase of the US government by private interest groups is merely the exercise of free speech. These rulings allow powerful corporate and financial interests to use their money-power to elect a government that serves their interests at the expense of the general welfare.

The control private interests exercise over the government is so complete that private interests have immunity to prosecution for crimes. At his retirement party on March 27, Securities and Exchange Commission prosecutor James Kidney stated that his prosecutions of Goldman Sachs and other "banks too big to fail" were blocked by superiors who "were focused on getting high-paying jobs after their government service." The SEC's top brass, Kidney said, did not "believe in afflicting the comfortable and powerful." In his report on Kidney's retirement speech, Eric Zuesse points out that the Obama regime released false statistics in order to claim prosecutions that did not take place in order to convince a gullible public that Wall Street crooks were being punished.[39]

Democracy and freedom require an independent and aggressive media, an independent and aggressive judiciary, and an independent and aggressive Congress. The United States has none of the above.

The US media consistently lies for the government. Reuters continues to report, falsely, that Russia invaded and annexed Crimea. The *Washington Post* ran an obviously false story planted in the paper by the

Obama regime that the massive protests in former Russian territories of Ukraine are "rent-a-mobs" instigated by the Russian government.

Not even Washington's stooges in Kiev believe that. Officials of the Washington-imposed government in Kiev acknowledged the need for some autonomy for the Russian-speaking regions and for a law permitting referendums, but this realistic response to widespread concerns among Ukrainians has apparently been squelched by Washington and its presstitute media. US Secretary of State John Kerry continues to turn a deaf ear to the Russian Foreign Minister and continues to demand that "Russia must remove its people from the South-East."

What is happening is very dangerous. Washington misjudged its ability to grab the Ukraine. Opposition to the US grab is almost total in the Russian-speaking areas. Local police and security forces have gone over to the protesters. The corrupt Obama regime and the presstitute media lie through their teeth that the protests are insincere and mere orchestrations by "Putin who wants to restore the Soviet empire." The Russian government keeps trying to end the conflict and unrest that Washington's reckless coup in Kiev has caused, short of having to reabsorb the former Russian territories as it was forced to do in Crimea. But Washington continues ignoring the Russian government and blaming the unrest on Russia.[40]

The Russian government knows that Washington does not believe what Washington is saying and that Washington is systematically provoking a continuation and worsening of the problem. The Russian government wonders what agenda Washington is pursuing. Is Washington in its arrogant stupidity and superpower hubris unable to acknowledge that its takeover of the Ukraine has run amok and to back off?

Does Washington not realize that the Russian government is no more able to accept the application of violence against Russian populations in Ukraine than it could accept violence against Russians in South Ossetia? If Washington doesn't come to its senses, the Russian government will have to send in troops as it had to do in Georgia.[41]

As this is clear, is it Washington's goal to start a war? Is that why Washington is massing NATO forces on Russia's borders and sending missile ships into the Black Sea? Washington is putting the entire world at risk. If Russia concludes that Washington intends to drive the Ukraine crisis to war rather than resolve the crisis, will Russia sit and wait, or will Russia strike first?

One would think that the Chancellor of Germany, the British Prime Minister, and the President of France would see the danger in the situation. Perhaps they do. However, there is a large difference between the aid that Russia gives countries and the aid given by Washington. Russia provides financial support to governments; Washington gives bagfuls of money to *individuals in the government* with the knowledge that individuals are more likely to act in their own interest than in the interest of their country. Therefore, European politicians are silent as Washington pushes a crisis toward war. If we don't get to war, the only reason will be that Putin comes up with a solution that Washington cannot refuse, as Putin did in Syria and Iran.

It is a paradox that Putin is portrayed unfavorably while Washington pretends to be the champion of "freedom and democracy." In the 21st century Washington has established as its hallmarks every manifestation of tyranny: illegal and unconstitutional execution of citizens without due process of law, illegal and unconstitutional indefinite detention of citizens without due process of law, illegal and unconstitutional torture, illegal and unconstitutional rendition, illegal and unconstitutional surveillance, and illegal and unconstitutional wars. The executive branch has established that it is unaccountable to law or to the Constitution. An unaccountable government is a tyranny.

Tired of being spied upon and lied to, the Senate Intelligence Committee has produced a thorough investigation of the CIA's torture programs. The investigation took four years to complete. The Committee found, unequivocally, that the CIA lied about the extent of the torture and kidnappings, that detainees did not undergo some mild form of "enhanced interrogation" but were subjected to brutal and inhumane torture, that the CIA, contrary to its claims, did not get even one piece of useful information from its grave crimes against humanity. The American presstitutes assisted the CIA in inaccurately portraying the effectiveness and mildness of the CIA's Gestapo practices. During the entirety of the investigation, the CIA illegally spied on the Senate staff conducting the investigation.

Is the public ever to see this report beyond the parts that have been leaked? Not if the CIA and Obama can prevent it. President "change" Obama has decided that it is up to the CIA to decide how much of the Senate Intelligence Committee's investigation will be made public. In other words, unless someone leaks the entire report, the American public will never know. How can they hate us for freedom and democracy that we don't have?

The Senate Intelligence Committee itself has the power to vote to declassify the entire report and to release it. The committee should do so immediately before the members of the committee are browbeaten, threatened, and propagandized into believing that they are endangering "national security" and providing those mistreated with grounds for a lawsuit.

The US government is the most corrupt government on earth. There is no independent judiciary or media, and Congress has acquiesced to executive branch encroachments on its powers. Consider the judiciary.

Michael Ratner of the Center for Constitutional Rights represented the father of the American citizen, whom Obama announced would be murdered by the US government on suspicion that he was associated with terrorism.

When Ratner asked the federal courts to block an illegal and unconstitutional execution of Anwar al-Awlaki, an American citizen without due process, the federal judge who heard the case ruled that the father of a son *about to be* murdered did not have standing to bring a case in behalf of his son.

After several lives were snuffed out by President "I'm good at killing people" Obama, Ratner represented relatives of Obama's murdered victims in a damage suit. Under US law it was clear as day that damages were due. But the federal judge ruled that "the government must be trusted."[42] Whether or not anyone has standing is entirely up to the government. The IRS takes a completely different position on the matter. Children have standing to have their tax refunds confiscated by the IRS if the IRS thinks the IRS may have overpaid the parents' Social Security benefits.[43]

So in "freedom and democracy" Amerika, children are responsible if the IRS "thinks"—no proof required—that it wrote parents too large of a Social Security check, but a father has no legal standing to bring a lawsuit to prevent the US government from the extra-legal murder of his son.

Thanks to the Republican Federalist Society and to the Republican judges the Federalist Society has managed to have appointed to the federal bench, the federal judiciary functions as a protector of executive branch tyranny. Whatever the executive branch asserts and does is permissible, especially if the executive branch invokes "national security."

In America today, the executive branch claims that "national security" is impaired unless the executive branch can operate illegally and unconstitutionally and unless citizens are willing to give up every constitutional right in order to be "made safe" in a total police state that spies on and documents every aspect of their lives.

Even the Government Accountability Office has been neutered. In 2013 the Government Accountability Office told the TSA to eliminate its behavior screening program as it is a waste of money and does not work. So what did the TSA do? Why, of course, it expanded the useless intrusion into the privacy of travelers.

This is Amerika today. Yet Washington prances around chanting "freedom and democracy" even as it displaces the worst tyrannies in human history with its own.

Only gullible Americans expect leaders and elites or voting to do anything about the institutionalization of tyranny. Elites are only interested in money. As long as the system produces more income and wealth for elites, elites don't give a hoot about tyranny or what happens to the rest of us.

WASHINGTON DRIVES THE WORLD TO WAR

April 14, 2014

The CIA director was sent to Kiev to launch a military suppression of the Russian separatists in the eastern and southern portions of Ukraine, former Russian territories for the most part that were foolishly attached to the Ukraine in the early years of Soviet rule.

Washington's plan to grab Ukraine overlooked that the Russian and Russian-speaking parts of Ukraine were not likely to go along with their insertion into the EU and NATO while submitting to the persecution of Russian speaking peoples. Washington has lost Crimea, from which Washington intended to eject Russia from its Black Sea naval base. Instead of admitting that its plan for grabbing Ukraine has gone amiss, Washington is unable to admit a mistake and, therefore, is pushing the crisis to more dangerous levels.

If Ukraine dissolves into secession with the former Russian territories reverting to Russia, Washington will be embarrassed that the result of its coup in Kiev was to restore the Russian provinces of Ukraine to Russia. To avoid this embarrassment, Washington is pushing the crisis toward war.

The CIA director instructed Washington's hand-picked stooge government in Kiev to apply to the United Nations for help in repelling "terrorists" who with alleged Russian help are allegedly attacking Ukraine.

In Washington's vocabulary, self-determination is a sign of Russian interference. As the UN is essentially a Washington-financed organization, Washington will get what it wants.

The Russian government has already made it completely clear some weeks ago that the use of violence against protesters in eastern and southern Ukraine would compel the Russian government to send in the Russian army to protect Russians, just as Russia had to do in South Ossetia when Washington instructed its Georgian puppet ruler to attack Russian peacekeeping troops and Russian residents of South Ossetia.

Washington knows that the Russian government cannot stand aside while one of Washington's puppet states attacks Russians. Yet, Washington is pushing the crisis to war.

The danger for Russia is that the Russian government will rely on diplomacy, international organizations, international cooperation, and on the common sense and self-interest of German politicians and politicians in other of Washington's European puppet states.

For Russia this could be a fatal mistake. There is no good will in Washington, only mendacity. Russian delay provides Washington with time to build up forces on Russia's borders and in the Black Sea and to demonize Russia with propaganda and whip up the US population into a war frenzy. The latter is already occurring.

Kerry has made it clear to Lavrov that Washington is not listening to Russia. As Washington pays well, Washington's European puppets are also not listening to Russia. Money is more important to European politicians than humanity's survival.

Washington does not want the Ukraine matters settled in a diplomatic and reasonable way. It might be the case that Russia's best move is immediately to occupy the Russian territories of Ukraine and re-absorb the territories into Russia from whence they came. This should be done before the US and its NATO puppets are prepared for war. It is more difficult for Washington to start a war when the objects of the war have already been lost. Russia will be demonized with endless propaganda from Washington whether or not Russia re-absorbs its traditional territories. If Russia allows these territories to be suppressed by Washington, the prestige and authority of the Russian government will collapse. Perhaps that is what Washington is counting on.

If Putin's government stands aside while Russian Ukraine is suppressed, Putin's prestige will plummet, and Washington will finish off the Russian government by putting into action its many hundreds of Washington-financed NGOs that the Russian government has so foolishly tolerated. Russia is riven with Washington's fifth columns.

In my opinion, the Russian and Chinese governments have made serious strategic mistakes by remaining within the US dollar-based international payments system. The BRICS and any others with a brain should instantly desert the dollar system, which is a mechanism for US imperialism. The countries of the BRICS should immediately create their own separate payments system and their own exclusive communications/ Internet system.

Russia and China have stupidly made these strategic mistakes, because reeling from communist failures and oppressions, they naively assumed that Washington was pure, that Washington was committed to its propagandistic self-description as the upholder of law, justice, mercy, and human rights.

In fact, Washington, the "exceptional, indispensable country," is committed to its hegemony over the world. Russia, China, and Iran are in the way of Washington's hegemony and are targeted for attack.

The attack on Russia is mounting.

WASHINGTON'S CORRUPTION AND MENDACITY IS WHAT MAKES AMERICA "EXCEPTIONAL"

April 18, 2014

As I have reported on several occasions, the US government pays foreign rulers to do Washington's bidding. There is no such thing as an independent government in the UK, Europe or Japan. On top of all the other evidence, it has now come to light that the US Agency for International Development has a large slush fund "where millions are paid to political figures in foreign countries."[44]

If you have four hours, watch President Putin's amazing open press conference with the Russian people[45] and then try to imagine an American or European leader capable of such a feat. The Russians have a real leader. We have two-bit punks.

The Obama regime has botched its takeover of Ukraine with its Kiev coup. The White House is embarrassed that so many Ukrainians prefer to be part of Russia than part of Washington's stooge "freedom and democracy" government in Kiev. The prostitute American and European media have thrown the propaganda into overdrive, demonizing Russia and President Putin in order to cover up Washington's blunder.

The latest deception cooked up by Washington or by the antisemitic, neo-Nazi Right Sector in western Ukraine consists of leaflets falsely issued under the name of one of the leaders of Russian secessionists in eastern Ukraine. The leaflet calls for Jews to sign a registration and list their property.

However, no such registration office exists. Washington's ambassador to Ukraine, Geoffrey Pyatt who assisted Assistant Secretary of State Victoria Nuland in orchestrating the overthrow of the elected Ukrainian government and installing Washington's stooges, declared the leaflets to be "the real deal."

But the Jewish community is suspicious and has issued a statement that the leaflet "smells like a provocation." Jewish residents of the Russian territories say that anti-Semitism has not been a feature of their lives in the Russian speaking areas.[46]

Washington and the prostitute media are purveyors of misinformation. Remember, Washington and its media prostitutes told you that Saddam Hussein had weapons of mass destruction and was a threat to America. Washington and its media prostitutes told you that Syria's President Assad used chemical weapons against his own people. Washington and its media prostitutes told you that "we are not spying on you." Remember, *The New York Times* sat on the first leak from a top NSA official that Americans were being illegally spied upon for one year until George W. Bush was safely reelected.

A government that relies on propaganda cannot be believed about anything.

WASHINGTON INTENDS RUSSIA'S DEMISE

May 2, 2014

Washington has no intention of allowing the crisis in Ukraine to be resolved. Having failed to seize the country and evict Russia from its Black Sea naval base, Washington sees new opportunities in the crisis.

One is to restart the Cold War by forcing the Russian government to occupy the Russian-speaking areas of present day Ukraine where protesters are objecting to the stooge anti-Russian government installed in Kiev by the American coup. These areas of Ukraine are former constituent parts of Russia herself.

Essentially, the protesters have established independent governments in the cities. The police and military units sent to suppress the protesters, called "terrorists" in the American fashion, have to date, for the most part, defected to the protesters.

With Obama's incompetent White House and State Department having botched Washington's takeover of Ukraine, Washington has been at work shifting the blame to Russia. According to Washington and its presstitute media, the protests are orchestrated by the Russian government and have no sincere basis. If Russia sends in military units to protect the Russian citizens in the former Russian territories, the act will be used by Washington to confirm Washington's propaganda of a Russian invasion (as in the case of Georgia), and Russia will be further demonized.

The Russian government is in a predicament. Moscow does not want financial responsibility for these territories but cannot stand aside and permit Russians to be put down by force. The Russian government has attempted to keep Ukraine intact, relying on the forthcoming elections in Ukraine to bring to office more realistic leaders than the stooges installed by Washington.

However, Washington does not want an election that might replace its stooges and return Ukraine to cooperating with Russia to resolve the situation. There is a good chance that Washington will tell its stooges in Kiev to declare that the crisis brought to Ukraine by Russia prevents an election. Washington's NATO puppet states would back up this claim.

It is almost certain that despite the Russian government's hopes, the Russian government is faced with the continuation of both the crisis and Washington puppet government in Ukraine.

On May 1 Washington's former ambassador to Russia, now NATO's "second-in-command" but the person who, being American, calls the shots, has declared Russia to no longer be a partner but an enemy.

The American, Alexander Vershbow, told journalists that NATO has given up on "drawing Moscow closer" and soon will deploy a large number of combat forces in Eastern Europe. Vershbow called this aggressive policy deployment of "defensive assets to the region."

In other words, here we have a ridiculous claim that the Russian government is going to forget all about its difficulties in Ukraine and launch attacks on Poland, the Baltic States, Romania, Moldova, and on the central Asian states of Georgia, Armenia, and Azerbaijan. The dissembler Vershbow wants to modernize the militaries of these American puppet states and "seize the opportunity to create the reality on the ground by accepting membership of aspirant countries into NATO."

What Vershbow has told the Russian government is: just keep on relying on Western good will and reasonableness while we set up sufficient military forces to prevent Russia from coming to the aid of its oppressed citizens in Ukraine. Our demonization of Russia is working. It has made you hesitant to act during the short period when you could preempt us and seize your former territories. By waiting you give us time to mass forces on your borders from the Baltic Sea to Central Asia. That will distract you and keep you from the Ukraine. The oppression we will inflict on your Russians in Ukraine will discredit you, and the NGOs we finance in the Russian Federation will appeal to nationalist sentiments and overthrow your government for failing to come to the aid of Russians and failing to protect Russia's strategic interests.

Washington is licking its chops, seeing an opportunity to gain Russia as a puppet state.

Will Putin sit there with his hopes awaiting the West's good will to work out a solution while Washington attempts to engineer his fall?

The time is approaching when Russia will either have to act to terminate the crisis or accept an ongoing crisis and distraction in its backyard. Kiev has launched military airstrikes on protesters in Slavyansk. On May 2 Russian government spokesman Dmitry Peskov said that Kiev's resort to violence had destroyed the hope for the Geneva agreement on de-escalating the crisis. Yet, the Russian government spokesman again expressed the hope of the Russian government that European governments and Washington will put a stop to the military strikes and pressure the Kiev government to accommodate the protesters in a way that keeps Ukraine together and restores friendly relations with Russia.

This is a false hope. It assumes that the Wolfowitz doctrine is just words, but it is not. The Wolfowitz doctrine is the basis of US policy toward Russia (and China). The doctrine regards any power sufficiently strong to remain independent of Washington's influence to be "hostile." The doctrine states:

> Our first objective is to prevent the re-emergence of a new rival, either on the territory of the former Soviet Union or elsewhere, that poses a threat on the order of that posed formerly by the Soviet Union. This is a dominant consideration underlying the new regional defense strategy and requires that we endeavor to prevent any hostile power from dominating a region whose resources would, under consolidated control, be sufficient to generate global power.

The Wolfowitz doctrine justifies Washington's dominance of all regions. It is consistent with the neoconservative ideology of the US as the "indispensable" and "exceptional" country entitled to world hegemony.

Russia and China are in the way of US world hegemony. Unless the Wolfowitz doctrine is abandoned, nuclear war is the likely outcome.

MILITARIST
BUNKUM

Did you know that 85 to 90 percent of war's casualties are noncombatant civilians? That is the conclusion reached by a nine-person research team in the June 2014 issue of the *American Journal of Public Health*. The deaths of soldiers who are fighting the war are a small part of the human and economic cost. Clearly, wars do not protect the lives of civilians. The notion that soldiers are the primary persons dying for us is false. Noncombatants are the main victims of war.

Keep that in mind for July 4th, which is arriving in six weeks.

July 4th is America's most important national holiday, celebrating American independence from Great Britain. On July 4th, 1776, America's Founding Fathers declared that the Thirteen Colonies were no longer colonies but an independent country in which the Rights of Englishmen would prevail for all citizens and not only for King George's administrators. (Actually, the Second Continental Congress voted in favor of independence on July 2, and historians debate whether the Declaration of Independence was signed on July 4 or August 2.)

In this American assertion of self-determination citizens of Great Britain were not allowed to vote.

Therefore, according to Washington's position on the votes in Crimea and in eastern Ukraine—the former Russian territories of Donetsk and Luhansk—America's Declaration of Independence was "illegitimate and illegal."

On July 4th all across America there will be patriotic speeches about our soldiers who gave their lives for their country. To an informed person these speeches are curious. I am hard pressed to think of any examples of our soldiers giving their lives for our country. US Marine General Smedley Butler had the same problem. He said that his Marines gave their lives for United Fruit Company's control of Central America. "War is a racket," said General Butler, pointing out that US participation in World War I produced 21,000 new American millionaires and billionaires.

When General Butler said "war is a racket," he meant that war is a racket for a few people to get rich on the backs of millions of dead people. According to the article in the *American Journal of Public Health*, during the 20th century 190 million deaths could be directly and indirectly related to war.

One hundred ninety million is 60 million more than the entire US population in the year that I was born.

The only war fought on US territory was the war against Southern Secession. In this war Irish immigrants fresh off the boat gave their lives for American Empire. As soon as the South was conquered, the Union forces were set loose on the Plains Indians and destroyed them as well.

Empire over life. That has always been Washington's guiding principle.

America's wars have always been fought elsewhere—Cuba, Haiti, Mexico, Philippines, Japan, Germany, Korea, Vietnam, Panama, Afghanistan, Iraq, Libya, Syria, and Somalia. Washington even attacks countries with which the US is not at war, such as Pakistan and Yemen, and engages in proxy wars. The article cited above reports: "The United States launched 201 overseas military operations between the end of World War II and 2001, and since then, others, including Afghanistan and Iraq."

Not a single one of these wars and military operations had anything whatsoever to do with defending the US population from foreign threats.

Not even Japan and Germany posed a threat to the US. Neither country had any prospect of invading the US and neither country had any such war plans.

Let's assume Japan had conquered China, Burma, and Indonesia. With such a vast territory to occupy, Japan could not have spared a single division with which to invade the US, and, of course, any invasion fleet would never have made it across the Pacific. Just as was the fate of the Japanese fleet at Midway, an invasion fleet would have been sitting ducks for the US Navy.

Assume Germany had extended its conquests over Europe to Great Britain, Russia and North Africa.

Germany would have been unable to successfully occupy such a vast territory and could not have spared a single soldier to send to invade America. Even the US superpower was unable to successfully occupy Iraq and Afghanistan, countries with small land areas and populations in comparison.

Except for its wars against the South, the Plains Indians, Haiti, Spain, Panama, Grenada, and Mexico, the US has never won a war. The Southern Confederates, usually outnumbered, often defeated the Union generals. Japan was defeated by its own lack of military resources. Germany was defeated by the Soviet Union. The allied invasion of Normandy did not occur until June 6, 1944, by which time the Red Army had ground up the Wehrmacht.

When the allies landed in Normandy, three-fourths of the German Army was on the Russian front. The allied invasion was greatly helped by Germany's shortage of fuel for mobilized units. If Hitler had not allowed hubris to lead him into invading the Soviet Union and, instead, just sat on his European conquests, no allied invasion would have been possible. Today Germany would rule all of Europe, including the UK. The US would have no European Empire with which to threaten Russia, China, and the Middle East.

In Korea in the 1950s, General Douglas MacArthur, victorious over Japan, was fought to a standstill by third world China. In Vietnam American technological superiority was defeated by a third world army.

The US rolled up mighty Grenada in the 1980s, but lost its proxy war against the Sandinistas in Nicaragua.

Is there anyone so foolish as to think that Grenada or the Sandinistas were a threat to the United States, that North Korea or North Vietnam comprised threats to the United States? Yet, the Korean and Vietnam wars were treated as if the fate of the United States hung in the balance. The conflicts produced voluminous dire predictions and strategic debates. The communist threat replaced the Hitler threat. The American Empire was at risk from third world peoples. Dominoes would fall everywhere.

Currently Washington is at work overturning President Reagan's accomplishment of ending the Cold War.

Washington orchestrated a coup that overthrew the elected government of Ukraine and installed a stooge government. Washington's stooges began issuing threats against Russia and the Russian speaking population in Ukraine. These threats resulted in those parts of Ukraine that were formerly part of Russia declaring their independence. Washington blames Russia, not itself, and is stirring the pot, demonizing Russia and recreating the Cold War with military deployments in the Baltics and Eastern Europe.

Washington needs to reinvent the Cold War in order to justify the hundreds of billions of dollars that Washington annually feeds the military/security complex, some of which recycles in political campaign donations. In contrast to Washington's propaganda, an honest view of the events in Ukraine can be found in Stephen Lendman's *Flashpoint in Ukraine*.[47]

In the United States patriotism and militarism have become synonyms. This July 4th, find the courage to remind the militarists that Independence Day celebrates the Declaration of Independence, not the American Empire. The Declaration of Independence was not only a declaration of independence from King George III but also a declaration of independence from unaccountable tyrannical government. The oath of office commits the US officeholder to the defense of the US Constitution from enemies "foreign and domestic."

In the 21st century Americans' worst enemies are not al Qaeda, Iran,

Russia, and China. America's worst enemies are our own presidents who have declared repeatedly that the orchestrated "war on terror" gives them the right to set aside the civil liberties guaranteed to every citizen by the US Constitution.

Presidential disrespect for the US Constitution is so extreme that Obama has nominated David Barron to the US Court of Appeals for the First Circuit. Barron is the Justice (sic) Department official who wrote the memos fabricating a legal justification for the Office of President to murder US citizens without due process of law.[48]

Having stripped US citizens of their civil liberties, executive branch agencies are now stocking up vast amounts of ammunition, and the Department of Agriculture has placed an order for submachine guns.

The Department for Homeland Security has acquired 2,717 mine-resistant armored personnel carriers.

Congress and the media are not interested in why the executive branch is arming itself so heavily against the American people.

During the entirety of the 21st century—indeed, dating from the Clinton regime at the end of the 20th century—the executive branch has declared its independence from law (both domestic and international) and from the Constitution, Congress, and the Judiciary. The executive branch, with the help of the Republican Federalist Society, has established that the office of the executive is a tyranny unaccountable to law, domestic or international, as long as the executive declares a state of war, even a war that is not conducted against another country or countries but a vague, undefined or ill-defined war against a vague stateless enemy such as al Qaeda, with which the US is currently allied against Syria.

Al Qaeda now has a dual role. Al Qaeda is Washington's agent for overthrowing the elected Assad government in Syria and al Qaeda is the evil force against which US civil liberties must be sacrificed.

The illegitimate power asserted by the Office of the President is not only a threat to every American but also to every living being on planet earth.

As the article in the *American Journal of Public Health* cited above reports: "Approximately 17,300 nuclear weapons are presently deployed in at least 9 countries, many of which can be launched and reach their targets within 45 minutes."

It only takes one fool—and Washington has thousands of fools—and all life on earth terminates in 45 minutes. The neoconservative belief that the United States is the exceptional, indispensable country chosen by history to rule the earth is a belief full of the arrogance and hubris that lead to war.

Keep your likely fate in mind as you watch the military bands and marches on July 4th and listen to the hot air of militarism.

WHY WAR
IS INEVITABLE

May 25, 2014

Memorial Day is when we commemorate our war dead. Like the Fourth of July, Memorial Day is being turned into a celebration of war.

Those who lose family members and dear friends to war don't want the deaths to have been in vain.

Consequently, wars become glorious deeds performed by noble soldiers fighting for truth, justice, and the American way. Patriotic speeches tell us how much we owe to those who gave their lives so that America could remain free.

The speeches are well-intentioned, but the speeches create a false reality that supports ever more wars.

None of America's wars had anything to do with keeping America free. To the contrary, the wars swept away our civil liberties, making us unfree.

President Lincoln issued an executive order for the arrest and imprisonment of northern newspaper reporters and editors. He shut down 300 northern newspapers and held 14,000 political prisoners. Lincoln arrested war critic US Representative Clement Vallandigham from Ohio and exiled him to the Confederacy. President Woodrow Wilson used WWI to suppress free speech, and President Franklin D. Roosevelt used WWII to intern 120,000 US citizens of Japanese descent on the grounds that race made them suspect. Professor Samuel Walker concluded that President George W. Bush used the "war on terror" for an across the board assault on US civil liberty, making the Bush regime the greatest danger American liberty has ever faced.

Lincoln forever destroyed states' rights. While the suspension of habeas corpus and free speech that went hand in hand with America's three largest wars was lifted at war's end, President George W. Bush's repeal of the Constitution has been expanded by President Obama and codified by Congress and executive orders into law. Far from defending our liberties, our soldiers who died in "the war on terror" died so that the president can indefinitely detain US citizens without due process of law and murder US citizens on suspicion alone without any accountability to law or the Constitution.

The conclusion is unavoidable that America's wars have not protected our liberty but, instead, destroyed liberty. As Alexander Solzhenitsyn said, "A state of war only serves as an excuse for domestic tyranny."

Southern secession did pose a threat *to Washington's empire, but not to the American people.* Neither the Germans of WWI vintage nor the Germans and Japanese of WWII vintage posed any threat to the US. As historians have made completely clear, Germany did not start WWI and did not go to war for the purpose of territorial expansion. Japan's ambitions were in Asia. Hitler did not want war with England and France.

Hitler's territorial ambitions were mainly to restore German provinces stripped from Germany as WWI booty in violation of President Wilson's guarantees. Any other German ambitions were to the East.

Neither country had any plans to invade the US. Japan attacked the US fleet at Pearl Harbor hoping to remove an obstacle to its activities in Asia, not as a precursor to an invasion of America.

Certainly the countries ravaged by Bush and Obama in the 21st century—Iraq, Afghanistan, Libya, Somalia, Syria, Pakistan, and Yemen—posed no military threat to the US. Indeed, these were wars used by a tyrannical executive branch to establish the basis of the Stasi State that now exists in the US.

The truth is hard to bear, but the facts are clear. America's wars have been fought in order to advance Washington's power, the profits of bankers and armaments industries, and the fortunes of US companies.

Marine General Smedley Butler said, " I served in all commissioned ranks from a second Lieutenant to a Major General. And during that time, I spent most of my time being a high-class muscle man for Big Business, for Wall Street, and for the bankers. In short, I was a racketeer for capitalism."

It is more or less impossible to commemorate the war dead without glorifying them, and it is impossible to glorify them without glorifying their wars.

For the entirety of the 21st century the US has been at war, not war against massed armies or threats to American freedom, but war against civilians, against women, children, and village elders, and war against our own liberty. Elites with a vested interest in these wars tell us that the wars will have to go on for another 20 to 30 years before we defeat "the terrorist threat."

This, of course, is nonsense. There was no terrorist threat until Washington began trying to create terrorists by military attacks, justified by lies, on Muslim populations.

Washington succeeded with its war lies to the point that Washington's audacity and hubris have outgrown Washington's judgment.

By overthrowing the democratically elected government in Ukraine, Washington has brought the United States into confrontation with Russia.

This is a confrontation that could end badly, perhaps for Washington and perhaps for the entire world.

If Gaddafi and Assad would not roll over for Washington, why does Washington think Russia will? Russia is not Libya or Syria. Washington is the bully who having beaten up the kindergarten kid, now thinks he can take on the college linebacker.

The Bush and Obama regimes have destroyed America's reputation with their incessant lies and violence against other peoples. The world sees Washington as the prime threat.

Worldwide polls consistently show that people around the world regard the US and Israel as the two countries that pose the greatest threat to peace.[49]

The countries that Washington's propaganda declares to be "rogue states" and the "axis of evil," such as Iran and North Korea, are far down the list when the peoples in the world are consulted. It could not be more clear that the world does not believe Washington's self-serving propaganda. The world sees the US and Israel as the rogue states.

The US and Israel are the only two countries in the world that are in the grip of ideologies. The US is in the grip of the Neoconservative ideology which has declared the US to be the "exceptional, indispensable country" chosen by history to exercise hegemony over all others. This ideology is buttressed by the Brzezinski and Wolfowitz doctrines that are the basis of US foreign policy.

The Israeli government is in the grip of the Zionist ideology that declares the right to a "greater Israel" from the Nile to the Euphrates. Many Israelis themselves do not accept this ideology, but it is the ideology of the "settlers" and those who control the Israeli government.

Ideologies are important causes of war. The Hitlerian ideology of German superiority is mirrored in the Neoconservative ideology of US superiority, and in the Zionist ideology that Israelis are superior to Palestinians. Washington and Israel's doctrines of superiority over others do not sit very well with the "others." When Obama declared in a speech that Americans are the exceptional people, Russia's President Putin responded, "God created us all equal."

To the detriment of its population, the Israeli government has made endless enemies. Israel has effectively isolated itself in the world. Israel's continued existence depends entirely on the willingness and ability of Washington to protect Israel. This means that Israel's power is derivative of Washington's power.

Washington's power is a different story. As the only economy standing after WWII, the US dollar became the world money. This role for the dollar has given Washington financial hegemony over the world, and is the main source of Washington's power. As other countries rise, Washington's hegemony is imperiled.

To prevent other countries from rising, Washington invokes the Brzezinski and Wolfowitz doctrines. To be brief, the Brzezinski doctrine says that in order to remain the only superpower, Washington must control the Eurasian land mass. Brzezinski is willing for this to occur peacefully by suborning the Russian government into Washington's empire. "A loosely confederated Russia ... a decentralized Russia would be less susceptible to imperial mobilization." In other words, break up Russia into associations of semiautonomous states whose politicians can be suborned by Washington's money.

Brzezinski propounded "a geo-strategy for Eurasia." In Brzezinski's strategy, China and "a confederated Russia" are part of a "transcontinental security framework," to be managed by Washington in order to perpetuate the role of the US as the world's only superpower.

I once asked my colleague, Brzezinski, that if everyone was allied with us, who were we organized against? My question surprised him, because I think that Brzezinski remains caught up in Cold War strategy even after the demise of the Soviet Union. In Cold War thinking it was important to have the upper hand or else be at risk of being eliminated as a player. The importance of prevailing became all consuming, and this consuming drive survived the Soviet collapse. *Prevailing over others is the only foreign policy that Washington knows.*

The mindset that America must prevail set the stage for the Neoconservatives and their 21st century wars, which, with Washington's overthrow of the democratically elected government of Ukraine, has resulted in a crisis that has brought Washington into direct conflict with Russia.

I know the strategic institutes that serve Washington. I was the occupant of the William E. Simon Chair in Political Economy, Center for Strategic and International Studies, for a dozen years. The idea is prevalent that Washington must prevail over Russia in Ukraine or Washington will lose prestige and its superpower status.

The idea of prevailing always leads to war once one power thinks it has prevailed.

The path to war is reinforced by the Wolfowitz Doctrine. Paul Wolfowitz, the neoconservative intellectual who formulated US military and foreign policy doctrine, wrote among many similar passages:

> Our first objective is to prevent the re-emergence of a new
> rival, either on the territory of the former Soviet Union or
> elsewhere [China], that poses a threat on the order of that
> posed formerly by the Soviet Union. This is a dominant
> consideration underlying the new regional defense strategy

and requires that we endeavor to prevent any hostile power from dominating a region whose resources would, under consolidated control, be sufficient to generate global power.

In the Wolfowitz Doctrine, any other strong country is defined as a *threat and a power hostile* to the US regardless of how willing that country is to get along with the US for mutual benefit.

The difference between Brzezinski and the Neoconservatives is that Brzezinski wants to suborn Russia and China by including them in the empire as important elements whose voices would be heard, if only for diplomatic reasons, whereas the Neoconservatives are prepared to rely on military force combined with internal subversion orchestrated with US financed NGOs and even terrorist organizations.

Neither the US nor Israel is embarrassed by their worldwide reputations as the two countries that pose the greatest threat. In fact, both countries are proud to be recognized as the greatest threats. The foreign policy of both countries is devoid of any diplomacy. US and Israeli foreign policy rests on violence alone.

Washington tells countries to do as Washington says or be "bombed into the stone age." Israel declares all Palestinians, even women and children, to be "terrorists," and proceeds to shoot them down in the streets, claiming that Israel is merely protecting itself against terrorists. Israel, which does not recognize the existence of Palestine as a country, covers up its crimes with the claim that Palestinians do not accept the existence of Israel.

"We don't need no stinking diplomacy. We got power."

This is an attitude that guarantees war, and that is where the US is taking the world. The prime minister of Britain, the chancellor of Germany, and the president of France are Washington's enablers. They provide the cover for Washington. Instead of war crimes, Washington has "coalitions of the willing" and military invasions that bring "democracy and women's rights" to non-compliant countries.

China gets much the same treatment. A country with four times the US population but a smaller prison population, China is constantly criticized by Washington as an "authoritarian state." China is accused of human rights abuses while US police brutalize the US population.

The problem for humanity is that Russia and China are not Libya and Iraq. These two countries possess strategic nuclear weapons. Their land mass greatly exceeds that of the US. The US, which was unable to successfully occupy Baghdad or Afghanistan, has no prospect of prevailing against Russia and China in conventional warfare. Washington will push the nuclear button. What else can we expect from a government devoid of morality?

The world has never experienced rogue states comparable to Washington and Israel. Both governments are prepared to murder anyone and everyone. Look at the crisis that Washington has created in Ukraine and the dangers thereof. On May 23, 2014, Russia's President Putin spoke to the St. Petersburg International Economic Forum, a three-day gathering of delegations from 62 countries and CEOs from 146 of the largest Western corporations.

Putin did not speak of the billions of dollars in trade deals that were being formalized. Instead Putin spoke of the crisis that Washington had brought to Russia, and he criticized Europe for being Washington's vassals for supporting Washington's propaganda against Russia and Washington's interference in vital Russian interests.

Putin was diplomatic in his language, but the message that powerful economic interests from the US and Europe received is that it will lead to trouble if Washington and European governments continue to ignore Russia's concerns and continue to act as if they can interfere in Russia's vital interests as if Russia did not exist.

The heads of these large corporations will carry this message back to Washington and European capitals.

Putin made it clear that the lack of dialogue with Russia could lead to the West making the mistake of putting Ukraine in NATO and establishing missile bases on Russia's border with Ukraine. Putin has learned that Russia cannot rely on good will from the West, and Putin made it clear, short of issuing a threat, that Western military bases in Ukraine are unacceptable.

Washington will continue to ignore Russia. However, European capitals will have to decide whether Washington is pushing them into a conflict with Russia that is against European interests. Thus, Putin is testing European politicians to determine if there is sufficient intelligence and independence in Europe for a rapprochement.

If Washington in its overbearing arrogance and hubris forces Putin to write off the West, the Russian/Chinese strategic alliance, which is forming to counteract Washington's hostile policy of surrounding both countries with military bases, will harden into preparation for the inevitable war.

The survivors, if any, can thank the Neoconservatives, the Wolfowitz doctrine and the Brzezinski strategy, for the destruction of life on earth.

There are a large number of misinformed people in the American public who think they know everything.

These people have been programmed by US and Israeli propaganda to equate Islam with political ideology. They believe that Islam, a religion, is instead a militarist doctrine that calls for the overthrow of Western civilization, as if anything remains of Western civilization.

Many believe this propaganda even in the face of evidence that the Sunnis and Shi'ites in Iraq were unable to unite against their Washington oppressor and occupier. The US has "departed" Iraq, but the carnage today is as high or higher than during the US invasion and occupation. The daily death tolls from the Sunni/Shi'ite conflict are extraordinary. A religion this disunited poses no threat to anyone except Islamists themselves. Washington successfully used Muslim disunity to overthrow Gaddafi, and is currently using Islamist disunity in an effort to overthrow the government of Syria. Muslims cannot even unite to defend themselves against Western aggression. There is no prospect of Muslims uniting in order to overthrow the West.

Even if Islam could do so, it would be pointless for Islam to overthrow the West. The West has overthrown itself. In the US the Constitution has been murdered by the Bush and Obama regimes.

Nothing remains. As the US *is* the Constitution, what was once the United States no longer exists. A different entity has taken its place.

Europe died with the European Union, which requires the termination of sovereignty of all member countries. A few unaccountable bureaucrats in Brussels have become superior to the wills of the French, German, British, Italian, Dutch, Spanish, Greek, and Portuguese peoples.

Western civilization is a skeleton. It still stands, barely, but there is no life in it. The blood of liberty has departed. Western peoples look at their governments and see nothing but enemies. Why else has Washington militarized local police forces, equipping them as if they were occupying armies? Why else has Homeland Security, the Department of Agriculture, and even the Postal Service and Social Security Administration ordered billions of rounds of ammunition and even submachine guns? What is this taxpayer-paid-for arsenal for if not to suppress US citizens?

As the prominent trends forecaster Gerald Celente spells out in the current *Trends Journal*, "uprisings span four corners of the globe." Throughout Europe angry, desperate and outraged peoples march against EU financial policies that are driving the peoples into the ground. Despite all of Washington's efforts with its well funded fifth columns known as NGOs to destabilize Russia and China, both the Russian and Chinese governments have far more support from their people than do the US and Europe.

In the 20th century Russia and China learned what tyranny is, and they have rejected it.

In the US tyranny has entered under the guise of the "war on terror," a hoax used to scare the sheeple into abandoning their civil liberties, thus freeing Washington from accountability to law and permitting Washington to erect a militarist police state. Ever since WWII Washington has used its financial hegemony and the "Soviet threat," now converted into the "Russian threat," to absorb Europe into Washington's empire.

Putin is hoping that the interests of European countries will prevail over subservience to Washington. This is Putin's current bet. This is the reason Putin remains unprovoked by Washington's provocations in Ukraine.

If Europe fails Russia, Putin and China will prepare for the war that Washington's drive for hegemony makes inevitable.

WHAT OBAMA
TOLD US AT
WEST POINT

June 2, 2014

At West Point Obama told us, to the applause of West Point cadets, that "American exceptionalism" is a doctrine that justifies whatever Washington does. If Washington violates domestic and international law by torturing "detainees" or violates the Nuremberg standard by invading countries that have undertaken no hostile action against the US or its allies, "exceptionalism" is the priest's blessing that absolves Washington's sins against law and international norms. Washington's crimes are transformed into Washington's affirmation of the rule of law. Here is Obama in his own words:

> I believe in American exceptionalism with every fiber of
> my being. But what makes us exceptional is not our ability
> to flout international norms and the rule of law; it is our
> willingness to affirm them through our actions.

Actions indeed. In the 21st century "American exceptionalism" has destroyed seven countries in whole or in part. Millions of people are dead, maimed, and displaced, and all of this criminal destruction is evidence of Washington's reaffirmation of international norms and the rule of law. Destruction and murder are merely collateral damage from Washington's affirmation of international norms.

"American exceptionalism" also means that US presidents can lie through their teeth and misrepresent those they choose to demonize. Listen to Obama's misrepresentations of the Putin and Assad governments: "Russia's aggression towards former Soviet states unnerves capitals in Europe . . . In Ukraine, Russia's recent actions recall the days when Soviet tanks rolled into Eastern Europe." Obama misrepresents Assad as "a dictator who bombs and starves his own people."

Did any of the cadets in Obama's West Point audience wonder why, if Assad is a brutal dictator who bombs and starves his own people, the Syrian people are supporting Assad instead of the American-backed "liberation forces," the combination of imported jihadists and al Qaeda fighters who object to Assad's government because it is secular? The US military is taught to respect its civilian commander-in-chief, but if West Point cadets actually do obtain an education, it is remarkable that Obama's audience did not break out in laughter.

The reference to Soviet tanks rolling into Eastern Europe is a reference to the Hungarian (1956) and Czech (1968) "revolutions" when the Hungarian and Czech communist leaders attempted to assert independence from Moscow. It is doubtful that Washington's response to countries attempting to exit NATO would be any different. A few months ago Washington responded to political talk in Germany and England about leaving the EU by informing both governments that it was not in Washington's interest for them to depart from the European Union.

Obama used the image of Soviet tanks in order to color Russia with the Soviet Threat, to mischaracterize Russia's response to the Georgian invasion of South Ossetia, and to misrepresent Crimea's vote in favor of reunification with Russia as "Russia's invasion and annexation of Crimea." These lies are still a mainstay in the US media and in Washington's official propaganda.

Obama's speech is probably the most disingenuous ever given by a Western politician. We could have fun for hours with all the crimes that Washington commits but buries in rhetoric directed at others. Perhaps my favorite is Obama evoking a world in which "individuals aren't slaughtered because of political belief." I am sure Obama was thinking of this just world when he murdered without due process of law American citizens Anwar al-Awlaki, Samir Khan, and Abdulrahman al-Awlaki "outside of areas of active hostilities."

Another favorite is the way Obama flushed the US Constitution of its meaning. Obama said, with reference to bringing the Guantanamo prisoners to the US, that "American values and legal traditions don't permit the indefinite detention of people beyond our borders." No, Obama, the US Constitution prevents the indefinite detention of US citizens by the US government anywhere on earth, especially within our borders.

By detaining prisoners without charge in Guantanamo and by murdering US citizens abroad without due process of law, Obama has violated his oath of office and should be impeached. It was only a short time ago that President Bill Clinton was impeached by the US House of Representatives (the Senate saved him from conviction) for lying about his sexual affair with a White House intern. How times change. Today a president who violates his oath of office to protect the Constitution from enemies foreign and domestic gets a free ride. The Constitution has lost its power to protect citizens from the arbitrary power of government. The US *is* the Constitution. Without the Constitution the US ceases to exist, and the country becomes a tyranny, both at home and abroad. Today the US is a tyranny cloaked in the garb of "freedom and democracy."

Instead of laughing our way through Obama's ridiculous speech to what apparently was a dumbed-down West Point graduating class, let's pay attention to Obama's bottom line: "America must always lead on the world stage. . . . The military is, and always will be, the backbone of that leadership."

In other words, Washington doesn't use diplomacy. Washington uses coercion. The favorite threat is: "Do as you are told or we will bomb you into the Stone Age." Obama's speech is a justification of Washington's criminal actions on the grounds that Washington acts for the exceptional Americans whose exceptionalism places them and, thereby, their government above law and international norms. In this way of thinking, only the failure to prevail constitutes failure.

Americans are the new *ubermensch*, the new master race. Inferior humans can be bombed, invaded, and sanctioned. Obama's West Point speech asserts American superiority over all others and Washington's determination to continue this superiority by preventing the rise of other powers. But this arrogant hubris was not enough for the *Washington Post* editorial board. The newspaper's editorial damned Obama for binding US power and limiting its use to "a narrow set of core interest," such as direct threats to America.

The American "liberal media" object that Obama's claim of exceptionalism is not broad enough for Washington's purposes. Obama's address, the *Washington Post* wrote, bound "US power" and "offered scant comfort" to those militarists who want to overthrow Syria, Iran, Russia, and China.

The world should take note that the most militarily aggressive American president in history is considered a wimp by the neoconized American media. The media drives wars, and the American media, firmly allied with the military/security complex, is driving the world to the final war.

ARE YOU READY
FOR NUCLEAR WAR?

June 3, 2014

Washington thinks nuclear war can be won and is planning for a first strike on Russia, and perhaps China, in order to prevent any challenge to Washington's world hegemony.

The plan is far advanced, and the implementation of the plan is underway. As I have reported previously, US strategic doctrine was changed and the role of nuclear missiles was elevated from a retaliatory role to a preemptive first strike role. US anti-ballistic missile (ABM) bases have been established in Poland on Russia's frontier, and other bases are planned. When completed Russia will be ringed with US missile bases.

Anti-ballistic missiles, known as "star wars," are weapons designed to intercept and destroy ICBMs. In Washington's war doctrine, the US hits Russia with a first strike, and whatever retaliatory force Russia might have remaining is prevented from reaching the US by the shield of ABMs.

The reason Washington gave for the change in war doctrine is the possibility that terrorists might obtain a nuclear weapon with which to destroy an American city. This explanation is nonsensical. Terrorists are individuals or a group of individuals, not a country with a threatening military. To use nuclear weapons against terrorists would destroy far more than the terrorists and be pointless as a drone with a conventional missile would suffice.

The reason Washington gave for the ABM base in Poland is to protect Europe from Iranian ICBMs.

Washington and every European government knows that Iran has no ICBMs and that Iran has not indicated any intent to attack Europe.

No government believes Washington's reasons. Every government realizes that Washington's reasons are feeble attempts to hide the fact that it is creating the capability on the ground to win a nuclear war.

The Russian government understands that the change in US war doctrine and the US ABM bases on its borders are directed at Russia and are indications that Washington plans a first strike with nuclear weapons on Russia.

China has also understood that Washington has similar intentions toward China. As I reported several months ago, in response to Washington's threat China called the world's attention to China's ability to destroy the US should Washington initiate such a conflict.

However, Washington believes that it can win a nuclear war with little or no damage to the US. This belief makes nuclear war likely.

As Steven Starr makes clear, this belief is based in ignorance. Nuclear war has no winner. Even if US cities were saved from retaliation by ABMs, the radiation and nuclear winter effects of the weapons that hit Russia and China would destroy the US as well. Pay close attention to Steven Starr's guest column, "The Lethality of Nuclear Weapons."[50]

The media, conveniently concentrated into a few hands during the corrupt Clinton regime, is complicit by ignoring the issue. The governments of Washington's vassal states in Western and Eastern Europe, Canada, Australia, and Japan are also complicit, because they accept Washington's plan and provide the bases for implementing it. The demented Polish government has probably signed the death warrant for humanity. The US Congress is complicit, because no hearings are held about the executive branch's plans for initiating nuclear war.

Washington has created a dangerous situation. As Russia and China are clearly threatened with a first strike, they might decide to strike first themselves. Why should Russia and China sit and await the inevitable while their adversary creates the ability to protect itself by developing its ABM shield? Once Washington completes the shield, Russia and China are certain to be attacked, unless they surrender in advance.

A 10 minute report from Russia Today makes it clear that Washington's secret plan for a first strike on Russia is not secret. The report also makes it clear that Washington is prepared to eliminate any European leaders who do not align with Washington. A transcript is provided by Global Research.[51]

Readers will ask me, "What can we do?" This is what you can do. You can shut down the Ministry of Propaganda by turning off Fox News, CNN, the BBC, ABC, NBC, CBS, by ceasing to read *The New York Times*, the *Washington Post*, the *LA Times*. Simply exit the official media. Do not believe one word that the government says. Do not vote. Realize that evil is concentrated in Washington. In the 21st century Washington has destroyed in whole or part seven countries. Millions of peoples murdered, maimed, displaced, and Washington has shown no remorse whatsoever. Neither have the "christian" churches. The devastation that Washington has inflicted is portrayed as a great success. Washington prevailed.

THE LIES GROW MORE AUDACIOUS

June 6, 2014

If there were any doubts that Western "leaders" live in a fantasy make-believe world constructed out of their own lies, the G-7 meeting and 70th anniversary celebration of the Normandy landing dispelled the doubts.

The howlers issuing from these occasions are enough to split your sides. Obama and his lap dog Cameron described the Normandy landing on June 6, 1944, as "the greatest liberation force that the world has ever known" and credited the US and Britain for the defeat of Hitler. No mention was made of the Soviet Union and the Red Army, *which for three years prior to the Normandy landing had been fighting and defeating the Wehrmacht.*

The Germans lost World War II at the Battle of Stalingrad, which was fought from August 23, 1942 until February 2, 1943, when most of the remnants of the powerful German Sixth Army surrendered, including 22 generals.

Nineteen months previously the largest invasion force ever assembled on planet earth invaded Russia across a one thousand mile front. *Three million* crack German troops; 7,500 artillery units, 19 panzer divisions with 3,000 tanks, and 2,500 aircraft rolled across Russia for 14 months.

By June 1944, three years later, very little of this force was left. The Red Army had chewed it up. When the so-called "allies" (a term which apparently excludes Russia) landed in France, there was little to resist them. The best forces remaining to Hitler were on the Russian front, which collapsed day by day as the Red Army approached Berlin.

The Red Army won the war with Germany. The Americans and the British showed up after the Wehrmacht was exhausted and in tatters and could offer little resistance. Joseph Stalin believed that Washington and London stayed out of the war until the last minute and left Russia with the burden of defeating Germany.

Hollywood and popular writers have, of course, buried the facts. Americans have all sorts of movies, such as "A Bridge Too Far," that portray insignificant events as heroic. Nevertheless, the facts are clear. The war was won on the Eastern front by Russia. Hollywood's movies are fun, but they are nonsense.

Russia is again on the outs with "the world community," because Obama's plan to seize Ukraine and to evict Russia from its Black Sea base in Crimea has come a cropper. Crimea has been a part of Russia for as long as the US has existed. Khrushchev, a Ukrainian, stuck Crimea into the Ukrainian Socialist Republic in 1954 when Russia and Ukraine were part of the same country.

When the Washington-imposed stooge government in Kiev recently declared that it was abolishing the use of the Russian language and arresting Ukrainians who had dual Russian citizenship and began tearing down Russian war memorials consecrated to the liberation of Ukraine from the Nazis, the people in Crimea used the ballot box to disassociate from Washington's stooge government in Kiev, first voting their independence and then voting for reunification with their mother country.

Washington, and the other G-7 countries following Washington's orders, described this Crimean act of self-determination, which is exactly comparable to the act of self-determination declared by Britain's American colonies, to be a case of "Russian invasion and annexation." Similar efforts to disassociate from Kiev are underway in other former Russian territories that today comprise eastern and southern Ukraine. Washington has equated self-determination in eastern and southern Ukraine with "terrorism" and has encouraged its stooge in Kiev to use military violence against protesting civilians. The reason for branding separatists "terrorists" is to make it OK to kill them.

It is extraordinary to any learned person that the President of the United States and the titular heads of state of the Western European countries would publicly declare such blatant lies to the world. The world has historians. The world has peoples whose knowledge vastly exceeds that of the "mainstream media," a.k.a., the Ministry of Propaganda, or, as Gerald Celente brands them, "the presstitutes." Whatever name we use, the Western media is a collection of well paid whores. They lie for money, dinner party invitations, speaking invitations with large honorariums and book contracts with large advances.

I know. They tried to recruit me.

Notice how narrowly Washington defines "the world community." The "world community" consists of the Group of 7. That's it. Seven countries make up the "world community." The "world community" consists of six white countries and Washington's puppet state of Japan. The "world community" is the US, Canada, Britain, Germany, France, Italy, and Japan. The other 190 countries are not part of Washington's "world community." In the neocon doctrine, they are not even part of humanity.

The "world community" doesn't have the population of single excluded countries, such as China or India.

I haven't done the calculation, but probably the land mass of Russia itself exceeds the land mass of the "world community."

So, what is this "world community?"

The "world community" is the assemblage of US vassal states. Britain, France, and Germany were important on the 20th century scene. Their histories are studied in universities. The populations had a decent standard of living, although not for all citizens. Their past is the reason for their present importance.

In effect, these countries were propelled forward by history, or by the history important to the West.

Japan, being an appendage of Washington, has tried to become "western." It is extraordinary how such a proud, war-like people became a puppet of America.

As I have finally stopped laughing at the presumed non-role of Russia in the defeat of Hitler, let's return to the G-7 meeting. The Big Happening of this meeting was Russia's exclusion and the shrinkage of the G-8 to the G-7.

This was the first time in 17 years that Russia was not allowed to participate in the meeting of which Russia is a member. Why?

Russia is being punished. Russia is being isolated from the 7 countries that constitute "the world community."

Obama's neocons thought that they could grab Crimea, evict Russia, and leave Russia without access to the Mediterranean, thus unable to hold on to its naval base in Tartus, Syria, the easier for Washington to invade Syria.

Crimea has been part of Russia since Russia completed the reconquest from the Tartars. I remember the Tarter, or Tater, ethnics from my visit to the tomb of Tamerlane the Great (Timur as he was also known) in Samarkand 53 years ago. Today Tamerlane's city is refurbished as a tourist site. Fifty-three years ago it was a desolate place in ruins, overgrown with trees growing out of the tops of the minarets.

As Obama's plan to seize Ukraine failed, like every one of his other plans has failed, Washington's spokesmen for the vested private interests have seized on the opportunity to demonize Putin and Russia and to restart the Cold War. Obama and his Group of 7 puppets or vassals used the occasion to threaten Russia with real sanctions, in place of the present propaganda sanctions that have no effect. According to Obama and his British lap dog, Putin must somehow prevent the Russian populations of eastern and southern Ukraine from protesting their subservience to a neo-Nazi government in Kiev backed by Washington, or else.

Putin is supposed to embrace the Oligarch, a former minister of the government that Washington overthrew, put in office by a fake vote in which turnout was a small percent of the population. Putin is supposed to kiss this corrupt Oligarch on both cheeks, pay Ukraine's natural gas bills and forgive its debts. In addition, Russia is supposed to repudiate the Crimean people, evict them from their re-unity with Russia and hand them over to the neo-Nazi Right Sector to be eliminated as retribution for Russia's victory over Nazi Germany. In exchange, Washington and NATO will put anti-ballistic missile bases on Ukraine's border with Russia in order to protect Europe from nonexistent Iranian nuclear ICBMs.

This is supposed to be a win-win deal for Russia.

The Obama regime used its well-paid NGOs in Ukraine to overthrow an elected, democratic government, a government no more corrupt than those in Western or Eastern Europe or Washington.

The political morons who have England, France, Germany, and Italy in their hands are shaking their fists at Russia, warning of more, this time real, sanctions. Do these morons really want their energy supplies cut off? There is no prospect, despite the propagandistic claims, of Washington supplying the energy on which German industry depends and on which Europeans depend so that they do not freeze in the winter.

Sanctions on Russia will wreck Europe and have little, if any, effect on Russia. Russia is already moving, with China and the BRICS, outside the dollar payments mechanism.

As the demand for dollars drops, the dollar's exchange value will drop. Initially, Washington will be able to force its vassals to support the dollar, but eventually this will become impossible as the supply of fiat money grows.

What the White House moron, the neoconized National Security Council, the presstitute media, and subservient Congress are doing is to support and uphold the policies based on hubris and arrogance that are leading the US into the abyss.

An abyss is like a black hole. You don't get out.

Washington's lies are so blatant and transparent that Washington is destroying its own credibility.

Consider the NSA spying. Documents released by Snowden and Greenwald make it completely clear that Washington spies not only on government leaders and ordinary people but also on foreign businesses in order to advance US commercial and financial interests. That the US steals Chinese business secrets is not in doubt. So what does Washington do? Washington not only denies what the documents prove but turns the charge around and indicts five Chinese generals for spying on US corporations.

The only purpose of these indictments hyped by the US attorney general is propaganda. The indictments are otherwise totally meaningless, not merely false. China is not about to turn over five Chinese generals to the liars in Washington. For the presstitute media the story is a way to move the NSA's spying out of the spotlight. China is substituted for the NSA as the guilty party.

Why doesn't China, Brazil, Germany and every other country issue arrest warrants for NSA's top officials, for Obama, and for the members of the congressional oversight committee? Why do other countries always allow Washington to control the explanation with propaganda first strikes? The answer is that other governments avoid the provocations that Washington substitutes for diplomacy.

Americans are very susceptible to propaganda. They seem to have a special taste for it. Consider the hate whipped up against Sgt. Bowe Bergdahl, a US soldier just released by the Taliban in a prisoner exchange with the US. The hatred and bloodlust that the presstitute media have whipped up against Bergdahl has caused his hometown to cancel the celebration of his release. The press engineered hatred of Bergdahl has spilled over into threats against Hailey, Idaho.

What is the basis for the attacks on Bergdahl? Apparently, the answer is that Bergdahl, like pro-football star Pat Tillman who turned down a $3.6 million contract to join the Army Rangers and go to defend freedom in Afghanistan, is suspected of coming down with a case of doubts about the war. Originally Pat Tillman's death was attributed to his heroic action and enemy fire. Then it emerged that Tillman was a victim of "friendly fire." Many concluded that he was murdered, because the government did not want a sports hero speaking out about the war. As Bergdahl is off the battlefield, he has to be murdered in the press—like Russia, China, Iran, Putin, Assad, Crimeans, and the Russian-speaking population in Ukraine.

In America hate and the cultivation of hate are alive and well, but moral virtues are in short supply.

WASHINGTON CAUGHT AGAIN IN A LIE

June 7, 2014

In case you didn't hear from the presstitute media, Syrian president Assad was just re-elected with 88.7% of the vote. Assad is the "brutal dictator" that Obama claims the Syrian people are trying to overthrow.

The vote clearly puts the lie, yet again, to Washington.

Voting was not possible in some parts of Syria where the Washington-backed Islamist jihadists hold sway.

Nevertheless, the vote clearly shows that it is Washington and not the Syrian people who want to overthrow Assad.

Washington and its British vassal had no choice but to allege, without any proof whatsoever as always, that the election was unfair and unfree.

When Washington puts out massive propaganda about how everyone in Syria wants to overthrow "a dictator" and then the people re-elect "the dictator" by 88.7% of the vote, Washington's propaganda is exposed.

WORLD WAR II: THE UNKNOWN WAR

June 9, 2014

In my June 6 column, "The Lies Grow More Audacious," I mentioned that Obama and the British prime minister, who Obama has as a lap dog, just as George Bush had Tony Blair as lap dog, had managed to celebrate the defeat of Nazi Germany at the 70th anniversary of the Normandy invasion without mentioning the Russians.

I pointed out the fact, well known to historians and educated people, that the Red Army defeated Nazi Germany long before the US was able to get geared up to participate in the war. The Normandy invasion most certainly did not defeat Nazi Germany. What the Normandy invasion did was to foreclose any likelihood of the Red Army overrunning all of Europe.

As I have reported in a number of columns, many, if not most, Americans have beliefs that are *not* fact-based, but instead are emotion-based. So I knew that at least one person would go berserk, and he did. JD from Texas wrote to set me straight. No one but "our American boys" won that war. JD didn't know that the Russians were even in the war.

JD had the option of consulting an encyclopedia or a history book or going online and consulting Wikipedia prior to making a fool of himself. But he chose instead to unload on me. JD epitomizes US foreign policy: rush into every fight that you know nothing about and start new ones hand over fist that someone else will win.

It occurred to me that World War II was so long ago that few are alive who remember it, and by now even these few probably remember the propaganda version that they have heard at every Memorial Day and July 4th occasion since 1945. Little wonder that neither Obama nor Cameron nor their pitiful speech writers knew anything about the war that they were commemorating.

Propaganda has always been with us. The difference is that in the 21st century Americans have nothing but propaganda. Nothing else at all.

Just lies. Lies are the American experience. The actual world as it exists is foreign to most Americans.

In 1973 a British television documentary series was released that chronicled WW II. Of the 28 episodes, only 3 and part of a 4th acknowledge Russian participation in the war. From the British standpoint, victory was an Anglo-American victory.

This did not sit well with the Soviet government. The Soviets offered their film archives to the West. In 1978 a 20 part series of 48 minutes per episode was released in an American documentary television series narrated by Burt Lancaster. The documentary was titled: "The Unknown War."

Certainly, it was a war unknown to most Americans, raised as they are on propaganda.

"The Unknown War" was a revelation to Americans because it demonstrated beyond all doubt that Nazi Germany lost World War II on the Russian front. Of the 20 episodes, "The Allies," that is, the Anglo- Americans and free French, feature only in number 17. One out of twenty is about the correct proportion of the West's participation in the defeat of Nazi Germany.

If you google "The Unknown War", you will find an entry on Wikipedia. The series might still be available on YouTube. It was taken off the air when the Soviets invaded Afghanistan, a folly repeated by Washington. It was more important to Washington that Russia be demonized than any truths should be presented, so the truth revealed in "The Unknown War" was removed from US TV. Later the documentary reappeared on the History Channel.

In my June 6 article, I said, following the consensus of historians, that Nazi Germany lost the war at Stalingrad. Historian Dr. Jacques R. Pauwels says that Germany lost the war 14 months earlier at the Battle of Moscow in December 1941.[52] He makes a good case. Whether one agrees or not, the facts he presents are eye openers for the "exceptional, indispensable Americans" who believe nothing happens without them.

Normandy, June 1944, is 2.5 years after Germany lost the war in the Battle of Moscow. As historians have made clear, by June 1944 Germany had little left with which to fight. Whatever was left of the German military was on the Eastern Front.

At the 70th annual Normandy landing celebration in France, Obama informed his French vassal, President Hollande, that he, Obama, the ruler of the Exceptional Country, would not sit down to dinner with the Russian Putin. Americans are too good to eat dinner with Russians. So Hollande had to have two dinners.

One for Obama, and then one for Putin. As food is still good in France thanks to the banning of GMOs, probably Holland didn't mind. I myself would have enjoyed being at both dinners for the food alone.

Like all news that is important, the dinner for Putin, and its meaning, escaped the attention of the American presstitute media, the world's greatest collection of whores. If memory serves, normally the Russians are left out of the Normandy commemoration celebrations. If the war was won in the West, what did the Russians have to do with it? Nothing, of course. "Our boys" did it all, just as JD informed me.

Russians? What Russians?

But this time France invited Putin to the Normandy celebration, and Putin was not too proud to come. Putin spoke with European politicians in the off moments, and these politicians saw a real person, unlike Obama, a total fake.

The superiority of Russian diplomacy over Washington's is clear to all. Putin's position is: "we are here for you, we can work things out." Washington's position is: "do as we say or we will bomb you into the stone age."

Russia is accommodating to its client states. Washington is not. Putin says that he is willing to work things out with the billionaire corrupt Oligarch imposed on Ukraine by Washington, but Washington has forced the Bulgarians to stop work on the South Stream Pipeline. This natural gas pipeline bypasses Ukraine by going under the Black Sea to Bulgaria. As Washington's new puppet state in Ukraine has not paid its multi-billion dollar natural gas bill to Russia and threatens to disrupt the pipeline to Europe and to steal gas from it, Russia, despite Western sanctions, made preparations for a new pipeline route in order that Europeans do not suffer from winter cold and have their industries shut down and economies collapse from lack of energy.

Washington sees Putin's commitment to Europe as a threat and has gone to work to prevent any Russian energy flows to Europe.

In contrast with Putin's position, Washington's position is: We don't give a hoot what happens to our European puppets. Like the rest of humanity, European puppets don't count and are dispensable, mere collateral damage, in the Indispensable Country's war for world hegemony.

All that is important to Washington is that Russia is damaged regardless of the damage done to the puppet regimes in Western and Eastern Europe, including the moronic Polish government, possibly the only government on earth more foolish than Obama's.

Washington is trying to break off Europe's economic relations with Russia. Washington is promising to supply Europe with US natural gas obtained by fracking. This promise is a lie, like everything else Washington says.

On May 20 the *Los Angeles Times* reported that "federal energy authorities have slashed by 96% the recoverable oil buried in California's vast Monterey Shale deposits." The Monterey Shale formation contains about two-thirds of the nation's shale oil reserves, and only 4% are recoverable.[53]

William Engdahl has reported that at best the US has 20 years of natural gas from fracking, and that the price of the gas will be the despoiling of US surface and ground waters. Experts have pointed out that the infrastructure for transporting US natural gas to Europe does not exist and that it would take three years to build the infrastructure. What will Europe do for three years while it waits for US energy to replace the cut-off Russian energy? Will Europe still be there?

Washington's European vassals should take note: Washington is prepared to destroy the economies of its vassals in order to score a one up on Russia.

How is it possible that by now Europe doesn't understand how Washington thinks? Those bags full of money must be very large.

As I have reported several times, the Assistant Secretary of Defense for International Security affairs told me years ago that Washington purchases European politicians with bags full of money. It remains to be seen if European "leaders" are willing to sacrifice their peoples and their own reputations in order to be complicit in the war that Washington is planning with Russia, a war that could mean the end of life on earth.

It is Europe's call. If leaders emerge who tell Washington, "no dice," the world is saved.

If instead European politicians want the money, the world is doomed.

Europe would be the first to go.

WASHINGTON'S IRAQ "VICTORY"

June 14, 2014

The citizens of the United States still do not know why their government destroyed Iraq. "National Security" will prevent them from ever knowing. "National Security" is the cloak behind which hides the crimes of the US government.

George Herbert Walker Bush, a former Director of the Central Intelligence Agency who became President courtesy of being picked as Ronald Reagan's Vice President, was the last restrained US President. When Bush the First attacked Iraq it was a limited operation, the goal of which was to evict Saddam Hussein from his annexation of Kuwait.

Kuwait was once a part of Iraq, but a Western colonial power created new political boundaries, as the Soviet Communist Party did in Ukraine. Kuwait emerged from Iraq as a small, independent oil kingdom.

According to reports, Kuwait was drilling at an angle across the Iraq/Kuwait border into Iraqi oil fields.

On July 25, 1990, Saddam Hussein, with Iraqi troops massed on the border with Kuwait, asked President George H. W. Bush's ambassador, April Glaspie, if the Bush administration had an opinion on the situation. Here is Ambassador Glaspie's reply:

> We have no opinion on your Arab-Arab conflicts, such as your dispute with Kuwait. Secretary [of State James] Baker has directed me to emphasize the instruction, first given to Iraq in the 1960's that the Kuwait issue is not associated with America.

According to this transcript, Saddam Hussein is further assured by high US government officials that Washington does not stand in his way in reunifying Iraq and putting a halt to a gangster family's theft of Iraqi oil.

At a Washington press conference called the next day, State Department spokesperson Margaret Tutweiler was asked by journalists: 'Has the United States sent any type of diplomatic message to the Iraqis about putting 30,000 troops on the border with Kuwait? Has there been any type of protest communicated from the United States government?' to which she responded: 'I'm entirely unaware of any such protest.'

On July 31st, two days before the Iraqi invasion [of Kuwait], John Kelly, Assistant Secretary of State for Near Eastern affairs, testified to Congress that the 'United States has no commitment to defend Kuwait and the U.S. has no intention of defending Kuwait if it is attacked by Iraq'.[54]

Was this an intentional a set-up of Saddam Hussein, or did the Iraqi takeover of Kuwait produce frantic calls from the Bush family's Middle Eastern business associates?

Whatever explains the dramatic, sudden, total change of position of the US government, the result produced military action that fell short of war on Iraq itself.

But when Bush II came along, we were told a passel of lies: Saddam Hussein had weapons of mass destruction that were a threat to America. The specter of a "mushroom cloud over an American city" was raised by the National Security Advisor. The Secretary of State was sent to the UN with a collection of lies with which to build acceptance of US naked aggression against Iraq. The icing on the cake was the claim that Saddam Hussein's secular government "had al Qaeda connections," al Qaeda bearing the blame for 9/11.

As neither Congress nor the US media have any interest to know the reason for Washington's about face on Iraq, the "Iraq Threat" will remain a mystery for Americans.

But the consequence of Washington's destruction of the secular government of Saddam Hussein, a government that managed to hold Iraq together without the American-induced violence that has made the country a permanent war zone, has been ongoing years of violence on a level equal to, or in excess of, the violence associated with the US occupation of Iraq.

Washington is devoid of humanitarian concerns. Hegemony is Washington's only concern. As in Afghanistan, Libya, Somalia, Pakistan, Yemen, Ukraine, Syria, and Iraq, Washington brings only death, and death is ongoing in Iraq.

On June 12, 500,000 residents of Mosul, Iraq's second largest city, benefactors of Washington's "freedom and democracy" liberation, fled the city as the American trained army collapsed and fled under attack by an al Qaeda splinter group, formerly al Qaeda in Iraq, now ISIS (Islamic State of Iraq and Syria). The Washington-installed government, fearing Baghdad is next, has asked Washington for air strikes against the ISIS fighters. Tikrit and Kirkuk have also fallen. Reportedly, Iran has sent two battalions of Revolutionary Guards to protect the Washington-installed government in Baghdad, but this is not confirmed by Iran.

(After this article was published, Iran's President Hassan Rouhani dismissed the widespread news reports—*Wall Street Journal*, *World Tribune*, the *Guardian*, *Telegraph*, CNBC, *Daily Mail*, *Times of Israel*, etc—that Iran has sent troops to help the Iraqi government. Once again the Western media has created a false reality with false reports.)

Does anyone remember the propaganda that Washington had to overthrow Saddam Hussein in order to bring "freedom and democracy and women's rights to Iraqis"? We had to defeat al Qaeda, which at the time was not present in Iraq, "over there before they came over here."

Do you remember the neoconservative promises of a "cakewalk war" lasting only a few weeks, of the war only costing $70 billion to be paid out of Iraqi oil revenues, of George W. Bush's economic advisor being fired for saying that the war would cost $200 billion? The true cost of the war was calculated by economist Joseph Stiglitz and Harvard University budget expert Linda Bilmes who showed that the Iraqi war cost US taxpayers $3 trillion dollars, an expenditure that threatens the US social safety net.

Do you remember Washington's promises that Iraq would be put on its feet by America as a democracy in which everyone would be safe and women would have rights?

What is the situation today?

Mosul, the second largest city in Iraq, has just been overrun by jihadist forces, an indication that Washington failed to bring democracy and stability to Iraq.

These are the forces that Washington has claimed a number of times to have completely defeated.

These "defeated" forces now control Iraq's second largest city and a number of provinces. The person Washington left in charge of Iraq is on his knees begging Washington for military help and air support against the jihadist forces that the incompetent Bush regime unleashed in the Muslim world.

What Washington has done in Iraq and Libya, and is trying to do in Syria, is to destroy governments that kept jihadists under control. Washington faces the prospect of a jihadist government encompassing Iraq and Syria. The Neoconservative conquest of the Middle East is becoming an al Qaeda conquest.

Washington has opened Pandora's Box. This is Washington's accomplishment in the Middle East.

Even as large swaths of Iraq fall to jihadists, Washington is supplying jihadists forces attacking Syria. Is it possible for a country to look more foolish than Washington looks?

One conclusion that we can reach is that the arrogance and hubris that defines the US government has rendered Washington incapable of making a rational, logical decision. Megalomania rules in Washington.

WASHINGTON IS BEATING THE WAR DRUMS

June 17, 2014

I wish I had only good news to bring to readers, or even one item of good news. Alas, goodness has ceased to be a feature of US policy and simply cannot be found in any words or deeds emanating from Washington or the capitals of its European vassal states. The Western World has succumbed to evil.

In an article published by Op-Ed News, Eric Zuesse supports my reports of indications that Washington is preparing for a nuclear first strike against Russia.[56]

US war doctrine has been changed. US nuclear weapons are no longer restricted to a retaliatory force, but have been elevated to the role of preemptive nuclear attack. Washington pulled out of the Anti-Ballistic Missile Treaty with Russia and is developing and deploying an ABM shield. Washington is demonizing Russia and Russia's President with shameless lies and propaganda, thus preparing the populations of the US and its client states for war with Russia.

Washington has been convinced by neoconservatives that Russian strategic nuclear forces are in run down and unprepared condition and are sitting ducks for attack. This false belief is based on out-of-date information, a decade old, such as the argument presented in "The Rise of U.S. Nuclear Primacy" by Keir A. Lieber and Daryl G. Press in the April 2006 issue of *Foreign Affairs*, a publication of the Council on Foreign Relations, an organization of American elites.[57]

Regardless of the condition of Russian nuclear forces, the success of Washington's first strike and degree of protection provided by Washington's ABM shield against retaliation, the May 30, 2014 article I posted by Steven Starr, "The Lethality of Nuclear Weapons," makes clear that nuclear war has no winners. Everyone dies.[58]

In an article published in the December 2008 issue of *Physics Today*, three atmospheric scientists point out that even the substantial reduction in nuclear arsenals that the Strategic Offensive Reductions Treaty hoped to achieve, from 70,000 warheads in 1986 to 1700-2200 warheads by the end of 2012, did not reduce the threat that nuclear war presents to life on earth. The authors conclude that in addition to the direct blast effects of hundreds of millions of human fatalities, "the indirect effects would likely eliminate the majority of the human population." The stratospheric smoke from firestorms would cause nuclear winter and agricultural collapse. Those who did not perish from blast and radiation would starve to death.[59]

Ronald Reagan and Mikhail Gorbachev understood this. Unfortunately, no successor US government has.

As far as Washington is concerned, death is what happens to others, not to "the exceptional people." (The SORT agreement apparently failed. According to the Stockholm International Peace Research Institute, the nine nuclear-armed states still possess a total of 16,300 nuclear weapons.)[60]

It is a fact that Washington has policymakers who think, incorrectly, that nuclear war is winnable and who regard nuclear war as a means of preventing the rise of Russia and China as checks on Washington's hegemony over the world. The US government, regardless of party in office, is a massive threat to life on earth. European governments, which think of themselves as civilized, are not, because they enable Washington's pursuit of hegemony. It is this pursuit that threatens life with extinction. The ideology that grants "exceptional, indispensable America" supremacy is an enormous threat to the world.

The destruction of seven countries in whole or in part by the West in the 21st century, with the support of "Western civilization" and the Western media, comprises powerful evidence that the leadership of the Western world is devoid of moral conscience and human compassion. Now that Washington is armed with its false doctrine of "nuclear primacy," the outlook for humanity is very bleak.

Washington has begun the run up to the Third World War, and Europeans seem to be on board. As recently as November 2012 NATO Secretary General Rasmussen said that NATO does not regard Russia as an enemy. Now that the White House and its European vassals have convinced Russia that the West is an enemy, Rasmussen declared that "we must adapt to the fact that Russia now considers us its adversary" by beefing up Ukraine's military along with those of Eastern and Central Europe.

Last month Alexander Vershbow, former US ambassador to Russia, currently NATO Deputy Secretary General, declared Russia to be the enemy and said that the American and European taxpayers need to fork over for the military modernization "not just of Ukraine, but also Moldova, Georgia, Armenia, Azerbaijan."

It is possible to see these calls for more military spending as just the normal functioning of agents for the US military/security complex. Having lost "the war on terror" in Iraq and Afghanistan, Washington needs a replacement and has set about resurrecting the Cold War.

This is probably how the armaments industry, its shills, and part of Washington sees it. But the neoconservatives are more ambitious. They are not pursuing merely more profits for the military/security complex. Their goal is Washington's hegemony over the world, which means reckless actions such as the strategic threat that the Obama regime, with the complicity of its European vassals, has brought to Russia in Ukraine.

Since last autumn the US government has been lying through its teeth about Ukraine, blaming Russia for the consequences of Washington's actions, and demonizing Putin exactly as Washington demonized Gaddafi, Saddam Hussein, Assad, the Taliban, and Iran. The presstitute media and the European capitals have seconded the lies and propaganda and repeat them endlessly. Consequently, the US public's attitude toward Russia moved sharply negative.

How do you think Russia and China see this? Russia has witnessed NATO brought to its borders, a violation of the Reagan-Gorbachev understandings. Russia has witnessed the US pull out of the ABM treaty and develop a "star wars" shield. (Whether or not the shield would work is immaterial. The purpose of the shield is to convince the politicians and the public that Americans are safe.) Russia has witnessed Washington change the role of nuclear weapons in its war doctrine from deterrent to preemptive first strike. And now Russia listens to a daily stream of lies from the West and witnesses the slaughter by Washington's vassal in Kiev of civilians in Russian Ukraine, branded "terrorists" by Washington, by such weapons as white phosphorus with not a peep of protest from the West.

Massive attacks by artillery and air strikes on homes and apartments in Russian Ukraine were conducted on the 25th anniversary of Tiananmen Square, while Washington and its puppets condemned China for an event that did not happen. As we now know, there was no massacre in Tiananmen Square. It was just another Washington lie like Tonkin Gulf, Saddam Hussein's weapons of mass destruction, Assad's use of chemical weapons, Iranian nukes, etc. It is an amazing fact that the world lives in a false reality created by Washington's lies.

The movie, The Matrix, is a true depiction of life in the West. The population lives in a false reality created for them by their rulers. A handful of humans have escaped the false existence and are committed to bringing humans back to reality. They rescue Neo, "The One," whom they believe correctly to have the power to free humans from the false reality in which they live. Morpheus, the leader of the rebels, explains to Neo:

The Matrix is a system, Neo. That system is our enemy.
But when you're inside, you look around, what do you
see? Businessmen, teachers, lawyers, carpenters. The very
minds of the people we are trying to save. But until we do,
these people are still a part of that system, and that makes
them our enemy. You have to understand, most of these
people are not ready to be unplugged. And many of them
are so inured, so hopelessly dependent on the system, that
they will fight to protect it.

I experience this every time I write a column. Protests from those
determined not to be unplugged arrive in emails and on those websites that
expose their writers to slander by government trolls in comment sections.
Don't believe real reality, they insist, believe the false reality.

The Matrix even encompasses part of the Russian and Chinese
population, especially those educated in the West and those susceptible to
Western propaganda, though on the whole those populations know the
difference between lies and truth. The problem for Washington is that the
propaganda that prevails over the Western peoples does not prevail over the
Russian and Chinese governments.

How do you think China reacts when Washington declares the South
China Sea to be an area of US national interest, allocates 60 percent of its
vast fleet to the Pacific, and constructs new US air and naval bases from the
Philippines to Vietnam?

Suppose all Washington intends is to keep taxpayer funding alive for
the military/security complex which launders some of the taxpayers' money
and returns it as political campaign contributions. Can Russia and China take
the risk of viewing Washington's words and deeds in this limited way?

So far the Russians (and Chinese), have remained sensible. Lavrov,
the Foreign Minister, said: "At this stage, we want to give our partners a
chance to calm down. We'll see what happens next. If absolutely baseless
accusations against Russia continue, it there are attempts to pressure us with
economic leverage, then we may reevaluate the situation."

If the White House, Washington's media whores and European
vassals convince Russia that war is in the cards, war will be in the cards. As
there is no prospect whatsoever of NATO being able to mount a conventional
offensive threat against Russia anywhere near the size and power of the
German invasion force in 1941 that met with destruction, the war will be
nuclear, which will mean the end of all of us.

Keep that firmly in mind as Washington and its media whores
continue to beat the drums for war. Keep in mind also that a long history

proves beyond all doubt that everything Washington and the presstitute media tells you is a lie serving an undeclared agenda. You cannot rectify the situation by voting Democrat instead of Republican or by voting Republican instead of Democrat.

Thomas Jefferson told us his solution: "The tree of liberty must be refreshed from time to time with the blood of patriots & tyrants. It is its natural manure."

There are few patriots in Washington but many tyrants.

PROFESSOR FRANCIS BOYLE ON IMPEACHMENT OF BUSH AND HIS CRIMINAL REGIME

June 17, 2014

As Democratic Representative Nancy Pelosi, the Richest Representative of the One Percent in the House of Representatives, said: "Impeachment is off the table." Nevertheless, Insouciant Californians still sent the bought-and-paid-for hireling to Washington.

In my day if an experienced professor of international and constitutional law, such as University of Illinois Professor Francis A. Boyle, called for impeachment of a president, it was a serious situation for the president. But no more. Today an American president can ride roughshod over constitutional lawyers, the US Constitution and US statutory law without any danger of impeachment. To avoid impeachment today, all a president has to do is to avoid having a sexual affair with a White House intern in the Oval Office, or is that the Oral Orifice.

America's last two presidents, Obama and George W. Bush, have established the precedent that impeachment is a "dead letter law." Impeachment is unlikely ever again to be a threat to a tyrannical president. Congress and the Federal Judiciary have accepted their impotence. Both "coequal" branches of government are happy in their subservience to the Executive Power. Members of Congress and the Judiciary are still permitted to pretend that they are important, like Roman Senators under the Caesars, but both are incapable of challenging the Executive Branch where a Caesar now rules independently of law and the Constitution.

I have received a communication from University of Illinois Law School Professor Francis A. Boyle, an internationally famous representative of human rights, with J.D. and Ph.D. degrees from Harvard University, a man revered in many countries of the world, although not in Washington:

On Tuesday 11 March 2003, with the Bush Jr. administration's war of aggression against Iraq staring the American People, Congress and Republic in their face, Congressman John Conyers of Michigan, the Ranking Member of the House Judiciary Committee (which has jurisdiction over Bills of Impeachment), convened an emergency meeting of forty or more of his top advisors, most of whom were lawyers. The purpose of the meeting was to discuss and debate immediately putting into the U.S. House of Representatives Bills of Impeachment against President Bush Jr., Vice President Dick Cheney, Secretary of Defense Donald Rumsfeld, and then Attorney General John Ashcroft in order to head off the impending war. Congressman Conyers kindly requested that Ramsey Clark and I come to the meeting in order to argue the case for impeachment.

This impeachment debate lasted for two hours. It was presided over by Congressman Conyers, who quite correctly did not tip his hand one way or the other on the merits of impeachment. He simply moderated the debate between Clark and I, on the one side, favoring immediately filing Bills of Impeachment against Bush Jr. et al. to stop the threatened war, and almost everyone else there who were against impeachment for partisan political reasons. Obviously no point would be served here by attempting to digest a two-hour-long vigorous debate among a group of well-trained lawyers on such a controversial matter at this critical moment in American history. But at the time I was struck by the fact that this momentous debate was conducted at a private office right down the street from the White House on the eve of war.

Suffice it to say that most of the 'experts' there opposed impeachment not on the basis of enforcing the Constitution and the Rule of Law, whether international or domestic, but on the political grounds that it might hurt the Democratic Party's effort to get their presidential candidate elected in the year 2004. As a political independent, I did not argue that point. Rather, I argued the merits of impeaching Bush Jr., Cheney, Rumsfeld, and Ashcroft under the United States Constitution, U.S. federal laws, U.S. treaties and other international agreements to which the United States is a party, etc. Article VI of the U.S. Constitution provides

that treaties 'shall be the supreme Law of the Land.' This
so-called Supremacy Clause of the U.S. Constitution also
applies to international executive agreements concluded
under the auspices of the U.S. President such as the 1945
Nuremberg Charter.

    Congressman Conyers was so kind as to allow me the
closing argument in the debate. Briefly put, the concluding
point I chose to make was historical: The Athenians lost
their democracy. The Romans lost their Republic. And if
we Americans did not act now we could lose our Republic!
The United States of America is not immune to the laws
of history!

After two hours of most vigorous debate among those in attendance,
the meeting adjourned with second revised draft Bills of Impeachment sitting
on the table.

    Professor Boyle said to former Attorney General Ramsey Clark on
the way out of the building after the two hour debate:

"Ramsey, I don't understand it. Why didn't those people
take me up on my offer to stick around, polish up my draft
bills of impeachment, and put them in there right away in
order to head off this war?
And Ramsey replied: 'I think most of the people there want
a war.'"

    And, indeed, they did. John Podesta representing the Democratic
National Committee told Conyers that the Democratic Party did not want
Conyers to pursue the impeachment effort. Instead, the Democratic Party
wanted to give Republicans Bush and Cheney their war on Iraq so that the
Democrats would fare better in the national elections in 2004. Think about
that, not just the stupidity of the Democratic Party—whenever has a party at
war been in danger of electoral defeat? Look and see! Here is the spokesman
for the Democratic Party telling Conyers: "Don't prevent a war, because we
will benefit politically from it. Let the Iraqi people die. Let our soldiers die.
We Democrats will benefit from it."

    You can listen to Professor Boyle tell the story on youtube.[61]

    Once upon a time Democrats were less vicious than Republicans,
but no more. I can remember when Democrats were the Humane Party. This
was before the corporations and their "free market" shills sent the industrial
and manufacturing jobs to Asia, destroying the industrial and manufacturing
basis of the Democratic Party in the working people. Today the Democrats

have to appeal to Wall Street, to the Military/Security Complex, and to the Environmental Despoilers in the Agribusiness, Timber, Mining, and Energy industries.

Obama completed George W. Bush's destruction of the US Constitution. Neither party represents you or America, unless you are the one percent. If you vote for a Republican or a Democrat you are voting for your dispossession and for war. You are voting in favor of a DHS sponsored SWAT team breaking into your home at night and murdering you or your wife or your children and most certainly the family pet dog.

Both political parties are irredeemably evil. Neither has any redeeming virtues.

If Americans cannot find leadership that can survive assassination, either by media slander or by SWAT Team bullet, America is lost.

How would you place your bet? Is America lost or is America the salt of the earth, the exceptional, indispensable people chosen by History to enjoy hegemony over Earth?

CAN PUTIN'S DIPLOMACY PREVAIL OVER WASHINGTON'S COERCION?

June 24, 2014

Russia's President Vladimir Putin is trying to save the world from war. We should all help him.

Today Putin's presidential press secretary Dmitry Peskov reported that President Putin has asked the Russian legislature to repeal the authorization to use force that was granted in order to protect residents of former Russian territories that are currently part of Ukraine from the rabid Russophobic violence that characterizes Washington's stooge government in Kiev.

Washington's neoconservatives are jubilant. They regard Putin's diplomacy as a sign of weakness and fear, and urge stronger steps that will force Russia to give back Crimea and the Black Sea naval base.

Inside Russia, Washington is encouraging its NGO fifth columns to undercut Putin's support with propaganda that Putin is afraid to stand up for Russians and has sold out Ukraine's Russian population. If this propaganda gains traction, Putin will be distracted by street protests. The appearance of Putin's domestic weakness would embolden Washington. Many members of Russia's young professional class are swayed by Washington's propaganda. Essentially, these Russians, brainwashed by US propaganda, are aligned with Washington, not with the Kremlin.

Putin has placed his future and that of his country on a bet that Russian diplomacy can prevail over Washington's bribes, threats, blackmail, and coercion. Putin is appealing to Western Europeans. Putin is saying, as did Saddam Hussein, Muammar Gaddafi and Bashir al-Assad before him, "I am not the problem. Russia is not the problem. We are reasonable. We are ignoring Washington's provocations. We want to work things out and to find a peaceful solution."

Washington is saying: "Russia is a threat. Putin is the new Hitler.

Russia is the enemy. NATO and the US must begin a military buildup against the Russian Threat, rush troops and jet fighters to Eastern European NATO bases on Russia's frontier. G-7 meetings must be held without Russia. Economic sanctions must be put on Russia regardless of the damage the sanctions do to Europe." And so forth.

Putin says: "I'm here for you. Let's work this out."

Washington says: "Russia is the enemy."

Putin knows that the UK is a complete vassal puppet state, that Cameron is just as bought-and-paid-for as Blair before him. Putin's hope for diplomacy over force rests on Germany and France. Both countries face Europe's budget and employment woes, and both countries have significant economic relations with Russia. German business interests are a counterweight to the Merkel government's subservience to Washington. Washington has stupidly angered the French by trying to steal $10 billion from France's largest bank. This theft, if successful, will destroy France's largest bank and deliver France to Wall Street.

If desire for national sovereignty still exists in the German or French governments, one or both could give the middle finger to Washington and publicly declare that they are unwilling for their country to be drawn into conflict with Russia for the sake of Washington's Empire and the financial hegemony of American banks.

Putin is betting on this outcome. If his bet is a bad one and Europe fails not only Russia but itself and the rest of the world by accommodating Washington's drive for world hegemony, Russia and China will have to submit to Washington's hegemony or be prepared for war.

WASHINGTON'S
CAPTIVE NATIONS

June 28, 2014

The Cold War made a lot of money for the military/security complex for four decades dating from Churchill's March 5, 1946 speech in Fulton, Missouri declaring a Soviet "Iron Curtain" until Reagan and Gorbachev ended the Cold War in the late 1980s. During the Cold War Americans heard endlessly about "the Captive Nations." The Captive Nations were the Baltics and the Soviet bloc, usually summarized as "Eastern Europe."

These nations were captive because their foreign policies were dictated by Moscow, just as these same Captive Nations, plus the UK, Western Europe, Canada, Mexico, Columbia, Japan, Australia, New Zealand, South Korea, Taiwan, the Philippines, Georgia, and Ukraine, have their foreign policies dictated today by Washington. Washington intends to expand the Captive Nations to include Azerbaijan, former constituent parts of Soviet Central Asia, Vietnam, Thailand, and Indonesia.

During the Cold War Americans thought of Western Europe and Great Britain as independent sovereign countries. Whether they were or not, they most certainly are not today. Seven decades have passed since WWII, and US troops still occupy Germany. No European government dares to take a stance different from that of the US Department of State.

Not long ago there was talk both in the UK and Germany about departing the European Union, and Washington told both countries that talk of that kind must stop as it was not in Washington's interest for any country to exit the EU. The talk stopped. Great Britain and Germany are such complete vassals of Washington that neither country can publicly discuss its own future.

When Baltasar Garzon, a Spanish judge with prosecuting authority, attempted to indict members of the George W. Bush regime for violating international law by torturing detainees, he was slapped down by the Spanish government on orders from Washington.

In *Modern Britain*, Stephane Aderca writes that the UK is so proud of being Washington's "junior partner" that the British government agreed to a one-sided extradition treaty under which Washington merely has to declare "reasonable suspicion" in order to obtain extradition from the UK, but the UK must prove "probable cause." Being Washington's "junior partner," Aderca reports, is an ego-boost for British elites, giving them a feeling of self-importance.

Under the rule of the Soviet Union, a larger entity than present day Russia, the captive nations had poor economic performance. Under Washington's rule, these same captives have poor economic performance due to their looting by Wall Street and the IMF.

As Giuseppe di Lampedusa said, "Things have to change in order to remain the same."

The looting of Europe by Wall Street has gone beyond Greece, Italy, Spain, Portugal, Ireland and Ukraine, and is now focused on France and Great Britain. The American authorities are demanding $10 billion from France's largest bank on a trumped-up charge of financing trade with Iran, as if it is any business whatsoever of Washington's who French banks choose to finance. And despite Great Britain's total subservience to Washington, Barclays bank has a civil fraud suit filed against it by the NY State Attorney General.

The charges against Barclays PLC are likely correct. But as no US banks were charged, most of which are similarly guilty, the US charge against Barclays means that big pension funds and mutual funds must flee Barclays as customers, because the pension funds and mutual funds would be subject to lawsuits for negligence if they stayed with a bank under charges.

The result, of course, of the US charges against foreign banks is that US banks like Morgan Stanley and Citigroup are given a competitive advantage and gain market share in their own dark pools.

So, what are we witnessing? Clearly and unequivocally, we are witnessing the use of US law to create financial hegemony for US financial institutions. The US Department of Justice (sic) has had evidence for five years of Citigroup's participation in the fixing of the LIBOR interest rate, but no indictment has been forthcoming.

The bought and paid for governments of Washington's European puppet states are so corrupt that the leaders permit Washington control over their countries in order to advance American financial, political, and economic hegemony.

Washington is organizing the world against Russia and China for Washington's benefit. On June 27 Washington's puppet states that comprise the EU issued an ultimatum to Russia. The absurdity of this ultimatum is obvious. Militarily, Washington's EU puppets are harmless. Russia could wipe out Europe in a few minutes. Here we have the weak issuing an ultimatum to the strong.

The EU, ordered by Washington, told Russia to suppress the opposition in southern and eastern Ukraine to Washington's stooge government in Kiev. But, as every educated person knows, including the White House,

10 Downing Street, Merkel, and Hollande, Russia is not responsible for the separatist unrest in eastern and southern Ukraine. These territories are former constituent parts of Russia that were added to the Ukrainian Soviet Republic by Soviet Communist Party leaders when Ukraine and Russia were two parts of the same country. These Russians want to return to Russia because they are threatened by the stooge government in Kiev that Washington has installed.

Washington, determined to force Putin into military action that can be used to justify more sanctions, is intent on forcing the issue, not on resolving the issue.

What is Putin to do? He has been given 72 hours to submit to an ultimatum from a collection of puppet states that he can wipe out at a moment's notice or seriously inconvenience by turning off the flow of Russian natural gas to Europe.

Historically, such a stupid challenge to power would result in consequences. But Putin is a humanist who favors peace. He will not willingly give up his strategy of demonstrating to Europe that the provocations are coming from Washington, not from Russia. Putin's hope, and Russia's, is that Europe will eventually realize that Europe is being badly used by Washington.

Washington has hundreds of Washington-financed NGOs in Russia hiding behind various guises such as "human rights," and Washington can unleash these NGOs on Putin at will, as Washington did with the protests against Putin's election. Washington's fifth columns claimed that Putin stole the election even though polls showed that Putin was the clear and undisputed winner.

In 1991 Russians were, for the most part, delighted to be released from communism and looked to the West as an ally in the construction of a civil society based on good will. This was Russia's mistake. As the Brzezinski and Wolfowitz doctrines make clear, Washington views Russia as the enemy whose rise to influence must be prevented at all cost.

Putin's dilemma is that he is caught between his heart-felt desire to reach an accommodation with Europe and Washington's desire to demonize and isolate Russia.

The risk for Putin is that his desire for accommodation is being exploited by Washington and explained to the EU as Putin's weakness and lack of courage. Washington is telling its European vassals that Putin's retreat under Europe's pressure will undermine his status in Russia, and at the right time Washington will unleash its many hundreds of NGOs to bring Putin to ruin.

This was the Ukraine scenario. With Putin replaced with a compliant Russian, richly rewarded by Washington, only China would remain as an obstacle to American world hegemony.

THE WEST IS TURNING THE PLANET INTO A GLOBAL BARRACKS

July 1, 2014

The remarks below are excerpted from President Putin's meeting with Russia's ambassadors on July 1, 2014.

Putin damns Washington's puppet president of Ukraine, an usurped position resulting from the overthrow of a democratically elected president, for taking "the path of violence which cannot lead to peace." Putin's remarks are simultaneous English translations as Putin speaks in Russian. Such translations are seldom good, but are usually adequate to convey the content.

Unfortunately, Ukrainian President Poroshenko has made the decision to resume military actions, and we—meaning myself and my colleagues in Europe—could not convince him that the way to reliable, firm and long-term peace can't lie through war. Previously, Petro Poroshenko had no direct relation to orders to take military action. Now he has taken on this responsibility in full.

Not only military, but also more importantly, politically.

On Monday [June 30], I spoke with France, Germany and Ukraine via telephone. I stressed the need to prolong the ceasefire and the creation of a reliable mechanism for monitoring compliance with the cease fire and that the Organization for Security and Cooperation in Europe (OSCE) should play an active role. I offered that checkpoints on the Russian side of the Ukrainian border could be monitored by representatives of Ukraine and by OSCE to insure joint control of the border.

Everything that's going on in Ukraine is of course

the internal business of Ukrainian government, but we are painfully sorry that civilians die. In my opinion, there is a deliberate attempt by Ukraine to eliminate representatives of the press. It concerns both Russian and foreign journalists.

The killing of journalists is absolutely unacceptable.

I hope pragmatism will prevail, that the West will get rid of its hegemonic ambitions and desire to arrange the world according to its preferences. I hope instead that the West will start building relations based on equal rights, mutual respect and good will toward others and respect for the interests of other countries.

Putin said that Washington had put pressure on France not to deliver the Mistral-class helicopter ships that the Russian/French contract specified. *"We know about the pressure that our American partners put on the French so that they would not deliver the Mistral ships to Russia. And we know that Washington hinted that if the French don't deliver Mistral, sanctions on the French bank will be minimized or removed. What is this, if not blackmail?"*

Putin said that Russia is willing to be a partner of the US and EU, but the partnership must be based on equality, not on America's partners following Washington's orders. *"We are not going to stop our relations with the US. The bilateral relations are not in the best shape, that is true. But this—and I want to emphasize—is not Russia's fault."*

While preparing this report I checked the BBC online news site. There was no mention of Putin's remarks. Ditto the online sites for CNN, the *Los Angeles Times, The New York Times*. The *Washington Post* did mention that Putin condemned the renewed violence in Ukraine at a meeting with Russia's ambassadors, but the importance of Putin's meeting with Russia's ambassadors was not conveyed by the *Post*'s report. Given Washington's arrogance, why does it matter what Putin says? America's loss to Belgium in the World Soccer Cup is more important to the American Propaganda Ministry than the President of Russia's attempt to end conflict and the drive toward war.

As I have previously observed, Americans live in The Matrix, not in the real world. One day Americans could wake up stunned by reality, or they could die from weapons of mass destruction and not wake up.

WASHINGTON'S WAR CRIMES SPREAD FROM AFRICA AND THE MIDDLE EAST TO UKRAINE

July 3, 2014

A person might think that revulsion in "the world community" against Washington's wanton slaughter of civilians in eight countries would have led to War Crimes Tribunal warrants issued for the arrest of Presidents Clinton, Bush, Obama and many officials in their regimes. But the vocal part of "the world community"—the West—has become inured to Washington's crimes against humanity and doesn't bother to protest. Indeed, many of these governments are complicit in Washington's crimes, and there could just as well be arrest warrants for members of European governments.

The one exception is Russia. The Ministry of Foreign Affairs of the Russian Federation has published a *White Book* on violations of human rights and the rule of law in Ukraine. Propagandized Americans think that all the violations in Ukraine are made by Russians. The *White Book* carefully and accurately documents reported violations that occurred in Ukraine for four months from December 2013 through March 2014. Another edition of the *White Book* covers July to November 2014.[62]

You will not hear much or anything about it from the presstitute US media, and it is unlikely to receive much coverage in Europe. The facts are so greatly at odds with the West's position that the *White Book* is a huge embarrassment to the West.

The slaughter of Ukrainians on Washington's orders by Washington's stooge government in Kiev has worsened considerably in the past three months, producing more than 100,000 Ukrainian refugees fleeing into Russia for protection from strikes against civilian housing from the air, artillery, and tanks.

Every effort by the Russian government to involve Washington, the European Union, and Kiev in negotiations to find a peaceful settlement has failed.

Washington is not interested in a settlement. Disturbed by its NATO vassals' dependence on Russian energy and the growing economic relationships between Russia and Europe, Washington is at work through its Kiev proxy murdering citizens in eastern and southern parts of present-day Ukraine that once were part of Russia. Washington has declared these civilians to be "terrorists" and is trying to force Russia to intervene militarily in order to protect them. Russia's protective intervention would then be denounced by Washington as "invasion and annexation." Washington would use this propaganda, which would blare from the Western media, to pressure Europe to support Washington's sanctions against Russia. The sanctions would effectively destroy the existing economic relationships between Russia and Europe.

Washington has not yet had success in imposing sanctions, because, although Washington's European vassals, such as Merkel, are willing, business interests in Germany, France, and Italy stand opposed.

Washington is hoping that by forcing Russia to act, Washington can sufficiently demonize Russia and silence the European business interests with propaganda.

To counter Washington's ploy, Putin had the Russian Duma rescind his authority to send Russian forces into Ukraine. Unlike the American presidents Clinton, Bush, and Obama, Putin does not claim the authority to use military forces without permission from the legislature.

Washington's response to Putin's stand down is to increase the slaughter of civilians, all the while denying that any such slaughter is occurring. Washington is determined not to acknowledge the existence of a slaughter for which it is responsible, although everyone knows that Kiev would not dare to take on Russia without Washington's backing.

Putin's bet is that European business interests will prevail over Washington's European lap dogs. This is a hopeful and optimistic bet, but Washington is already at work threatening and undermining the resistance of European business interests. Using concocted charges, Washington has stolen $9 billion from France's largest bank for doing business with countries disapproved by Washington. This was Washington's warning to European business to comply with Washington's sanctions. Washington even told France that the fine would be rescinded or reduced if France broke its contract with Russia to supply two helicopter carriers. Other such moves against European businesses are in the works. The purpose is to intimidate European businesses from opposing sanctions against Russia.

Washington's arrogance that Washington can decide with whom

a French bank can do business is astonishing. It is even more astonishing that France and the bank would accept such arrogance and infringement of France's sovereignty. France's acceptance of Washington's hegemony shows that one risk in Putin's bet is that the bet assumes European business interests can prevail over Washington's strategic interest.

Another risk in Putin's bet is that by standing down and tolerating Washington's slaughter of civilians, Putin is becoming complicit in Washington's crimes against humanity. The longer the slaughter goes on, the more complicit the Russian government becomes. Moreover, the passage of time allows Kiev to increase its forces and NATO to supply these forces with more deadly weapons. A Russian intervention, which previously would have met with easy success, becomes more costly and more drawn out as Kiev's forces increase.

Washington's puppet in Kiev has made it clear that he is not going to accommodate any Russian interests or any opposition of Ukrainian provinces to the radical anti-Russian policies of Washington's stooge government. As Washington acknowledges no responsibility whatsoever for the situation, how long can Putin wait for Merkel or Hollande to break ranks with Washington?

Putin's alternative is to come to the defense of the Ukrainians who are being attacked. Putin could accept the requests of the rebellious provinces to rejoin Russia as he did with Crimea, declare Washington's stooge, Petro Poroshenko, to be a war criminal and issue a warrant for his arrest, and send in the Russian military to face down the forces sent by Kiev.

Outside the West, this would establish Putin as a defender of human rights. Inside the West it would make it completely clear to Washington's European vassals that the consequence of their alignment with Washington is that they will be drawn into war with Russia and, likely, also with China. Europeans have nothing to gain from these wars.

Sooner than later Putin needs to realize that his reasonableness is not reciprocated by Washington. Washington is taking advantage of Putin's reasonableness, and Washington is pushing Russia harder.

Putin has done what he can to avoid conflict. Now he needs to do the right thing, as he did in Georgia and Crimea.

WASHINGTON'S ARROGANCE WILL DESTROY ITS EMPIRE

July 9, 2014

Alone among the governments in the world, Washington requires sovereign governments to follow Washington's laws even when Washington's laws contradict the laws of sovereign countries.

The examples are endless. For example, Washington forced Switzerland to violate and to repeal Switzerland's historic bank secrecy laws. Washington executes citizens of other countries, as well as its own citizens, without due process of law. Washington violates the sovereignty of other countries and murders the countries' citizens with drones, bombs, and special forces teams. Washington kidnaps abroad citizens of other countries and either brings them to the US to be tried under US law or sends them to another country to be tortured in secret torture centers. Washington tells banks in other countries with whom they can do business and when the banks disobey, Washington blackmails them into compliance or imposes fines that threaten their existence. Last week Washington forced a French bank to pay Washington $9 billion dollars or be banned from its US operations, because the bank financed trade with countries disapproved by Washington.

Washington issues ultimatums to sovereign nations to do as they are told or "be bombed into the stone age."

Washington violates diplomatic immunity and forces down the planes of presidents of sovereign countries to be illegally searched.

Washington ordered its UK vassal to violate the laws and conventions governing political asylum and to refuse free passage to Julian Assange to Ecuador.

Washington ordered Russia to violate its laws and to hand over Edward Snowden.

Russia is strong enough to refuse to comply with Washington's orders.

So what did Washington do?

The city upon the hill, the light unto the world, the "indispensable, exceptional government," kidnapped Roman Seleznyov, the son of a Russian MP, in a foreign country, the Republic of the Maldives, an island nation in the Indian Ocean. Seleznyov was seized by Washington as he boarded a flight to Moscow and was spirited away on a private plane to US controlled territory where he was arrested on bogus fraud charges.

The Russian Foreign Ministry accused Washington of kidnapping a Russian citizen in "a new hostile move by Washington" against the Russian people.

There is no doubt whatsoever that Seleznyov's kidnapping is illegal— as is everything Washington has done since the Clinton regime. Seleznyov's father, a member of the Russian legislative body, believes that Washington kidnapped his son in order to exchange him for Edward Snowden.

Seleznyov was immediately, without any evidence, charged with imaginary offenses amounting to 30 years in prison. The fascist head of Homeland Security declared that the completely illegal action by the Washington Gestapo is an "important arrest" that "sends a clear message" that "the long arm of justice—and this Department—will continue to disrupt and dismantle sophisticated criminal organizations."

The US Secret Service declared the Russian MP's son to be "one of the world's most prolific traffickers of stolen financial information."

What utter bullshit!

As the entire world now knows, the greatest thief of financial information is Washington's National Stasi Agency. Washington's Stasi Agency has stolen for the benefit of US corporations that make generous political contributions financial information from companies in Brazil, Germany, France, China, Japan, indeed, everywhere. Washington's Stasi have even stolen the Chancellor of Germany's private cell phone conversations.

The world was stupid to trust American information systems which serve as spy devices. Anyone who purchases an American brand name computer, or relies on American Internet services, can know for a fact that Washington's National Stasi Agency has complete information about them.

The other governments thought that they had a free ride on US capital investment, but what this free ride meant was that no government and no population had proprietary information and secrets.

The US National Stasi Agency can blackmail the entire population of the world.

According to the neoconservatives, the right to spy on the world is the right of the "indispensable" people, as represented by the "exceptional government" in Washington.

The world is stupid in many other ways in the trust misplaced in Washington. NGOs funded by Washington operate in many countries and serve as Washington's Fifth Columns. Washington can call out its NGOs into the streets to challenge and overthrow non-cooperating governments or to create for Washington propaganda against targeted governments, as Washington did when it called out its Russian NGOs to protest in the Russian streets that Putin stole the election. These NGOs are proud of the blood that they have, or soon will have, on their hands. It shows that they are important agents of the Empire.

With a captive Western media and European governments plus Japan, Australia, Canada, New Zealand, S. Korea and the Philippines, Washington can brazen out its lies and false charges. "Saddam Hussein has weapons of Mass Destruction." No one has been punished for this costly lie. "Assad of Syria used chemical weapons against his own people." No one has been punished for this costly lie. "Russia invaded Ukraine." No one has been punished for this costly lie. "Edward Snowden is a Chinese/Russian/someone's spy and a traitor to boot for telling Americans about the illegal actions of their government."

No one has been punished for this lie. "Julian Assange is a spy for making leaked documents of Washington's crimes available on the Internet."

No one has been punished for this lie.

Every American opposed to Wall Street's and Washington's hegemony has been declared to be persona non grata. Such Americans are "domestic extremists," who are now the focus of the Gestapo Homeland Security, a well armed military force, in contravention of the Posse Comitatus Act. Homeland Security is an illegal and unconstitutional force directed at the American people. The American sheeple are forced to pay for it as their homes are foreclosed or invaded by goon thug SWAT teams.

Environmentalists are in the way of capitalist profits, and the capitalists rule, not the environmentalists.

Environmentalists are "domestic extremists."

War protesters are investigated as "agents of foreign powers."

People concerned with the fate of animals and the decline of species due to habitat destruction by greedy, short-term motivated corporations, are on the list of "domestic extremists."

The Supreme Court is owned by the private interest groups who have bought our government. The US Supreme Court is the great enemy of the US Constitution.

Law is misused to send millions of innocents, especially the young, and Americans whose violations are inconsequential to prison in order to support the revenue needs of the privatized prison system and the career needs of prosecutors.

It is difficult to imagine a country as wrong as the US, where government serves not the people but a tiny handful of the one percent, a government incapable of delivering any kind of justice, a government that if it uttered truth would destroy itself.

Washington reeks of evil. And the world is beginning to realize it.

SANCTIONS
AND
AIRLINERS

July 17, 2014

NOTE: Photos are now available of the wreckage from the Malaysian airliner crash.[63] Notice the extensive debris and the large section of fuselage. You are observing remains of an airliner that was shot down by a fighter jet or hit with a missile at 33,000 feet and fell to impact land. Remember, no such debris was present at the site where the airliner is alleged to have hit the Pentagon and at the alleged crash site in Pennsylvania of the 4th 9/11 hijacked airliner. Give that some thought. No doubt the 9/11 Commission will conclude that only Malaysian airliners leave debris.

The unilateral US sanctions announced by Obama on July 16 blocking Russian weapons and energy companies' access to US bank loans demonstrate Washington's impotence. The rest of the world, including America's two largest business organizations, turned their backs on Obama. The US Chamber of Commerce and the National Association of Manufacturers placed ads in *The New York Times*, *Wall Street Journal*, and *Washington Post* protesting US sanctions. NAM said that the manufacturer's association is "disappointed that the US is extending sanctions in increasingly unilateral ways that will undermine US commercial engagement." Bloomberg reported that "meeting in Brussels, leaders of the European Union refused to match the US measures."

In attempting to isolate Russia, the White House has isolated Washington.

The sanctions will have no effect on the Russian companies. The Russian companies can get more bank loans than they need from China.

The three traits that define Washington—arrogance, hubris, and corruption—make Washington a slow learner.

With its sanctions Washington is undermining its own power and influence. Sanctions are encouraging countries to withdraw from the dollar payments system that is the foundation of US power. Christian Noyer,

Governor of the Bank of France and a member of the European Central Bank's Governing Council, said that Washington's sanctions are driving companies and countries out of the dollar payments system. The huge sum extorted from the French bank, BNP Paribas, for doing business with countries disapproved by Washington, makes clear the increased legal risks that arise from using the dollar when Washington makes the rules.

Washington's attack on the French bank was the occasion for many to remember the numerous past sanctions and to contemplate future sanctions, such as those that loom for Germany's Commerzbank. A movement to diversify the currencies used in international trade is inevitable. Noyer pointed out that trade between Europe and China does not need to use the dollar and can be fully paid in Euros or Renminbi.

The phenomenon of US rules expanding to all US dollar-denominated transactions around the world is accelerating the movement away from the dollar payment system. Some countries have already arranged bilateral agreements with trading partners to make their trade payments in their own currencies. The BRICS are establishing new payment methods independently of the dollar and are setting up their own International Monetary Fund to finance trade imbalances.

The US dollar's exchange value depends on its role in the international payments system. As this role shrivels, so will demand for dollars and the dollar's exchange value. Inflation will enter the US economy via import prices, and already hard-pressed Americans will experience more compression of their living standards.

In the 21st century distrust of Washington has been growing. Washington's lies, such as Iraq's "weapons of mass destruction," "Assad's use of chemical weapons," and "Iranian nukes" are recognized as lies by other governments. The lies were used by Washington to destroy countries and to threaten others with destruction, keeping the world in constant turmoil. Washington delivers no benefit that offsets the turmoil that Washington inflicts on everyone else. Washington's friendship requires complying with Washington's demands, and governments are concluding that Washington's friendship is not worth the high cost.

The NSA spy scandal and Washington's refusal to apologize and desist has deepened the distrust of Washington by its own allies. World polls show that other countries regard the US as the greatest threat to peace. The American people themselves have little confidence in their government. Polls show that a large majority of Americans believe that politicians, the presstitute media, and private interest groups such as Wall Street and the military/security complex rig the system to serve themselves at the expense of the American people.

Washington's empire is beginning to crack, a circumstance that will bring desperate action from Washington. Today (July 17) I heard a BBC news report on National Public Radio about a Malaysian airliner being shot down in Ukraine. The reporting might have been honest, but it sounded like a frame-up of Russia and the Ukrainian "separatists." As the BBC solicited more biased opinions, the broadcast ended with a report from social media that separatists had brought down the airliner with a Russian weapon system.

No one on the program wondered what the separatists had to gain by shooting down an airliner. Instead, the discussion was whether, once Russian responsibility was established, this would force the EU to endorse tougher US sanctions against Russia. The BBC was following Washington's script and heading the story where Washington wanted it to go.

The appearance of a Washington operation is present. All the warmongers were ready on cue. US Vice President Joe Biden declared that the airliner was "blown out of the sky." It was "not an accident." Would a person without an agenda be so declarative prior to having any information? Clearly, Biden was not implying that it was Kiev that blew the airliner out of the sky. Biden was at work in advance of the evidence blaming Russia. Indeed, the way Washington operates, it will pile on blame until it needs no evidence.

Senator John McCain jumped on the supposition that there were US citizens aboard to call for punitive actions against Russia before the passenger list and the cause of the airliner's fate are known.

The probability is high that we are going to have more fabricated evidence, such as the fabricated evidence presented by US Secretary of State Colin Powell to the UN "proving" the existence of the nonexistent Iraqi "weapons of mass destruction." Washington has succeeded with so many lies, deceptions and crimes that it believes that it can always succeed.

At this writing, we have no reliable information about the airliner, but the Roman question always pertains: "Who benefits?" There is no conceivable motive for separatists to shoot down an airliner, but Washington did have a motive—to frame-up Russia—and possibly a second motive. Among the reports or rumors there is one that says Putin's presidential plane flew a similar route to that of the Malaysian airliner, the two flying within 37 minutes of one another. This report has led to speculation that Washington decided to rid itself of Putin and mistook the Malaysian airliner for Putin's jet. RT reports that the two airplanes are similar in appearance.[64]

Before you say Washington is too sophisticated to mistake one airliner for another, keep in mind that when Washington shot down an Iranian airliner over Iranian air space, the US Navy claimed that it thought the 290 civilians that it murdered were in an Iranian fighter jet, a F-14 Tomcat fighter, a US-made fighter that was a mainstay of the US Navy. If the US Navy cannot tell its own workhorse fighter aircraft from an Iranian airliner, clearly the US can confuse two airliners that the RT report shows appear very similar.

During the entire BBC frame-up of Russia, no one mentioned the Iranian passenger airliner that the US "blew out of the sky." No one put sanctions on Washington.

Whatever the outcome of the Malaysian airliner incident, it demonstrates a danger in Putin's soft policy toward Washington's ongoing hard intervention in Ukraine. Putin's decision to respond with diplomacy instead of with military means to Washington's provocations in Ukraine gave Putin a winning hand, as evidenced by the opposition to Obama's sanctions by the EU and US business interests. However, by not bringing a quick forceful end to the Washington-sponsored conflict in Ukraine, Putin has left the door open for the devious machinations in which Washington specializes.

If Putin had accepted the requests of the former Russian territories in eastern and southern Ukraine to rejoin Mother Russia, the Ukrainian imbroglio would have come to an end months ago, and Russia would not be running risks of being framed.

Putin did not get the full benefit of refusing to send troops into the former Russian territories, because Washington's official position is that Russian troops are operating in Ukraine. When facts do not support Washington's agenda, Washington disposes of the facts. The US media blames Putin as the perpetrator of violence in Ukraine. It is Washington's accusation, not any known facts, that is the basis for the sanctions.

Russia seems hypnotized by the West and motivated to be included as a part of the West. This desire for acceptance plays into Washington's hands. Russia does not need the West, but Europe needs Russia. One option for Russia is to tend to Russian interests and wait for Europe to come courting.

The Russian government should not forget that Washington's attitude toward Russia is formed by the Wolfowitz Doctrine.

WHAT HAS HAPPENED TO THE MALAYSIAN AIRLINER?

July 19, 2014

Washington's propaganda machine is in such high gear that we are in danger of losing the facts that we do have.

One fact is that the separatists *do not* have the expensive Buk anti-aircraft missile system or the trained personnel to operate it.

Another fact is that the separatists have no incentive to shoot down an airliner and neither does Russia.

Anyone can tell the difference between low-flying attack aircraft and an airliner at 33,000 feet.

The Ukrainians do have Buk anti-aircraft missile systems, and a Buk battery was operational in the region and deployed at a site from which it could have fired a missile at the airliner.

Just as the separatists and the Russian government have no incentive to shoot down an airliner, neither does the Ukrainian government nor, one would think, even the crazed extreme Ukrainian nationalists—unless there was a plan to frame Russia.

One Russian general familiar with the weapon system offered his opinion that it was a mistake made by the Ukrainian military untrained in the weapon's use. The general said that although Ukraine has a few of the weapons, Ukrainians have had no training in their use in the 23 years since Ukraine separated from Russia. The general thinks it was an accident due to incompetence.

This explanation makes a certain amount of sense and far more sense than Washington's propaganda. The problem with the general's explanation is that it does not explain why the Buk anti-aircraft missile system was deployed near or in a separatist territory. *The separatists have no aircraft.* It seems odd for Ukraine to have an expensive missile system in an area in which it is of no military use and where the position could be overrun and captured by separatists.

As Washington, Kiev, and the presstitute media are committed to the propaganda that Putin did it, *we are not going to get any reliable information from the US media.* We will have to figure it out for ourselves.

One way to begin is to ask: Why was the missile system where it was? Why risk an expensive missile system by deploying it in a conflict environment in which it is of no use? Incompetence is one answer, and another is that the missile system did have an intended use.

What intended use? News reports and circumstantial evidence provide two answers. One is that the ultranationalist extremists intended to bring down Putin's presidential airliner and confused the Malaysian airliner with the Russian airliner.

Now the Interfax news agency, citing anonymous sources, apparently air traffic controllers, has reported that the Malaysian airliner and Putin's airliner were traveling almost the identical route within a few minutes of one another. Interfax quotes its source: "I can say that Putin's plane and the Malaysian Boeing intersected at the same point and the same echelon. That was close to Warsaw on 330-m echelon at the height of 10,100 meters. The presidential jet was there at 16:21 Moscow time and the Malaysian aircraft at 15:44 Moscow time. The contours of the aircrafts are similar, linear dimensions are also very similar, as for the coloring, at a quite remote distance they are almost identical."

I have not seen an official Russian denial, but according to news reports, the Russian government in response to the Interfax news report said that Putin's presidential plane no longer flies the Ukraine route since the outbreak of hostilities.

Before we take the denial at face value, we need to be aware that the implication that Ukraine attempted to assassinate the president of Russia implies war, which Russia wants to avoid. It also implies Washington's complicity as it is highly unlikely that Washington's puppet in Kiev would risk such a dangerous act without Washington's backing. The Russian government, being intelligent and rational, would obviously deny reports of an attempted assassination of the Russian president by Washington and its Kiev puppet. Otherwise, Russia has to do something about it, and that means war.

The second explanation is that the neo-Nazi extremists, who operate outside the official Ukrainian military, hatched a plot to down an airliner in order to cast the blame on Russia. If such a plot occurred, it likely originated with the CIA or some operative arm of Washington and was intended to force the EU to cease resisting Washington's sanctions against Russia and to break off Europe's valuable economic relationships with Russia. Washington is frustrated that its sanctions are unilateral, unsupported by its NATO puppets or any other countries in the world except possibly the lapdog British PM.

There is considerable circumstantial evidence in support of this second explanation. There is the youtube video which purports to be a conversation between a Russian general and separatists who are discussing having mistakenly brought down a civilian airliner. According to reports, expert examination of the code in the video reveals that it was made *the day before the airliner was hit.*

Another problem with the video is that whereas we could say that separatists conceivably could confuse an airliner at 33,000 feet with a military attack plane, the Russian military would not. The only conclusion is that by involving the Russian military, the video doubly discredited itself.

The circumstantial evidence easiest for non-technical people to understand is the *on cue* news programs organized to put the blame on Russia *prior to the knowledge of any facts.*

In my previous article I reported on the BBC news report which was obviously primed to place all blame on Russia. The program ended with a BBC correspondent breathlessly reporting that he has just seen the youtube video and that the video is the smoking gun that proved Russia did it. There is no longer any doubt, he said. Somehow the information got on a video and on youtube before it reached the Ukrainian government or Washington.

So the evidence that Putin did it is a video made prior to the attack on the airliner. The entire BBC report aired over National Public Radio was orchestrated for the sole purpose of establishing prior to any evidence that Russia was responsible.

Indeed the entire Western media spoke as one: Russia did it. And the presstitutes are still speaking the same way.

Possibly, this uniform opinion merely reflects the pavlovian training of the Western media to automatically line up with Washington. No media source wants to be subject to criticism for being unamerican or to find itself isolated by majority opinion, which carries the day, and earn black marks for being wrong. As a former journalist for, and contributor to, America's most important news publications, I know how this works.

On the other hand, if we discount the pavlovian conditioning, the only conclusion is that the entire news cycle pertaining to the downing of the Malaysian airliner is orchestrated in order to lay the blame on Putin.

Romesh Ratnesar, deputy editor of Bloomberg Businessweek, provides convincing evidence for orchestration in his own remarks of July 17.[65]

Ratnesar's opinion title is: "The Malaysia Airlines Shootdown Spells Disaster for Putin." Ratnesar does not mean that Putin is being framed. He means that prior to Putin having the Malaysian airliner shot down, "to the vast majority of Americans, Russia's meddling in Ukraine has largely seemed of peripheral importance to U.S. interests. That calculus has changed. . . . It may take months, even years, but Putin's recklessness is bound to catch up to him. When it does, the downing of MH 17 may be seen as the beginning of his undoing."

As a former *Wall Street Journal* editor, anyone who handed me propaganda like Ratnesar published would have been fired. Look at the insinuations when there is no evidence to support them. Look at the lie that Washington's coup is "Russia's meddling in Ukraine." What we are witnessing is the total corruption of Western journalism by Washington's imperial agenda. Journalists have to get on board with the lies or get run over.

Look around for still honest journalists. Who are they? Glenn Greenwald, who is under constant attack by his fellow journalists, all of whom are whores. Who else can you think of? Julian Assange, locked away in the Ecuadoran Embassy in London on Washington's orders. The British puppet government won't permit free transit to Assange to take up his asylum in Ecuador. The last country that did this was the Soviet Union, which required its Hungarian puppet to keep Cardinal Mindszenty interred in the US Embassy in Budapest for 15 years from 1956 until 1971. Mindszenty was granted political asylum by the United States, but Hungary, on Soviet orders, would not honor his asylum, just as Washington's British puppet, on Washington's orders, will not honor Assange's asylum.

If we are honest and have the strength to face reality, we will realize that the Soviet Union did not collapse. It simply moved, along with Mao and Pol Pot, to Washington and London.

The flaw in Putin's diplomacy is that Putin's diplomacy relies on good will and on truth prevailing.

However, the West has no good will, and *Washington is not interested in truth prevailing but in Washington prevailing*. What Putin confronts is not reasonable "partners," but a propaganda ministry aimed at him.

I understand Putin's strategy, which contrasts Russian reasonableness with Washington's threats, but it is a risky bet. Europe has long been a part of Washington, and there are no Europeans in power who have the vision needed to separate Europe from Washington. Moreover, European leaders are paid large sums of money to serve Washington. One year out of office and Tony Blair was worth $50 million dollars.

After the disasters that Europeans have experienced, it is unlikely that European leaders think of anything other than a comfortable existence for themselves. That existence is best obtained by serving Washington.

As the successful extortion of Greece by banks proves, European people are powerless.

The official statement of the Russian Defense Ministry is available on GlobalResearch.ca.[66]

Washington's propaganda assault against Russia is a double tragedy, because it has diverted attention from Israel's latest atrocity against the

Palestinians locked up in the Gaza Ghetto. Israel claims that its air attack and invasion of Gaza is merely Israel's attempt to find and close the alleged tunnels through which Palestinian terrorists pour into Israel inflicting carnage. The tunnels and terrorist carnage in Israel are largely propaganda.

One might think that at least one journalist somewhere in the American media would ask why bombing hospitals and civilian housing closes underground tunnels into Israel. But that is too much to ask of the whores that comprise the US media.

Expect even less from the US Congress. Both the House and Senate have passed resolutions supporting Israel's slaughter of Palestinians. Two Republicans—the despicable Lindsey Graham and the disappointing Rand Paul—and two democrats—Bob Menendez and Ben Cardin–sponsored the Senate resolution backing Israel's premeditated murder of Palestinian women and children. The resolution passed the "exceptional and indispensable" people's Senate unanimously.

As a reward for Israel's policy of genocide, the Obama regime is immediately transferring $429 million of US taxpayers' money to Israel to pay for the slaughter.

Contrast the US government's support for Israel's war crimes with the propaganda onslaught against Russia based on lies. We are living all over again "Saddam Hussein's weapons of mass destruction," "Assad's use of chemical weapons," "Iranian nukes."

Washington has lied for so long that it can't do anything else.

GUILT BY INSINUATION: HOW AMERICAN PROPAGANDA WORKS

July 21, 2014

Why hasn't Washington joined Russian President Putin in calling for an objective, non-politicized international investigation by experts of the case of the Malaysian jetliner?

The Russian government continues to release facts, including satellite photos showing the presence of Ukrainian Buk anti-aircraft missiles in locations from which the airliner could have been brought down by the missile system and documentation that a Ukrainian SU-25 fighter jet rapidly approached the Malaysian airliner prior to its downing. The head of the Operations Directorate of Russian military headquarters said at a Moscow press conference today (July 21) that the presence of the Ukrainian military jet is confirmed by the Rostov monitoring center.

The Russian Defense Ministry pointed out that at the moment of destruction of MH-17 an American satellite was flying over the area. The Russian government urges Washington to make available the photos and data captured by the satellite.

President Putin has repeatedly stressed that the investigation of MH-17 requires "a fully representative group of experts to be working at the site under the guidance of the International Civil Aviation Organization (ICAO)." Putin's call for an independent expert examination by ICAO does not sound like he is a person with anything to hide.

Turning to Washington Putin stated: "In the meantime, no one [not even the "exceptional nation"] has the right to use this tragedy to achieve their narrowly selfish political goals."

Putin reminded Washington: "We repeatedly called upon all conflicting sides to stop the bloodshed immediately and to sit down at the negotiating table. I can say with confidence that if military operations were not resumed [by Kiev] on June 28 in eastern Ukraine, this tragedy wouldn't have happened."

What is the American response?

Lies and insinuations.

Yesterday (July 20) the US Secretary of State, John Kerry, confirmed that pro-Russian separatists were involved in the downing of the Malaysian airliner and said that it was "pretty clear" that Russia was involved. Here are Kerry's words: "It's pretty clear that this is a system that was transferred from Russia into the hands of separatists. We know with confidence, with confidence, that the Ukrainians did not have such a system anywhere near the vicinity at that point and time, so it obviously points a very clear finger at the separatists."

Kerry's statement is just another of the endless lies told by US secretaries of state in the 21st century.

Who can forget Colin Powell's package of lies delivered to the UN about Saddam Hussein's "weapons of mass destruction" or Kerry's lie repeated endlessly that Assad "used chemical weapons against his own people" or the endless lies about "Iranian nukes"?

Remember that Kerry on a number of occasions stated that the US had proof that Assad crossed the "red line" by using chemical weapons. However, Kerry was never able to back up his statements with evidence. The US had no evidence to give the British prime minister whose effort to have Parliament approve Britain's participation with Washington in a military attack on Syria was voted down. Parliament told the prime minister, "no evidence, no war."

Again here is Kerry declaring "confidence" in statements that are directly contradicted by the Russian satellite photos and endless eye witnesses on the ground.

Why doesn't Washington release its photos from its satellite?

The answer is for the same reason that Washington will not release all the videos it confiscated and that it claims prove that a hijacked 9/11 airliner hit the Pentagon. The videos do not support Washington's claim, and the US satellite photos do not support Kerry's claim.

The UN weapons inspectors on the ground in Iraq reported that Iraq had no weapons of mass destruction.

However, the fact did not support Washington's propaganda and was ignored. Washington started a highly destructive war based on nothing but Washington's intentional lie.

The International Atomic Energy Agency's inspectors on the ground in Iran and all 16 US intelligence agencies reported that Iran had no nuclear weapons program. However, the fact was inconsistent with Washington's agenda and was ignored by both the US government and the presstitute media.

We are witnessing the same thing right now with the assertions in the absence of evidence that Russia is responsible for the downing of the Malaysian airliner.

Not every member of the US government is as reckless as Kerry and John McCain. In place of direct lies, many US officials use insinuations.

US Senator Diane Feinstein is the perfect example. Interviewed on the presstitute TV station CNN, Feinstein said: "The issue is where is Putin? I would say, 'Putin, you have to man up. You should talk to the world. You should say, if this is a mistake, which I hope it was, say it.'"

Putin has been talking to the world nonstop calling for an expert non-politicized investigation, and Feinstein is asking Putin why he is hiding behind silence. We know you did it, Feinstein insinuates, so just tell us whether you meant to or whether it was an accident.

The way the entire Western news cycle was orchestrated with blame instantly being placed on Russia long in advance of real information suggests that the downing of the airliner was a Washington operation. It is, of course, possible that the well-trained presstitute media needed no orchestration from Washington in order to lay the blame on Russia. On the other hand, some of the news performances seem too scripted not to have been prepared in advance.

We also have the advanced preparation of the youtube video that purports to show a Russian general and Ukrainian separatists discussing having mistakenly downed a civilian airliner. As I pointed out earlier, this video is twice damned. It was made prior to the event and overlooked that the Russian military can tell the difference between a civilian airliner and a military airplane. The existence of the video itself implies that there was a plot to down the airliner and blame Russia.

I have seen reports that the Russian anti-aircraft missile system, as a safety device, is capable of contacting aircraft transponders in order to verify the type of aircraft. If the reports are correct and if the transponders from MH-17 are found, they might record the contact.

I have seen reports that Ukrainian air control changed the route of MH-17 and directed it to fly over the conflict area. The transponders should also indicate whether this is correct. If so, there clearly is at least circumstantial evidence that this was an intentional act on the part of Kiev, an act which would have required Washington's blessing.

There are other reports that there is a divergence between the Ukrainian military and the unofficial militias formed by the right-wing Ukrainian extremists who apparently were the first to attack the separatists. It is possible that Washington used the extremists to plot the airliner's destruction in order to blame Russia and use the accusations to pressure the EU to go along with Washington's unilateral sanctions against Russia. We do know that Washington is desperate to break up the growing economic and political ties between Russia and Europe.

If it was a plot to down an airliner, any safety device on the missile system could have been turned off so as to give no warning or leave any telltale sign. That could be the reason a Ukrainian fighter was sent to inspect the airliner. Possibly the real target was Putin's airliner and incompetence in implementing the plot resulted in the destruction of a civilian airliner.

As there are a number of possible explanations, let's keep open minds and resist Washington's propaganda until facts and evidence are in. At the very least Washington is guilty of using the incident to blame Russia in advance of the evidence. All Washington has shown us so far are accusations and insinuations. If that is all Washington continues to show us, we will know where the blame resides.

In the meantime, remember the story of the boy who cried "wolf!" He lied so many times that when the wolf did come, no one believed him. Will this be Washington's ultimate fate?

Instead of declaring war on Iraq, Afghanistan, Libya, Somalia, and Syria, why did Washington hide behind lies? If Washington wants war with Iran, Russia, and China, why not simply declare war? The reason that the US Constitution requires war to begin with a declaration of war by Congress is to prevent the executive branch from orchestrating wars in order to further hidden agendas. By abdicating its constitutional responsibility, the US Congress is complicit in the executive branch's war crimes. By approving Israel's premeditated murder of Palestinians, the US government is complicit in Israel's war crimes.

Ask yourself this question: Would the world be a safer place with less death, destruction and displaced peoples and more truth and justice if the United States and Israel did not exist?

US INTELLIGENCE: RUSSIA DIDN'T DO IT

July 23, 2014

After days of placing hostile blame for the downing of the Malaysian airliner on Russia, the White House permitted US intelligence officials to tell reporters that there is no evidence of the Russian government's involvement.

Obviously, the US satellite photos do not support the Obama regime's lies. If the White House had any evidence of Russian complicity, it would have released it to great fanfare days ago.

We are fortunate that the analytical side of the CIA, in contrast with the black ops side, retains analysts with integrity even after the purge of the agency ordered by Dick Cheney. Incensed that the CIA did not immediately fall in line with all of the Bush regime's war lies, Cheney had the agency purged. The black ops side of the agency is a different story. Many believe that it should be defunded and abolished as this part of the CIA operates in violation of statutory US law.

Don't hold your breath until Washington abolishes black-ops operations or the Obama regime apologizes to the Russian government for the unfounded accusations and insinuations leveled by the White House at Russia.

Despite this admission by US intelligence officials, the propaganda ministry is already at work to undermine the admission. The intelligence officials themselves claim that Russia is, perhaps, indirectly responsible, because Russia "created the conditions" that caused Kiev to attack the separatists.

In other words, Washington's coup overseen by US State Department official Victoria Nuland, which overthrew an elected democratic Ukrainian government and brought extreme Russophobes into power in Kiev who attacked dissenting former Russian territories that were attached to Ukraine by Soviet communist party leaders when Russia and Ukraine were part of the same country, has no responsibility for the result.

Washington is innocent. Russia is guilty. End of story.

The previous day, State Department spokeswoman Marie Harf, one of the Obama regime's brainless warmonger women, angrily turned on reporters who asked about the Russian government's official denial of responsibility. Don't you understand, she demanded, that what the US government says is credible and what the Russian government says is not credible!

Rest assured that the owners of the media and the editors of the reporters received calls and threats. I wouldn't be surprised if the reporters have lost their jobs for doing their jobs.

There you have it. America's free press. The American press is free to lie for the government, but mustn't dare exercise any other freedom.

Washington will never permit official clarification of MH-17. Today (July 23) the BBC (the British Brainwashing Corporation) declared: "Whitehall sources say information has emerged that MH17 crash evidence was deliberately tampered-with, as the plane's black boxes arrive in the UK."

After making this claim of tampered with black boxes, the BBC contradicted itself: "The Dutch Safety Board, which is leading the investigation, said 'valid data' had been downloaded from MH17's cockpit voice recorder (CVR) which will be 'further analyzed'. The board said: 'The CVR was damaged but the memory module was intact. Furthermore no evidence or indications of manipulation of the CVR was found.'"

The BBC does not tell us how the black boxes got into British and Dutch hands when the separatists gave the black boxes to the Malaysians with the guarantee that the black boxes would be turned over to the International Civil Aviation Organization (ICAO) for expert and non-politicized examination.

So where are the black boxes? If the Malaysians gave them to the British, Whitehall will tell whatever lie Washington demands. If Washington's British puppet actually has the black boxes, we will never know the truth. Judging from the hostile and unsupported accusations against Russia from the bought-and-paid-for Netherlands prime minister, we can expect the Dutch also to lie for Washington. Apparently, Washington has succeeded in removing the "investigation" from the ICAO's hands and placing the investigation in the hands of its puppets.

The problem with writing columns based on Western news reports is that you have no idea of the veracity of the news reports.

From all appearances, the Obama regime intends to turn the "international investigation" into an indictment of Russia, and the Dutch seem to be lined up behind this corrupt use of the investigation. As the *Washington Post* story makes clear, there is no room in the investigation for any suspicion that Kiev and Washington might be responsible.[67]

By continuing to trust a corrupt West that is devoid of integrity and of good will toward Russia, the separatists and the Russian government have again set themselves up for vilification. Will they never learn?

As I write, more confusion is added to the story. It has just come across my screen that Reuters reports that Alexander Khodakovsky, "a powerful Ukrainian rebel leader has confirmed that pro-Russian separatists had an anti-aircraft missile of the type Washington says was used to shoot down the Malaysia Airlines flight MH17 and it could have originated in Russia." Reuters says that this separatist commander (or perhaps former commander, as later in its report Reuters describes Khodakovsky as "a former head of the 'Alpha' anti-terrorism unit of the security service in Donetsk") is in dispute with other commanders about the conduct of the war.

Khodakovsky makes clear that he doesn't know which unit might have had the missile or from where it was fired. He makes it clear that he has no precise or real information. His theory is that the Ukrainian government tricked the separatists into firing the missile by launching airstrikes in the area over which the airliner was flying and by sending military jets to the vicinity of the airliner to create the appearance of military aircraft. Reuters quotes Khodakovsky, ""Even if there was a BUK, and even if the BUK was used, Ukraine did everything to ensure that a civilian aircraft was shot down"

Not knowing the nature of Khodakovsky's dispute with other commanders or his motivation, it is difficult to assess the validity of his story, but his tale does explain why Ukrainian air control would route the Malaysian airliner over the combat area, a hitherto unexplained decision.

After the sensational part of its story, Reuters seems to back away a bit. Reuters quotes Khodakovsky saying that the separatist movement has different leaders and "our cooperation is somewhat conditional."

Khodakovsky then becomes uncertain as to whether the separatists did or did not have operational BUK missiles. According to Reuters, Khodakovsky "said none of the BUKs captured from Ukrainian forces were operational." This implies that Russia provided the working missile to the separatists if such a missile existed.

I find the separatists' reply convincing. If we have these missiles why do the fools in Kiev send aircraft to bomb us, and why is their bombing so successful? The separatists do have shoulder fired ground to air missiles of the kind that the US supplied to Afghanistan during the Soviet invasion. These missiles are only capable of striking low flying aircraft. They cannot reach 33,000 feet.

According to Reuters, the reporting of its story was by one person, the writing by a second, and the editing by a third. From my experience in journalism, this means that we don't know whose story it is, how the story was changed, or what its reliability might be.

We can safely conclude that the obfuscations are just beginning, and like 9 /11 and John F. Kennedy's assassination, there will be no alternative to individuals forming their own opinion from researching the evidence. The

United States government will never come clean, and the British government and presstitute media will never stop telling lies for Washington.

Washington's bribes and threats can produce whatever story Washington wants. Keep in mind that a totally corrupt White House, over the objections of its own intelligence agencies, sent the Secretary of State to the United Nations to lie to the world about Iraqi weapons of mass destruction that the White House knew did not exist. The consequences are that millions were killed, maimed, and displaced for no other reason than Washington's lie.

The Obama regime lied on the basis of concocted "evidence" that Assad had used chemical weapons against the Syrian people, thus crossing the "red line" that the White House had drawn, justifying a US military attack on the Syrian people. The Russian government exposed the fake evidence, and the British Parliament voted down any UK participation in the Obama regime's attack on Syria. Left isolated, the Obama regime dared not assume the obvious role of war criminal.

Blocked in this way, the Obama regime financed and supplied outside jihadist militants to attack Syria, with the consequence that a radical Islamic State is in the process of carving out a new Caliphate from parts of Iraq and Syria.

Keep in mind that both the George W. Bush and Obama regimes have also lied through their teeth about "Iranian nukes."

The only possible conclusion is that a government that consistently lies is not believable.

Since the corrupt Clinton regime, American journalists have been forced by their bosses to lie for Washington. It is a hopeful sign that in their confrontation with Marie Harf some journalists found a bit of courage. Let's hope it takes root and grows.

I do not think that the United States can recover from the damage inflicted by the neoconservatives who determined the policies of the Clinton, George W. Bush and Obama governments, but whenever we see signs of opposition to the massive lies and deceptions that define the US government in the 21st century, we should cheer and support those who confront the lies.

Our future, and that of the world, depend on it.

WASHINGTON IS ESCALATING THE ORCHESTRATED UKRAINE "CRISIS" TO WAR

July 24, 2014

Despite the conclusion by US intelligence that there is no evidence of Russian involvement in the destruction of the Malaysian airliner and all lives onboard, Washington is escalating the crisis and shepherding it toward war.

Twenty-two US senators have introduced into the 113th Congress, Second Session, a bill, S.2277, "To prevent further Russian aggression toward Ukraine and other sovereign states in Europe and Eurasia, and for other purposes."[68]

Note that prior to any evidence of *any* Russian aggression, there are already 22 senators lined up in behalf of preventing *further Russian aggression.*

Accompanying this preparatory propaganda move to create a framework for war, hot or cold with Russia, NATO commander General Philip Breedlove announced his plan for a deployment of massive military means in Eastern Europe that would permit lightning responses against Russia in order to protect Europe from Russian aggression.

There we have it again: Russian Aggression. Repeat it enough and it becomes real.

The existence of "Russian aggression" is assumed, not demonstrated. Neither Breedlove nor the senators make any reference to Russian war plans for an attack on Europe or any other countries. There are no references to Russian position papers and documents setting forth a Russian expansionist ideology or a belief declared by Moscow that Russians are "exceptional, indispensable people" with the right to exercise hegemony over the world. No evidence is presented that Russia has infiltrated the communication systems of the entire world for spy purposes. There is no evidence that Putin has Obama's or Obama's daughters' private cell phone conversations or that Russia downloads US corporate secrets for the benefit of Russian businesses.

Nevertheless, the NATO commander and US senators see an urgent need to create blitzkrieg capability for NATO on Russia's borders.

Senate bill 2277 consists of three titles: "Reinvigorating the NATO Alliance," "Deterring Further Russian Aggression in Europe," and "Hardening Ukraine and other European and Eurasian States Against Russian Aggression." Who do you think wrote this bill? Hint: it wasn't the senators or their staffs.

Title I deals with strengthening US force posture in Europe and Eurasia and strengthening the NATO alliance, with accelerating the construction of ABM (anti-ballistic missile) bases on Russia's borders so as to degrade the Russian strategic nuclear deterrent, and to provide more money for Poland and the Baltic states and strengthen US-German cooperation on global security issues, that is, to make certain that the German military is incorporated as part of the US empire military force.

Title II is about confronting "Russian aggression in Europe" with sanctions and with financial and diplomatic "support for Russian democracy and civil society organizations," which means to pump billions of dollars into NGOs (non-governmental organizations) that can be used to destabilize Russia in the way that Washington used the NGOs it funded in Ukraine to overthrow the elected government. For 20 years Russian government negligence permitted Washington to organize fifth columns inside Russia that pose as human rights organizations, etc.

Title III deals with military and intelligence assistance for Ukraine, putting Ukraine, Georgia, and Moldova on a NATO track, expediting US natural gas exports in order to remove European and Eurasian energy dependence on Russia, preventing recognition of Crimea as again a part of Russia, expanding broadcasting (propaganda) into Russian areas, and again "support for democracy and civil society organizations in countries of the former Soviet Union," which means to use money to subvert the Russian federation.

However you look at this, it comprises a declaration of war. Moreover, these provocative and expensive moves are presented as necessary to counter Russian aggression for which there is no evidence.

How do we characterize a bill that is not merely thoughtless, unnecessary, and dangerous, but also more Orwellian than Orwell? I am open to suggestions.

Ukraine as it currently exists is an a-historical state with artificial boundaries. Ukraine presently consists of part of what was once a larger entity plus former Russian provinces added to the Ukrainian Soviet Republic by Soviet leaders. When the Soviet Union collapsed and Russia permitted Ukraine's independence, under US pressure Russia mistakenly permitted Ukraine to take with it the former Russian provinces.

When Washington executed its coup in Kiev in 2014, the Russophobes who grabbed power began threatening in word and deed the Russian populations in eastern and southern Ukraine. The Crimeans voted to reunite with Russia and were accepted. This reunification was grossly misrepresented by Western propaganda. When other former Russian provinces voted likewise, the Russian government, kowtowing to Western propaganda, did not grant their requests. Instead, Russian president Putin called for Kiev and the former Russian provinces to work out an agreement that would keep the provinces within Ukraine.

Kiev and its Washington master did not listen. Instead, Kiev launched military attacks on the provinces and was conducting bombing attacks on the provinces at the moment the Malaysian airliner was downed.

Washington and its European vassals have consistently misrepresented the situation in Ukraine and denied their responsibility for the violence, instead placing all blame on Russia. But it is not Russia that is conducting bombing raids and attacking provinces with troops, tanks, and artillery. Just as Israel's current military assault against Palestinian civilians fails to evoke criticism from Washington, European governments, and the Western media, Kiev's assault on the former Russian provinces goes unreported and uncriticized. Indeed, it appears that few Americans are even aware that Kiev is attacking civilian areas of the provinces that wish to return to their mother country.

Sanctions should be imposed on Kiev, from which the military violence originates. Instead, Kiev is receiving financial and military support, and sanctions are placed on Russia which is not militarily involved in the situation.

When the outbreak of violence against the former Russian provinces began, the Russian Duma voted Putin the power to intervene militarily. Instead of using this power, Putin requested that the Duma rescind the power, which the Duma did. Putin preferred to deal with the problem diplomatically in a reasonable and unprovocative manner.

Putin has received neither respect nor appreciation for encouraging a non-violent resolution of the unfortunate Ukrainian situation created by Washington's coup against a democratically elected government that was only months away from a chance to elect a different government.

The sanctions that Washington has applied and that Washington is pressuring its European puppets to join send the wrong information to Kiev. It tells Kiev that the West approves and encourages Kiev's determination to resolve its differences with the former Russian provinces with violence rather than with negotiation.

This means war will continue, and that is clearly Washington's intent. The latest reports are that US military advisors will soon be in Ukraine to aid the conquest of the former Russian provinces that are in revolt.

The presstitute nature of the Western media ensures that the bulk of the American and European populations will remain in the grip of Washington's anti-Russian propaganda.

At some point the Russian government will have to face the fact that it doesn't have "Western partners."

Russia has Western enemies who are being organized to isolate Russia, to injure Russia economically and diplomatically, to surround Russia militarily, to destabilize Russia by calling the American-funded NGOs into the streets, and in the absence of a coup that installs an American puppet in Moscow, to attack Russia with nuclear weapons.

I respect Putin's reliance on diplomacy and good will in the place of force. The problem with Putin's approach is that Washington has no good will, so there is no reciprocity.

Washington has an agenda. Europe consists of captive nations, and these nations are without leaders capable of breaking free of Washington's agenda.

I hope that I am wrong, but I think Putin has miscalculated. If Putin had accepted the former Russian provinces' requests to reunite with Russia, the conflict in Ukraine would be over. I am certain that Europe would not have joined Washington in any invasion with the purpose of recovering for Ukraine former provinces of Russia herself. When Washington says that Putin is responsible for downing the Malaysian airliner, Washington is correct in a way that Washington doesn't suspect. Had Putin completed the task begun with Crimea and reunited the Russian provinces with Russia, there would have been no war during which an airliner could have been downed, whether by accident or as a plot to demonize Russia. Ukraine has no capability of confronting Russia militarily and would have no alternative but to accept the reunification of the Russian territories.

Europe would have witnessed a decisive Russian decision and would have put a great distance between itself and Washington's provocative agenda. This European response would have precluded Washington's ability to escalate the crisis by gradually turning the temperature higher without the European frog jumping out of the pot.

In its dealings with Washington Europe has grown accustomed to the efficacy of bribes, threats, and coercion. Captive nations are inured to diplomacy's impotence. Europeans see diplomacy as the weak card played by the weak party. And, of course, all the Europeans want money, which Washington prints with abandon.

Russia and China are disadvantaged in their conflict with Washington.

Russia and China have emerged from tyranny. People in both countries were influenced by American Cold War propaganda. Both countries have educated people who think that America has freedom, democracy, justice, civil liberty, economic wellbeing and is a welcoming friend of other countries that want the same thing.

This is a dangerous delusion. Washington has an agenda. Washington has put in place a police state to suppress its own population, and Washington believes that history has conveyed the right to Washington to exercise hegemony over the world. Last year President Obama declared to the world that he sincerely believes that America is the exceptional nation on whose leadership the world depends.

In other words, all other countries and peoples are unexceptional. Their voices are unimportant. Their aspirations are best served by Washington's leadership. Those who disagree—Russia, China, Iran, and the new entity ISIS—are regarded by Washington as obstacles to history's purpose. Anything, whether an idea or a country, that is in the way of Washington is in the way of History's Purpose and must be run over.

In the late 18th and early 19th centuries Europe faced the determination of the French Revolution to impose Liberty, Equality, Fraternity upon Europe. Today Washington's ambition is larger. The ambition is to impose Washington's hegemony on the entire world.

Unless Russia and China submit, this means war.

DOES RUSSIA (AND HUMANITY) HAVE A FUTURE?

July 25, 2014

The Russian government has finally realized that it has no Western "partners," and is complaining bitterly about the propagandistic lies and disinformation issued without any evidence whatsoever against the Russian government by Washington, its European vassals, and presstitute media.

Perhaps the Russian government thought that only Iraq, Libya, Syria, China, and Edward Snowden would be subjected to Washington's lies and demonization.

It was obvious enough that Russia would be next.

The Russian government and Europe need to look beyond Washington's propaganda, because the reality is much worse.

NATO commander General Breedlove and Senate bill 2277 clearly indicate that Washington is organizing itself and Europe for war against Russia.

Europe is reluctant to agree with Washington to put Ukraine in NATO. Europeans understand that if Washington or its stooges in Kiev cause a war with Russia Europe will be the first casualty. Washington finds its vassals' noncompliance tiresome. Remember Assistant Secretary of State Victoria Nuland's "fuck the EU." That is just what Washington is about to do.

The US Senate's Russian Aggression Prevention Act does even more mischief than I previously reported.

If the bill passes, which it likely will, Washington becomes empowered to bypass NATO and to grant the status of "allied nation" to Ukraine independent of NATO membership. By so doing, Washington can send troops to Ukraine and thereby commit NATO to a war with Russia.

Notice how quickly Washington escalated the orchestrated Ukrainian "crisis" without any evidence into "Russian aggression." Overnight we have the NATO commander and US senators taking actions against "Russian aggression" of which no one has seen any evidence.

With Iraq, Libya, and Syria, Washington learned that Washington could act on the basis of bald-faced lies.

No one, not Great Britain, not France, not Germany, not Italy, not the Netherlands, not Canada, not Australia, not Mexico, not New Zealand, not Israel, nor Japan, nor S. Korea, nor Taiwan, nor (substitute your selection) stepped forward to hold Washington accountable for its blatant lies and war crimes, just as the UN accepted the package of blatant and obviously transparent lies that Colin Powell delivered to the UN, which had already been refuted by the UN's own weapons inspectors. Remember how the UN then gave the go-ahead for a devastating war?

The only conclusion is that all the whores were paid off. The whores can always count on Washington paying them off. For money the whores are selling out civilization to Washington's war, which likely will be nuclear and terminate life on earth. The whores' money will incinerate with them.

It is hardly surprising that Washington now targets Russia. The world has given Washington carte blanche to do as it pleases. We have now had three administrations of US war criminals welcomed and honored wherever the war criminals go. The heads of other governments continue to desire invitations to the White House as indications of their own worth. To be received by war criminals has become the highest honor.

Even the president of China comes to Washington to receive acceptance by the Evil Empire.

The world did not notice Washington's war crimes against Serbia and didn't puke when Washington then put the Serbian president, who had tried to prevent his country from being torn apart by Washington, on trial as a war criminal.

The world has made no effort to hold Washington responsible for its destruction of Iraq, Afghanistan, Libya, and now Syria and Gaza. The world has not demanded that Washington stop murdering people in Pakistan and Yemen, countries with which Washington is not at war. The world looks the other way as Washington creates the US Africa Command. The world looks the other way as Washington sends deadly weapons to Israel with which to murder women and children in the Gaza Ghetto. Washington passes Senate and House Resolutions cheering on the Israeli murder of Palestinians.

Washington is accustomed to its free pass, granted by the world, to murder and to lie, and now is using it against Russia.

Russian President Putin's bet that by responding to Washington's aggression in Ukraine in an unprovocative and reasonable manner would demonstrate to Europe that Russia was not the source of the problem has not paid off. European countries are captive nations. They are incapable of thinking and acting for themselves. They bend to Washington's will. Essentially, Europe is a nonentity that follows Washington's orders.

If the Russian government hopes to prevent war with Washington, the Russian government needs to act now and end the problem in Ukraine by accepting the separatist provinces' request to be reunited with Russia. Once S.2277 passes, Russia cannot retrieve the situation without confronting the US militarily, because Ukraine will have been declared an American ally.

Putin's bet was reasonable and responsible, but Europe has failed him. If Putin does not use Russian power to bring an end to the problem with which Washington has presented him in Ukraine while he still can, Washington's next step will be to unleash its hundreds of NGOs inside Russia to denounce Putin as a traitor for abandoning the Russian populations in the former Russian provinces that Soviet leaders thoughtlessly attached to Ukraine.

The problem with being a leader is that you inherit festering problems left by previous leaders. Putin has the problems bequeathed by Boris Yeltsin, Washington's puppet. Yeltsin was a disaster for Russia. It is not certain that Russia will survive Yeltsin's mistakes.

If Washington has its way, Russia will survive only as an American puppet state.

In a previous chapter I described the article in *Foreign Affairs*, the journal of the Washington foreign policy community, that makes a case that the US has such strategic advantage over Russia at this time that a "window of opportunity" exists for the US to remove Russia as a restraint on US hegemony with a preemptive nuclear attack.

It is almost certain that Obama is being told that President John F. Kennedy had this window of opportunity and did not use it, and that Obama must not let the opportunity pass a second time.

As Steven Starr explained, there are no winners of nuclear war. Even if the US escapes retaliatory strikes, everyone will die.

The view in Washington of the neoconservatives, who control the Obama regime, is that nuclear war is winnable. No expert opinion supports their assumption, but the neocons, not the experts, are in power.

The American people are out to lunch. They have no comprehension of their likely fate. Americans are an uninformed people, distracted by their mounting personal and financial problems. If Europeans are aware, they have decided to live for the moment on Washington's money.

DON'T EXPECT
TO LIVE
MUCH LONGER

July 26, 2014

European governments and the Western media have put the world at risk by enabling Washington's propaganda and aggression against Russia.

Washington has succeeded in using transparent lies to demonize Russia as a dangerous aggressive country led by a new Hitler or a new Stalin, just as Washington succeeded in demonizing Saddam Hussein in Iraq, the Taliban in Afghanistan, Gaddafi in Libya, Assad in Syria, Chavez in Venezuela, and, of course, Iran.

The real demons—Clinton, Bush, Obama—are "the exceptional and indispensable people" above the reach of demonization. Their horrific real crimes go unnoticed, while fictitious crimes are attributed to the unexceptional and dispensable people and countries.

The reason that Washington demonizes a leader and a country is to permit the creation of circumstances that Washington can use to act with force against a leader and a country.

Washington's incessant lies alleging "Russian aggression" have created Russian aggression out of thin air.

John Kerry and the State Department's Marie Harf issue new lies daily, but never with any supporting evidence. With the stage set, the US Senate, the NATO commander and the Chairman of the US Joint Chiefs of Staff are busy at work oiling the wheels of war.

Senate bill 2277 provides for beefing up forces on Russia's borders and for elevating Ukraine's status to "ally of the US" so that US troops can assist the war against "terrorists" in Ukraine.[69]

NATO commander Breedlove is preparing his plans for stockpiling war material on Russia's borders so that US/NATO troops can more quickly strike Russia.[70]

Chairman of the US Joint Chiefs of Staff, General Martin Dempsey, is at work preparing American opinion for the upcoming war.

On July 24 Dempsey told the Aspen Security Forum, a high level group where US opinion is formed, that Putin's aggression in Ukraine is comparable to Stalin's invasion of Poland in 1939 and that the Russian threat was not limited to Ukraine or Eastern Europe but was global.[71]

The intellectuals in the Aspen Forum did not break out laughing when Dempsey told them that Russia's (alleged but unproven) involvement in Ukraine was the first time since 1939 that a country made a conscious decision to use its military force inside another sovereign nation to achieve its objectives. No one asked Dempsey what Washington has been doing during the last three presidential regimes: Clinton in Serbia, Bush and Obama in Afghanistan, Iraq, Somalia, Pakistan, and Yemen, Obama in Libya and Syria.

Here are Dempsey's words: "You've got a Russian government that has made a conscious decision to use its military force inside another sovereign nation to achieve its objectives. It's the first time since 1939 or so that that's been the case. They clearly are on a path to assert themselves differently not just in Eastern Europe, but Europe in the main, and towards the United States."

Washington's view that the world is its oyster is so ingrained that neither Dempsey nor his upper echelon audience at the Aspen Forum noticed the absurdity of his statement. *Washington and the brainwashed US population take it for granted that the "exceptional, indispensable nation" is not limited in its actions by the sovereignty of other countries.*

Washington takes it for granted that US law prevails in other countries over the countries' own laws—just ask France or Switzerland—that Washington can tell foreign financial institutions and corporations with whom they can do business and with whom they cannot—just ask every country and company prevented from doing business with Iran—that Washington can invade any country whose leader Washington can demonize and overthrow—just ask Iraq, Honduras, Libya, Serbia, and so forth, and that Washington can conduct military operations against peoples in foreign countries, such as Pakistan and Yemen, with which Washington is not at war.

All of this is possible because Washington has claimed the title from Israel of being "God's Chosen People." Of course, Israel's loss of the title has not stopped Israel from acting the same way.

Washington now has in motion the wheels of war. Once the wheels of war begin to turn, momentum carries them forward. The foolish, indeed utterly stupid, governments and media in Europe seem unaware of Washington's orchestration of their future or lack thereof, or they are indifferent to it. They are dooming themselves and all of humanity by their insouciance. Heaven help it if the British PM or French president or German chancellor were not invited to the White House or the Polish nonentity did not get his Washington stipend.

Here is a suggested solution:

Putin should take his case to the UN. If Washington can send Colin

Powell to the UN *unarmed with any truth* to make Washington's case for war against Iraq, Putin should be able to take his case to the UN against Washington's war against Russia.

The case that the emperor has no clothes is an easy one to make.

Unlike Washington, Putin is willing to share the evidence that Russia has about who is doing what in Ukraine. It is a simple matter to establish that Washington organized a coup that overthrew an elected government, supports violence against those who object to the coup, and has turned a deaf ear to Russia's repeated pleas for Kiev and the separatists to negotiate their differences.

Putin should make it clear to the world that Washington continues with provocative military steps against Russia, with force buildups on Russia's borders and calls for more buildups, with S.2277 which reads like a US preparation for war, with provocative actions and accusations by top US generals and government officials against Russia, and with efforts to isolate Russia and to inflict economic and political injury on Russia.

Putin should make it clear to the world that there is a limit to the provocations that Russia can accept and that Russia believes that Russia is in danger of preemptive nuclear attack by Washington. Putin can describe Washington's withdrawal from the ABM treaty, the construction of ABM bases on Russia's borders, and the announced change in Washington's war doctrine that elevates US nuclear forces from a retaliatory role to a preemptive first strike role. These actions are clearly directed at Russia (and China— wake up China! You are next!).

Putin must state clearly that the likely consequence of the world continuing to enable Washington's lies and aggression will be not merely another disastrous war but the termination of life.

The governments of the world, especially Washington's vassals in Europe, Canada, Australia, and Japan, need to be told that it is their responsibility to stop their enabling of Washington's aggression or to accept their responsibility for World War III.

At least we could all have the enjoyment of watching the arrogant U.S. Ambassador Samantha Powers and the craven British lapdog rise and walk out of the UN proceedings. There is no doubt whatsoever that Washington is unable to answer the charges.

ANOTHER STATE DEPARTMENT HOAX?

July 27, 2014

I have an email that purports to be from the State Department Press Office. It is dated today, Sunday, July 27, 2014 at 8:45 AM EDT. It reads:

State Department Press Corps:
Sharing with you the attached document with DNI images — evidence of Russia firing into Ukraine.
Regards,
State Department Press Office

There is a 1.1MB file attached with pictures and a few words saying that the pictures indicate Russian firing into Ukraine territory.

As one with news and government experience, I am confident that information as important as this purports to be would not be released in this way. For several days reporters have been asking State Department press office spokeswoman Marie Harf for evidence to back her claims that the Russian military is attacking Ukrainian forces. Harf has told the reporters that she cannot provide evidence. In other words, Harf's evidence is like John Kerry's evidence that he could never provide that Assad had used chemical weapons.

Suddenly the evidence appears in an email and is spread via social media. This is not credible. Such evidence if it actually exists would be released in a Washington press conference by top government officials with experts present to explain the meaning of the photos to the journalists and to answer questions. No real journalists, if any are left, are going to believe that such hot information would be released in an email. Moreover, the photos are meaningless to the uninitiated, and there is no way to judge their authenticity.

Additionally, it is not credible that such important information would be released at a news dead time—8:45 AM EDT on a Sunday morning when the West Coast is still asleep.

What are we to make of this?

One explanation is that kids, unaware of the seriousness of the matter, concocted a hoax for fun.

Another explanation is that, unable to substantiate any of its charges against the Russian government, the State Department decided to use social media to spread disinformation in behalf of its propaganda assault on Russia. It was Geoffrey Pyatt, the US Ambassador to Ukraine who posted the images on Twitter. Pyatt was Victoria Nuland's partner in orchestrating the coup against the Ukrainian government.

As of 5:45PM EDT Sunday, to my knowledge, no State Department official has verified that this is a State Department news release. Indeed, email on Sunday morning is such an unprofessional way to release important news that I do not believe even the incompetent Marie Harf could be responsible for releasing information that was valid in this way.

The intent of the "news release" is to use social media to build the image of a dangerous Russia among an unsophisticated public independently of having to convince reporters. Once this image is created, Washington can use it to build public support for its purposes, such as more military spending or sending US troops to Ukraine.

In my opinion, it is reckless for Washington to convince Russia that Washington is going to continue to lie in order to discredit Russia in world opinion, and to continue to dismiss out of hand Russia's protests.

Washington is conveying to Russia that Washington has launched a very aggressive propaganda campaign against Russia, a campaign that could easily push the world to war.

In my day, if Washington had such information as the email purports to be, Washington would have used the information to defuse the situation. The Russian ambassador would have been called in and asked to explain. The ambassador would understand that he needed to tell the Kremlin to back off or the information would be released in a news conference.

Today, with the Obama regime seeking confrontation with Russia, the regime would have released the information in a press conference with all the important bureau chiefs present. For journalists of my vintage, releasing it in an indiscriminate email targeted to social media would have completely discredited the information.

The UK *Daily Mail* took the bait, reproducing the images and reported them as official government releases, but the State Department has made no official statement in behalf of the email, instead passing inquiries off to the US embassy in Ukraine. Russian media have skeptically reported the charges, thus helping to spread the propaganda.

UPDATE ON
THE LATEST US
GOVERNMENT HOAX

July 28, 2014

The Russian Ministry of Defense has declared the purported satellite photos placed on Twitter by the US Ambassador in Ukraine as fakes.[72]

I could tell that the images were fakes not only from their low resolution and absence of proper designation, but also from the unprofessional way in which the information was released.[73]

Of course, many users of social media would have no experience and could easily fall for the hoax, which was clearly the US government's intention.

The anti-Russian propaganda campaign being conducted by Washington follows in the footsteps of the campaigns conducted against Saddam Hussein, Gaddafi, Assad, and Iran. Washington's campaign of lies against Russia proves the absence of integrity in the US government and is reckless as it can lead to war.

Peter Duveen, who commented on my article exposing the State Department hoax, explained that having foreknowledge of news events that Washington orchestrates allows Washington to control the explanation before any evidence is available. By the time evidence is gathered, the narrative is established and the evidence ignored:

> Part of the US propaganda mill's effort is into forming the conversation. Once certain narratives take hold, true or untrue, they edge out other narratives. So the effort is to get control of the narrative, to form the conversation with whatever materials, usually false, are available. Then, of course, the false information will be referenced as true, and the direction of the narrative will be fixed. The narrative being lowered into place, for example, is that Russia was somehow responsible for the downing of Flight 17. With the help of the media, the hope is that the narrative will

gain momentum. Eventually, if it catches properly, it will be impossible to question, just as people are considered freaks who question the official narrative of 9-11. That is why the narratives are introduced as quickly as possible. Thus, we saw how quickly it was announced that Flight 17 was brought down by a surface to air missile. That would lead me to believe that it was actually not brought down by a surface to air missile. So also with this incredibly amateurish effort regarding Russian shelling of Ukrainian positions. Russian reaction is never obtained in the articles about it, and it is no longer mentioned that Russian territory has been shelled by the Ukrainian military.

The Russian Foreign Minister Lavrov has expressed the Russian government's concern that Washington will corrupt the official investigation of MH-17: "We are concerned by the fact that some of our partners are trying to organize the investigation by means of holding separate bilateral talks with the Ukrainian authorities." Lavrov said that Russia hopes that "only honest, open participation of all who possess information on the catastrophe" is considered to be the appropriate way to proceed and that "no one will try to cover tracks."[74]

WAR
IS COMING

July 28, 2014

The extraordinary propaganda being conducted against Russia by the US and UK governments and Ministries of Propaganda, a.k.a., the "Western media," has the purpose of driving the world to a war that no one can win. European governments need to rouse themselves from insouciance, because Europe will be the first to be vaporized due to the US missile bases that Europe hosts to guarantee its "security."

As reported by Tyler Durden of *Zero Hedge*, the Russian response to the extra-legal ruling of a corrupt court in the Netherlands is telling. The court, which had no jurisdiction over the case on which it ruled, awarded $50 billion dollars from the Russian government to shareholders of Yukos, a corrupt entity that was looting Russia and evading taxes. Asked what Russia would do about the ruling, an advisor to President Putin replied, "There is a war coming in Europe. Do you really think this ruling matters?"

The West has ganged up on Russia, because the West is totally corrupt. The wealth of the elites is based not only on looting weaker countries whose leaders can be purchased (read John Perkins' *Confessions of an Economic Hit Man* for instruction on how the looting works), but also on looting their own citizens.

The American elites excel at looting their fellow citizens and have financially wiped out most of the US middle class in the new 21st century.

Russia has emerged from tyranny and from a government based on lies, while the US and UK submerge into tyranny shielded by lies. Western elites desire to loot Russia, a juicy prize, and there stands Putin in the way. The solution is to get rid of him like they got rid of President Yanukovich in Ukraine.

The looting elites and the neoconservative hegemonists have the same goal: make Russia a vassal state.

This goal unites the Western financial imperialists with the political imperialists.

I have recorded for readers the propaganda that is used in order to demonize Putin and Russia. But even I was stunned by the astounding and vicious lies in the UK publication *The Economist* on July 26. Putin's face in a spider web is on the cover and, you guessed it, the cover story is "A Web of Lies." There is no evidence whatsoever in the story to support *The Economist*'s wild accusations and demand for the end of Western "appeasement" of Russia and the harshest possible action against Putin.

This kind of reckless lies and transparent propaganda has no other purpose than to drive the world to war.

The Western elites and governments are not merely totally corrupt, they are insane. As I have previously written, don't expect to live much longer. In this video one of Putin's advisors and Russian journalists speak openly of US plans for a first strike on Russia.[75]

THE MORAL
FAILURE
OF THE WEST

July 29, 2014

Readers are asking for my take on the Israel-Gaza situation, and, believe it or not, Oxford University's famous debating society, the Oxford Union, invited me to debate the issue.

I replied to the Oxford Union that I was unprepared to take responsibility for the Palestinians without undergoing the extensive preparation that an Oxford Union debate deserves and requires. Unless things have changed since my time at Oxford, one prevails in a Union debate by anticipating every argument of one's opponent and smashing the arguments with humor and wit. Facts seldom, if ever, carry the day, and sometimes not even wit and humor if the audience is already committed to the outcome by the prevailing propaganda. There is no time or energy in my overfull schedule for such preparation plus time away and jet lag.

Moreover, I am not an expert on Israel's conquest and occupation of Palestine. I know more than most people. I was rescued from Zionist propaganda by Israeli historians, such as Ilan Pappe, by Jewish intellectuals, such as Noam Chomsky and Norman Finkelstein, by documentary film makers, such as John Pilger, by Israeli journalists such as Uri Avnery and the Israeli newspaper Haaretz, and by an Israeli houseguest who is an Israeli member of an Israeli peace group that opposes Israeli destruction of Palestinian homes, villages, and orchards in order to build apartment blocks for settlers.

There is only one take on the current Israeli slaughter of Palestinians, which Netanyahu, the demonic Israeli leader, declares will be a "protracted campaign" this time. We are witnessing yet again Israeli war crimes that are supported by the Great Moral West that is so concerned about the deaths of 290 passengers on MH-17 that they are about to drive the world to a major war, while Palestinian casualties pile up so fast that they are out of date by the time you put the numbers in a column. So far more than 1,200 deaths, with injuries to 2,000 children, 1,170 women, and 257 elderly.

Reading the Western Media, watching Western TV, and listening to Western radio, one is left with the propaganda that the Palestinians are to blame for the Israeli attack on Gaza, just as one is left with the propaganda that the Malaysian airliner deaths are Russia's fault. There is no evidence, but propaganda does not require evidence. Just repetition.

The Gaza strip, a ghetto full of Palestinians evicted from their homes and villages in the West Bank, is one of the most densely populated areas on earth where life with scant resources is difficult. Israel is currently in the process of shrinking Gaza by 44 percent, while Senate Majority Leader Harry Reid, a Democrat, is preparing another "emergency" aid package consisting of US tax dollars to finance Israel's slaughter and compression of Palestinian lives.[76]

One would think that the Great Moral West would be discussing sanctions on Israel and on Washington's stooge government in Kiev, which is bombing civilian homes, apartment complexes, and infrastructure in provinces where the people object to the Russophobic government installed by Washington in place of the one that they elected. But the Great Moral West only aids the perpetrators of death and destruction, not the victims.

Palestinians are being dispossessed and exterminated exactly as were the native American Indians. On occasion Israeli officials have said that they are only following America's lead in clearing the land of undesirables. This is my take on what is one of the West's great moral failings.

Israel Is Stealing and Murdering Its Way Through Palestine

As Zionists have endeavored to teach the world for decades, Israel is not subject to criticism. Only Jewhaters, anti-Semites, and people who want to gas Jews and boil them in oil criticize Israel. Israel is above criticism, because Israelis are God's Chosen People and despite being God's Chosen People suffered the Holocaust.

This means that the Israeli government, like the one in Washington, can do whatever it wants and remain above criticism.

Since the 1940s Zionists have been stealing Palestine from the Palestinians. The majority of Palestinians have been removed from their homes and their country. They exist in refugee camps in other countries and 1.5 million are concentrated in the Gaza Ghetto, which is blockaded by Israel on one end and by the Washington paid Egyptians on the other.

This makes it convenient for Israel from time to time to attack the civilian population and civilian infrastructure in Gaza with military force. So far in Israel's latest war crime, Israel has murdered more than 1,200 Palestinians, largely women and children. You will seldom see the photos of the destruction in the American media, but RT provides a few glimpses.[77]

Israel is always the aggressor but always takes the role of the victim. Palestinian women and children are all subhumans—"snakes" as one Israeli politician put it—who sneak into Israel wearing suicide bomb belts and blow up innocent Israelis along with themselves while Israelis sit in cafes peacefully discussing philosophical issues and the latest news. To stop this slaughter of innocent Israelis, Israel has to blow up Palestinian hospitals, schools, and civilian homes and apartment blocks.

These unmistakable war crimes, these crimes against humanity are all ignored by the great moral arbiters of the world—the Governments of the West who are shaking their fingers not at Israel but their fists at Russia.

Western governments ignore Israel's war crimes but not all Western peoples comply with this neglect.

Many thousands of demonstrators against Israel have been in the streets in South America, London, Paris, Germany, Dublin, and Israel's own Tel Aviv.[78] But don't look for much reporting of these demonstrations in the American presstitute media.

The American presstitute media is focused on those who died in the downing of the Malaysian airliner in eastern Ukraine, in order to blame those 290 deaths on Russia. As far as the American presstitute media is concerned, the murder of 1,200 Palestinian deaths is not happening or if it is, the Palestinians deserve it for responding to Israel's oppression by firing in frustration primitive rockets that seldom, if ever, hit their targets.

What is another 1,200 murdered Palestinians? Who cares? Not Washington or the British PM in Whitehall and certainly not the Israelis. As far as Israel and the Great Moral West are concerned, 1,200 murdered Palestinians amount to nothing. They are not even chafe in the wind.

The last time Israel attacked the civilians in Gaza, a distinguished Israeli jurist, himself a Zionist, prepared a case for the UN that Israel had committed war crimes. On Israel's orders the craven but very obedient US Congress passed a resolution denouncing the distinguished jurist for defaming the pure and innocent Israeli government. The pressure from Washington and Israel on the jurist broke his commitment to truth, and Goldstone retracted his findings.

This is what the Israel Lobby and the craven American presstitute media do to everyone who criticizes Israel's crimes against humanity and Washington's protection of Israel's crimes. Anytime you see a person attacked by the Israel Lobby, you know for certain that the person under attack is the salt of the earth. The distinctive mark of a moral human being is to be attacked by the Israel Lobby and the presstitute American media.

While Israel murders Palestinians in Gaza with attacks on hospitals, schools, and civilian apartment blocks, Washington and its puppets in Kiev attack civilians in apartment blocks in the former Russian provinces of

Ukraine who object to Washington's overthrow of the democratically elected government in Ukraine and Washington's installation of a Russophobic government in its place.

Washington has declared those in Ukraine who object to Washington's takeover of their country to be "terrorists" and is seeking legislation that will permit US troops legally to enter Ukraine to suppress the "terrorists."

David Ward, a Member of the British Parliament, who has the right as a British citizen and member of Parliament to express his opinion, said that if he lived in Gaza under Israeli oppression, he would likely fire a rocket into Israel.

The British media and government is yet to criticize Israel for its crimes, but instantly attacked Ward for his "vile comments." A Conservative member of Parliament, Nadhim Zahawi, wrote the Metropolitan Police demanding an investigation into Ward's statement "as a matter of urgency." The Conservative party chairman, Grant Shapps, declared Ward's statement to be an "incitement to violence," a felony. The craven Labour Party declared Ward's opinion to be "so vile and irresponsible" that "it defied belief."[79]

The Liberal Democrats of which Ward is a member "utterly condemned" Ward's remarks and declared that Ward would be subject to disciplinary hearings and may permanently be expelled from the party.

There you have it. A Member of Parliament in the country that invented freedom of speech expresses an honest opinion, and he is dead meat. Ward's harmless remarks killed no one. The Israelis with weapons supplied by Washington have, at this time of writing, murdered more than 1,200 people. But it is Ward who must be restrained, not Israel. Ward's remarks are declared "vile and irresponsible" but not Israel's murder of 1,200 people.

The US and UK pretend to be countries that are not afraid of the truth, where there is free inquiry and freedom to express one's views, but it is all a great lie.

The US and UK are the two greatest threats to free speech on the face of the earth. In the UK no truth contrary to the line is permissible. In the US people who speak the truth are put on a Watch List.

How much longer will the governments of the rest of the world regard the US and UK as homes of free speech and uplifting Western morality?

In America the success of Israeli propaganda, never challenged of course by the US media, exceeds the success of Washington's own propaganda. Most Americans believe that Palestinian women and children are outfitted with explosive suicide belts and that "the snakes," as they are described by Israeli politicians, walk into Israeli cafes and blow everyone up including themselves.

The fact of the matter is that Palestinians cannot get into Israel. Gaza is blockaded as are the few remaining Palestinian settlements in the

West Bank. Israel has stolen almost all of Palestine. The few Palestinian settlements still permitted to exist are cut off by a massive wall from Israel and from each other by barbed wire and check points, cut off from hospitals and schools, from water, and from their fields and olive groves, which are being destroyed to make room for settlers' apartment blocks.

People this hemmed in are helpless, and the extreme right-wing Israeli settlers are moving into the few remaining Palestinian settlements evicting the Palestinians from their properties with the aid of US-provided Caterpillar tractors especially designed for uprooting Palestinian olive groves and demolishing Palestinian houses, just like the Caterpillar tractor that the Israelis ran over US citizen Rachel Corrie, murdering this protesting US citizen in cold blood. Yes, you are correct, the Great Moral US government did nothing about it. Israel learned when it murdered the crew of the *USS Liberty* in 1967 that Israel had carte blanche from Washington to murder US citizens.

When you view the photos of Palestinians who have undergone an Israeli attack, what do you see? You see unarmed people crying, hugging dead children in their arms and one another. You never see a resolute armed people prepared to repel the next Israeli attack. You see devastated hospitals, schools, and apartment complexes and Palestinians in tears—and no weapons.

What is striking about the success of Israeli propaganda is its success when all evidence is that Palestinians are pacifists, incapable of resistance. The bulk of the people in Gaza are refugees from the West Bank where their land and homes were stolen by the Great Democratic State of Israel. The Israeli destruction of Palestine has been going on for almost seven decades. And still Palestinians are not armed and have no effective military units.

After seven decades the Palestinian people remain unarmed. Hamas has a few ineffective weapons, but the people themselves are unarmed. Their response to the Israeli murders of their children, wives, husbands, brothers, sisters, parents, cousins, and friends is to cry. This is not the response of a warlike people.

In contrast, there are reports that Israeli civilians sit atop the hill overlooking Gaza on sofas that they bring along with their drinks and food and watch in glee, clapping and cheering as Israeli bombs destroy Palestinians in their homes, children in their schools, and the ill in hospitals. If this is the true face of "the only democracy in the Middle East," it is the face of evil.

Photos from *The New York Times* show Israelis gathered to enjoy the slaughter of Palestinians.[80] If Hamas' rockets were a threat, these Israelis would be dead.

The view brainwashed into the West that Palestinians are a threat to Israel is absurd. If Palestinians are a threat and a danger to Israel, how is it possible that Palestinians are locked away into sealed ghettos in the remnants of their own country or into refugee camps in foreign countries?

As Israel's most distinguished historian, Ilan Pappe, has related, the story of Israel is the story of *The Ethnic Cleansing of Palestine*. This story has been hidden by Western "moral" governments and by a corrupt Western media.

WASHINGTON THREATENS THE WORLD

August 8, 2014

The consequence of Washington's reckless and irresponsible political and military interventions in Iraq, Libya, and Syria has been to unleash evil. The various sects that lived in peace under the rule of Saddam Hussein, Gaddafi, and Assad are butchering one another, and a new group, ISIS, is in the process of creating a new state out of parts of Iraq and Syria.

The turmoil brought into the Middle East by the Bush and Obama regimes has meant death and displacement for millions and untold future deaths. As I write, 40,000 Iraqis are stranded on a mountain top without water awaiting death at the hands of ISIS, a creation of US meddling.

The reality in the Middle East stands in vast contradiction to the stage managed landing of George W. Bush on the US aircraft carrier *Abraham Lincoln* where Bush declared "Mission Accomplished" on May 1, 2003. The mission that Washington accomplished was to wreck the Middle East and the lives of millions of people and to destroy America's reputation in the process. Thanks to the demonic neoconservative Bush regime, today America is regarded by the rest of the world as the greatest threat to world peace.

The Clinton regime's attack on Serbia set the pattern. Bush upped the ante with Washington's naked aggression against Afghanistan, which Washington clothed in Orwellian language—"Operation Enduring Freedom."

Washington brought ruin, not freedom, to Afghanistan. After 13 years of blowing up the country, Washington is now withdrawing, the "superpower" having been defeated by a few thousand lightly armed Taliban, but leaving a wasteland behind for which Washington will accept no responsibility.

Another source of endless Middle East turmoil is Israel whose theft of Palestine is Washington-enabled. In the middle of Israel's latest attack on civilians in Gaza, the US Congress passed resolutions in support of Israel's war crimes and voted hundreds of millions of dollars to pay for Israel's ammunition. Here we witness Great Moral America 100 percent in support of unambiguous war crimes against essentially defenseless people.

When Israel murders women and children, Washington calls it "Israel's right to defend their own country"—a country that Israel stole from Palestinians—but when Palestinians retaliate Washington calls it "terrorism." By supporting Israel, declared to be a terrorist state by a few moral governments that still exist, and accused of war crimes by the UN General Secretary, Washington is in violation of its own laws against supporting terrorist states.

Of course, Washington itself is the leading terrorist state. Therefore, it is illegal under US law for Washington to support itself. Washington, however, does not accept law, either domestic or international, as a constraint on its actions. Washington is "exceptional, indispensable." No one else counts. No law, no Constitution, and no humane consideration has authority to constrain Washington's will. Washington's claims surpass those of the Third Reich.

As horrific as Washington's recklessness toward the Middle East is, Washington's recklessness toward Russia is many orders of magnitude greater. Washington has convinced nuclear armed Russia that Washington is planning a nuclear first strike. In response Russia is beefing up its nuclear forces and testing US air defense reactions.[81] It is difficult to imagine a more irresponsible act than to convince Russia that Washington intends to hit Russia with a preemptive first strike. One of Putin's advisers has explained to the Russian media Washington's first strike intentions, and a member of the Russian Duma has made a documented presentation of Washington's first strike intentions.[82] By marshaling the evidence, I have pointed out in my columns that it is impossible for Russia to avoid this conclusion.

China is aware that China faces the same threat from Washington. China's response to Washington's war plans against China was to demonstrate how China's nuclear forces would be used in response to Washington's attack on China to destroy the US. China made this public, hoping to create opposition among Americans to Washington's war plans against China.[83] Like Russia, China is a rising country that does not need war in order to succeed.

The only country on earth that needs war is Washington, and that is because Washington's goal is the neoconservative one of exercising hegemony over the world.

Prior to the Bush and Obama regimes, every previous US president went to great effort to avoid telegraphing any nuclear threat. US war doctrine was careful to keep nuclear weapons limited to retaliation in the event the US suffered a nuclear attack. The purpose of nuclear forces was to prevent the use of such weapons. The reckless George W. Bush regime elevated nuclear weapons to preemptive first use, thus destroying the constraint placed on the use of nuclear weapons.

The overriding purpose of the Reagan administration was to end the Cold War and, thereby, the threat of nuclear war. The George W. Bush regime and the Obama regime's demonization of Russia have overturned President Reagan's unique achievement and made nuclear war likely.

When the incompetent Obama regime decided to overthrow the democratically elected government in Ukraine and install a puppet government of Washington's choosing, the Obama State Department, run by neoconservative ideologues, forgot that the eastern and southern portions of Ukraine consist of former Russian provinces that were attached to the Ukraine Soviet Socialist Republic by Communist Party leaders when Ukraine and Russia were part of the same country—the Soviet Union. When the Russophobic stooges that Washington installed in Kiev demonstrated in word and deed their hostility to Ukraine's Russian population, the former Russian provinces declared their desire to return to mother Russia. This is not surprising, nor is it something that can be blamed on Russia.

Crimea succeeded in returning to Russia, where Crimea resided since the 1700s, but Putin, hoping to defuse the propaganda war that Washington was mounting against him, did not accept the pleas from the other former Russian provinces. Consequently, Washington's stooges in Kiev felt free to attack the protesting provinces and have been following the Israeli policy of attacking civilian populations, civilian residences, and civilian infrastructure.

The presstitute Western media ignored the facts and accused Russia of invading and annexing parts of Ukraine. This lie is comparable to the lies that US Secretary of State Colin Powell told the UN about Iraqi weapons of mass destruction in behalf of the criminal Bush regime, lies that Colin Powell later apologized for to no avail as Iraq had been destroyed by his lies.

When the Malaysian airliner was destroyed, before any facts were known Russia was blamed. The British media was especially primed to blame Russia almost the instant it was known the airliner was downed. I heard the BBC's gross misrepresentation and blatant lies on American National Public Radio, and only the *Daily Mail*'s propagandistic account was worse. The entire "news" event has the appearance of orchestration prior to the event, which, of course, suggests that Washington was behind it.

The airliner deaths became all important for Washington's propaganda war. The 290 casualties are unfortunate, but they are a small fraction of the deaths that Israel was inflicting on Palestinians at the same moment without provoking any protests from Western governments, as distinct from Western people in the streets, people whose protests were conveniently suppressed for Israel by Western security forces.

Washington used the downing of the airliner, which probably was Washington's responsibility, as an excuse for another round of sanctions and to pressure its European puppets to join the sanctions with sanctions of their own, which Washington's EU puppets did.

Washington relies on accusations and insinuations and refuses to release the evidence from the satellite photos, because the photos do not support Washington's lies. Facts are not permitted to interfere with Washington's demonization of Russia any more than facts interfered with Washington's demonization of Iraq, Libya, Syria, and Iran.

Twenty-two reckless and irresponsible US senators have introduced the "Russian Aggression Prevention Act of 2014," US Senate bill 2277, sponsored by Senator Bob Corker, who well represents in his ignorance and stupidity what appears to be the majority of the American population or the majority of voters in the state of Tennessee. Corker's bill is a mindless piece of legislation designed to start a war that would be likely to leave no survivors. Apparently, idiotic Americans will elect any fool to power.

The belief that Russia is responsible for the downed Malaysian airliner has become fact in Western capitals despite the total absence of even a tiny scrap of evidence in behalf of the claim. Moreover, even if the accusation were true, is one airliner worth a World War?

The UK Defense Committee has concluded that a broke and militarily impotent UK must "focus on the defense of Europe against Russia." The military spending drums, if not the war drums, are beating and the entire West has joined in. A militarily impotent Britain is going to defend Europe from a non-existent, although much proclaimed, attack from the Russian bear.

US and NATO military dignitaries and the Pentagon chief are issuing Russia Threat Warnings based on alleged but non-existent Russian troop-buildups on Ukraine's border. According to the Western Ministry of Propaganda, if Russia defends the Russian populations in Ukraine from military attack from Washington's stooge government in Kiev, it is proof that Russia is the villain.

Washington's propaganda campaign has succeeded in turning Russia into a threat. Polls show that 69 percent of Americans now regard Russia as a threat, and that the confidence of Russians in American leadership has vanished.

Russians and their government observe the identical demonization of their country and their leader as they observed of Iraq and Saddam Hussein, of Libya and Gaddafi, of Syria and Assad, and of Afghanistan and the Taliban just prior to military assaults on these countries by the West. For a Russian, the safest conclusion from the evidence is that Washington intends war on Russia.

It is my opinion that the irresponsibility and recklessness of the Obama regime is without precedent.

Never before has the United States government or the government of any nuclear power gone to such great efforts to convince another nuclear power that that power was being set up for attack. It is difficult to imagine a more provocative act that more endangers life on earth. Indeed, the White House Fool has doubled up, convincing both Russia and China that Washington is planning a preemptive first strike on both.

Republicans want to sue or to impeach Obama over relatively inconsequential issues, such as ObamaCare.

Why don't Republicans want to impeach Obama over such a critical issue as subjecting the world to the risk of nuclear Armageddon?

The answer is that the Republicans are as crazed as the Democrats. Their leaders, such as John McCain and Lindsey Graham, are determined that "we stand up to the Russians!" Wherever one looks in American politics one sees crazed people, psychopaths and sociopaths who should not be in political office.

Washington long ago gave up diplomacy. Washington relies on force and intimidation. The US government is utterly devoid of judgment. This is why polls show that the rest of the world regards the US government as the greatest threat to world peace. Today (August 8, 2014) *Handelsblatt*, Germany's *Wall Street Journal*, wrote in a signed editorial by the publisher:

> The American tendency to move from verbal escalation to military escalation—the isolation, demonization, and attacking of enemies—has not proven effective. The last successful major military action the US conducted was the Normandy landing [in 1944]. Everything else—Korea, Vietnam, Iraq, and Afghanistan—was a clear failure. Moving NATO units towards the Polish border with Russia and thinking about arming Ukraine is a continuation of relying on military means in the absence of diplomacy.

Washington's puppet states—all of Europe, Japan, Canada, and Australia—enable Washington's unrivaled danger to the world by their support of Washington's agenda of exercising hegemony over the entire world.

The 100th anniversary of World War I is upon us. And the folly that caused this war is being repeated.

WWI destroyed a civilized Western world, and it was the work of a mere handful of scheming people.

The result was Lenin, the Soviet Union, Hitler, the rise of American Imperialism, Korea, Vietnam, the military interventions that created ISIS, and the now resurrected conflict between Washington and Russia that President Reagan and Mikhail Gorbachev had ended.

As Stephen Starr has pointed out on my website, if merely 10% of the nuclear weapons in the US and Russian arsenals are used, life on earth terminates.

Dear readers, ask yourselves, when has Washington told you anything that was not a lie? Washington's lies have caused millions of casualties. Do you want to be a casualty of Washington's lies?

Do you believe that Washington's lies and propaganda about the Malaysian airliner and Ukraine are worth risking life on earth? Who is so gullible that he cannot recognize that Washington's lies about Ukraine are like Washington's lies about Hussein's weapons of mass destruction, Iranian nukes, and Assad's use of chemical weapons?

Do you think that the neoconservative influence that prevails in Washington, regardless of the political party in office, is too dangerous to be tolerated?

WASHINGTON
CHOKES TRUTH
WITH LIES

August 13, 2014

Are Western propagandists fooling anyone but themselves?

The latest absurdity coming out of Ukraine, the EU and Washington is that the humanitarian aid that Russia and the Red Cross are trucking into the former Russian territories that comprise eastern Ukraine is a trick, a deception, a pretext for Russia's invasion forces. Such a preposterous lie tells us that Western propagandists have no respect whatsoever for the intelligence of Western peoples.

Even a moron should understand that if Russia wants to send military forces into Ukraine, Russia doesn't need any pretext, much less a joint humanitarian venture with the Red Cross. The eastern Ukraine, following Crimea's lead, has already voted both independence from Kiev and in favor of rejoining Russia.

If Russia needed an excuse, the decisions by the eastern Ukrainians made months ago suffice. But Russia needs no excuse to rescue Russians from being slaughtered by Washington's stooges like the Palestinians in Gaza.

By its inaction, the Russian government is providing Washington's vassal states in Europe time to comprehend that Washington, not Russia, is the problem, and that Washington intends for the cost of its conflict with Russia to fall on Europeans.

The opposition from Washington, Washington's EU vassals, and Washington's stooges in Kiev to the inflow of humanitarian aid is due to the West's desperate attempt to keep the world from knowing about the massive destruction by Washington and its stooges of civilian lives, housing, and infrastructure in those former Russian territories who are directly threatened by the Russophobic extremists that Washington has installed in power in Kiev.

The Western presstitute media has added yet another failure to its long inglorious history by failing to report the atrocities inflicted on a people who see no future for themselves in a country ruled by murderous Russophobic criminals installed in power by Washington.

185

The demented NATO generals, Pentagon chief, and US senators are spreading hysteria about a looming Russian invasion not only of Ukraine but also of the Baltics, Poland, indeed, all of Europe. This hysteria is engulfing the West despite the total lack of any sign whatsoever of Russian preparations or motives for such invasions. The lie is being spread by Washington that Putin intends to reconstitute the Soviet Empire.

This is the same Putin who had the former Russian province of Georgia in his hands and let it go.

Washington's propaganda is working. Polls reveal that a majority of Americans, who should be awake by now after being lied to about Afghanistan, Iraq, Somalia, Libya, Syria, and Iran, have again, in their infinite gullibility, fallen victim to the propaganda and regard Russia as a threat.

Among the misinformed and propagandized American population, the question of the day is: "How are we going to stop the Russians?" Thus has the corrupt and deceitful Obama regime again prepared Americans for war.

The hope for peace is that the Russian counter-sanctions, a response to the sanctions against Russia that Washington forced its European vassals to implement, will end up falling on the deluded American taxpayers. The Polish government has demanded that Washington purchase the apples and agricultural products that Washington has made impossible for Poland to sell to Russia. As Poland is Washington's choice for the US missile base directed at Russia, the Polish government has leverage. Once Washington gives in to Poland, Washington will be faced with similar demands from hard-hit Greece and Austria and from the rest of Europe to compensate Europeans for the costs that Washington's sanctions have imposed on its vassal populations.

The fraud perpetuated on the world by the United States in the 21st century is extraordinary. Nothing comparable has ever been witnessed in history. Not only are there the frauds of the numerous wars (Afghanistan, Iraq, Somalia, Iraq, Syria, Ukraine, almost Iran and Washington's illegal military actions within the borders of Pakistan and Yemen), but also the vast financial frauds perpetuated on the world.

Among the costs of Wall Street's frauds are the European debt crisis, the infringements of national sovereignty of European countries by the IMF bailouts of sovereign debt, and the impoverishment of "rescued" Greece, Italy, Spain, Portugal, and Ireland, along with Eastern Europe.

One day the Europeans will wake up. When they do, they will realize that Washington does nothing for them except to protect them from a non-existent "Russian threat," while imposing dramatic costs upon them by employing Europeans as levies in Washington's war for hegemony over the world. Sooner or later Europeans must realize that this role assigned to them by Washington is not in their interest and leads directly to World War III in which Europeans will be the first casualties.

WASHINGTON HAS PLACED THE WORLD ON THE ROAD TO WAR

August 14, 2014

Update: A fabricated report was spread by the UK Guardian *newspaper and BBC that a Russian armored convoy entered Ukraine and was destroyed by the Ukrainian military. The German media including* Die Welt *picked up the false report and spread the hysteria. Once again we have confirmation that the Western media is corrupt and unreliable.*

The drums for war are being loudly beaten in Washington, European capitals, and the presstitute Western media. A headline in the *Asia Times* is "NATO Is Desperate For War."[84] This time the target is Russia, a major nuclear power.

The deadly consequences of such a war would extend beyond Russia, Europe, and the US to the entire world. The Western use of lies to demonize Russia endangers life on earth and reveals the West to be both reckless and irresponsible. Yet, few voices are raised against this recklessness and irresponsibility.

Ron Unz brings to our attention the important voice of a distinguished Dutch journalist, Karel Van Wolferen.[85] Wolferen and Unz himself[86] are important offsets to what Unz regards, correctly in my opinion, as "the utter corruption and unreliability of the mainstream American media."

Wolferen's article is long but very important. Readers will see analysis akin to my own.

Wolferen shows how the Washington hegemon has captured Europe within an Atlanticist ideology that forecloses any independent thinking or foreign policy on the part of Europeans who are reduced to a state of vassalage. Wolferen concludes that as Washington drives Europe toward war, "Europeans cannot bring themselves to believe in the dysfunction and utter irresponsibility of the American state."

With no internal checks on Washington's recklessness from allies, the media, and US Senators, the only brake on Washington's drive to war is Russian, Chinese, Indian, and South American diplomacy. If this diplomacy fails, Fukushima, as bad as it is, becomes a mere raindrop in the ocean.[87]

The slaughter by Washington, Washington's Kiev stooges and Washington's EU vassals of civilians in the former Russian territories that comprise the southern and eastern borders of present-day Ukraine is not only largely unreported in the Western media, but also denied or blamed on Russia.

The crimes that Washington is perpetrating while blaming Russia have aroused a high level of anger among the Russian people. Such anger is dangerous as it could force Putin, who continues to emphasize non-confrontation,[88] to turn away from diplomacy to violence.

Egor Prosvirnin, the chief editor of a Russian news site, shows us the extent of the anger in Russia caused by the dangerous mixture of Washington's broken promises with the vicious propaganda war against Russia and the German government's complicity.[89]

Prosvirnin expresses anger that is white hot: "Germans have failed their test. When Evil has returned again to Europe, you do not even attempt to resist it, and immediately fall prostrate at its feet like a slave." As Russians see it, all of Europe is a slave to the evil emanating from Washington.

Why did Merkel allow Washington to force Germany into a conflict with Russia that has produced enormous Russian anger toward Germany? What accounts for Merkel's total failure as a leader?

The Clinton, Bush, and Obama regimes have set the world on the path to the final war. How is it possible for their evil to go unrecognized?

The two murderous states are the US and Israel. By tolerating their endless slaughters and endless lies, the world prepares its own demise.

The only hope for life and truth is that the countries of the world unite against these two criminal governments, isolate them diplomatically and economically, and make it impossible for their government officials to travel abroad without being arrested and placed on trial.

Why does the world need Washington and Israel? Unless the world has a death wish, the world does not need Washington and Israel.

IN THE WEST RESPECT FOR TRUTH NO LONGER EXISTS

August 17, 2014

The Western media have proved for all to see that the Western media comprises either a collection of ignorant and incompetent fools or a whorehouse that sells war for money.

The Western media fell in step with Washington and blamed the downed Malaysian airliner on Russia. No evidence was provided. In its place the media used constant repetition. Washington withheld the evidence that proved that Kiev was responsible. The media's purpose was not to tell the truth, but to demonize Russia.

Now we have the media story of the armored Russian column that allegedly crossed into Ukraine and was destroyed by Ukraine's rag-tag forces that ISIS would eliminate in a few minutes. British reporters fabricated this story or were handed it by a CIA operative working to build a war narrative. The disreputable BBC hyped the story without investigating. The German media, including *Die Welt*, blared the story throughout Germany without concern at the absence of any evidence. Reuters news agency, also with no investigation, spread the story. Readers tell me that CNN has been broadcasting the fake story 24/7. Although I cannot stand to watch it, I suspect Fox "news" has also been riding this lame horse hard.

Readers tell me that my former newspaper, the *Wall Street Journal*, which has fallen so low as to be unreadable, also spread the false story. I hope they are wrong. One hates to see the complete despoliation of one's former habitat.

The media story is preposterous for a number of reasons that should be obvious to a normal person.

The first reason is that the Russian government has made it completely clear that its purpose is to deescalate the situation. When other former Russian territories that are part of present day Ukraine followed Crimea, voted their independence and requested reunification with Russia,

President Putin refused. To underline his de-escalation, President Putin asked the Russian Duma to rescind his authority to intervene militarily in Ukraine in behalf of the former Russian provinces. As the Russian government, unlike Washington or EU governments, stresses legality and the rule of law, Russian military forces would not be sent into Ukraine prior to the Duma renewing Putin's authority so to do.

The second reason the story is obviously false is that if the Russian government decides to invade Ukraine, Russia would not send in one small armored group unprotected by air cover or other forces. If Russia invades Ukraine, it will be with a force capable of rolling up the rag-tag Ukrainian forces, most of which are semi-private militias organized by Nazis. The "war" would last a few hours, after which Ukraine would be in Russia's hands where it resided for hundreds of years prior to the dissolution of the Soviet Union and Washington's successful efforts in 1991 to take advantage of Russian weakness to break apart the constituent provinces of Russia herself.

The third reason that the story is obviously false is that not a single Western news organization hyping the story has presented a shred of evidence in its behalf.

What we witness in this fabricated story is the total lack of integrity in the entirety of the Western media.

A story totally devoid of any evidence to support it has been broadcast worldwide. The White House has issued a statement saying that it cannot confirm the story, but nevertheless the White House continues to issue accusations against Russia for which the White House can supply no evidence. Consequently, Western repetition of bald-faced lies has become truth for huge numbers of peoples. As I have emphasized in my columns, these Western lies are dangerous, because they provoke war.

The same group in Washington and the same Western "media" are telling the same kind of lies that were used to justify Washington's wars in Iraq (weapons of mass destruction), Afghanistan (Taliban = al Qaeda), Syria (use of chemical weapons), Libya (an assortment of ridiculous charges), and the ongoing US military murders in Pakistan, Yemen, and Somalia.

The city upon the hill, the light unto the world, the home of the exceptional, indispensable people is the home of Satan's lies where truth is prohibited and war is the end game.

Update: After pretending that the Russian humanitarian truck convoy contained a hidden invasion force, the stooge Kiev government was forced by facts on the ground to officially acknowledge that the trucks only contained aid for those that the Kiev stooge government has been bombing and attacking with artillery.[90]

UKRAINE
CRISIS
CONTINUES

August 20, 2014

Having served Washington's propaganda purposes, the downed Malaysian airliner and the alleged Russian armored column that entered Ukraine and was allegedly destroyed have dropped out of the news even though both stories remain completely and totally unresolved.

Washington's stooge government in Ukraine has not released the records of communications between Ukrainian air traffic control and Malaysian flight 17, and Washington has not released the photos from its satellite which was directly overhead at the time of the airliner's demise.

We can safely and conclusively conclude from this purposeful withholding of evidence that the evidence does not support Washington and Kiev's propaganda.

We can also safely and conclusively conclude that the Western media's sudden disinterest in the unresolved story and failure to demand the evidence kept secret by Washington and Kiev is in keeping with the Western media's role as a Ministry of Propaganda.

In other words, Washington and its presstitutes are protecting the lie that Washington and its media vassals successfully spread around the world and have used as the basis for further sanctions that escalate the conflict with Russia. Washington could not possibly make it clearer that Washington intends to escalate, not defuse, the conflict that Washington alone orchestrated.

Ditto for the alleged Russian armored column. The Russian government has labeled the story a fantasy, which it clearly is, but nevertheless Washington and its media vassals have left the story in place.

As English is the world language and as the European press follows the lead of the American presstitutes, the propaganda war is stacked against Russia (and China). Russian and Chinese are not world languages.

Indeed, these languages are difficult for others to learn and are not well known outside the countries themselves. The Western media follows Washington's lead, not Moscow's or Beijing's.

As facts are not relevant to the outcome, Moscow and Beijing are in a losing situation in the propaganda war.

The same holds for diplomacy. Washington does not engage in diplomacy. The exceptional country uses bribes, threats, and coercion. The Russian government's diplomatic efforts come to naught. As Russian President Putin has complained, "Washington doesn't listen, the West doesn't hear us."

And yet the Russian government continues to try to deal with the Ukrainian situation with facts and diplomacy. This approach is proving to be very costly to the residents of the former Russian territories in eastern and southern Ukraine. These people are being killed by air and artillery strikes against their homes and infrastructure. Large numbers of these people have been displaced by the Ukrainian attacks and are refugees in Russia. The Western media does not report the violence that Washington's stooge government in Kiev is inflicting on these people. The Western media speaks only with Washington's voice: "It is all Russia's fault."

The crisis would have been prevented if the Russian government had accepted the provinces request to be reunited with Russia as in the case of Crimea. However, the Russian government decided to avoid any decision that Washington could misrepresent as "invasion and annexation," thinking that Europe would see Russia's unprovocative behavior as reassuring and resist Washington's pressure to enter into conflict with Russia.

In my opinion the Russian government over-estimated the power of diplomacy in the West. Washington is interested in fomenting crises, not in resolving them.

In the 23 years since the collapse of the Soviet Union, many Russians have been of the opinion that Washington, not the Soviet government, was the party to be trusted in the Cold War. What the Russian government has learned recently is that Washington cannot be trusted and that the Soviet government's suspicions of the West were very well founded.

Kiev's military assault on eastern and southern Ukraine is not going to stop because Europeans finally see the light and object. Europeans not only stood aside for 13 years while Washington bombed civilians in Afghanistan, Iraq, Libya, Somalia, Pakistan, Yemen, and organized outside forces to attack Syrians, while isolating Iran for military attack, but also actively participated in the attacks. Europe has stood aside while Israel has massacred Palestinians on numerous occasions. For Russia to rely on Europe's moral conscience is to rely on something that does not exist.

The continued slaughter and destruction of the Russian populations in eastern and southern Ukraine will eventually demoralize the Russian people and undermine their support of Putin's government for failing to halt it. The Russian government's acceptance of the slaughter makes Russia look weak and encourages more aggression against Russia.

If the Russian government intends to resolve its problems in Ukraine and to forestall Washington's ability to further erode Russia's political and economic relationships with Europe with more sanctions, the Russian government will have to turn to more forceful measures.

In Ukraine the Russian government has two alternatives. One is to announce that the ongoing slaughter and the unresponsiveness of Kiev and its Western backers to Russia's efforts to end the killing with a diplomatic settlement has caused Russia to reconsider the provinces' requests to be reunited with Russia and that any further attacks on these territories will be regarded as attacks on Russia and be met with a devastating military response.

The other alternative is for Putin to meet privately with Washington's stooge and convey to the corrupt oligarch that enough is enough and that if the attacks continue Russia will accept the requests for reunification and protect the provinces. Putin would explain to Washington's stooge that if he wants to retain the former Russian territories as part of Ukraine, he will have to work out satisfactory arrangements with the provinces. In other words, Putin would deliver an ultimatum, one that required an immediate answer so that the stooge couldn't run to Washington and Washington would not have time to create a new propaganda.

Karl Marx regarded morality as a rationale for class interests. As each class created a morality to justify its interests, there was no basis for good will between people. With reform impossible, violence becomes the only effective method of change. Washington has its own version of Marx's doctrine. As the exceptional country, history has chosen the US to prevail over other countries' interests. Prevailing rules out diplomacy which requires compromise. Therefore, Washington, like Marx, relies on violence.

The Russian government cannot rely on diplomacy and good will if the West is relying on violence.

Perhaps a solution could be found by President Putin meeting separately with Merkel and Hollande and explaining that Russia cannot indefinitely accept sanctions based on lies and propaganda without taking more determined steps than Russian sanctions against European agricultural products. Putin could make it clear that if Europe continues to accommodate Washington's assault on Russia, the flow of energy could be restricted or be turned off.

Additionally, President Putin might explain to the European leaders that the dynamics of Washington's campaign to demonize Russia can escape control and result in war that would devastate Europe. Putin could tell Europeans that by disassociating from Washington's foreign policy and adopting foreign policies that serve their own interests instead of Washington's, Europeans have nothing to lose but their chains of vassalage.

Putin could explain to Europeans that Russia is prepared to guarantee

Europe's security and, therefore, that Europe does not need Washington's guarantee against a nonexistent Russian threat.

   If this very reasonable and diplomatic approach to Europe fails, then Russia and China know that they must prepare for war.

THE LENINIST
IN THE
WHITE HOUSE

August 27, 2014

According to Lenin, the Soviet government rested "directly on force, not limited by anything, not restricted by any laws, nor any absolute rules."[94]

In the 21st century the US government has echoed Lenin. No laws, domestic or international, restrain the US from torture. Laws do not prevent the US from attacking sovereign countries or from conducting military operations within the borders of sovereign countries. Constitutional protections and due process do not prevent the US from detaining citizens indefinitely or from murdering them on suspicion or accusation alone.

The latest manifestation of Washington's Leninism is Washington's announcement that the US government has no plans to coordinate US attacks on ISIS on Syrian territory with the Syrian government. Washington recognizes no limitations on its use of force, and the sovereignty of countries provides no inhibition.

In Washington coercion has supplanted the rule of law.

Syria has every right to be nervous. The reason ISIS is operating on Syrian territory is that Washington armed them and sent them to Syria. Washington's air strikes on ISIS could very well be cover for air strikes on Syrian armed forces.

Here we see the complete failure of the Obama regime. As in Libya, the Obama regime set jihadists lose on Syria, pretending that they were fighting for democracy against a dictator. But Washington lost control over its monster which has gobbled up large parts of Syria and Iraq and is forming them into a new country hostile both to the West and to the Muslim vassals of the West.

Simultaneously, the US is threatening Russia with war. And everywhere hostility is rising against Washington. Without diplomacy Washington only has coercion. Does Washington have enough coercion to subdue the world?

The government of Washington's ally, Israel, has also endorsed

Leninism and is using the same principle of boundless coercion against the Palestinians.

Of all the governments in the world, only Washington and Zionist Israel have declared themselves to be unaccountable and above law. They are models not of democracy but of tyranny.

WASHINGTON PILES
LIE UPON LIE

August 28, 2014

The latest Washington lie, this one coming from NATO, is that Russia has invaded Ukraine with 1,000 troops and self-propelled artillery.

How do we know that this is a lie? Is it because we have heard nothing but lies about Russia from NATO, from US ambassador to the UN Samantha Power, from assistant secretary of state Victoria Nuland, from Obama and his entire regime of pathological liars, and from the British, German, and French governments along with the BBC and the entirety of the Western media?

This, of course, is a good reason for knowing that the latest Western propaganda is a lie. Those who are pathological liars don't suddenly start telling the truth.

But there are even better reasons for understanding that Russia has not invaded Ukraine with 1,000 troops.

One reason is that Putin has invested heavily in diplomacy backed by unprovocative behavior. He would not risk his bet on diplomacy by sending in troops too few in number to have a decisive effect on the outcome.

Another reason is that if Putin decides he has no alternative to sending the Russian military to protect the Russian residents in eastern and southern Ukraine, Putin will send in enough troops to do the job quickly as he did in Georgia when the American and Israeli trained Georgian army invaded South Ossetia and was destroyed in a few hours by the Russian response. If you hear that 100,000 Russian troops accompanied by air cover have invaded Ukraine, it would be a more believable claim.

A third reason is that the Russian military does not need to send troops into Ukraine in order to stop the bombing and artillery shelling of the Russian populations by Washington's puppet government in Kiev.

The Russian air force can easily and quickly destroy the Ukrainian air force and artillery and, thereby, stop the Ukrainian attack on the secessionist provinces.

It was only two weeks ago that a fabricated report spread by the UK *Guardian* and the BBC that a Russian armored convoy entered Ukraine and was destroyed by the Ukrainian Military. And two weeks prior to that we had the hoax of the satellite images allegedly released by the US State Department that the corrupt US ambassador in Kiev spread around the world on social media allegedly showing that Russian forces were firing into Ukraine. One or two weeks from now we will have another lie, and another a week or two after that, and so on.

The cumulative effect of lie piled upon lie for most people is to build the view that the Russians are up to no good. Once this view is established, Western governments can take more serious moves against Russia.

The alleged entry of 1,000 Russian soldiers into Ukraine has been declared by NATO Brigadier General Niko Tak to be a "significant escalation in Russia's military interference in Ukraine." The champion liar Samantha Power told the UN Security Council that "Russia has to stop lying." The UK ambassador to the UN said that Russia was guilty of "a clear violation of sovereign Ukrainian territory." UK Prime Minister Cameron warned Russia of "further consequences." German chancellor Merkel announced that there would be more sanctions. A German Security Council advisor declared that "war with Russia is an option." Polish foreign minister Sikorski called it Russian aggression that required international action.

French president Hollande declared Russia's behavior to be "intolerable." Ukraine's security council imposed mandatory conscription.

This suicidal drive toward war with Russia by Europe's leaders is based entirely on a transparent lie that 1,000 Russian troops crossed into Ukraine.

Of course the Western media followed in lock-step. The BBC, CNN, and *Die Welt* are among the most reckless and irresponsible.

The mountain of lies piled up by Western governments and media has obscured the true story. The US government orchestrated the overthrow of the elected government in Ukraine and imposed a US puppet in Kiev. Washington's puppet government began issuing threats and committing violent acts against the Russian populations in the former Russian territories that Soviet leaders attached to Ukraine. The Russian people in eastern and southern Ukraine resisted the threat brought to them by Washington's puppet government in Kiev.

Washington continually accuses the Russian government of supporting the people in the territories who have voted their separation from Ukraine. There would be no war, Washington alleges, except for Russian support. But, of course, Washington could easily stop the violence by ordering its puppet government in Kiev to stop the bombing and shelling of the former Russian provinces. If Russia can tell the "separatists" not to fight, Washington can tell Kiev not to fight.

The only possible conclusion from the facts is that Washington is determined to involve Europe in a war with Russia or at least in an armed standoff in order to break up Europe's political and economic relations with Russia.

Europe's leaders are going along with this because European countries, except for Charles de Gaulle's France, have not had independent foreign policies since the end of World War II. They follow Washington's lead and are well paid for doing so.

The inability of Europe to produce independent leadership dooms Russian President Putin's diplomacy to failure. If European capitals cannot make decisions independently of Washington, there is no scope for Putin's diplomacy.

Notice that the very day after Putin met with Washington's Ukrainian vassal in an effort to resolve the situation, the new lie of Russian invasion was issued in order to ensure that no good can come of the meeting in which Putin invested his time and energy.

Washington's only interest is in hegemony. Washington has no interest in resolving the situation that Washington itself created in order to bring discomfort and confusion to Russia. With the caveat that the situation could be resolved by Ukrainian economic collapse, otherwise the longer Putin waits to resolve the situation by force, the more difficult the task will be.

UKRAINE DISSOLVES

August 30, 2014

"Every time you come to Russia with a sword,
from a sword you will perish."

Washington's coup in Kiev has resulted in the dismemberment of Ukraine. First Crimea returned to Russia, and now the Donetsk and Luhansk regions are independent republics.

Donetsk and Luhansk, former Russian provinces which Soviet party leaders carelessly attached to Ukraine at a time when it seemed to make no difference as all were part of the Soviet Union, are now independent republics with their own governments. The West pretends that this isn't so, because Washington and its puppet capitals don't recognize the independence of formerly captive peoples. But the West's opinion no longer counts.

In the last couple of days the newly formed military units of the Donetsk National Republic have defeated and surrounded large portions of the remaining Ukrainian military. Russian President Putin asked the Donetsk Republic to allow the defeated Ukrainians to return home to their wives and mothers. The Donetsk Republic agreed to Putin's mercy request as long as the Ukrainians left their weapons behind.

The Donetsk Republic is short on weapons as, contrary to Western lies, the Donetsk Republic is not supplied with weapons by Russia.

Washington's puppet government in Kiev declined the mercy extended to its troops and said they had to fight to the death. Shades of Hitler at Stalingrad. Western Ukraine has remained the repository of Nazism since 1945, and it is Western Ukraine with which Washington is allied against self-determination, freedom and democracy.

Thanks to The Saker we are provided with a press conference with English subtitles that Alexander Zakharchenko, Chairman of the Council of Ministers of the Donetsk National Republic, held with media.

Present are Russian and Western press.

You will be impressed with the ease with which Zakharchenko handles the corrupt Western media representatives, and your sides will burst with laughter at his reply to the media question: "Are there regular Russian military units fighting on your side?"

The British and American journalists were the most stupid, as we already knew. You will die laughing at the response to the question, "why did you parade the prisoners?"

Zakharchenko puts to shame every politician in the US, Europe, Canada, Australia, Japan, all of the puppet politicians of the American Empire. If only the United States had people of the character and quality of Zakharchenko.

Now that Zakharchenko has revealed himself and made mincemeat of the ridiculous Western media, he will be demonized and misrepresented. So use this opportunity to see for yourself who has integrity and character. Hint: no one in political and media circles in the West.[91] You might have to put the video on full screen to read the subtitles.

Zakharchenko is amazed that the Western media is so incompetent that reporters are unable to discern what a Russian invasion of Ukraine would look like. Zakharchenko describes it for the idiot reporters

"If you think that Russia is sending its regular units here, then let me tell you something. If Russia was sending its regular troops, we wouldn't be talking about the battle of Elenovka here. We'd be talking about a battle of Kiev or a possible capture of Lvov."[92]

Lvov is in western Ukraine near the border with Poland. In other words, if Russia invades Ukraine, the fighting will move from the east side to the west side of the country.

Demitry Orlov also describes what a Russian invasion would look like:[93]

FORMER CIA OFFICIAL CALLS FOR PUTIN'S ASSASSINATION

September 2, 2014

Herbert E. Meyer, a nutcase who was a special assistant to the CIA director for a period during the Reagan administration, has penned an article calling for Russian President Putin's assassination. If we have "to get him out of the Kremlin feet-first with a bullet hole in the back of his head, that would be okay with us."[95]

As the crazed Meyer illustrates, the insanity that Washington has released upon the world knows no restraint. Jose Manuel Barroso, installed as Washington's puppet as European Commission President, misrepresented his recent confidential telephone conversation with Russia's President Putin by telling the media that Putin issued a threat: "If I want to, I can take Kiev in two weeks."

Clearly, Putin did not issue a threat. A threat would be inconsistent with Putin's entire unprovocative approach to the strategic threat that Washington and its NATO puppets have brought to Russia in Ukraine.

Russia's permanent representative to the EU, Vladimir Chizhov, said that if Barroso's lie stands, Russia will make public the full recording of the conversation.

Anyone familiar with the disparity between the Ukrainian and Russian militaries knows full well that it would take the Russian military 14 hours, not 14 days, to take all of Ukraine. Just remember what happened to the American and Israeli trained and equipped Georgian Army when Washington set its stupid Georgian puppets on South Ossetia. The American and Israeli trained and equipped Georgian army collapsed under Russian counterattack in 5 hours.

The lie that Washington's puppet Barroso told was not worthy of a serious person. But where in Europe is there a serious person in power? Nowhere. The few serious people are all out of power. Consider the NATO Secretary General, Anders Rasmussen. He was a prime minister of Denmark who saw he could rise beyond Denmark by serving as Washington's puppet. As prime minister he strongly supported Washington's illegal invasion of

202

Iraq, declaring that "we know that Saddam Hussein has weapons of mass destruction." Of course, the fool didn't know any such thing, and why would it matter if Iraq did have such weapons. Many countries have weapons of mass destruction.

According to the rule that anyone who serves Washington is elevated, the cipher Rasmussen was elevated.

The problem with elevating unprincipled fools is that they risk the world for their career. Rasmussen has now put the entirety of Eastern and Western Europe at risk of annihilation. Rasmussen has announced the creation of a blitzkrieg spearhead force capable of blitzkrieg attack on Russia. What Washington's puppet calls "the Readiness Action Plan" is justified as a response to "Russia's aggressive behavior in Ukraine."

Rasmussen's "lightening spearhead force" would be wiped out along with every European capital. What kind of idiot provokes a nuclear superpower in this way?

Rasmussen asserts "Russia's aggressive behavior" but has no evidence of it. Russia has stood on the sidelines while Washington's puppet government in Kiev has shelled and bombed civilian housing, hospitals, schools in eastern and southern Ukraine and issued a constant stream of lies against Russia.

Russia denied the requests of the now independent eastern and southern provinces of Ukraine, former Russian territories, to be reunited with Russia. As readers know, I regard Putin's decision as a mistake, but events might prove me wrong and that is OK with me. For now, the fact is that every act of aggressive behavior is the result of the US and EU support of the Kiev Nazis. It is the Ukrainian Nazi militias that are attacking civilians in the former Russian territories of eastern and southern Ukraine. A number of regular Ukrainian military units have defected to the independent republics.

Yes, Nazis. Western Ukraine is the home of the Ukrainian SS division that fought for Hitler. Today the militias organized by the Right Sector and other right-wing political organizations wear the Nazi insignia of the Ukrainian SS divisions. These are the people that Washington and the EU support. If the Ukrainian Nazis could win against Russia, which they cannot, they would turn on the West, just as has the Washington-funded ISIS that Washington unleashed on Libya and Syria. Now ISIS is remaking the Middle East, and Washington appears helpless.

William Binney, a former high level official in the US National Security Agency, and colleagues from the CIA and military intelligence services have written to German chancellor Merkel advising her to beware of Obama's lies at the upcoming NATO summit in Wales. The US intelligence officials advise Merkel to remember Iraq's "weapons of mass destruction" and don't again be deceived, this time into conflict with Russia.[96]

The question is: who does Merkel represent? Washington or Germany? So far Merkel has represented Washington, not German business interests, not the German people, and not Germany's interests as a country. Here is a protest in Dresden where a crowd prevents Merkel's speech with shouts of "kriegstreiber" (warmonger), "liar, liar," and "no war with Russia."[97]

My Ph.D. dissertation chairman, who became a high Pentagon official assigned to wind down the Vietnam War, in answer to my question about how Washington gets Europeans to always do what Washington wants, replied: "Money, we give them money." "Foreign aid?" I asked. "No, we give the European political leaders bagfuls of money. They are for sale, we bought them. They report to us."

Perhaps this explains Tony Blair's $50 million fortune one year out of office.

The Western media, the largest brothel on earth, is desperate for war. The editorial board of the *Washington Post*, now a trophy newspaper in the hands of Amazon.com's billionaire owner, ran an editorial on August 31 that projected all of Washington's (and the *Post*'s) lies upon Putin.

Amazon.com's owner might know how to market products on the Internet, but he is hopeless when it comes to running a newspaper. His editors at the *Washington Post* have made his trophy a worldwide laughing stock.

Here are the mindless accusations against Putin from the editors that the billionaire put in charge of his trophy newspaper in an editorial of today's date:

- Putin, bitterly resentful at the loss of power from the Soviet collapse, has "resurrected the tyranny of the Big Lie" in order to reconstitute the Russian Empire.
- "Russian sponsored militias in Ukraine" are responsible for the "shoot-down of the Malaysian airliner in July." The "Russian state-controlled media" lied and misrepresented to the Russian people the party responsible for downing the airliner.
- "In the absence of independent and free reporting, few Russians realize that Russian soldiers and armaments are in action in eastern Ukraine, albeit (as in Crimea) in uniforms and vehicles stripped of their identifying insignia and license plates. With no free media, Russians are left to fend for themselves against a firestorm of falsehoods."
- "Mr. Putin's Big Lie shows why it is important to support a free press where it still exists and outlets like Radio Free Europe that bring the truth to people who need it."

As a former *Wall Street Journal* editor, I can say with complete confidence that such extraordinary propaganda posing as an editorial would have resulted in the immediate firing of all concerned. In my days on the Congressional staff, the *Washington Post* was regarded as a CIA asset. Today the *Post* has sunk far below this status.

I have seen much media propaganda in my day, but this *Washington Post* editorial takes the cake. The editorial shows that either the editorial writers are completely ignorant or they are completely corrupt and also assume that their readers are completely ignorant. If Russian military units were in action in eastern Ukraine, the situation would be precisely as Alexander Zakharchenko and Dmitry Orlov describe.

Ukraine would no longer exist. Ukraine would again be part of Russia where it was for centuries prior to Washington taking advantage of the Soviet collapse to tear Ukraine away from Russia.

The question before us is: how long will Russia's patience last with the West's enormous lies and provocations? No matter how restrained Russia is, Russia is accused of the worst. Therefore, Russia might as well inflict the worst.

At what point will the Russian government decide that Washington's mendacity, and that of its European puppets and corrupt Western media, render hopeless Russia's efforts to resolve the situation with diplomacy and unprovocative behavior? As Russia is constantly accused falsely of invading Ukraine, when will the Russian government decide that as Western propaganda has established that Russia has invaded Ukraine and has imposed sanctions and new military bases on Russia's borders because of the alleged invasion, Russia might as well go ahead and rid themselves of the problem Washington has brought to Russia and invade Ukraine?

There is nothing that NATO could do about it if Russia decides that Ukraine in Washington's hands is too much of a strategic threat to Russia and reincorporates Ukraine again into Russia where it has resided for centuries. Any NATO force sent would start a war that NATO can't win. The German population, remembering the consequences of war with Russia, would overthrow Washington's puppet government.

NATO and the EU would collapse as Germany departed the absurd construct that serves Washington's interest at the expense of Europe.

Once this happens, the world will have peace. But not until.

For those who care to understand how the land of lies works, Washington's puppet government in Kiev attributes the defeat of its military forces by the Donetsk Republic to the presence in the Donetsk army of Russian military units. This is the propaganda that has gone out to western Ukraine and to the presstitute western media, a collection of whores that echo the propaganda without any investigation whatsoever.

In other words, Kiev is at war, which raises a problem for an IMF loan. The IMF lends for balance of payments problems. The IMF is not supposed to finance war or lend to countries involved in war or civil war because repayment is in doubt.

In the 21st century West, lawlessness has displaced charters, constitutions, and law. The IMF is not supposed to lend in support of government budget deficits. Regardless, the IMF became involved in the sovereign debt crisis in Europe. Now the IMF is a war financier.

The disregard of standards, mores, and legal, moral and behavioral norms is endemic in the West. The call by a former US government official for the assassination of the president of Russia exemplifies the West's descent into lawlessness and barbarism.

THE ROAD TO WAR
PAVED WITH
LIES

September 5, 2014

Official statements from the Russian government indicate that the president and foreign minister continue to rely on the good will of "our Western partners" to work out a reasonable diplomatic solution to the trouble in Ukraine caused by Washington. Not only is there no evidence of this good will in Western capitals, the hostile measures against Russia are increasing. Moreover, hostile measures are on the rise even though their main effect is to disadvantage Europe.

Francois Hollande, the socialist president of France, has followed Washington's orders and refused to deliver a ship that it owes to Russia under contract. The news reports are so incompetent that they do not say whether Russia has paid for the ship or whether payment was awaiting completion. If Russia has not already paid, then the failure to deliver will harm whoever financed the construction of the ship. If Russia has paid, then the idiot French president has placed France in violation of a contract and under international law France is subject to heavy financial penalties.

It is not clear how this hurts Russia. It is Russia's strategic nuclear force that the West has to fear, not a helicopter carrier. What Hollande has taught Russia is not to do business with France or any country in NATO.

Russia should promptly take the contract violation to court. Either France will be sanctioned with penalties that could exceed the value of the contract or the West will prove that in its hands international law is meaningless. If I were Russia, I would give up a helicopter ship in order to establish this point.

Marine Le Pen, the only leader France has, is not in power, although her support is growing. Le Pen says that Hollande's obedience to Obama "will have a huge cost for France: the lost of millions of working hours and a fine of 5 to 10 billion euro."

Hollande sought to justify his kowtowing to Washington with a lie:

"Russia's recent actions in the east of Ukraine contravene the fundamental principles of European security."

To the complete contrary. It is the stupid actions of Hollande, Chancellor Merkel, and Prime Minister Cameron who are endangering European security by enabling Washington's drive to war with Russia.

According to news reports for whatever they are worth, Washington and its EU puppet are preparing more sanctions against Russia. Considering the incompetence of Washington and the EU, it is unclear who will be bitten by the sanctions—Russia or Europe. The point is that Russia has done nothing to deserve any sanctions.

The sanctions are based on Washington's lie that, in Obama's words (September 3), "Russian combat forces with Russian weapons in Russian tanks" are deployed in eastern Ukraine. As Professor Michel Chossudovsky reports on Global Research, observers from the Organization for Security and Cooperation in Europe (OSCE) "have registered no troops, ammunition or weapons crossing the Russian-Ukrainian border over the past two weeks."

These passages are from Professor Chossudovsky's report on the OSCE findings:

> The OSCE Observer Mission is deployed at the Russian Checkpoints of Gukovo and Donetsk at the request of Russia's government. The decision was taken in a consensus agreement by all 57 OSCE participating States, many of which are represented at the NATO Summit in Wales.
>
> The OSCE report contradicts the statements made by the Kiev regime and its US-NATO sponsors. It confirms that NATO accusations pertaining to the influx of Russian tanks are an outright fabrication.
>
> NATO backed up Obama's statements with fake satellite images (28 August 2014) that allegedly 'show Russian combat forces engaged in military operations inside the sovereign territory of Ukraine'. These statements are refuted by a detailed report of the OSCE monitoring mission stationed at the Russia-Ukraine border. The NATO reports including its satellite photos were based on fake evidence.
>
> It is worth noting that the OSCE carefully categorizes movements across the border, which largely consist of refugees.

Just as Iraq, Afghanistan, and Libya were attacked on the basis of transparent lies and Syria and Iran were set up for attack on the basis of transparent lies, the sanctions against Russia rest solely on transparent lies. According to the UK *Telegraph*, the new sanctions will ban all Russian state-owned oil and defense companies from raising funds in European capital markets. In other words, any Western oil enterprises operating in Russia would be exempted.

One Russian response to sanctions should be to confiscate any Western firms operating in Russia as compensation for damages inflicted by the sanctions.

Another response is to obtain financing from China.

Another response is to self-finance energy and defense needs. If the US can print money in order to keep 4 or 5 mega-banks afloat, Russia can print money to finance its needs.

The lesson that Washington is teaching the larger part of the world is that a country has to be insane to do business with the West. The West views business as a hegemonic tool that is used to punish, exploit, and loot. It is astonishing that after so many lessons, countries still seek IMF loans. It is impossible not to know by now that an IMF loan has two purposes: the looting of the country by the West and the subordination of the country to Western hegemonic policy. Yet idiot governments still apply for IMF loans.

All of the escalation of the Ukrainian situation is caused by the US, EU, and Kiev. Apparently, Washington interprets Russia's low-key response as evidence that the Russian government is intimidated.

But when Putin holds all the cards and can wreck Europe by turning off the flow of natural gas and can reincorporate the entire Ukraine back into Russia in two weeks or less, how can Washington impose its will?

Is Russia so desperate to be part of the West that it will succumb to being another of Washington's puppet states?

THE UKRAINE CRISIS REMAINS UNRESOLVED

September 9, 2014

Some Western commentators interpret the ceasefire in Ukraine obtained by President Putin as a victory for Russia. The reasoning is that the ceasefire leaves Ukraine with disputed borders, which rules out Ukraine's membership in NATO.

But will the cease fire hold? The right-wing Kiev militias, whose members often wear Nazi insignias, are not under Kiev's complete control. These militias can easily violate the ceasefire, and there are already reports of violations. Moreover the billionaire oligarch that Washington has installed in Kiev as president of Ukraine will violate the ceasefire on Washington's orders, unless, of course, Putin has put the fear of God in him.

To a military strategist the passive Russian response to the trouble that Washington has caused Russia in Ukraine, longer a part of Russia than the US has existed, is a mystery. Russia lost Ukraine because of its weakness when the Soviet Union collapsed, and Washington forced Russia to permit an independent Ukraine, which served Washington's purpose of breaking up the Russian Federation.

The western Ukrainians, who fought for Hitler during World War II, maintained an impressive lobby organization in Washington and secured their independent country, but they did not control Ukraine because much of the country consists of former Russian territories made part of Ukraine by Soviet leaders in the 20th century.

Blood ties from intermarriage over centuries and tied economic interrelationships between Russia and Ukraine achieved over centuries essentially left Ukraine as part of Russia, where it has resided for centuries.

This frustrated the World Empire Neoconservatives, who have controlled the US government since the corrupt Clintons, whose regime brought Third World corruption into American political life. Remember

Robert Reich, Clinton's university friend and Secretary of Labor who resigned from Clinton's cabinet on principle. Clinton betrayed the constituency that elected him, as did Obama. Clinton's two-timed wife, allied with Zionist Israel, the banksters, and the military/security complex, is the Democrats' current favorite for their next presidential nominee.

As it was in Rome, dynasties are now the sources of US presidential leadership. And as it was in Rome, the US is on the path to destruction, which occurs when the ambitions of leaders take precedence over the fate of the country.

Keeping Ukraine out of NATO is no doubt a goal of the Russian government. However, the trouble that Washington brought to Russia in Ukraine—by orchestrating a coup, installing a puppet government, and unleashing violence against the residents of the former Russian territories that Soviet leaders attached to Ukraine—is being used for wider purposes than to incorporate Ukraine within NATO.

In other words, Washington's strategic goals go beyond NATO membership for Ukraine.

One goal is to break apart the economic and political relationships between Europe and Russia.

By using Ukraine to demonize Russia, Washington has pushed the European Union into imposing sanctions on Russia that disrupt the trade relationships and create distrust.

The distrust serves Washington's purpose. Washington has demonstrated to Russia that Washington's bought and-paid-for European politicians are unwilling to have foreign policies independent of Washington's. Europe's lack of an independent policy means that the Russian government is hampered in its use of diplomacy.

Another Washington goal is to build up military forces on Russia's borders. NATO has used the "crisis" to stoke fear of Russia in the Baltics and in Poland. Washington and NATO generals speak of Russian attacks as if it is a foregone conclusion that Russia intends to invade Eastern Europe. To protect against the "Russian threat," NATO has created a "quick reaction force" and is building up supplies of military equipment and new bases on Russia's borders. Whatever the outcome in Ukraine, Washington has used Ukraine to start a new Cold War.

The Western presstitute media, a collection of government propagandists, has misrepresented the situation in Ukraine from the beginning. In place of news coverage, there has been propaganda against Russia. Consequently, Western peoples who rely on the media are misinformed about Ukraine and place all blame on Russia. The fact that the American people are misinformed makes it easy for Washington to continue to orchestrate events to Russia's disadvantage.

Washington has no interest in resolving the troubles in Ukraine. Washington has successfully used Ukraine to create fear of Russia both in Europe and in the United States. Washington has successfully used Ukraine to damage European-Russian economic and political relations, and Washington has succeeded in starting a new Cold War that will keep profits flowing into the US military/security complex.

As the Kiev government is Washington's puppet, there is no reason to expect a resolution of the conflict that Washington brought to Ukraine and to Russia.

It is not only Washington that rejects a resolution of the Ukrainian difficulties created by Washington, but also the EU. Washington's puppet, Herman Van Rompuy, President of the Washington front group—the European Council—announced, if news reports are correct, which they seldom are, that the European Union is imposing sanctions on the Russian energy firms Rosneft, Gazpromneft and Transneft as well as state-run companies with turnover of more than $27 billion a year.

The Russian response to this audacity should be to turn off the gas in the winter without warning.

All of it. As Putin's interest is to separate Europe from Washington's control, this would do it. All of East and West Europe and Ukraine would be on their knees in Moscow begging for the energy to be turned back on. All Putin would have to say is "only non-NATO members get gas."

That would bring an end to Washington's assault on Russia.

The American neoconservatives, a deranged cadre of warmongers, are denouncing Obama for "weakness" for not sending troops to Ukraine. The neocons, who have involved the US since the Clinton regime in costly and failed US military aggressions abroad, claim that Obama's leadership has resulted in NATO losing its will and its muscle.

It remains for the Russian government to demonstrate that all muscle over Ukraine and Europe resides in Moscow.

9/11
AFTER
13 YEARS

September 10, 2014

The tragedy of September 11, 2001, goes far beyond the deaths of those who died in the towers and the deaths of firefighters and first responders who succumbed to illnesses caused by inhalation of toxic dust.

For thirteen years a new generation of Americans has been born into the 9/11 myth that has been used to create the American warfare/police state.

The corrupt Bush and Obama regimes used 9/11 to kill, maim, dispossess and displace millions of Muslims in seven countries, none of whom had anything whatsoever to do with 9/11.

A generation of Americans has been born into disdain and distrust of Muslims.

A generation of Americans has been born into a police state in which privacy and constitutional protections no longer exist.

A generation of Americans has been born into continuous warfare while needs of citizens go unmet.

A generation of Americans has been born into a society in which truth is replaced with the endless repetition of falsehoods.

According to the official story, on September 11, 2001, the vaunted National Security State of the World's Only Superpower was defeated by a few young Saudi Arabians armed only with box cutters. The American National Security State proved to be totally helpless and was dealt the greatest humiliation ever inflicted on any country claiming to be a power.

That day no aspect of the National Security State worked. Everything failed.

The US Air Force for the first time in its history could not get intercepter jet fighters into the air.

The National Security Council failed.

All sixteen US intelligence agencies failed as did those of America's NATO and Israeli allies.

213

Air Traffic Control failed.

Airport Security failed four times at the same moment on the same day.

The probability of such a failure is zero. If such a thing had actually happened, there would have been demands from the White House, from Congress, and from the media for an investigation. Officials would have been held accountable for their failures. Heads would have rolled.

Instead, the White House resisted for one year the 9/11 families' demands for an investigation. Finally, a collection of politicians was assembled to listen to the government's account and to write it down. The chairman, vice chairman, and legal counsel of the 9/11 Commission have said that information was withheld from the commission, lies were told to the commission, and that the commission "was set up to fail." The worst security failure in history resulted in not a single firing. No one was held responsible.

Washington concluded that 9/11 was possible because America lacked a police state.

The PATRIOT Act, which was awaiting the event, was quickly passed by Congress. The Act established executive branch independence of law and the Constitution. The Act and follow-up measures have institutionalized a police state in "the land of the free."

Osama bin Laden, originally a CIA asset then dying of renal failure, was blamed despite his explicit denial. For the next ten years Osama bin Laden was the bogyman that provided the excuse for Washington to kill countless numbers of Muslims.

Then suddenly on May 2, 2011, Obama claimed that US Navy SEALs had killed bin Laden in Pakistan.

Eyewitnesses on the scene contradicted the White House's story. Osama bin Laden became the only human in history to survive renal failure for ten years. There was no dialysis machine in what was said to be bin Laden's hideaway. The numerous obituaries of bin Laden's death in December 2001 (see my book, *How America Was Lost*) went down the memory hole. And the SEAL unit that supplied the team died a few weeks later in a mysterious helicopter crash in Afghanistan. The thousands of sailors on the aircraft carrier from which bin Laden was said to have been dumped into the Indian Ocean wrote home that no such burial took place.

The fairy tale story of bin Laden's murder by Seal Team Six served to end the challenge by disappointed Democrats to Obama's nomination for a second term. It also freed the "war on terror" from the bin Laden constraint. Washington wanted to attack Libya, Syria, and Iran, countries in which bin Laden was known not to have organizations, and the succession of faked bin Laden videos, in which bin Laden grew progressively younger as the fake bin Laden claimed credit for each successive attack, had lost credibility among experts.

Watching the twin towers and WTC 7 come down, it was obvious to me that the buildings were not falling down as a result of structural damage. When it became clear that the White House had blocked an independent investigation of the only three steel skyscrapers in world history to collapse as a result of low temperature office fires, it was apparent that there was a cover-up.

After 13 years people at home and abroad find the government's story less believable. The case made by independent experts is now so compelling that mainstream media has opened to it. Richard Gage of Architects & Engineers for 9/11 Truth addresses the issue on C-SPAN.[98]

After years of persistence a group in New York has secured the necessary number of valid signatures to put on the ballot a vote to investigate the cause of the collapse of the three WTC buildings. The official account, if correct, means that existing fire and building codes are insufficient to protect the public and that all other steel high rise structures are subject to the same failure. The group has been clever to frame the issue in terms of public safety and not in terms of 9/11 truth.

New York authorities, of course, continue to oppose the initiative. The question now rests on a judge's ruling. It is difficult to imagine a judge going against the government in such a major way, *but the group will have made the point that the government has no confidence in the truth of its own story.*

Over these 13 years, physicists, chemists, architects, engineers, and first responders have provided massive evidence that completely disproves the official account of the failure of the three skyscrapers.

The response to experts has been for non-experts to call experts "conspiracy theorists." In other words, the defenders of the government's story have no scientific or factual basis on which to stand. So they substitute name-calling.

9/11 was used to fundamentally alter the nature of the US government and its relationship to the American people. Unaccountable executive power has replaced due process and the checks and balances established by the US Constitution. In the name of National Security, executive power knows no restraints.

Essentially, Americans today have no rights if the government targets them.

Those Americans born after 9/11 were born into a different country from the rest of us. Having never experienced constitutional government, they will not know what they have lost.

The anthrax attacks of October 2001 have been forgotten, but Professor Graeme MacQueen in *The 2001 Anthrax Deception* (Clarity Press, 2014) shows that the anthrax attacks played an essential role in setting the stage for the government's acquisition of unaccountable police state power. Two Democratic Senate committee chairmen, Thomas Daschle and Patrick Leahy, were disturbed by the Bush regime's overreach for carte blanche power, and were in a position to block the coming police state legislation and the ability of the executive branch alone to take America to war.

Both senators received anthrax letters, as did major news organizations. The TV network news anchors, such as Dan Rather, who compared the collapse of WTC skyscrapers to buildings brought down by controlled demolition, had not yet been fired by Republicans on framed-up charges.

Initially, the anthrax letters, which caused the deaths of some USPS employees, were seen as the second stage of the 9/11 attack. Fear multiplied. The senators and media shut up. Then it was discovered that the anthrax was a unique kind produced only by a US government military facility.

The response to this monkey wrench thrown into the government's propaganda, was the FBI's frame-up of a dead man, Bruce Edwards Ivins, who had been employed in the military lab that produced the anthrax and was driven to suicide by the false charges. The dead man's colleagues did not believe one word of the government's false story, and nothing in the dead man's past indicated any motive or instability that would have led him to such a deed.

Initially, the US government tried to frame up Steven Jay Hatfill, but despite the best efforts of *The New York Times* and Nicholas Kristof the attempt to frame Hatfill failed. Hatfill received $5 million from the US government for the false accusation that ruined his life. So the corrupt US government moved on to Ivins.

Ivins was dead and couldn't defend himself, but his colleagues did.

The anthrax episode stinks to high heaven. In April 2015 Richard Lambert, the FBI agent in charge of the anthrax investigation, filed suit in federal court. In the court filing Lambert says that as the agent in charge of the anthrax investigation he was obstructed and impeded in his investigation for four years by the FBI's Washington Field Office, by apathy and error from the FBI Laboratory, by erroneous legal decisions, and by politically motivated communication embargoes from FBI Headquarters.[99]

Most Americans are unaware of the extent to which the federal government owns the experts who can contradict its fairy tales. For example, no competent physicist can possibly believe the official story of the destruction of the three WTC buildings. But physics departments in US universities are heavily dependent on federal money. Any physicist who speaks his mind jeopardizes not only his own career but also the career of all of his colleagues. Physicist Steven Jones, who first pointed to the use of thermite in the destruction of the two towers, had to agree to having his university buy out his tenure or his university was faced with losing all federal financing.

The same constraints operate in the private sector. High rise architects and structural engineers who express doubts about the official explanation of the collapse of three skyscrapers are viewed by potential clients as Muslim apologists and conspiracy kooks. The clients, of course, have no expert knowledge with which to assess the issue, but they are indoctrinated with ceaseless, endless, repetition that 9/11 was Osama bin Laden's attack on America. Their indoctrination makes them immune to facts.

The 9/11 lie has persisted for 13 years. Millions of Muslims have paid for this lie with their lives, the destruction of their families, and with their dislocation. Most Americans remain comfortable with the fact that their government has destroyed in whole or part seven countries based on a lie Washington told to cover up an inside job that launched the crazed neoconservatives' drive for Washington's World Empire.[100]

WASHINGTON'S WAR AGAINST RUSSIA

September 14, 2014

The new sanctions against Russia announced by Washington and Europe do not make sense as merely economic measures. I would be surprised if Russian oil and military industries were dependent on European capital markets in a meaningful way. Such a dependence would indicate a failure in Russian strategic thinking. The Russian companies should be able to secure adequate financing from Russian Banks or from the Russian government. If foreign loans are needed, Russia can borrow from China.

If critical Russian industries are dependent on European capital markets, the sanctions will help Russia by forcing an end to this debilitating dependence. Russia should not be dependent on the West in any way.

The real question is the purpose of the sanctions. My conclusion is that the purpose of the sanctions is to break up and undermine Europe's economic and political relations with Russia. When international relations are intentionally undermined, war can be the result. Washington will continue to push sanctions against Russia until Russia shows Europe that there is a heavy cost for serving as Washington's tool.

Russia needs to break up this process of ever more sanctions in order to derail the drive toward war. In my opinion this is easy for Russia to do. Russia can tell Europe that since you do not like our oil companies, you must not like our gas company, so we are turning off the gas. Or Russia can tell Europe, we don't sell natural gas to NATO members, or Russia can say we will continue to sell you gas, but you must pay in rubles, not in dollars. This would have the additional benefit of increasing the demand for rubles in exchange markets, thus making it harder for speculators and the US government to drive down the ruble.

The real danger to Russia is a continuation of its low-key, moderate response to the sanctions. This is a response that encourages more sanctions. To stop the sanctions, Russia needs to show Europe that the sanctions have serious costs for Europe.

A Russian response to Washington would be to stop selling to the US the Russian rocket engines on which the US satellite program is dependent. This could leave the US without rockets for its satellites for six years between the period 2016 and 2022.

Possibly the Russian government is worried about losing the earnings from gas and rocket engine sales.

However, Europe cannot do without the gas and would quickly abandon its participation in the sanctions, so no gas revenues would be lost. The Americans are going to develop their own rocket engine anyhow, so the Russian sales of rocket engines to the US have at most about 6 more years. But the US with an impaired satellite program for six years would mean a great relief to the entire world from the American spy program. It would also make difficult US military aggression against Russia during the period.

Russian President Putin and his government have been very low-key and unprovocative in responding to the sanctions and to the trouble that Washington continues to cause for Russia in Ukraine. The low-key Russian behavior can be understood as a strategy for undermining Washington's use of Europe against Russia by presenting a non-threatening face to Europe. However, another explanation is the presence inside Russia of a fifth column that represents Washington's interest and constrains the power of the Russian government.

Donetsk leader Igor Strelkov describes the American fifth column.[103]

The Saker describes the two power groups inside Russia as the Eurasian Sovereignists who stand behind Putin and an independent Russia and the Atlantic Integrationists, the fifth column that works to incorporate Russia in Europe under US hegemony or, failing that, to help Washington break up the Russian Federation into several weaker countries that are too weak to constrain Washington's use of power.[104]

Russia's Atlantic Integrationists share the Brzezinski and Wolfowitz doctrines with Washington. These doctrines are the basis for US foreign policy. The doctrines define the goal of US foreign policy in terms of preventing the rise of other countries, such as Russia and China, that could limit Washington's hegemony.

Washington is in a position to exploit the tensions between these two Russian power groups.

Washington's fifth column is not best positioned to prevail. However, Washington can at least count on the struggle causing dissent within the Eurasian Sovereignists over Putin's low-key response to Western provocations. Some of this dissent can be seen in Strelkov's defense of Russia and more can be seen online.[105] Russia, thinking the Cold War ended with the collapse of the Soviet Union, opened herself to the West.

Russian governments trusted the West, and as a result of Russia's gullibility, the West was able to purchase numerous allies among the Russian elites. Depending on the alignment of the media, these compromised elites are capable of assassinating Putin and attempting a coup.

One would think that by now Putin's government would recognize the danger and arrest the main elements of the fifth column, followed by trial and execution for treason, in order that Russia can stand united against the Western Threat. If Putin does not take this step, it means either than Putin does not recognize the extent of the threat or that his government lacks the power to protect Russia from the internal threat.

It is clear that Putin has not achieved any respite for his government from the West's propaganda and economic assault by refusing to defend the Donbass area from Ukrainian attack and by pressuring the Donetsk Republic into a ceasefire when its military forces were on the verge of a major defeat of the disintegrating Ukrainian army. All Putin has achieved is to open himself to criticism among his supporters for betraying the Russians in eastern and southern Ukraine.

The European politicians and elites are so deeply in Washington's pocket that Putin has little chance of courting Europe with a Russian show of good will. I have never believed that this strategy could work, although I would be pleased if it did. Only a direct threat to deprive Europe of energy has a chance of producing within Europe a foreign policy independent of Washington. I do not think Europe can survive a cutoff of the Russian natural gas. Europe would abandon sanctions in order to guarantee the flow of gas.

If Washington's hold on Europe is so powerful that Europe is willing to endure a major disruption of its energy supply as the price of its vassalage, Russia will know to cease its futile attempts at diplomacy and to prepare for war.

If China sits on the sidelines, China will be the next isolated target and will receive the same treatment.

Washington intends to defeat both countries, either through internal dissent or through war.

Nothing said by Obama or any member of his government or any influential voice in Congress has signaled any pullback in Washington's drive for hegemony over the world.

The US economy is now dependent on looting and plunder, and Washington's hegemony is essential to this corrupted form of capitalism.

HOW MUCH PATIENCE
CAN RUSSIA AND
CHINA AFFORD?

September 25, 2014

Obama's September 24 speech at the UN is the most absurd thing I have heard in my entire life. It is absolutely amazing that the president of the United States would stand before the entire world and tell what everyone knows are blatant lies while simultaneously demonstrating Washington's double standards and belief that Washington alone, because the US is exceptional and indispensable, has the right to violate all law.

It is even more amazing that every person present did not get up and walk out of the assembly.

The diplomats of the world actually sat there and listened to blatant lies from the world's worst terrorist.

They even clapped their approval.

The rest of the speech was self-congratulatory platitudes: "We stand at a crossroads," "signposts of progress," "reduced chance of war between major powers," "hundreds of millions lifted from poverty," and while ebola ravages Africa "we've learned how to cure disease and harness the power of the wind and the sun." We are now God. "We" is comprised of the "exceptional people"—Americans. No one else counts. "We" are it.

It is impossible to pick the most absurd statement in Obama's speech or the most outrageous lie. Is it this one? "Russian aggression in Europe recalls the days when large nations trampled small ones in pursuit of territorial ambition." This is precisely what Washington has been doing in the Middle East and Africa in the 21st century.

Or is it this one? "After the people of Ukraine mobilized popular protests and calls for reform, their corrupt president fled. Against the will of the government in Kiev, Crimea was annexed. Russia poured arms into eastern Ukraine, fueling violent separatists and a conflict that has killed thousands. When a civilian airliner was shot down from areas that these proxies controlled, they refused to allow access to the crash for days. When Ukraine started to reassert control over its territory, Russia gave up the pretense of merely supporting the separatists, and moved troops across the border."

The entire world knows that Washington overthrew the elected Ukrainian government, that Washington refuses to release its satellite photos of the destruction of the Malaysian airliner, that Ukraine refuses to release its air traffic control instructions to the airliner, that Washington has prevented a real investigation of the airliner's destruction, that European experts on the scene have testified that both sides of the airliner's cockpit demonstrate machine gun fire, an indication that the airliner was shot down by the Ukrainian jets that were following it. Indeed, there has been no explanation why Ukrainian jets were close on the heels of an airliner directed by Ukrainian air traffic control.

The entire world knows that if Russia had territorial ambitions, when the Russian military defeated the American trained and supplied Georgian army that attacked South Ossetia, Russia would have kept Georgia and reincorporated it within Russia where it resided for centuries.

Notice that it is not aggression when Washington bombs and invades seven countries in 13 years without a declaration of war. Aggression occurs when Russia accepts the petition of Crimeans who voted 97 percent in favor of reuniting with Russia where Crimea resided for centuries before Khrushchev attached it to the Soviet Socialist Republic of Ukraine in 1954 when Ukraine and Russia were part of the same country.

And the entire world knows that, as the separatist leader of the Donetsk Republic said, "If Russian military units were fighting with us, the news would not be the fall of Mariupol but the fall of Kiev and Lviv."

Which is "the cancer of violent extremism"—ISIS which cut off the heads of four journalists, or Washington which has bombed seven countries in the 21st century, murdering hundreds of thousands of civilians and displacing millions?

Who is the worst terrorist—ISIS, a group that is redrawing the artificial boundaries created by British and French colonialists, or Washington with its Wolfowitz Doctrine, the basis of US foreign policy, which declares Washington's dominant objective to be US hegemony over the world?

ISIS is the creation of Washington. ISIS consists of the jihadists Washington used to overthrow Gaddafi in Libya and then sent to Syria to overthrow Assad. If ISIS is a "network of death," a "brand of evil" with which negotiation is impossible as Obama declares, it is a network of death created by the Obama regime itself. If ISIS poses the threat that Obama claims, how can the regime that created the threat be credible in leading the fight against it?

Obama never mentioned in his speech the central problem that the world faces. That problem is Washington's inability to accept the existence of strong independent countries such as Russia and China.

The neoconservative Wolfowitz Doctrine commits the United States to maintaining its status as the sole Uni-power. This task requires Washington "to prevent any hostile power from dominating a region whose resources would, under consolidated control, be sufficient to generate global power." A "hostile power" is any country that has sufficient power or influence to be able to limit Washington's exercise of power.

The Wolfowitz Doctrine explicitly targets Russia: "Our first objective is to prevent the re-emergence of a new rival, either on the territory of the former Soviet Union or elsewhere." A "rival" is defined as any country capable of defending its interests or those of allies against Washington's hegemony.

In his speech, Obama told Russia and China that they can be part of Washington's world order on the condition that they accept Washington's hegemony and do not interfere in any way with Washington's control. When Obama tells Russia that the US will cooperate with Russia "if Russia changes course," Obama means that Moscow must accept the primacy of Washington's interest over Russia's own interest.

Clearly, this is an inflexible and unrealistic position. If Washington keeps to it, war with Russia and China will ensue.

Obama told China that Washington intended to continue to be a Pacific power in China's sphere of influence, "promoting peace, stability, and the free flow of commerce among nations" by building new US air and naval bases from the Philippines to Vietnam so that Washington can control the flow of resources in the South China Sea and cut off China at will.

As far as I can tell, neither the Russian nor Chinese governments sufficiently understand the seriousness of the threat that Washington represents. Washington's claim to world hegemony seems too farfetched to Russia and China to be real. But it is very real.

By refusing to take the threat seriously, Russia and China have not responded in ways that would bring an end to the threat without the necessity of war.

For example, the Russian government could most likely destroy NATO by responding to sanctions imposed by Washington and the EU by informing European governments that Russia does not sell natural gas to members of NATO. Instead of using this power, Russia has foolishly allowed the EU to accumulate record amounts of stored natural gas to see homes and industry through the coming winter.

Has Russia sold out its national interests for money?

Much of Washington's power and financial hegemony rests on the role of the US dollar as world reserve currency. Russia and China have been slow, even negligent from the standpoint of defending their sovereignty, to take advantage of opportunities to undermine this pillar of Washington's power. For example, the BRICS' talk of abandoning the dollar payments system has been more talk than action.

Russia doesn't even require Washington's European puppet states to pay for Russian natural gas in rubles.

One might think that a country such as Russia experiencing such extreme hostility and demonization from the West would at least use the gas sales to support its own currency instead of Washington's dollar. If the Russian government is going to continue to support the economies of European countries hostile to Russia and to prevent the European peoples from freezing during the coming winter, shouldn't Russia in exchange for this extraordinary subsidy to its enemies at least arrange to support its own currency by demanding payment in rubles? Unfortunately for Russia, Russia is infected with Western trained neoliberal economists who represent Western, not Russian, interests.

When the West sees such extraordinary weakness on the part of the Russian government, Obama knows he can go to the UN and tell the most blatant lies about Russia with no cost whatsoever to the US or Europe. Russian inaction subsidizes Russia's demonization.

China has been no more successful than Russia in using its opportunities to destabilize Washington. For example, it is a known fact, as Dave Kranzler and I have repeatedly demonstrated, that the Federal Reserve uses its bullion bank agents to knock down the gold price in order to protect the dollar's value from the Federal Reserve's policies. The method used is for the bullion banks to drive down the gold price with enormous amounts of naked shorts during periods of low or nonexistent volume.

China or Russia or both could take advantage of this tactic by purchasing every naked short sold plus all covered shorts, if any, and demanding delivery instead of settling the contracts in cash. Neither New York Comex nor the London market could make delivery, and the system would implode. The consequence of the failure to deliver possibly could be catastrophic for the Western financial system, but in the least it would demonstrate the corrupt nature of Western financial institutions.

Or China could deal a more lethal blow. Choosing a time of heightened concern or disruptions in US financial markets, China could dump its trillion dollar plus holdings of US treasuries, or indeed all its holdings of US financial instruments, on the market. The Federal Reserve and the US Treasury could try to stabilize the prices of US financial instruments by creating money with which to purchase the bonds and other instruments. This money creation would increase concern about the dollar's value, and at that point China could dump the trillion dollars plus it receives from its bond sales on the exchange market.

The Federal Reserve cannot print foreign currencies with which to buy up the dollars. The dollar's exchange value would collapse and with it the dollar's use as world reserve currency. The US would become just another broke country unable to pay for its imports.

Possibly, Washington could get Japan and the European Central Bank to print enough yen and euros to buy up the dumped dollars. However, the likelihood is that this would bring down the yen and euro along with the dollar.

Flight would occur into the Chinese and Russian currencies, and financial hegemony would depart the West.

By their restraint, Russia and China enable Washington's attack upon them. Last week Washington put thousands of its NGO operatives into the Moscow streets protesting "Putin's war against Ukraine."

Foolishly, Russia has permitted foreign interests to buy up its newspapers, and these interests continually denounce Putin and the Russian government to their Russian readers.

Did Russia sell its soul and communication system for dollars? Did a few oligarchs sell out Russia for Swiss and London bank deposits?

Both Russia and China have Muslim populations among whom the CIA operates encouraging disassociation, rebellion, and violence. Washington intends to break up the Russian Federation into smaller, weaker countries that could not stand in the way of Washington's hegemony. Russian and Chinese fear of discord among their own Muslim populations has caused both governments to make the extremely serious strategic mistake of aligning with Washington against ISIS and with Washington's policy of protecting Washington's status quo in the Muslim world.

If Russia and China understood the deadly threat that Washington presents, both governments would operate according to the time honored principle that "the enemy of my enemy is my friend." Russia and China would arm ISIS with surface to air missiles to bring down the American planes and with military intelligence in order to achieve an American defeat. With defeat would come the overthrow of Saudi Arabia, Bahrain, Qatar, the United Arab Emirates, Jordan, Egypt and all of the American puppet rulers in the area. Washington would lose control over oil, and the petro-dollar would be history. It is extraordinary that instead Russia and China are working to protect Washington's control over the Middle East and the petro-dollar.

China is subject to a variety of attacks. The Rockefeller Foundation creates American agents in Chinese universities, or so I am informed by Chinese academics. American companies that locate in China create Chinese boards on which they place the relatives of local and regional party officials. This shifts loyalty from the central government to the American money. Moreover, China has many economists educated in the US who are imbued with the neoliberal economics that represents Washington's interests.

Both Russia and China have significant percentages of their populations who wish to be western. The failure of communism in both countries and the success of American Cold War propaganda have created loyalties to America in place of their own governments. In Russia they go by the designation "Atlanticist Integrationists." They are Russians who wish to be integrated into the West. I know less about the Chinese counterpart, but among youth Western materialism and lack of sexual restraint is appealing.

The inability of the Russian and Chinese governments to come to terms with the threat posed to their existence as sovereign countries by the neoconservative insistence on American world hegemony makes nuclear war more likely. If Russia and China catch on too late in the game, their only alternative will be war or submission to Washington's hegemony. As there is no possibility of the US and NATO invading and occupying Russia and China, the war would be nuclear.

To avoid this war, which, as so many experts have shown, would terminate life on earth, the Russian and Chinese governments must soon become far more realistic in their assessment of the evil that resides in what Washington has turned into the world's worst terrorist state—the US.

It is possible that Russia, China, and the rest of the world will be saved by American economic collapse.

The US economy is a house of cards. Real median family incomes are in long-term decline. Universities produce graduates with degrees and heavy debts but no jobs. The bond market is rigged by the Federal Reserve which necessitates rigging the bullion markets in order to protect the dollar. The stock market is rigged by the outpouring of money from the Federal Reserve, by the Plunge Protection Team, and by corporations repurchasing their own stock. The dollar is supported by tradition, habit, and currency swaps.

The American House of Cards continues to stand only as a result of the tolerance of the world for vast corruption and disinformation and because greed is satisfied by the money made from a rigged system.

Russia and/or China could pull down this House of Cards whenever either country or both had leadership capable of it.

WASHINGTON'S SECRET AGENDAS

One might think that by now even Americans would have caught on to the constant stream of false alarms that Washington sounds in order to deceive the people into supporting its hidden agendas.

The public fell for the lie that the Taliban in Afghanistan are terrorists allied with al Qaeda. Americans fought a war for 13 years that enriched former US vice president Dick Cheney's firm, Halliburton, and other private interests only to end in another Washington failure.

The public fell for the lie that Saddam Hussein in Iraq had "weapons of mass destruction" that were a threat to America and that if the US did not invade Iraq Americans risked a "mushroom cloud going up over an American city." With the rise of ISIS, this long war apparently is far from over. Billions of dollars more in profits will pour into the coffers of the US military security complex as Washington fights those who are redrawing the false Middle East boundaries created by the British and French after WW I when the British and French seized territories of the former Ottoman Empire.

The American public fell for the lies told about Gaddafi in Libya. The formerly stable and prosperous country is now in chaos.

The American public fell for the lie that Iran has, or is building, nuclear weapons. Sanctioned and reviled by the West, Iran has shifted toward an Eastern orientation, thereby removing a principal oil producer from Western influence.

The public fell for the lie that Assad of Syria used "chemical weapons against his own people." The jihadists that Washington sent to overthrow Assad have turned out to be, according to Washington's propaganda, a threat to America.

The greatest threat to the world is Washington's insistence on its hegemony. The ideology of a handful of neoconservatives is the basis for this insistence. We face the situation in which a handful of American neoconservative psychopaths claim to determine the fate of countries.

Many still believe Washington's lies, but increasingly the world sees Washington as the greatest threat to peace and life on earth. The claim that America is "exceptional and indispensable" is used to justify Washington's right to dictate to other countries.

The casualties of Washington's bombings are invariably civilians, and the deaths will produce more recruits for ISIS. Already there are calls for Washington to reintroduce "boots on the ground" in Iraq.

Otherwise, Western civilization is doomed, and our heads will be cut off. The newly created propaganda of a "Russian threat" requires more NATO spending and more military bases on Russia's borders. A "quick reaction force" is being created to respond to a nonexistent threat of a Russian invasion of the Baltics, Poland, and Europe.

Usually it takes the American public a year, or two, three, or four to realize that it has been deceived by lies and propaganda, but by that time the public has swallowed a new set of lies and propaganda and is all concerned about the latest "threat." The American public seems incapable of understanding that just as the first, second, third, fourth, and fifth, threat was a hoax, so is the sixth threat, and so will be the seventh, eighth, and ninth.

Moreover, none of these American military attacks on other countries has resulted in a better situation, as Vladimir Putin honestly states. Yet, the public and its representatives in Congress support each new military adventure despite the record of deception and failure.

Perhaps if Americans were taught their true history in place of idealistic fairy tales, they would be less gullible and less susceptible to government propaganda. I have recommended Oliver Stone and Peter Kuznick's *The Untold History of the United States*, Howard Zinn's *A People's History of the United States*, and now I recommend Stephen Kinzer's *The Brothers*, the story of the long rule of John Foster and Allen Dulles over the State Department and CIA and their demonization of reformist governments that they often succeeded in overthrowing. Kinzer's history of the Dulles brothers' plots to overthrow six governments provides insight into how Washington operates today.

In 1953 the Dulles brothers overthrew Iran's elected leader, Mossadegh and imposed the Shah, thus poisoning American-Iranian relations through the present day. Americans might yet be led into a costly and pointless war with Iran, because of the Dulles brothers poisoning of relations in 1953.

The Dulles brothers overthrew Guatemala's popular president Arbenz, because his land reform threatened the interest of the Dulles brothers' Sullivan & Cromwell law firm's United Fruit Company client. The brothers launched an amazing disinformation campaign depicting Arbenz as a dangerous communist who was a threat to Western civilization. The brothers enlisted dictators such as Somoza in Nicaragua and Batista in Cuba against Arbenz. The CIA organized air strikes and an invasion force. But nothing could happen until Arbenz's strong support among the people in Guatemala could be shattered. The brothers arranged this through Cardinal Spellman, who enlisted Archbishop Rossell y Arellano. "A pastoral letter was read on April 9, 1954 in all Guatemalan churches."

A masterpiece of propaganda, the pastoral letter misrepresented Arbenz as a dangerous communist who was the enemy of all Guatemalans. False radio broadcasts produced a fake reality of freedom fighter victories and army defections. Arbenz asked the UN to send fact finders, but Washington prevented that from happening. American journalists, with the exception of James Reston, supported the lies.

Washington threatened and bought off Guatemala's senior military commanders, who forced Arbenz to resign. The CIA's chosen and well paid "liberator," Col. Castillo Armas, was installed as Arbenz's successor.

We recently witnessed a similar operation in Ukraine.

President Eisenhower thanked the CIA for averting "a Communist beachhead in our hemisphere," and Secretary of State John Foster Dulles gave a national TV and radio address in which he declared that the events in Guatemala "expose the evil purpose of the Kremlin." This despite the uncontested fact that the only outside power operating in Guatemala was the Dulles brothers.

What had really happened is that a democratic and reformist government was overthrown because it compensated United Fruit Company for the nationalization of the company's fallow land at a value listed by the company on its tax returns. America's leading law firm or perhaps more accurately, America's foreign policy-maker, Sullivan & Cromwell, had no intention of permitting a democratic government to prevail over the interests of the law firm's client, especially when senior partners of the firm controlled both overt and covert US foreign policy. The two brothers, whose family members were invested in the United Fruit Company, simply applied the resources of the CIA, State Department, and US media to the protection of their private interests. The extraordinary gullibility of the American people, the corrupt American media, and the indoctrinated and impotent Congress allowed the Dulles brothers to succeed in overthrowing a democracy.

Keep in mind that this use of the US government in behalf of private interests occurred 60 years ago, long before the corrupt Clinton, George W. Bush, and Obama regimes. And no doubt in earlier times as well.

The Dulles brothers next intended victim was Ho Chi Minh. Ho, a nationalist leader, asked for America's help in freeing Vietnam from French colonial rule. But John Foster Dulles, a self-righteous anticommunist, miscast Ho as a Communist Threat who was springing the domino theory on the

Western innocents. Nationalism and anti-colonialism, Foster declared, were merely a cloak for communist subversion.

Paul Kattenburg, the State Department desk officer for Vietnam, suggested that instead of war, the US should give Ho $500 million in reconstruction aid to rebuild the country from war and French misrule, which would free Ho from dependence on Russian and Chinese support, and, thereby, influence. Ho appealed to Washington several times, but the demonic inflexibility of the Dulles brothers prevented any sensible response. Instead, the hysteria whipped-up over the "communist threat" by the Dulles brothers landed the United States in the long, costly, fiasco known as the Vietnam War. Kattenburg later wrote that it was suicidal for the US "to cut out its eyes and ears, to castrate its analytic capacity, to shut itself off from the truth because of blind prejudice." Unfortunately for Americans and the world, castrated analytic capacity is Washington's strongest suit.

The Dulles brothers' next targets were President Sukarno of Indonesia, Prime Minister Patrice Lumumba of Congo, and Fidel Castro. The plot against Castro was such a disastrous failure that it cost Allen Dulles his job. President Kennedy lost confidence in the agency and told his brother Bobby that after his reelection he was going to break the CIA into a thousand pieces. When President Kennedy removed Allen Dulles, the CIA understood the threat and struck first.

Warren Nutter, my Ph.D. dissertation chairman, later Assistant Secretary of Defense for International Security Affairs, taught his students that for the US government to maintain the people's trust, which democracy requires, the government's policies must be affirmations of our principles and be openly communicated to the people. Hidden agendas, such as those of the Dulles brothers and the Clinton, Bush and Obama regimes, must rely on secrecy and manipulation and, thereby, arouse the distrust of the people. If Americans are too brainwashed to notice, many foreign nationals are not.

The US government's secret agendas have cost Americans and many peoples in the world tremendously.

Essentially, the Dulles brothers created the Cold War with their secret agendas and anti-communist hysteria. Secret agendas committed Americans to long, costly, and unnecessary wars in Vietnam and the Middle East. Secret CIA and military agendas intending regime change in Cuba were blocked by President John F. Kennedy and resulted in the assassination of a president, who, for all his faults, was likely to have ended the Cold War twenty years before Ronald Reagan seized the opportunity.

Secret agendas have prevailed for so long that the American people themselves are now corrupted. As the saying goes, "a fish rots from the head." The rot in Washington now permeates the country.

THE NEOCON
UNI-POWER
THREATENS
WORLD WAR

October 6, 2014

The aggressive and mindless stance that Washington's warmongers have taken toward Russia and China has shattered the accomplishment of Reagan and Gorbachev.

Reagan and Gorbachev ended the Cold War and removed the threat of nuclear Armageddon. Now the neocons, the US budget-dependent (taxpayer dependent) US military/security complex, and the US politicians dependent on campaign funds from the military/security complex have resurrected the nuclear threat.

The corrupt and duplicitous Clinton regime broke the agreement that the George H.W. Bush administration gave Moscow in 1990. In exchange for Moscow permitting a reunified Germany to be a NATO member, Washington agreed that there would be no expansion of NATO to the east. Gorbachev, US Secretary of State James Baker, US ambassador to Moscow Jack Matlock, and declassified documents all testify to the fact that Moscow was assured that there would be no expansion of NATO into Eastern Europe.

In 1999 President Bill Clinton made a liar of the administration of President George H.W. Bush. The corrupt Clinton brought Poland, Hungary, and the newly formed Czech Republic into NATO.

President George W. Bush also made a liar out of his father, George H.W. Bush, and his father's trusted Secretary of State, James Baker. "Dubya" brought Estonia, Latvia, Lithuania, Slovenia, Slovakia, Bulgaria, and Romania into NATO in 2004. The corrupt and hopeless Obama regime added Albania and Croatia in 2009.

In other words, over the past 21 years three two-term US presidents have taught Moscow that the word of the US government is worthless.

Today Russia is surrounded by US and NATO military bases, with more to come in Ukraine (part of Russia for centuries), Georgia (part of Russia for centuries and the birthplace of Joseph Stalin), Montenegro, Macedonia, Bosnia-Herzegovina, and perhaps also Azerbaijan.

A large land expanse that was formerly part of the Soviet Empire is now part of Washington's Empire. The "coming of democracy" simply meant the changing of masters.

Washington always picks the puppet who serves as Secretary General of NATO. The latest is a former Norwegian politician and prime minister, Jens Stoltenberg. On Washington's orders, the puppet quickly antagonized Moscow with the statement that NATO has a powerful army that has a global policing role and can be deployed wherever Washington wishes. This claim is a total contradiction of NATO's purpose and charter.

Igor Korotchenko, a member of the Russian Defense Ministry Public Council replied to Washington's puppet Stoltenberg: "Such statements run counter to the system of international security, as the NATO alliance poses a threat to Russia. Therefore, it will cause responsive measures."

The responsive measures are what you would expect: enough nuclear capability to wipe out the United States and Europe many times over.

The arrogance of Washington wallowing in hubris as "the indispensable nation" has provoked Moscow to the point that Russia now has more deployed nuclear weapons than the US. As a result of Washington breaking its word and putting ABM missile bases on Russia's border, Russia has developed supersonic ICBMs that can rapidly change their trajectory and cannot be shot down by any missile defense system.

Of course, the US corporations making billions of dollars selling Washington a useless ABM system will deny this.

Moreover, those countries, such as Poland, whose governments are sufficiently stupid to accept US ABM bases, would be obliterated before the bases could function. The utter stupidity of Eastern Europe's bought-and-paid-for governments to put trust in Washington is likely to be the main cause of WW III.

The happy participant in the new Armageddon is the American military/security complex. These greedy "private corporations" whose revenues are entirely public funds are guaranteed more money regardless of the potential cost in human life. Their US Senate spokesperson, Jim Inhofe, a member of the Senate Armed Services Subcommittee on Strategic Forces, has resurrected the argument from 60 years ago that America is falling behind in the arms race. Restarting the arms race is essential to the profits of the US military/security complex and to the campaign contributions of senators.

It is not only Russia's strategic nuclear forces that the fools in Washington have revived and activated, but China's as well. Last year China released a pictorial description of how China's nuclear forces could destroy the US. This was China's response to Washington's insane plan of building new air and naval bases from the Philippines to Vietnam in order to control the flow of resources in the South China Sea.

What kind of idiotic government does America have that thinks China is going to put up with this kind of interference in China's sphere of influence?

China has now added to its nuclear arsenal a new variant of one of its mobile ICBMs. Washington does not know much about this new missile, because the CIA is too busy arranging protests in Hong Kong.

Both Russia and China were content to be part of the world economy and to improve the economic situation of their citizens by developing their economies. But along comes the Neocon Unipower, a collection of arrogant psychopaths who declare that Washington will not permit any other country, not even Russia and China, to rise to a capability of exercising a foreign policy independent of Washington's purposes.

Nuclear war is back into the picture. First Washington threatens those it perceives as rivals. When the perceived rivals don't submit, Washington demonizes them.

In the histories written by Washington's court historians, the greatest demons of modern times are the WW II governments of Japan and Germany along with the post-WW II Soviet government of Joseph Stalin. These American court historians ignore the facts. Many think WWII began with Germany's invasion of France. However, the German invasion of France was a response to the French and British declaration of war against Germany that resulted from Britain's irresponsible "guarantee" to Poland that disrupted Hitler's negotiations with the Polish military government for the return of German territory given to Poland after WWI. Japan was forced into war by Washington, which cut off Japan's access to resources. Japan was then nuked twice while the Japanese government was trying to surrender.

All of US president Woodrow Wilson's promises made to Germany in order to end WW I, such as no territorial loses and no reparations, were broken. Germany was torn apart and German territory was handed over to Poland, France, and Czechoslovakia. Despite US president Woodrow Wilson's promise to the contrary, impossible reparations were imposed on Germany by the Treaty of Versailles. The prescient John Maynard Keynes declared that the reparations would result in a second world war. If memory serves, portions of Germany were also given to Belgium and Denmark.

This humiliation of an industrious and powerful people, whose armies occupied foreign territories when WW I ended, demonstrated the folly of the so-called "Western powers." The French, British, and Americans paved the way for Adolph Hitler. By 1935 Hitler was sufficiently ensconced to denounce the Versailles Treaty. If Hitler had not succumbed to hubris and sent the German armies marching off into Russia where they were destroyed, he, or his successors, would still be ruling Europe today.

True history is very different from what Washington pretends and Americans are taught.

PUTIN SPEAKS: HOPE THAT WASHINGTON HEARS

October 15, 2014

In an interview today with *Politika*, a Serbian newspaper, Russia's president, Vladimir Putin, said that it is futile and dangerous for the US and its European puppets to blackmail Russia and that the Exceptional Nation and its vassals should consider the risks that are inherent in aggressive disputes between countries heavily armed with nuclear weapons. Putin noted that Obama took a hostile attitude toward Russia in Obama's UN speech to the General Assembly on September 24 when Obama declared Russia to be one of the three threats to the world along with the Islamic State and ebola. President Putin said that unilateral and punitive actions taken against Russia can provoke a crisis, and that if Washington's purpose is to "isolate our country, it is an absurd and illusory goal."

Here are some of President Putin's direct quotes:

"How can we talk about de-escalation in Ukraine while the decisions on new sanctions are introduced almost simultaneously with the agreements on the peace process?"

"Together with the sanctions against entire sectors of our economy, this approach can be called nothing but hostile."

"We hope that our partners will realize the futility of attempts to blackmail Russia and remember what consequences discord between major nuclear powers could bring for strategic stability."

If we don't all die from nuclear blasts, radiation, and nuclear winter, it will be because of the humanity and common sense—both of which are missing in Washington—of the President of Russia.

Look around you. The economies of Western civilization are in retreat, and the energies of the Exceptional Government are focused on combating the Islamic State, a creature created by Washington itself, and on demonizing Russia.

"THE CIA OWNS EVERYONE OF ANY SIGNIFICANCE IN THE MAJOR MEDIA"

October 16, 2014

As a former member of the major media prior to its
concentration in few hands by the Clinton regime,
I have reported on many occasions that the Western
media is a Ministry of Propaganda for Washington.
In the article below one of the propagandists confesses.
Published on Russia Insider News [104]

*"The CIA owns everyone of any significance in the major
media." — former CIA Director William Colby*

Our Exclusive Interview with German Editor Turned CIA Whistleblower

Fascinating details emerge. Leading US-funded think-tanks and German secret service are accessories. Attempted suppression by legal threats. Blackout in German media.

Exclusively for RI, Dutch journalist Eric van de Beek interviews the senior German editor who is causing a sensation with his allegations that the CIA pays German media professionals to spin stories to follow US government goals.

We wrote about this two weeks ago, and the article shot up in views, becoming one of the most read articles on our site.

Udo Ulfkotte reveals in his bestseller *Bought Journalists*, how he was "taught to lie, to betray and not to tell the truth to the public."

The former editor of *Frankfurter Allgemeine Zeitung*, which is one of Germany's largest newspapers, was secretly on the payroll of the CIA and German secret service, spinning the news in a way that was positive for the United States and bad for its opponents.

236

In his latest interview, Ulfkotte alleges that some media are nothing more than propaganda outlets of political parties, secret services, international think tanks and high finance entities.

Repenting for collaborating with various agencies and organisations to manipulate the news, Ulkotte laments, "I'm ashamed I was part of it. Unfortunately I cannot reverse this."

Some highlights from the interview:

• "I ended up publishing articles under my own name written by agents of the CIA and other intelligence services, especially the German secret service."

• "Most journalists from respected and big media organisations are closely connected to the German Marshall Fund, the Atlantik-Brücke or other so-called transatlantic organisations…once you're connected, you make friends with selected Americans. You think they are your friends and you start cooperating. They work on your ego, make you feel like you're important. And one day one of them will ask you 'Will you do me this favor'…"

• "When I told the *Frankfurter Allgemeine* that I would publish the book, their lawyers sent me a letter threatening with all legal consequences if I would publish any names or secrets – but I don't mind."

• "[The *Frankfurter Allgemeine Zeitung*] hasn't sued me. They know that I have evidence on everything."

• *"No German mainstream journalist is allowed to report about [my] book. Otherwise he or she will be sacked. So we have a bestseller now that no German journalist is allowed to write or talk about."*

• "We're talking about puppets on a string, journalists who write or say whatever their masters tell them to say or write. If you see how the mainstream media is reporting about the Ukraine conflict and if you know what's really going on, you get the picture. The masters in the background are pushing for war with Russia and western journalists are putting on their helmets."

And you were one of them, and now you are the first to blow the whistle.

"I'm ashamed I was part of it. Unfortunately I cannot reverse this. Although my superiors at the *Frankfurter Allgemeine Zeitung* approved of what I did, I'm still to blame. But yes, to my knowledge I am the first to accuse myself and to prove many others are to blame."

How did you become a bought journalist?

"It started very soon after I started working at the *Frankfurter Allgemeine Zeitung*. I learned to regard luxury invitations as quite acceptable and to write positive articles in return. Later on I was invited by the German Marshall Fund of The United States to travel the United States. They paid for all my expenses and put me in contact with Americans they'd like me to meet. In fact, most journalists from respected and big media organizations are closely connected to the German Marshall Fund, the Atlantik-Brücke or other so-called transatlantic organizations. Many of them are even members or 'fellows'. I am a fellow of the German Marshall Fund. The thing is, once you're connected, you make friends with selected Americans.

You think they are your friends and you start cooperating. They work on your ego, make you feel like you're important. And one day one of them will ask you 'Will you do me this favor' and then another will ask you 'Will you do me that favor'. Bye and bye you get completely brainwashed. I ended up publishing articles under my own name written by agents of the CIA and other intelligence services, especially the Bundesnachrichtendienst."

You said your superiors approved of that?

"They did. From my private point of view, in retrospective, they even sent me to spy. For instance in 1988 they put me on a plane to Iraq, where I traveled to the border with Iran. In those days Saddam Hussein was still seen as a good guy, a close ally to the US. The Americans supported him in his war against Iran.

About 35 kilometers from the border, in an Iranian place called Zubaidad, I witnessed the Iraqis killing and injuring thousands of Iranians by throwing poison gas at them. I did exactly what my superiors had asked me to do. I made photos of the gas attacks. Back in Frankfurt it appeared my superiors didn't show much interest in the atrocities I had witnessed. They allowed me to write an article about it, but they severely limited the size of it as if it wasn't of much importance. At the same time they asked me to hand over the photos that I had made to the German association of chemical companies in Frankfurt, Verband der Chemischen Industrie. This poison gas that had killed so many Iranians was made in Germany."

What's your opinion on press trips? Journalists usually excuse themselves by saying they are perfectly able to follow their own judgment and that they don't commit themselves to anything or anybody.

"I've been on a thousand press trips and never reported bad about those who paid all the expenses. You don't bite the hand that feeds you. That's where corruption starts. And that's the reason why magazines like *Der Spiegel* don't allow their journalists to accept invitations to press trips unless they pay for their own expenses."

The consequences of becoming a whistleblower can be serious. Do you have any indications people tried to prevent the publication of your book?

"When I told the *Frankfurter Allgemeine* that I would publish the book, their lawyers sent me a letter threatening with all legal consequences if I would publish any names or secrets—but I don't mind. You see, I don't have children to take care of. And you must know I was severely injured during the gas attack I witnessed in Iran in 1988. I'm the sole German survivor from a German poison gas attack. I'm still suffering from this. I've had three heart attacks. I don't expect to live for more than a few years."

In your book you mention many names of bought journalists. How are they doing now? Are they being

sacked? Are they trying to clear their names?

"No German mainstream journalist is allowed to report about the book. Otherwise he or she will be sacked. So we have a bestseller now that no German journalist is allowed to write or talk about. More shocking: We have respected journalists who seem to have gone deep sea diving for a long time. It's an Interesting situation. I expected and hoped that they would sue me and bring me to court. But they have no idea what to do. The respected *Frankfurter Allgemeine* just announced they will fire 200 employees, because they're losing subscribers very rapidly and in high numbers. But they don't sue me. They know that I have evidence on everything."

RUSSIAN FOREIGN MINISTER LAVROV SPEAKS TO THE WORLD

October 17, 2014

Russian Foreign Minister Sergey Lavrov's speech to the United Nations and President Putin's remarks in his Serbian press conference clearly indicate that the moral leader of the world is Russia, not Washington

The Russians have come out of tyranny as America descends into tyranny. Washington's barbarity in the world is unprecedented. For 13 years Americans have permitted their government to bomb women, children and village elders in seven countries based entirely on lies and the selfish interests of the ruling elite. Washington has spewed depleted uranium everywhere, causing massive birth defects and health problems. We must remember that Washington is the only government that dropped nuclear weapons on helpless civilian populations. The victims were Japanese when the Japanese government was trying to surrender.

Putin's warning to the White House that humanity's existence requires that Obama "remember what consequences discord between major nuclear powers could bring for strategic stability" is a pointed demand that the White House halt Washington's aggression toward Russia. We have had enough, Putin said. We are a patient people, but we are running out of patience with your idiocy.

It is not Ebola but Washington that is a plague upon the world. Washington has declared itself to be above both the US Constitution and international law. Washington has destroyed the sovereignty of Great Britain, all of Europe, and Japan and permits none of the countries in its empire of captive nations to have a foreign policy independent of Washington. Europe and Japan are nothing but punk puppet states whose "leaders" are well paid for their subservience to Washington.

Insouciant Americans are told that as they are the exceptional, indispensable people, their government has a right to be unaccountable to law. Law is what Washington imposes on others. Washington's hegemony over others is the right of the "exceptional nation." No other country counts or has any rights.

Russia and China disagree with Washington. Russia formed between the third and eighth centuries and reformed after the Mongol invasion. China has been around for five thousand years. The US is 238 years old, and judging by its behavior remains a two-year old.

Here is Lavrov speaking for Russia to the world. No one in the US government is capable of giving such a speech. The speech follows after these excerpts:

> "Attempts to put pressure on Russia and to compel it to abandon its values, truth, and justice have no prospects whatsoever for success."

> "The [US] policy of ultimatums and the philosophy of supremacy and domination do not meet the requirements of the 21st century, and run counter to the objective process of developing a polycentric and democratic world order."

> "Washington has openly declared its right to the unilateral use of military force anywhere to advance its own interests. Military interference has become a norm, even despite the dismal outcome of all operations of force that the US has carried out over recent years. The sustainability of the international system has been severely shaken by the NATO bombardment of Yugoslavia, intervention in Iraq, the attack against Libya, and the failure in Afghanistan."

No One Has A Monopoly on Truth — Sergey Lavrov

Ladies and gentlemen,

There is growing evidence today of a contradiction for collective and purposive efforts in the interest of developing adequate responses to challenges common to all of us, and the aspiration of a number of states for domination and a revival of the archaic block thinking based on military drill discipline and the erroneous logic of friend or foe.

The US-led western alliance that portrays itself as a

champion of democracy, the rule of law, and human rights within individual countries acts from a directly opposite position in the international arena, rejecting the democratic principles of sovereign equality of states, and trying to decide for everyone what is good and what is evil.

Washington has openly declared its right to the unilateral use of military force anywhere to advance its own interests. Military interference has become a norm, even despite the dismal outcome of all operations of force that the US has carried out over recent years. The sustainability of the international system has been severely shaken by the NATO bombardment of Yugoslavia, intervention in Iraq, the attack against Libya, and the failure in Afghanistan.

Only due to intensive diplomatic efforts was the aggression against Syria prevented in 2013.

There was an involuntary impression that the goal of various color revolutions and other projects to change unsuitable regimes is to create chaos and instability. Today, Ukraine has fallen victim to this arrogant policy. The situation there has revealed the remaining deep-rooted systematic flaws of the existing architecture in the Euro-Atlantic area. The West has embarked on a course towards vertical structuring of humanity, tailored to its own far-from-inoffensive standards.

After they declared victory in the Cold War and the so-called End of History, the US and the EU have opted to expand the geopolitical area that is under their control without taking into account the balance of legitimate interests of all people of Europe. The western partners did not heed our numerous warnings of the inadmissibility of violating the principles of the UN Charter and the Helsinki Final Act. Time and again, they have avoided serious joint work to establish a common space of equal and indivisible security and cooperation, from the Atlantic to the Pacific Ocean.

The Russian proposal to draft the European Security Treaty was rejected. We were told directly that the legally binding guarantees of security are only meant for the members of the North Atlantic Alliance, and at this time they continue to expand to the East in spite of the promises that were given to the contrary. The instantaneous switch of NATO to hostile rhetoric, to the drawdown of its cooperation with Russia even to the detriment of the West's own interests, and the buildup of military infrastructure on Russia's borders reveal the inability of the alliance to change its genetic code which it created during the Cold War.

The US and the EU supported the coup d'état in Ukraine and reverted to outright justification of any acts by the self-proclaimed Kiev authorities that opted for suppression by force of the part of the Ukraine people which had rejected attempts to impose throughout the country an anti-constitutional order and wanted to defend its right to its native language, culture, and history. It is precisely the aggressive assault on these rights that helped the population of Crimea to take its destiny in its own hands and make a choice in favor of self-determination.

This was an absolutely free choice, no matter what was invented by those who are primarily responsible for the internal conflict in Ukraine. General attempts to distort the truth and hide facts behind blanket accusations have been undertaken at all stages of the Ukrainian crisis. Nothing has been done to try to hold to account those responsible for the bloody February events at Maidan, and the massive loss of human life in Odessa, Mariupol, and other regions of Ukraine. The scale of appalling humanitarian disaster provoked by the acts of the Ukrainian army in Southeastern Ukraine has been deliberately ignored.

Recently, new horrifying facts have been brought to light, when mass graves were discovered in the suburbs of Donetsk. Despite UN Security Council Resolution 2166, a thorough and independent investigation of the circumstance of the loss of the Malaysian airliner over the territory of the Ukraine has been drawn out. The perpetrators of all these crimes must be identified and brought to justice, otherwise it will be difficult to count on national reconciliation occurring in Ukraine.

Russia is sincerely interested in the restoration of peace in this neighboring country, and this should be well understood by all who are slightly acquainted with the history of the deep-rooted and fraternal ties between these two peoples. The way towards political settlement is well known.

Last April, Kiev already took upon itself an obligation

in the Geneva Declaration of Russia, Ukraine, the US, and EU to immediately begin a broad national dialogue with the participation of all regions and political forces in Ukraine, with a view to carrying out constitutional reform. The implementation of this obligation would allow all Ukrainians to agree on how to live in accordance with their traditions and culture, and would enable Ukraine to restore its organic role as a binding link between the various parts of the European space, which naturally implies the preservation and respect by all of its neutral and non-block status.

We are convinced that with goodwill and the refusal to support the party of war in Kiev which is trying to push the Ukrainian people into the abyss of national catastrophe, a way out of the crisis is within our reach. The way to overcome a crisis has been opened with the achievement of the ceasefire agreement in Southeastern Ukraine on the basis of initiatives by Presidents Poroshenko and Putin. With the participation of their representatives of Kiev, Donetsk, Lugansk, as well as the OSCE and Russia, practical measures are being agreed upon for the successive implementation of those agreements, including the separation of the parties to the conflict, the removal of heavy weapons of Ukraine and militia forces, and the setting up of monitoring through the OSCE.

Russia is prepared to continue to actively promote the political settlement under the well known Minsk process as well as other formats. However, it should be crystal clear that we are doing this for the sake of peace, tranquility, and the well-being of the Ukrainian people—rather than to appease someone's ambitions. Attempts to put pressure on Russia and to compel it to abandon its values, truth, and justice have no prospects whatsoever for success.

Allow me to recall some history from not so long ago. As a condition for establishing diplomatic relations with the Soviet Union in 1933, the US government demanded of Moscow guarantees of non-interference into the domestic affairs of the United States and obligations not to take any actions with a view to changing the political or social order in America. At that time, Washington feared a revolutionary virus, and those guarantees were put on record. And this was the basis for, of course, reciprocity between the US and the Soviet Union. Perhaps it makes sense to return to this topic and reproduce the demands of that time of the US government—on a universal scale.

Why would the General Assembly not adopt a declaration on the inadmissibility of interference into the internal affairs of sovereign states and the non-recognition of a coup d'état as the method for the change of power? The time has come to completely exclude from international interactions attempts to exert illegitimate pressure by some states on others. The senselessness and counter-productive nature of unilateral sanctions is obvious if we look at the example of the US blockade on Cuba.

The policy of ultimatums and the philosophy of supremacy and domination do not meet the requirements of the 21st century, and run counter to the objective process of developing a polycentric and democratic world order.

Russia is promoting a positive and unifying agenda. We always were, and continue to be, open to discussion of the most complex issues no matter how unresolvable they may seem to be in the beginning. We will be prepared to search for compromises and a balance of interests, and even to exchange concessions, but only if the discussion will be truly respectful and equitable. The Minsk agreements of 5 and 19 September, on the way out of the Ukrainian crisis, and the compromise on the timeline of the agreement between Kiev and the EU are good examples to follow as is the declaration, finally, of the readiness of Brussels to begin negotiations on the establishment of a free-trade agreement between the European Union and the Customs Union of Russia, Belarus, Kazakhstan as had been proposed by President Putin back in January of this year.

Russia has consistently called for the harmonization of integration projects in Europe and Eurasia.

The political on political benchmarks and timelines of such a convergence of integrations would make a real contribution to the work of the OSCE on the topic of Helsinki Plus 40.

Another crucial area of this work would be to launch a pragmatic discussion, free from ideology, about the political and military architecture of the Euro-Atlantic region, so that not only members of NATO but all countries of the region including Ukraine, Moldova, and Georgia would experience equal and indivisible security, and would not have to make a false choice of 'either with us, or against us'. New dividing lines in Europe must not be allowed, even more so because in the era of globalization those lines can turn into a watershed divide between the West and the rest of the world.

It should be stated honestly that no one has a monopoly on truth and no one is now capable of tailoring global and regional processes to their own needs. There is no alternative today to the development of consensus regarding the rules of sustainable governance and new historical circumstances with full respect of the cultural and civilizational diversity of the world, and a multiplicity of models of development. It will be a difficult and perhaps a tiresome task to achieve such a consensus on every issue, but the recognition of the fact that democracy in every state is the worst form of government except for all the others also took time to break its way through, until Churchill proclaimed his verdict.

The time has come to realize the inevitability of this fundamental truth in international affairs, where today there is a huge deficit of democracy. Of course, some will have to shatter centuries-old ideas and abandon claims to eternal uniqueness, but there is no other way forward. Joint efforts can only be built on the principle of mutual respect and taking into account one another's interests, as is the case for example in the framers of the United Nations Security Council, the G20, BRICS, and the SCO.

The theory of the value of collective work has been reaffirmed by practice, and this includes progress in the settlement of the situation around the Iranian nuclear program and the successful conclusion of the chemical de-militarization of Syria. On the point, speaking of chemical weapons, we would like to receive authentic information on the state of the chemical arsenals in Libya. We understand that our NATO colleagues, having bombed this country in contravention of UN Security Council resolutions, would not like to stir up the mayhem that they have created.

However, the problem of uncontrolled Libyan chemical arsenals is too serious to turn a blind eye to.

We think that the UN Secretary General has an

obligation to show proof of his responsibility on this issue as well. What is important at this point is to see the global priorities and to avoid holding them hostage to a unilateral agenda. There is an urgent need to refrain from double standards and approaches to conflict settlement. Generally, everyone agrees that the key issue is to resolutely counter terrorists who are attempting to bring under their control increasingly broader territories in Iraq, Syria, Afghanistan, the Sahara-Sahel area.

That being the case, this task should not be sacrificed to ideological schemes or the desire to settle personal scores. Terrorists, no matter what slogans they hide behind, should remain outside the law. Moreover, it goes without saying that the fight against terrorism should rely on a solid foundation of international law. An important phase in this matter was the unanimous adoption by a number of UN security resolutions, including those on the issue of foreign terrorist fighters, and, to the contrary, attempts to contravene the charter of our organization do not contribute to the success of joint efforts.

The struggle against terrorists on the territory of Syria should be organized in cooperation with the Syrian government, which has clearly stated its readiness to join it. Damascus has already shown its capability of cooperating with international programs when it participated in the destruction of its chemical arsenals. From the very beginning of the Arab Spring, Russia called for it not to be left to extremists and for the establishment of a united front to counter the growing terrorist threat. We went against the temptation to make allies of almost anyone who proclaimed himself an enemy of Bashar Al Assad, whether it be Al Qaeda, Al Nusra, or other fellow travelers seeking regime change, including ISIL, which today is the focus of our attention.

As the saying goes, better late than never. It is not for the first time that Russia is making a very real contribution to the fight against both ISIL and other terrorist factions in the region. We have sent large supplies of weapons and military equipment to the governments of Iraq, Syria, and other countries in the Middle East and North Africa, and we will continue to support their efforts to suppress terrorists. The terrorist threat requires a comprehensive approach; we want to eradicate its root cause rather than be condemned to react only to the symptoms. ISIL is only part of the problem.

We propose to launch, under the auspices of the United Nations Security Council, an in-depth and broad study on extremist and terrorist threats and aspects of their threat in the Middle East and North African region.

This integrated approach implies also the long-standing conflict should be considered primarily between the Arabs and Israel. The absence of a settlement of the Israel-Palestine issue over several decades remains and is widely recognized one of the main factors of instability in the region which is helping the extremists to recruit more and more jihadists.

Another literally urgent area of our common work together is the joining of our efforts to implement decisions of the UN General Assembly and Security Council to combat the Ebola virus. Our doctors are already working in Africa. There are plans to send additional humanitarian assistance, equipment, medical instruments, medicines, and teams of experts to assist the UN programs in Guinea, Liberia, and Sierra Leone.

The United Nations was established on the ruins of World War II, and it is entering the year of its 70th anniversary. It is an obligation for us all to celebrate in an appropriate manner the anniversary of the great victory, and to give tribute to the memory of all who perished for freedom and the right of each people to determine its own destiny.

The lessons of that terrible war, and the entire course of events in today's world, require us to join efforts and forget about unilateral interests and national election cycles. When it comes to countering global threats to all humanity, it should not be allowed for national egoism to prevail over collective responsibility.

VLADIMIR PUTIN IS THE LEADER OF THE MORAL WORLD

October 24, 2014

Today (October 24, 2014) at the Valdai International Discussion Club meeting in Sochi, Russia's President Putin correctly and justifiably denounced Washington for destabilizing the world in order to serve its own narrow and selfish interest and the interests of the private interest groups that control Washington at the expense of the rest of the world. It is about time a world leader denounced the thuggish neocon regime in Washington. Putin described Washington's double standards with the Roman phrase: "What is allowed for God [the US] is not allowed for cattle [the rest of the world]."

PRESIDENT OF RUSSIA VLADIMIR PUTIN:

Colleagues, ladies and gentlemen, friends, it is a pleasure to welcome you to the XI meeting of the Valdai International Discussion Club. It was mentioned already that the club has new co-organizers this year. They include Russian non-governmental organizations, expert groups and leading universities. The idea was also raised of broadening the discussions to include not just issues related to Russia itself but also global politics and the economy.

I hope that these changes in organization and content will bolster the club's influence as a leading discussion and expert forum. At the same time, I hope the 'Valdai spirit' will remain—this free and open atmosphere and chance to express all manner of very different and frank opinions.

Let me say in this respect that I will also not let you down and will speak directly and frankly.

Some of what I say might seem a bit too harsh, but if

we do not speak directly and honestly about what we really think, then there is little point in even meeting in this way. It would be better in that case just to keep to diplomatic get-togethers, where no one says anything of real sense and, recalling the words of one famous diplomat, you realize that diplomats have tongues so as not to speak the truth.

We get together for other reasons. We get together so as to talk frankly with each other. We need to be direct and blunt today not so as to trade barbs, but so as to attempt to get to the bottom of what is actually happening in the world, try to understand why the world is becoming less safe and more unpredictable, and why the risks are increasing everywhere around us.

Today's discussion took place under the theme: New Rules or a Game without Rules. I think that this formula accurately describes the historic turning point we have reached today and the choice we all face. There is nothing new of course in the idea that the world is changing very fast. I know this is something you have spoken about at the discussions today. It is certainly hard not to notice the dramatic transformations in global politics and the economy, public life, and in industry, information and social technologies.

Let me ask you right now to forgive me if I end up repeating what some of the discussion's participants have already said. It's practically impossible to avoid. You have already held detailed discussions, but I will set out my point of view. It will coincide with other participants' views on some points and differ on others.

As we analyze today's situation, let us not forget history's lessons. First of all, changes in the world order—and what we are seeing today are events on this scale—have usually been accompanied by if not global war and conflict, then by chains of intensive local-level conflicts.

Second, global politics is above all about economic leadership, issues of war and peace, and the humanitarian dimension, including human rights.

The world is full of contradictions today. We need to be frank in asking each other if we have a reliable safety net in place. Sadly, there is no guarantee and no certainty that the current system of global and regional security is able to protect us from upheavals. This system has become seriously weakened, fragmented and deformed. The international and regional political, economic, and cultural cooperation organizations are also going through difficult times.

Yes, many of the mechanisms we have for ensuring the world order were created quite a long time ago now, including and above all in the period immediately following World War II. Let me stress that the solidity of the system created back then rested not only on the balance of power and the rights of the victor countries, but on the fact that this system's 'founding fathers' had respect for each other, did not try to put the squeeze on others, but attempted to reach agreements.

The main thing is that this system needs to develop, and despite its various shortcomings, needs to at least be capable of keeping the world's current problems within certain limits and regulating the intensity of the natural competition between countries.

It is my conviction that we could not take this mechanism of checks and balances that we built over the last decades, sometimes with such effort and difficulty, and simply tear it apart without building anything in its place. Otherwise we would be left with no instruments other than brute force.

What we needed to do was to carry out a rational reconstruction and adapt it to the new realities in the system of international relations.

But the United States, having declared itself the winner of the Cold War, saw no need for this.

Instead of establishing a new balance of power, essential for maintaining order and stability, they took steps that threw the system into sharp and deep imbalance.

The Cold War ended, but it did not end with the signing of a peace treaty with clear and transparent agreements on respecting existing rules or creating new rules and standards. This created the impression that the so-called 'victors' in the Cold War had decided to pressure events and reshape the world to suit their own needs and interests. If the existing system of international relations, international law and the checks and balances in place got in the way of these aims, this system was declared worthless, outdated and in need of immediate demolition.

Pardon the analogy, but this is the way nouveaux riches behave when they suddenly end up with a great fortune, in this case, in the shape of world leadership and domination. Instead of managing their wealth wisely, for their own benefit too of course, I think they have committed many follies.

We have entered a period of differing interpretations and deliberate silences in world politics.

International law has been forced to retreat over and over by the onslaught of legal nihilism.

Objectivity and justice have been sacrificed on the altar of political expediency. Arbitrary interpretations and biased assessments have replaced legal norms. At the same time, total control of the global mass media has made it possible when desired to portray white as black and black as white.

In a situation where you had domination by one country and its allies, or its satellites rather, the search for global solutions often turned into an attempt to impose their own universal recipes.

This group's ambitions grew so big that they started presenting the policies they put together in their corridors of power as the view of the entire international community. But this is not the case.

The very notion of 'national sovereignty' became a relative value for most countries. In essence, what was being proposed was the formula: the greater the loyalty towards the world's sole power centre, the greater this or that ruling regime's legitimacy.

We will have a free discussion afterwards and I will be happy to answer your questions and would also like to use my right to ask you questions. Let someone try to disprove the arguments that I just set out during the upcoming discussion.

The measures taken against those who refuse to submit are well-known and have been tried and tested many times. They include use of force, economic and propaganda pressure, meddling in domestic affairs, and appeals to a kind of 'supra-legal' legitimacy when they need to justify illegal intervention in this or that conflict or toppling inconvenient regimes. Of late, we have increasing evidence too that outright blackmail has been used with regard to a number of leaders.

It is not for nothing that 'big brother' is spending billions of dollars on keeping the whole world, including its own closest allies, under surveillance.

Let's ask ourselves, how comfortable are we with this, how safe are we, how happy living in this world, and how fair and rational has it become? Maybe, we have no real reasons to worry, argue and ask awkward questions? Maybe the United States' exceptional position and the way they are carrying out their leadership really is a blessing for us all, and their meddling in events all around the world is bringing peace, prosperity, progress, growth and democracy, and we should maybe just relax and enjoy it all?

Let me say that this is not the case, absolutely not the case.

A unilateral diktat and imposing one's own models produces the opposite result. Instead of settling conflicts it leads to their escalation, instead of sovereign and stable states we see the growing spread of chaos, and instead of democracy there is support for a very dubious public ranging from open neo-fascists to Islamic radicals.

Why do they support such people? They do this because they decide to use them as instruments along the way in achieving their goals but then burn their fingers and recoil. I never cease to be amazed by the way that our partners just keep stepping on the same rake, as we say here in Russia, that is to say, make the same mistake over and over.

They once sponsored Islamic extremist movements to fight the Soviet Union. Those groups got their battle experience in Afghanistan and later gave birth to the Taliban and Al-Qaeda. The West if not supported, at least closed its eyes, and, I would say, gave information, political and financial support to international terrorists' invasion of Russia (we have not forgotten this) and the Central Asian region's countries. Only after horrific terrorist attacks were committed on US soil itself did the United States wake up to the common threat of terrorism. Let me remind you that we were the first country to support the American people back then, the first to react as friends and partners to the terrible tragedy of September 11.

During my conversations with American and

European leaders, I always spoke of the need to fight terrorism together, as a challenge on a global scale. We cannot resign ourselves to and accept this threat, cannot cut it into separate pieces using double standards. Our partners expressed agreement, but a little time passed and we ended up back where we started. First there was the military operation in Iraq, then in Libya, which got pushed to the brink of falling apart.

Why was Libya pushed into this situation? Today it is a country in danger of breaking apart and has become a training ground for terrorists.

Only the current Egyptian leadership's determination and wisdom saved this key Arab country from chaos and having extremists run rampant. In Syria, as in the past, the United States and its allies started directly financing and arming rebels and allowing them to fill their ranks with mercenaries from various countries. Let me ask where do these rebels get their money, arms and military specialists? Where does all this come from? How did the notorious ISIL manage to become such a powerful group, essentially a real armed force?

As for financing sources, today, the money is coming not just from drugs, production of which has increased not just by a few percentage points but many-fold, since the international coalition forces have been present in Afghanistan. You are aware of this. The terrorists are getting money from selling oil too. Oil is produced in territory controlled by the terrorists, who sell it at dumping prices, produce it and transport it. But someone buys this oil, resells it, and makes a profit from it, not thinking about the fact that they are thus financing terrorists who could come sooner or later to their own soil and sow destruction in their own countries.

Where do they get new recruits? In Iraq, after Saddam Hussein was toppled, the state's institutions, including the army, were left in ruins. We said back then, be very, very careful. You are driving people out into the street, and what will they do there? Don't forget (rightfully or not) that they were in the leadership of a large regional power, and what are you now turning them into?

What was the result? Tens of thousands of soldiers, officers and former Baath Party activists were turned out into the streets and today have joined the rebels' ranks. Perhaps this is what explains why the Islamic State group has turned out so effective? In military terms, it is acting very effectively and has some very professional people. Russia warned repeatedly about the dangers of unilateral military actions, intervening in sovereign states' affairs, and flirting with extremists and radicals. We insisted on having the groups fighting the central Syrian government, above all the Islamic State, included on the lists of terrorist organizations. But did we see any results? We appealed in vain.

We sometimes get the impression that our colleagues and friends are constantly fighting the consequences of their own policies, throw all their effort into addressing the risks they themselves have created, and pay an ever-greater price.

Colleagues, this period of unipolar domination has convincingly demonstrated that having only one power center does not make global processes more manageable. On the contrary, this kind of unstable construction has shown its inability to fight the real threats such as regional conflicts, terrorism, drug trafficking, religious fanaticism, chauvinism and neo-Nazism. At the same time, it has opened the road wide for inflated national pride, manipulating public opinion and letting the strong bully and suppress the weak.

Essentially, the unipolar world is simply a means of justifying dictatorship over people and countries. The unipolar world turned out too uncomfortable, heavy and unmanageable a burden even for the self-proclaimed leader. Comments along this line were made here just before and I fully agree with this. This is why we see attempts at this new historic stage to recreate a semblance of a quasi-bipolar world as a convenient model for perpetuating American leadership.

It does not matter who takes the place of the centre of evil in American propaganda, the USSR's old place as the main adversary. It could be Iran, as a country seeking to acquire nuclear technology, China, as the world's biggest economy, or Russia, as a nuclear superpower.

Today, we are seeing new efforts to fragment the world, draw new dividing lines, put together coalitions not built for something but directed against someone, anyone, create the image of an enemy as was the case during the Cold War years, and obtain the right to this leadership, or diktat if you wish. The situation was presented this way during the Cold War. We all understand this and know this. The United States always told its allies: "We have a common enemy, a terrible foe, the centre of evil, and we are defending you, our allies, from this foe, and so we have the right to order you around, force you to sacrifice your political and economic interests and pay your share of the costs for this collective defense, but we will be the ones in charge of it all of course." In short, we see today attempts in a new and changing world to reproduce the familiar models of global management, and all this so as to guarantee their [the US'] exceptional position and reap political and economic dividends.

But these attempts are increasingly divorced from reality and are in contradiction with the world's diversity. Steps of this kind inevitably create confrontation and countermeasures and have the opposite effect to the hoped-for goals. We see what happens when politics rashly starts meddling in the economy and the logic of rational decisions gives way to the logic of confrontation that only hurts one's own economic positions and interests, including national business interests.

Joint economic projects and mutual investment objectively bring countries closer together and help to smooth out current problems in relations between states. But today, the global business community faces unprecedented pressure from Western governments. What business, economic expediency and pragmatism can we speak of when we hear slogans such as "the homeland is in danger", "the free world is under threat", and "democracy is in jeopardy"? And so everyone needs to mobilize. That is what a real mobilization policy looks like.

Sanctions are already undermining the foundations of world trade, the WTO rules and the principle of inviolability of private property. They are dealing a blow to the liberal model of globalization based on markets, freedom and competition, which, let me note, is a model that has primarily benefited precisely the Western countries. And now they risk losing trust as the leaders of globalization.

We have to ask ourselves, why was this necessary? After all, the United States' prosperity rests in large part on the trust of investors and foreign holders of dollars and US securities. This trust is clearly being undermined and signs of disappointment in the fruits of globalization are visible now in many countries.

The well-known Cyprus precedent and the politically motivated sanctions have only strengthened the trend towards seeking to bolster economic and financial sovereignty and countries' or their regional groups' desire to find ways of protecting themselves from the risks of outside pressure.

We already see that more and more countries are looking for ways to become less dependent on the dollar and are setting up alternative financial and payments systems and reserve currencies. I think that our American friends are quite simply cutting the branch they are sitting on. You cannot mix politics and the economy, but this is what is happening now. I have always thought and still think today that politically motivated sanctions were a mistake that will harm everyone, but I am sure that we will come back to this subject later.

We know how these decisions were taken and who was applying the pressure. But let me stress that Russia is not going to get all worked up, get offended or come begging at anyone's door.

Russia is a self-sufficient country. We will work within the foreign economic environment that has taken shape, develop domestic production and technology and act more decisively to carry out transformation. Pressure from outside, as has been the case on past occasions, will only consolidate our society, keep us alert and make us concentrate on our main development goals.

Of course the sanctions are a hindrance. They are trying to hurt us through these sanctions, block our development and push us into political, economic and cultural isolation, force us into backwardness in other words. But let me say yet again that the world is a very different place today. We have no intention of shutting ourselves off from anyone and choosing some kind of closed development road, trying to live in autarky. We are always open to dialogue, including on normalizing our economic and political relations. We are counting here on the pragmatic approach and position of business communities in the leading countries.

Some are saying today that Russia is supposedly turning its back on Europe—such words were probably spoken already here too during the discussions—and is looking for new business partners, above all in Asia. Let me say that this is absolutely not the case. Our active policy in the Asian-Pacific region began not just yesterday and not in response to sanctions, but is a policy that we have been following for a good many years now. Like many other countries, including Western countries, we saw that Asia is playing an ever greater role in the world, in the economy and in politics, and there is simply no way we can afford to overlook these developments.

Let me say again that everyone is doing this, and we will do so too, all the more so as a large part of our country is geographically in Asia. Why should we not make use of our competitive advantages in this area? It would be extremely shortsighted not to do so.

Developing economic ties with these countries and carrying out joint integration projects also creates big incentives for our domestic development. Today's demographic, economic and cultural trends all suggest that dependence on a sole superpower will objectively decrease. This is something that European and American experts have been talking and writing about too.

Perhaps developments in global politics will mirror the developments we are seeing in the global economy, namely, intensive competition for specific niches and frequent change of leaders in specific areas. This is entirely possible.

There is no doubt that humanitarian factors such as education, science, healthcare and culture are playing a greater role in global competition. This also has a big impact on international relations, including because this 'soft power' resource will depend to a great extent on real achievements in developing human capital rather than on sophisticated propaganda tricks.

At the same time, the formation of a so-called polycentric world (I would also like to draw attention to this, colleagues) in and of itself does not improve stability; in fact, it is more likely to be the opposite. The goal of reaching global equilibrium is turning into a fairly difficult puzzle, an equation with many unknowns.

So, what is in store for us if we choose not to live by the rules—even if they may be strict and inconvenient—but rather live without any rules at all? And that scenario is entirely possible; we cannot rule it out, given the tensions in the global situation. Many predictions can already be made, taking into account current trends, and unfortunately, they are not optimistic. If we do not create a clear system of mutual commitments and agreements, if we do not build the mechanisms for managing and resolving crisis situations, the symptoms of global anarchy will inevitably grow.

Today, we already see a sharp increase in the likelihood of a whole set of violent conflicts with either direct or indirect participation by the world's major powers. And the risk factors include not just traditional multinational conflicts, but also the internal instability in separate states, especially when we talk about nations located at the intersections of major states' geopolitical interests, or on the border of cultural, historical, and economic civilizational continents.

Ukraine, which I'm sure was discussed at length and which we will discuss some more, is one example of such sorts of conflicts that affect the international power balance, and I think it will certainly not be the last. From here emanates the next real threat of destroying the current system of arms control agreements. And this dangerous process was launched by the United States of America when it unilaterally withdrew from the Anti-Ballistic Missile Treaty in 2002, and then set about and continues today to actively pursue the creation of its global missile defense system.

Colleagues, friends, I want to point out that we did not start this. Once again, we are sliding into the times when, instead of the balance of interests and mutual guarantees, it is fear and the balance of mutual destruction that prevent nations from engaging in direct conflict. In absence of legal and political instruments, arms are once again becoming the focal point of the global agenda; they are used wherever and however, without any UN Security Council sanctions. And if the Security Council refuses to produce such decisions, then it is immediately declared to be an outdated and ineffective instrument.

Many states do not see any other ways of ensuring their sovereignty but to obtain their own bombs. This is extremely dangerous. We insist on continuing talks; we are not only in favor of talks, but insist on continuing talks to reduce nuclear arsenals. The fewer nuclear weapons we have in the world, the better. And we are ready for the most serious, concrete discussions on nuclear disarmament—but only serious discussions without any double standards.

What do I mean? Today, many types of high-precision weaponry are already close to mass-destruction weapons in terms of their capabilities, and in the event of full renunciation of nuclear weapons or radical reduction of nuclear potential, nations that are leaders in creating and producing high-precision systems will have a clear military advantage. Strategic parity will be disrupted, and this is likely to bring destabilization. The use of a so-called first global pre-emptive strike may become tempting. In short, the risks do not decrease, but intensify.

The next obvious threat is the further escalation of ethnic, religious, and social conflicts. Such conflicts are dangerous not only as such, but also because they create zones of anarchy, lawlessness, and chaos around them, places that are comfortable for terrorists and criminals, where piracy, human trafficking, and drug trafficking flourish.

Incidentally, at the time, our colleagues tried to somehow manage these processes, use regional conflicts and design 'color revolutions' to suit their interests, but the genie escaped the bottle. It looks like the controlled chaos theory fathers themselves do not know what to do with it; there is disarray in their ranks.

We closely follow the discussions by both the ruling elite and the expert community. It is enough to look at the headlines of the Western press over the last year. The same people are called fighters for democracy, and then Islamists; first they write about revolutions and then call them riots and upheavals. The result is obvious: the further expansion of global chaos.

Colleagues, given the global situation, it is time to start agreeing on fundamental things. This is incredibly important and necessary; this is much better than going back to our own corners. The more we all face common problems, the more we find ourselves in the same boat, so to speak.

And the logical way out is in cooperation between nations, societies, in finding collective answers to increasing challenges, and in joint risk management. Granted, some of our partners, for some reason, remember this only when it suits their interests.

Practical experience shows that joint answers to challenges are not always a panacea; and we need to understand this. Moreover, in most cases, they are hard to reach; it is not easy to overcome the differences in national interests, the subjectivity of different approaches, particularly when it comes to nations with different cultural and historical traditions. But nevertheless, we have examples when, having common goals and acting based on the same criteria, together we achieved real success.

Let me remind you about solving the problem of chemical weapons in Syria, and the substantive dialogue on the Iranian nuclear program, as well as our work on North Korean issues, which also has some positive results. Why can't we use this experience in the future to solve local and global challenges?

What could be the legal, political, and economic basis for a new world order that would allow for stability and security, while encouraging healthy competition, not allowing the formation of new monopolies that hinder development? It is unlikely that someone could provide absolutely exhaustive, ready-made solutions right now. We will need extensive work with participation by a wide range of governments, global businesses, civil society, and such expert platforms as ours.

However, it is obvious that success and real results are only possible if key participants in international affairs can agree on harmonizing basic interests, on reasonable self-restraint, and set the example of positive and responsible leadership. We must clearly identify where unilateral actions end and we need to apply multilateral mechanisms, and as part of improving the effectiveness of international law, we must resolve the dilemma between the actions by the international community to ensure security and human rights and the principle of national sovereignty and non-interference in the internal affairs of any state.

Those very collisions increasingly lead to arbitrary external interference in complex internal processes, and time and again, they provoke dangerous conflicts between leading global players.

The issue of maintaining sovereignty becomes almost paramount in maintaining and strengthening global stability.

Clearly, discussing the criteria for the use of external force is extremely difficult; it is practically impossible to separate it from the interests of particular nations. However, it is far more dangerous when there are no agreements that are clear to everyone, when no clear conditions are set for necessary and legal interference.

I will add that international relations must be based on international law, which itself should rest on moral principles such as justice, equality and truth. Perhaps most important is respect for one's partners and their interests. This is an obvious formula, but simply following it could radically change the global situation.

I am certain that if there is a will, we can restore the effectiveness of the international and regional institutions system. We do not even need to build anything anew, from scratch; this is not a "green field," especially since the institutions created after World War II are quite universal and can be given modern substance, adequate to manage the current situation.

This is true of improving the work of the UN, whose central role is irreplaceable, as well as the OSCE, which, over the course of 40 years, has proven to be a necessary mechanism for ensuring security and cooperation in the Euro-Atlantic region. I must say that even now, in trying to resolve the crisis in southeast Ukraine, the OSCE is playing a very positive role.

In light of the fundamental changes in the international environment, the increase in uncontrollability and various threats, we need a new global consensus of responsible forces. It's not about some local deals or a division of spheres of influence in the spirit of classic diplomacy, or somebody's complete global domination. I think that we need a new version of interdependence. We should not be afraid of it. On the contrary, this is a good instrument for harmonizing positions.

This is particularly relevant given the strengthening and growth of certain regions on the planet, which process objectively requires institutionalization of such new poles, creating powerful regional organizations and developing rules for their interaction. Cooperation between these centers would seriously add to the stability of global security, policy and economy. But in order to establish such a dialogue, we need to proceed from the assumption that all regional centers and integration projects forming around them need to have equal rights to development, so that they can complement each other and nobody can force them into conflict or opposition artificially.

Such destructive actions would break down ties between states, and the states themselves would be subjected to extreme hardship, or perhaps even total destruction.

I would like to remind you of the last year's events. We have told our American and European partners that hasty backstage decisions, for example, on Ukraine's association with the EU, are fraught with serious risks to the economy. We didn't even say anything about politics; we spoke only about the economy, saying that such steps, made without any prior arrangements, touch on the interests of many other nations, including Russia as Ukraine's main trade partner, and that a wide discussion of the issues is necessary. Incidentally, in this regard, I will remind you that, for example, the talks on Russia's accession to the WTO lasted 19 years. This was very difficult work, and a certain consensus was reached.

Why am I bringing this up? Because in implementing Ukraine's association project, our partners would come to us with their goods and services through the back gate, so to speak, and we did not agree to this, nobody asked us about this. We had discussions on all topics related to Ukraine's association with the EU, persistent discussions, but I want to stress that this was done in an entirely civilized manner, indicating possible problems, showing the obvious reasoning and arguments. Nobody wanted to listen to us and nobody wanted to talk. They simply told us: this is none of your business, period, end of discussion. Instead of a comprehensive but—I stress—civilized dialogue, it all came down to a government overthrow; they plunged the country into chaos, into economic and social collapse, into a civil war with enormous casualties.

Why? When I ask my colleagues why, they no longer have an answer; nobody says anything.

That's it. Everyone's at a loss, saying it just turned out that way. Those actions should not have been encouraged—it wouldn't have worked. After all (I already spoke about this), former Ukrainian President Yanukovych signed everything, agreed with everything. Why do it? What was the point? What is this, a civilized way of solving problems? Apparently, those who constantly throw together new 'color revolutions' consider themselves 'brilliant artists' and simply cannot stop.

I am certain that the work of integrated associations, the cooperation of regional structures, should be built on a transparent, clear basis; the Eurasian Economic Union's formation process is a good example of such transparency. The states that are parties to this project informed their partners of their plans in advance, specifying the parameters of our association, the principles of its work, which fully correspond with the World Trade Organization rules.

I will add that we would also have welcomed the start of a concrete dialogue between the Eurasian and European Union. Incidentally, they have almost completely refused us this as well, and it is also unclear why—what is so scary about it?

And, of course, with such joint work, we would think that we need to engage in dialogue (I spoke about this many times and heard agreement from many of our western partners, at least in Europe) on the need to create a common space for economic and humanitarian cooperation stretching all the way from the Atlantic to the Pacific Ocean.

Colleagues, Russia made its choice. Our priorities are further improving our democratic and open economy institutions, accelerated internal development, taking into account all the positive modern trends in the world, and consolidating society based on traditional values and patriotism.

We have an integration-oriented, positive, peaceful

agenda; we are working actively with our colleagues in the Eurasian Economic Union, the Shanghai Cooperation Organization, BRICS and other partners. This agenda is aimed at developing ties between governments, not dissociating.

We are not planning to cobble together any blocs or get involved in an exchange of blows.

The allegations and statements that Russia is trying to establish some sort of empire, encroaching on the sovereignty of its neighbors, are groundless. Russia does not need any kind of special, exclusive place in the world—I want to emphasize this. While respecting the interests of others, we simply want for our own interests to be taken into account and for our position to be respected.

We are well aware that the world has entered an era of changes and global transformations, when we all need a particular degree of caution, the ability to avoid thoughtless steps. In the years after the Cold War, participants in global politics lost these qualities somewhat. Now, we need to remember them. Otherwise, hopes for a peaceful, stable development will be a dangerous illusion, while today's turmoil will simply serve as a prelude to the collapse of world order.

Yes, of course, I have already said that building a more stable world order is a difficult task. We are talking about long and hard work. We were able to develop rules for interaction after World War II, and we were able to reach an agreement in Helsinki in the 1970s. Our common duty is to resolve this fundamental challenge at this new stage of development.

Thank you very much for your attention.

VLADIMIR PUTIN (commenting on statements by former Prime Minister of France, Dominique de Villepin, and former Federal Chancellor of Austria, Wolfgang Schuessel):

I would like to begin by saying that overall I agree with what both Wolfgang and Dominique have said. I fully support everything they said. However, there are a few things I would like to clarify.

I believe Dominique referred to the Ukrainian crisis as the reason for the deterioration in international relations. Naturally, this crisis is a cause, but this is not the principal cause. The crisis in Ukraine is itself a result of a misbalance in international relations. I have already said in my address why this is happening, and my colleagues have already mentioned it. I can add to this, if necessary. However, primarily this is the outcome of the misbalance in international relations.

As for the issues mentioned by Wolfgang, we will get back to them: we will talk about the elections, if necessary, and about the supply of energy resources to Ukraine and Europe.

However, I would like to respond to the phrase "Wolfgang is an optimist, while life is harder for pessimists." I already mentioned the old joke we have about a pessimist and an optimist, but I cannot help telling it again. We have this very old joke about a pessimist and an optimist: a pessimist drinks his cognac and says, "It smells of bedbugs," while an optimist catches a bedbug, crushes it, then sniffs it and says, "A slight whiff of cognac."

I would rather be the pessimist who drinks cognac than the optimist who sniffs bedbugs.

(Laughter)

Though it does seem that optimists have a better time, our common goal is to live a decent life (without overindulging in alcohol). For this purpose, we need to avoid crises, together handle all challenges and threats and build such relations on the global arena that would help us reach these goals.

Later I will be ready to respond to some of the other things mentioned here. Thank you.

BRITISH JOURNALIST SEUMAS MILNE (retranslated from Russian): I would like to ask a two-in-one question.

First, Mr. President, do you believe that the actions of Russia in Ukraine and Crimea over the past months were a reaction to rules being broken and are an example of state management without rules? And the other question is: does Russia see these global violations of rules as a signal for changing its position? It has been said here lately that Russia cannot lead in the existing global situation; however, it is demonstrating the qualities of a leader. How would you respond to this?

VLADIMIR PUTIN: I would like to ask you to reword the second part of your question, please.

What exactly is your second question?

SEUMAS MILNE (retranslated from Russian): It has been said here that Russia cannot strive for leading positions in the world considering the outcomes of the Soviet Union's collapse, however it can influence who the leader will be. Is it possible that Russia would alter its position, change its focus, as you mentioned, regarding the Middle East and the issues connected with Iran's nuclear program?

VLADIMIR PUTIN: Russia has never altered its position. We are a country with a traditional focus on cooperation and search for joint solutions. This is first.

Second. We do not have any claims to world leadership. The idea that Russia is seeking some sort of exclusivity is false; I said so in my address. We are not demanding a place under the sun; we are simply proceeding from the premise that all participants in international relations should respect each other's interests. We are ready to respect the interests of our partners, but we expect the same respect for our interests.

We did not change our attitude to the situation in the Middle East, to the Iranian nuclear program, to the North Korean conflict, to fighting terrorism and crime in general, as well as drug trafficking. We never changed any of our priorities even under the pressure of unfriendly actions on the part of our western partners, who are led, very obviously in this case, by the United States.

We did not even change the terms of the sanctions.

However, here too everything has its limits. I proceed from the idea that it might be possible that external circumstances can force us to alter some of our positions, but so far there have not been any extreme situations of this kind and we have no intention of changing anything. That is the first point.

The second point has to do with our actions in Crimea. I have spoken about this on numerous occasions, but if necessary, I can repeat it. This is Part 2 of Article 1 of the United Nations' Charter—the right of nations to self-determination. It has all been written down, and not simply as the right to self-determination, but as the goal of the United Nations. Read the article carefully.

I do not understand why people living in Crimea do not have this right, just like the people living in, say, Kosovo. This was also mentioned here. Why is it that in one case white is white, while in another the same is called black? We will never agree with this nonsense. That is one thing.

The other very important thing is something nobody mentions, so I would like to draw attention to it. What happened in Crimea? First, there was this anti-state overthrow in Kiev. Whatever anyone may say, I find this obvious—there was an armed seizure of power.

In many parts of the world, people welcomed this, not realizing what this could lead to, while in some regions people were frightened that power was seized by extremists, by nationalists and right-wingers including neo-Nazis. People feared for their future and for their families and reacted accordingly. In Crimea, people held a referendum.

I would like to draw your attention to this. It was not by chance that we in Russia stated that there was a referendum. The decision to hold the referendum was made by the legitimate authority of Crimea—its Parliament, elected a few years ago under Ukrainian law prior to all these grave events. This legitimate body of authority declared a referendum, and then based on its results, they adopted a declaration of independence, just as Kosovo did, and turned to the Russian Federation with a request to accept Crimea into the Russian state.

You know, whatever anyone may say and no matter how hard they try to dig something up, this would be very difficult, considering the language of the United Nations court ruling, which clearly states (as applied to the Kosovo precedent) that the decision on self-determination does not require the approval of the supreme authority of a country.

In this connection I always recall what the sages of the past said. You may remember the wonderful saying: Whatever Jupiter is allowed, the Ox is not.

We cannot agree with such an approach. The ox may not be allowed something, but the bear will not even bother to ask permission. Here we consider it the master of the taiga, and I know for sure that it does not intend to move to any other climatic zones—it will not be comfortable there.

However, it will not let anyone have its taiga either. I believe this is clear.

What are the problems of the present-day world order? Let us be frank about it, we are all experts here. We talk and talk, we are like diplomats. What happened in the world? There used to be a bipolar system. The Soviet Union collapsed, the power called the Soviet Union ceased to exist.

All the rules governing international relations after World War II were designed for a bipolar world. True, the Soviet Union was referred to as 'the Upper Volta with missiles'. Maybe so, and there were loads of missiles. Besides, we had such brilliant politicians like Nikita Khrushchev, who hammered the desk with his shoe at the UN. And the whole world, primarily the United States and NATO, thought: this Nikita is best left alone, he might just go and fire a missile, they have lots of them, we should better show some respect for them.

Now that the Soviet Union is gone, what is the situation and what are the temptations? There is no need to take into account Russia's views, it is very dependent, it has gone through transformation during the collapse of the Soviet Union, and we can do whatever we like, disregarding all rules and regulations.

This is exactly what is happening. Dominique here mentioned Iraq, Libya, Afghanistan and Yugoslavia before that. Was this really all handled within the framework of international law? Do not tell us those fairy-tales.

This means that some can ignore everything, while we cannot protect the interests of the Russian-speaking and Russian population of Crimea. This will not happen.

I would like everyone to understand this. We need to get rid of this temptation and attempts to arrange the world to one's liking, and to create a balanced system of interests and relations that has long been prescribed in the world, we only have to show some respect.

As I have already said, we understand that the world has changed, and we are ready to take heed of it and adjust this system accordingly, but we will never allow anyone to completely ignore our interests.

Does Russia aim for any leading role? We don't need to be a superpower; this would only be an extra load for us. I have already mentioned the taiga: it is immense, illimitable, and just to develop our territories we need plenty of time, energy and resources.

We have no need of getting involved in things, of ordering others around, but we want others to stay out of our affairs as well and to stop pretending they rule the world. That is all. If there is an area where Russia could be a leader—it is in asserting the norms of international law.

QUESTION: The peaceful process between the Palestinians and Israelis has completely collapsed. The United States never let the quartet work properly. At the same time, the growth of illegal Israeli settlements on the occupied territories renders impossible the creation of a Palestinian state. We have recently witnessed a very severe attack on the Gaza Strip. What is Russia's attitude to this tense situation in the Middle East? And what do you think of the developments in Syria?

One remark for Mr Villepin as well. You spoke of humiliation. What can be more humiliating than the occupation that Palestine has been experiencing all these years?

VLADIMIR PUTIN: Regarding Palestine and the Israeli conflict. It is easy for me to speak about this because, first, I have to say and I believe everyone can see that our relations with Israel have transformed seriously in the past decade. I am referring to the fact that a large number of people from the former Soviet Union live in Israel and we cannot remain indifferent to their fate. At the same time, we have traditional relations with the Arab world, specifically with Palestine.

Moreover, the Soviet Union, and Russia is its legal successor, has recognized Palestinian statehood. We are not changing anything here.

Finally, regarding the settlements. We share the views of the main participants in international relations. We consider this a mistake. I have already said this to our Israeli partners. I believe this is an obstacle to normal relations and I strongly expect that the practice itself will be stopped and the entire process of a peaceful settlement will return to its legal course based on agreement.

We proceed from the fact that that Middle East conflict is one of the primary causes of destabilization not only in the region, but also in the world at large. Humiliation of any people living in the area, or anywhere else in the world is clearly a source of destabilization and should be done away with. Naturally, this should be done using such means and measures that would be acceptable for all the participants in the process and for all those living in the area.

This is a very complicated process, but Russia is ready to use every means it has for this settlement, including its good relations with the parties to this conflict.

DIRECTOR, KIEV CENTER FOR POLITICAL AND CONFLICT STUDIES, MIKHAIL POGREBINSKY: Mr. President, I have come from Ukraine. For the first time in 70 years, it is going through very hard times. My question has to do with the possibility of a settlement. In this connection, I would like to go back in history. You mentioned that there was a moment when a trilateral format was under consideration: Russia-Ukraine-Europe. Back then, Europe did not agree to it, after which a series of tragic events took place, including the loss of Crimea, the death of thousands of people and so forth.

Recently, Europe together with Ukraine and Russia agreed that this format is possible after all; moreover, a corresponding resolution was passed. At that moment, there was hope that Russia together with Europe and Ukraine would manage to reach agreement and could become the restorer of peace in Ukraine. What happened next? What happened between Moscow and Brussels, Moscow and Berlin—because now the situation seems completely insane? It is unclear what this might lead to. What do you think happened to Europe?

VLADIMIR PUTIN: You know, what happened can be described as nothing happened. Agreements were reached, but neither side complied with them in full. However, full compliance by both sides might be impossible.

For instance, Ukrainian army units were supposed to leave certain locations where they were stationed prior to the Minsk agreements, while the militia army was supposed to leave certain settlements they were holding prior to these agreements. However, neither is the Ukrainian army withdrawing from the locations they should leave, nor is the militia army withdrawing from the settlements they have to move out of, referring, and I will be frank now—to the fact that their families remain there (I mean the militia) and they fear for their safety. Their families, their wives and children live there. This is a serious humanitarian factor.

VLADIMIR PUTIN: We are ready to make every effort to ensure the implementation of the Minsk agreements. I would like to take advantage of your question to stress Russia's position: we are in favor of complete compliance with the Minsk agreements by both sides.

What is the problem? In my view, the key problem is that we do not see the desire on the part of our partners in Kiev, primarily the authorities, to resolve the issue of relations with the country's southeast peacefully, through negotiations. We keep seeing the same thing in various forms: suppression by force. It all began with Maidan, when they decided to suppress Yanukovych by force. They succeeded and raised this wave of nationalism and then it all transformed into some nationalistic battalions.

When people in southeast Ukraine did not like it, they tried to elect their own bodies of government and management and they were arrested and taken to prison in Kiev at night. Then, when people saw this happening and took to arms, instead of stopping and finally resorting to peaceful dialogue, they sent troops there, with tanks and aircraft.

Incidentally, the global community keeps silent, as if it does not see any of this, as if there is no such thing as 'disproportionate use of force'. They suddenly forgot all about it. I remember all the frenzy around when we had a complicated situation in the Caucasus. I would hear one and the same thing every day. No more such words today, no more 'disproportionate use of force'. And that's while cluster bombs and even tactical weapons are being used.

You see, under the circumstances, it is very difficult for us in Russia to arrange to work with people in southeast Ukraine in a way that would induce them to fully comply with all the agreements. They keep saying that the authorities in Kiev do not fully comply with the agreements either.

However, there is no other way. I would like to stress that we are for the full implementation of the agreements by both parties, and the most important thing I want to say—and I want everyone to hear that—if, God forbid, anyone is again tempted to use force for the final settlement of the situation in southeast Ukraine, this will bring the situation to a complete deadlock.

In my view, there is still a chance to reach agreement. Yes, Wolfgang spoke about this, I understood him. He spoke of the upcoming elections in Ukraine and in the southeast of the country. We know it and we are constantly discussing it. Just this morning I had another discussion with the Chancellor of Germany about it. The Minsk agreements do stipulate that elections in the southeast should be held in coordination with Ukrainian legislation, not under Ukrainian law, but in coordination with it.

This was done on purpose, because nobody in the southeast wants to hold elections in line with Ukrainian law. Why? How can this be done, when there is shooting every day, people get killed on both sides and they have to hold elections under Ukrainian law? The war should finally stop and the troops should be withdrawn. You see? Once this is achieved, we can start considering any kind of rapprochement or cooperation. Until this happens, it is hard to talk about anything else.

They spoke of the date of the elections in the southeast, but few know that there has been an agreement that elections in southeast Ukraine should be held by November 3. Later, the date was amended in the corresponding law, without consulting anyone, without consulting with the southeast. The elections were set for December 7, but nobody talked to them. Therefore, the people in the southeast say, "See, they cheated us again, and it will always be this way."

You can argue over this any way you like. The most important thing is to immediately stop the war and move the troops away. If Ukraine wants to keep its territorial integrity, and this is something we want as well, they need to understand that there is no sense in holding on to some village or other—this is pointless. The idea is to stop the bloodshed and to start normal dialogue, to build relations based on this dialogue and restore at least some communication, primarily in the economy, and gradually other things will follow. I believe this is what should be achieved first and then we can move on.

PROFESSOR OF POLITICAL SCIENCE, DIRECTOR OF THE CENTER FOR GOVERNANCE AND PUBLIC POLICY AT CARLETON UNIVERSITY (OTTAWA), PIOTR DUTKIEWICZ: Mr. President, if I may I would like to go back to the issue of Crimea, because it is of key importance for both the East and the West. I would like to ask you to give us your picture of the events that lead to it, specifically why you made this decision. Was it possible to do things differently? How did you do it? There are important details—how Russia did it inside Crimea. Finally, how do you see the consequences of this decision for Russia, for Ukraine, for Europe and for the normative world order? I am asking this because I believe millions of people would like to hear your personal reconstruction of those events and of the way you made the decision.

VLADIMIR PUTIN: I do not know how many times I spoke about this, but I will do it again.

On February 21, Viktor Yanukovych signed the well-known documents with the opposition. Foreign ministers of three European countries signed their names under this agreement as guarantors of its implementation.

In the evening of February 21, President Obama called me and we discussed these issues and how we would assist in the implementation of these agreements. Russia undertook certain obligations.

I heard that my American colleague was also ready to undertake some obligations. This was the evening of the 21st. On the same day, President Yanukovych called me to say he signed the agreement, the situation had stabilized and he was going to a conference in Kharkov. I will not conceal the fact that I expressed my concern: how was it possible to leave the capital in this situation. He replied that he found it possible because there was the document signed with the opposition and guaranteed by foreign ministers of European countries.

I will tell you more, I told him I was not sure everything would be fine, but it was for him to decide. He was the president, he knew the situation, and he knew better what to do. "In any case, I do not think you should withdraw the law enforcement forces from Kiev," I told him. He said he understood. Then he left and gave orders to withdraw all the law enforcement troops from Kiev.

Nice move, of course.

We all know what happened in Kiev. On the following day, despite all our telephone conversations, despite the signatures of the foreign ministers, as soon as Yanukovych left Kiev his administration was taken over by force along with the government building. On the same day, they shot at the cortege of Ukraine's Prosecutor General, wounding one of his security guards.

Yanukovych called me and said he would like us to meet to talk it over. I agreed. Eventually we agreed to meet in Rostov because it was closer and he did not want to go too far. I was ready to fly to Rostov. However, it turned out he could not go even there. They were beginning to use force against him already, holding him at gunpoint. They were not quite sure where to go.

I will not conceal it; we helped him move to Crimea, where he stayed for a few days. That was when Crimea was still part of Ukraine. However, the situation in Kiev was developing very rapidly and violently, we know what happened, though the broad public may not know— people were killed, they were burned alive there. They came into the office of the Party of Regions, seized the technical workers and killed them, burned them alive in the basement. Under those circumstances, there was no way he could return to Kiev. Everybody forgot about the agreements with the opposition signed by foreign ministers and about our telephone conversations. Yes, I will tell you frankly that he asked us to help him get to Russia, which we did. That was all.

Seeing these developments, people in Crimea almost immediately took to arms and asked us for help in arranging the events they intended to hold. I will be frank; we used our Armed Forces to block Ukrainian units stationed in Crimea, but not to force anyone to take part in the elections.

This is impossible, you are all grown people, and you understand it. How could we do it? Lead people to polling stations at gunpoint?

People went to vote as if it were a celebration,

everybody knows this, and they all voted, even the Crimean Tatars. There were fewer Crimean Tatars, but the overall vote was high. While the turnout in Crimea in general was about 96 or 94 percent, a smaller number of Crimean Tatars showed up. However 97 percent of them voted 'yes'. Why? Because those who did not want it did not come to the polling stations, and those who did voted 'yes'.

I already spoke of the legal side of the matter. The Crimean Parliament met and voted in favor of the referendum. Here again, how could anyone say that several dozen people were dragged to parliament to vote? This never happened and it was impossible: if anyone did not want to vote they would get on a train or plane, or their car and be gone.

They all came and voted for the referendum, and then the people came and voted in favor of joining Russia, that is all. How will this influence international relations? We can see what is happening; however if we refrain from using so-called double standards and accept that all people have equal rights, it would have no influence at all. We have to admit the right of those people to self-determination.[105]

PRESIDENTIAL CRIMES: THEN AND NOW

November 3, 2014

Not much remains of the once vibrant American left-wing. Among the remnants there is such a hatred of Richard Nixon and Ronald Reagan that the commitment of these two presidents to ending dangerous military rivalries is unrecognized. Whenever I write about the illegal invasions of other countries launched by Clinton, George W. Bush, and Obama, leftists point to Chile, Nicaragua and Grenada and say that nothing has changed. But a great deal has changed. In the 1970s and 1980s Nixon and Reagan focused on reducing Cold War tensions. Courageously, Nixon opened to China, and Reagan negotiated with Gorbachev the end of the dangerous Cold War.

Beginning with the Clinton regime, the neoconservative doctrine of the US as the Uni-power exercising hegemony over the world has resurrected tensions between nuclear-armed powers. Clinton trashed the word of the Reagan and George H.W. Bush administrations and expanded NATO throughout Eastern Europe and brought the military alliance to Russia's border. The George W. Bush regime withdrew from the anti-ballistic missile treaty and revised US war doctrine to permit pre-emptive nuclear attack, thus bringing major security problems to Russia. The Obama regime announced the "pivot to Asia" with the purpose of controlling shipping in the South China Sea. Additionally, the Clinton, George W. Bush, and Obama regimes fomented wars across a wide swath of the planet from Yugoslavia and Serbia through the Middle East to South Ossetia and now in Ukraine.

The neoconservative ideology rose from the post-Reagan collapse of the Soviet Union. The doctrine met the need of the US military/security complex for a new enemy in order to avoid downsizing. Washington's pursuit of empire is a principal danger to life itself.

Unlike Clinton, George W. Bush, and Obama, Nixon and Reagan went against the military/security complex. Nixon opened to China and made arms reduction agreements with the Soviets. Reagan negotiated with Gorbachev the end of the Cold War. The military/security complex was displeased with these presidential initiatives. Both left and right accused Nixon and Reagan of nefarious machinations. Right-wing Republicans said that Nixon and Kissinger were selling America out to the communists and that the scheming Soviets would take advantage of the old movie actor. "Communists," we were assured, "only understand force."

Nixon and Reagan focused on eliminating dangerous rivalries, and the three stooges—Clinton, Bush, and Obama—have resurrected the rivalries. Those who cannot see the astonishing difference are blinded by prejudices.

In this chapter I describe unappreciated aspects of the Nixon and Reagan presidencies. What I provide is neither a justification nor a denunciation, but an explanation. Here is what Patrick Buchanan, who was in the White House with both presidents, wrote to me in response to my explanation:

> *Craig, you are dead on in what you write about both Nixon and Reagan and what they sought in their presidencies. Reagan often talked of those "godawful weapons," meaning nukes. I was at Reykjavik with him, and was stunned at Hofde House to learn that RR pretty much wanted to trade them all away. And when, years later, Tom Wicker wrote favorably about the Nixon presidency, he accurately titled his book* One of Us. *All his life Nixon sought the approbation of the Establishment. Am deep into a new book, based on my experiences and my White House files, and all through it I am urging him [Nixon] to be and to become the kind of conservative president I wanted, but he never was. My thanks for bringing in* The Greatest Comeback, *which covered the period when I was closest to him.*
> *All the best, Pat.*

Writing for Americans is not always an enjoyable experience. Many readers want to have their prejudices confirmed, not challenged. Emotions rule their reason, and they are capable of a determined resistance to facts and are not inhibited from displays of rudeness and ignorance. Indeed, some are so proud of their shortcomings that they can't wait to show them to others. Some simply cannot read and confuse explanations with justifications as if the act of explaining something justifies the person or event explained. Thankfully, all readers are not handicapped in these ways or there would be no point in trying to inform the American people.

In a recent column I used some examples of Clinton-era scandals to make a point about the media, pointing out that the media and the American people were more interested in Clinton's sexual escapades and in his choice

of underwear than in the many anomalies associated with such serious events as the Oklahoma City bombing, Waco, the mysterious death of a White House legal counsel, sanctions on Iraq that took the lives of 500,000 children, and illegal war against Serbia.

Reaganphobes responded in an infantile way, remonstrating that the same standards should be applied to "your dear beloved Ray-Gun" as to Clinton. Those readers were unable to understand that the article was not about Clinton, but about how the media sensationalizes unimportant events in order to distract attention from serious ones. Examples from the Clinton era were used, because no question better epitomizes the level of the American public's interest in political life than the young woman's question to President Clinton: "boxers or briefs?"

It is doubtful that journalists and historians are capable of providing accurate understandings of any presidential term. Even those personally involved often do not know why some things happened. I have been in White House meetings from which every participant departed with a different understanding of what the president's policy was. This was not the result of lack of clarity on the president's part, but from the various interests present shaping the policy to their agendas.

Many Americans regard the White House as the lair of a powerful being who can snap his fingers and make things happen. The fact of the matter is that presidents have little idea of what is transpiring in the vast cabinet departments and federal agencies that constitute "their" administration. Many parts of government are empires unto themselves. The "Deep State," about which Mike Lofgren, formerly a senior member of the Congressional staff has written, is unaccountable to anyone. But even the accountable part of the government isn't. For example, the information flows from the cabinet departments, such as defense, state, and treasury, are reported to Assistant Secretaries, who control the flow of information to the Secretaries, who inform the President. The civil service professionals can massage the information one way, the Assistant Secretaries another, and the Secretaries yet another. If the Secretaries report the information to the White House Chief of Staff, the information can be massaged yet again. In my day before George W. Bush and Dick Cheney gave us the Gestapo-sounding Department of Homeland Security, the Secret Service reported to an Assistant Secretary of the Treasury, but the official had no way of evaluating the reliability of the information. The Secret Service reported whatever it suited the Secret Service to report.

Those who think that "the President knows" can test their conviction by trying to keep up with the daily announcements from all departments and agencies of the government. It is a known fact that CEOs of large corporations, the relative size of which are tiny compared to the US government, cannot know all that is happening within their organizations.

Nixon: Villain or Centrist Reformer?

I am not particularly knowledgeable about the terms of our various presidents. Nevertheless, I suspect that the Nixon and Reagan terms are among the least understood. Both presidents had more ideological opponents among journalists and historians than they had defenders. Consequently, their stories are distorted by how their ideological opponents want them to be seen and remembered. For example, compare your view of Richard Nixon with the portrait Patrick Buchanan provides in his latest book, *The Greatest Comeback*. A person doesn't have to agree with Buchanan's view of the issues of those years, or with how Buchanan positioned, or tried to position, Nixon on various issues, to learn a great deal about Nixon. Buchanan can be wrong on issues, but he is not dishonest.

For a politician, Richard Nixon was a very knowledgeable person. He travelled widely, visiting foreign leaders. Nixon was the most knowledgeable president about foreign policy we have ever had. He knew more than Obama, Bush I and II, Clinton, Reagan, Carter, Ford, and Johnson combined.

The liberal-left created an image of Nixon as paranoid and secretive with a long enemies list, but Buchanan shows that Nixon was inclusive, a "big tent" politician with a wide range of advisors. There is no doubt that Nixon had enemies. Many of them continue to operate against him long after his death.

Indeed, it was Nixon's inclusiveness that made conservatives suspicious of him. To keep conservatives in his camp, Nixon used their rhetoric, and Nixon's rhetoric fueled Nixon-hatred among the liberal-left. The inclination to focus on words rather than deeds is another indication of the insubstantiality of American political comprehension.

Probably the US has never had a more liberal president than Nixon. Nixon went against conservatives and established the Environmental Protection Agency (EPA) by executive order. He supported the Clean Air Act of 1970. Nixon federalized Medicaid for poor families with dependent children and proposed a mandate that private employers provide health insurance to employees. He desegregated public schools and implemented the first federal affirmative action program.

Declaring that "there is no place on this planet for a billion of its potentially most able people to live in angry isolation," Nixon engineered the opening to Communist China. He ended the Vietnam War and replaced the draft with the volunteer army. He established economic trade with the Soviet Union and negotiated with Soviet leader Brezhnev landmark arms control treaties—SALT I and the Anti-Ballistic Missile Treaty in 1972, which lasted for 30 years until the neoconized George W. Bush regime violated and terminated the treaty in 2002.

These are astonishing achievements for any president, especially a

Republican one. But if you ask Americans what they know about Nixon, the response is Watergate and President Nixon's forced resignation.

I am convinced that Nixon's opening to China and Nixon's arms control treaties and de-escalation of tensions with the Soviet Union threatened the power and profit of the military/security complex. Watergate was an orchestration used to remove the threat. If you read the Watergate reporting by Woodward and Bernstein in the *Washington Post*, there is no real information in it. In place of information, words are used to create an ominous presence and sinister atmosphere that is transferred to Nixon.

There was nothing in the Watergate scandal that justified Nixon's impeachment, but his liberal policies had alienated conservative Republicans. Conservatives never forgave Nixon for agreeing with Zhou Enlai that Taiwan was part of China. When the *Washington Post*, John Dean, and a missing segment of a tape got Nixon in trouble, conservatives did not come to his defense. The liberal-left was overjoyed that Nixon got his comeuppance for supporting the exposure and prosecution of Alger Hiss two decades previously.

I do not contend that the left-wing has no legitimate reasons for hostility against Nixon. Nixon wanted out of Vietnam, but "with honor" so that conservatives would not abandon him. Nixon did not want to become known as the President who forced the US military to accept defeat. He wanted to end the war, but if not with victory then with a stalemate like Korea. He or Kissinger gave the US military carte blanche to produce a situation that the US could exit "with honor." This resulted in the secret bombing in Laos and Cambodia. The shame of the bombings cancelled any exit with real honor.

The Reagan era is also misunderstood. Just as President Jimmy Carter was regarded as an outsider by the Democratic Washington Establishment, Ronald Reagan was an outsider to the Republican Establishment whose candidate was George H. W. Bush. Just as Carter's presidency was neutered by the Washington Establishment with the frame-up of Carter's Budget Director and Chief of Staff, Reagan was partially neutered before he assumed office, and the Establishment removed in succession two national security advisors who were loyal to Reagan.

Reagan's Priorities and the Establishment's Agenda

When Reagan won the Republican presidential nomination, he was told that although he had defeated the Establishment in the primaries, the voters would not be able to come to his defense in Washington. He must not make Goldwater's mistake and shun the Republican Establishment, but pick its presidential candidate for his vice president. Otherwise, the Republican Establishment would work to defeat him in the presidential election just as Rockefeller had undermined Goldwater.

As a former movie star, Nancy Reagan put great store on personal appearance. Reagan's California crew was a motley one. Lynn Nofziger, for example, sported a beard and a loosely knotted tie if a tie at all. He moved around his office in sock feet without shoes. When Nancy saw Bush's man, Jim Baker, she concluded that the properly attired Baker was the person that she wanted standing next to her husband when photos were made. Consequently, Reagan's first term had Bush's most capable operative as Chief of Staff of the White House.

To get Reagan's program implemented with the Republican Establishment occupying the chief of staff position was a hard fight.

I don't mean that Jim Baker was malevolent and wished to damage Reagan. For a member of the Republican Establishment, Jim Baker was very intelligent, and he is a hard person to dislike. The problem with Baker was two-fold. He was not part of the Reagan team and did not understand what we were about or why Reagan was elected. Americans wanted the stagflation that had destroyed Jimmy Carter's presidency ended, and they were tired of the ongoing Cold War with the Soviet Union and its ever present threat of nuclear Armageddon.

It is not that Baker (or VP Bush) were personally opposed to these goals. The problem was, and still is, that the Establishment, whether Republican or Democratic, is responsive not to solving issues but to accommodating the special interest groups that comprise the Establishment. For the Establishment, preserving power is the primary issue.

The Republican Establishment and the Federal Reserve did not understand Reagan's Supply-Side economic policy. In the entire post World War II period, reductions in tax rates were associated with the Keynesian demand management macroeconomic policy of increasing aggregate demand. The Reagan administration had inherited high inflation, and economists, Wall Street, and the Republican Establishment misunderstood Reagan's Supply-side policy as a stimulus to consumer demand that would cause inflation, already high, to explode. On top of this, conservatives in Congress were disturbed that Reagan's policy would worsen the deficit—in their opinion the worst evil of all.

Reagan's supply-side economic policy was designed not to increase aggregate demand, but to increase aggregate supply. Instead of prices rising, output and employment would rise. This was a radically new way of using fiscal policy, but instead of helping people to understand the new policy, the media ridiculed and mischaracterized the policy as "voodoo economics," "trickle-down economics," and "tax cuts for the rich." These mischaracterizations are still with us three decades later. Nevertheless, the supply-side policy was partially implemented. It was enough to end stagflation and provided the basis for Clinton's economic success. It also provided the economic basis that made credible Reagan's strategy of forcing the Soviets to choose between a new arms race or negotiating the end of the Cold War.

Ending the Cold War and Bad CIA Advice

President Reagan's goal of ending the Cold War was upsetting to both conservatives and the military/security complex. Conservatives warned that wily Soviets would deceive Reagan and gain from the negotiations. The military/security complex regarded Reagan's goal of ending the Cold War as a threat comparable to Nixon's opening to China and arms limitations treaties with the Soviet Union. President John F. Kennedy had threatened the same powerful interests when he realized from the Cuban Missile Crisis that the US must put an end to the risk of nuclear confrontation with the Soviet Union.

With the success of his economic policy in putting the US economy back on its feet, Reagan intended to force a negotiated end to the Cold War by threatening the Soviets with an arms race that their suffering economy could not endure. However, the CIA advised Reagan that if he renewed the arms race, he would lose it, because the Soviet economy, being centrally planned, was in the hands of Soviet leaders, who, unlike Reagan, could allocate as much of the economy as necessary to win the arms race. Reagan did not believe the CIA. He created a secret presidential committee with authority to investigate the CIA's evidence for its claim, and he appointed me to the committee. The committee concluded that the CIA was wrong.

Reagan always told us that his purpose was to end, not win, the Cold War. He said that the only victory he wanted was to remove the threat of nuclear annihilation. He made it clear that he did not want a Soviet scalp. Like Nixon, to keep conservatives on board, he used their rhetoric.

Curing stagflation and ending the Cold War were the main interests of President Reagan. Perhaps I am mistaken, but I do not think he paid much attention to anything else.

Grenada and the Contras in Nicaragua were explained to Reagan as necessary interventions to make the Soviets aware that there would be no further Soviet advances and, thus, help to bring the Soviets to the negotiating table to end the nuclear threat. Unlike the George W. Bush and Obama regimes, the Reagan administration had no goal of a universal American Empire exercising hegemony over the world. Grenada and Nicaragua were not part of an empire-building policy. Reagan understood them as a message to the Soviets that "you are not going any further, so let's negotiate."

Conservatives regarded the revolutionary movements in Grenada and Nicaragua as communist subversion, and were concerned that these movements would ally with the Soviet Union, thus creating more Cuba-like situations. Even President Carter opposed the rise of a left-wing government in Nicaragua. Grenada and Nicaragua were reformist movements rather than communist-inspired, and the Reagan administration should have supported them, but could not because of the hysteria of American conservatives. Reagan knew that if his constituency saw him as "soft on communism," he would lack the domestic support that he needed in order to negotiate with the Kremlin the end of the Cold War.

America Playing the Foreign Policy Game

Today Western governments support and participate in Washington's invasions, but not then. The invasion of Grenada was criticized by both the British and Canadian governments. The US had to use its UN Security Council veto to save itself from being condemned for "a flagrant violation of international law."

The Sandinistas in Nicaragua were reformers opposed to the corruption of the Somoza regime that catered to American corporate and financial interests. The Sandinistas aroused the same opposition from Washington as every reformist government in Latin America always has. Washington has traditionally regarded Latin American reformers as Marxist revolutionary movements and has consistently overthrown reformist governments in behalf of the United Fruit Company and other private interests that have large holdings in countries ruled by unrepresentative governments.

Washington's policy was, and still is, short-sighted and hypocritical. The United States should have allied with representative governments, not against them. However, no American president, no matter how wise and well-intentioned, would have been a match for the combination of the interests of politically-connected US corporations and the fear of more Cubas. Remember Marine General Smedley Butler's confession that he and his US Marines served to make Latin America safe for the United Fruit Company and "some lousy investment of the bankers."[106]

Information is Power

Americans, even well informed ones, dramatically over-estimate the knowledge of presidents and the neutrality of the information that is fed to them by the various agencies and advisors. Information is power, and presidents get the information that Washington wants them to receive. In Washington private agendas abound, and no president is immune from these agendas. A cabinet secretary, budget director, or White House chief of staff who knows how Washington works and has media allies is capable, if so inclined, of shaping the agenda independently of the president's preferences.

The Establishment prefers a nonentity as president, a person without experience and a cadre of knowledgeable supporters to serve him. Harry Truman was, and Obama is, putty in the hands of the Establishment.

If you read Oliver Stone and Peter Kuznick's *The Untold History of the US*, you will see that the Democratic Establishment, realizing that FDR would not survive his fourth term, forced his popular Vice President Henry Wallace off the ticket and put in his place the inconsequential Truman. With Truman in place, the military/security complex was able to create the Cold War.

From Bad to Worse

The transgressions of law that occurred during the Nixon and Reagan years are small when compared to the crimes of Clinton, George W. Bush and Obama, and the crimes were punished. Nixon was driven from office and numerous Reagan administration officials were prosecuted and convicted. Neither Nixon nor Reagan could have run roughshod over both Constitution and statutory law, setting aside habeas corpus and due process and detaining US citizens indefinitely without charges and convictions, authorizing and justifying torture, spying without warrants, and executing US citizens without due process of law.

Moreover, unlike the Clinton, Bush, and Obama regimes, the Reagan administration prosecuted those who broke the law. Assistant Secretary of State Elliott Abrams was convicted, National Security Advisor Robert McFarlane was convicted, Chief of CIA Central American Task Force Alan Fiers was convicted, Clair George, Chief of the CIA's Division of Covert Operations was convicted. Richard Secord was convicted. National Security Advisor John Poindexter was convicted. Oliver North was convicted. North's conviction was later overturned, and President George H.W. Bush pardoned others. But the Reagan Administration held its operatives accountable to law. No American President since Reagan has held the government accountable.

Clair George was convicted of lying to congressional committees. Richard Secord was convicted of lying to Congress. John Poindexter was convicted of lying to Congress. Alan Fiers was convicted of withholding information from Congress. Compare these convictions then with James R. Clapper now. President Obama appointed Clapper Director of National Intelligence on June 5, 2010, declaring that Clapper "possesses a quality that I value in all my advisers: a willingness to tell leaders what we need to know even if it's not what we want to hear." With this endorsement, Clapper proceeded to lie to Congress under oath, a felony. Clapper was not indicted and prosecuted. He was not even fired or forced to resign. For executive branch officials, perjury is now a dead letter law.

The destruction of the rule of law and accountable government has extended to state and local levels. Police officers no longer "serve and protect" the public. The most dangerous encounter most Americans will ever experience is with police, who brutalize citizens without cause and even shoot them down in their homes and on their streets. A police badge has become a license to kill, and police use it to the hilt. During the Iraq War, more Americans were murdered by police than the military lost troops in combat. And nothing is done about it. The country is facing the November 4 elections, and the abuse of US citizens by "their" police is not an issue. Neither are the many illegal interventions by Washington into the internal affairs of other sovereign countries or the unconstitutional spying that violates citizens' privacy.

The fact that Washington is gearing up for yet another war in the Middle East is not an important issue in the election.

In the US the rule of law, and with it liberty, have been lost. With few exceptions, Americans are too ignorant and unconcerned to do anything about it. The longer the rule of law is set aside, the more difficult it is to reestablish it. Sooner or later the rule of law ceases even as a memory. No candidate in the upcoming election has made the rule of law an issue.

Americans have become a small-minded divided people, ruled by petty hatreds, who are easily set against one another and against other peoples by their rulers.

THE NEXT PRESIDENTIAL ELECTION WILL MOVE THE WORLD CLOSER TO WAR

November 16, 2014

Glenn Greenwald has revealed that Hillary Clinton is the presidential candidate of the banksters and warmongers.[107] Pam and Russ Martens note that Elizabeth Warren is the populist alternative.[108] I doubt that a politician who represents the people can acquire the campaign funds needed to run a campaign. If Warren becomes a threat, the Establishment will frame her with bogus charges and move her aside.

Hillary as president would mean war with Russia. With neocons such as Robert Kagan and Max Boot running her war policy and with Hillary's comparison of Russia's President Putin to Adolf Hitler, war would be a certainty. As I, Michel Chossudovsky and Noam Chomsky have written, the war would be nuclear.

If Hillary is elected president, the financial gangsters and profiteering war criminals would complete their takeover of the country. It would be forever or until Armageddon.

To understand what we would be getting with Hillary, recall the Clinton presidency. The Clinton presidency was transformative in ways not generally recognized. Clinton destroyed the Democratic Party with "free trade" agreements, deregulated the financial system, launched Washington's ongoing policy of "regime change" with illegal military attacks on Yugoslavia and Iraq, and his regime used deadly force without cause against American civilians and covered up the murders with fake investigations. These were four big changes that set the country on its downward spiral into a militarized police state with massive income and wealth inequality.

One can understand why Republicans wanted the North American Free Trade Agreement, but it was Bill Clinton who signed it into law. "Free trade" agreements are devices used by US corporations to offshore their production of goods and services sold in American markets. By moving production abroad, labor cost savings increase corporate profits and share prices, bringing capital gains to shareholders and multimillion dollar performance bonuses to executives. The rewards to capital are large, but the rewards come at the expense of US manufacturing workers and the tax base of cities and states.

When plants are closed and the work shipped overseas, middle class jobs disappear. Industrial and manufacturing unions are eviscerated, destroying the labor unions that financed the Democrats' election campaigns. The countervailing power of labor against capital was lost, and Democrats had to turn to the same sources of funding as Republicans. The result is a one party state.

The weakened tax base of cities and states has made it possible for Republicans to attack the public sector unions. Today the Democratic Party no longer exists as a political party financed by the union dues of ordinary people. Today both political parties represent the interests of the same powerful interest groups: the financial sector, the military/security complex, the Israel Lobby, the extractive industries, and agribusiness.

Neither party represents voters. Thus, the people are loaded up with the costs of financial bailouts and wars, while the extractive industries and Monsanto destroy the environment and degrade the food supply.

Elections no longer deal with real issues such as the loss of constitutional protections and a government accountable to law. Instead the parties compete on issues such as homosexual marriage and federal funding of abortion.

Clinton's repeal of the Glass-Steagall Act was the initiating move followed by the removal of more constraints that allowed the financial system to transform itself into a gambling casino where bets are covered by the public and the Federal Reserve. The full consequences of this remain to be seen.

The Clinton regime's attack on the Serbs was a war crime under international law, but it was the Yugoslavian president who tried to defend his country who was put on trial as a war criminal. When the Clinton regime murdered Randy Weaver's family at Ruby Ridge and 76 people at Waco, subjecting the few survivors to a show trial, the regime's crimes against humanity went unpunished. Thus did Clinton set the precedents for 14 years of Bush/Obama crimes against humanity in seven countries. Millions of people have been killed, maimed, and displaced, and it is all acceptable.

It is easy enough for a government to stir up its population against foreigners as the successes of Clinton, George W. Bush, and Obama demonstrate. But the Clinton regime managed to stir up Americans against their fellows as well. When the FBI gratuitously murdered Randy Weaver's wife and young son, propagandistic denunciations of Randy Weaver took the place of accountability. When the FBI attacked the Branch Davidians, a religious movement that split from the Seventh-day Adventist Church, with tanks and poison gas, causing a fire that burned 76 people, mainly women and children, to death, the mass murder was justified by the Clinton regime with wild and unsubstantiated charges against the government's murdered victims.

All efforts to bring accountability to the crimes were blocked. These were the precedents for the executive branch's successful drive to secure immunity from law. This immunity has now spread to local police who routinely abuse and murder US citizens on their streets and in their homes.

Washington's international lawlessness about which the Russian and Chinese governments increasingly complain originated with the Clinton regime. Washington's lies about Saddam Hussein's "weapons of mass destruction" originated in the Clinton regime, as did the goal of "regime change" in Iraq and Washington's illegal bombings and embargoes that costs the lives of 500,000 Iraqi children, lost lives that Clinton's Secretary of State said were "worth it".

The US government has done wicked things in the past. For example, the Spanish-American war was a grab for empire, and Washington has always protected the interests of US corporations from Latin American reformers, but the Clinton regime globalized the criminality. Regime change has become reckless bringing with it danger of nuclear war. It is no longer Grenada and Honduras whose governments are overthrown. Today it is Russia and China that are targeted. Former parts of Russia herself—Georgia and Ukraine—have been turned into Washington's vassal states. Washington-financed NGOs organize "student protests" in Hong Kong, hoping that the protests will spread into China and destabilize the government. The recklessness of these interventions in the internal affairs of nuclear powers is unprecedented.

Hillary Clinton is a warmonger, as will be the Republican candidate. The hardening anti-Russian rhetoric issuing from Washington and its punk EU puppet states places the world on the road to extinction. The arrogant neoconservatives, with their hubristic belief that the US is the "exceptional and indispensable" country, would regard a de-escalation of rhetoric and sanctions as backing down. The more the neocons and politicians such as senators John McCain and Lindsey Graham escalate the rhetoric, the closer we come to war.

As the US government now embraces pre-emptive arrest and detention of those who might someday commit a crime, the entire cadre of neocon warmongers should be arrested and indefinitely detained before they destroy humanity.

The Clinton years produced a spate of books documenting the numerous crimes and cover-ups—the Oklahoma City bombing, Ruby Ridge, Waco, the FBI crime lab scandal, Vincent Foster's death, CIA involvement in drug running, the militarization of law enforcement, Kosovo, you name it. Most of these books are written from a libertarian or conservative viewpoint as no one realized while it was happening the nature of the transformation of American governance. Those who have forgotten and those too young ever to have known owe it to themselves to acquaint or re-acquaint themselves with the Clinton years.

Recently I wrote about Ambrose Evans-Pritchard's book, *The Secret Life of Bill Clinton*. Another book with substantial documentation is James Bovard's *Feeling Your Pain*. Congress and the media aided and abetted the extensive cover-ups, focusing instead on the relatively unimportant Whitewater real estate deals and Clinton's sexual affair with White House intern Monica Lewinsky.

Clinton and his corrupt regime lied about many important things, but only his lie about his affair with Monica Lewinsky caused the House of Representatives to impeach him. By ignoring numerous substantial grounds for impeachment and selecting instead an insubstantial reason, Congress and the media were complicit in the rise of an unaccountable executive branch. This lack of accountability has brought us tyranny at home and war abroad, and these two evils are enveloping us all.

OPENING THE GATES TO WORLD WAR III

November 23, 2014

"The US wants to subdue Russia, to solve US problems at Russia's expense. No one in history ever managed to do this to Russia, and no one ever will." Vladimir Putin, November 17, 2014.

According to news reports, Washington has decided to arm Ukraine for renewed military assault on Russian ethnics in Donetsk and Luhansk.

A Russian foreign ministry official condemned Washington's reckless decision to supply weapons to Kiev as a violation of agreements that would make a political resolution of the conflict less likely. This statement is perplexing. It implies that the Russian government has not yet figured out that Washington has no interest in resolving the conflict. Washington's purpose is to use the hapless Ukrainians against Russia. The worse the conflict becomes, the happier Washington is.

The Russian government made a bet that Europe would come to its senses and the conflict would be peacefully resolved. The Russian government has lost that bet and must immediately move to preempt a worsening crisis by uniting the separatist provinces with Russia or by reading the riot act to Europe.

It would be a costly humiliation for the Russian government to abandon the ethnic Russians to a military assault. If Russia stands aside while Donetsk and Luhansk are destroyed, the next attack will be on Crimea. By the time Russia is forced to fight Russia will face a better armed, better prepared, and more formidable foe.

By its inaction the Russian government is aiding and abetting Washington's onslaught against Russia. The Russian government could tell Europe to call this off or go without natural gas. The Russian government could declare a no-fly zone over the separatist provinces and deliver an ultimatum to Kiev. The Russian government could accept the requests from Donetsk and Luhansk for unification or reunification with Russia. Any one of these actions would suffice to resolve the conflict before it spins out of control and opens the gates to World War III.

The American people are clueless that Washington is on the brink of starting a dangerous war. Even informed commentators become sidetracked in refuting propaganda that Russia has invaded Ukraine and is supplying weapons to the separatists. These commentators are mistaken if they think establishing the facts will do any good.

Washington intends to remove Russia as a constraint on Washington's power.

THE CIA'S TORTURE PROGRAM

December 11, 2014

UPDATE: Congress fails to hold executive branch accountable for its massive violations of human rights as documented in the released summary of the CIA Torture Report, but passes sanctions on Venezuela for "human rights violations."[109]

Readers have asked for my take on the CIA torture report. There is so much information and commentary available that it is unnecessary.

Igor Volsky provides a concise summary.[110]

President George W. Bush signed off on torture and then told the gullible people that "this government does not torture people." According to the Senate Intelligence Committee's report, the torture was horrific.

The CIA even tortured its own informers. Two American psychologists who designed the torture program were paid $81 million.

CIA torturers received cash awards for "consistently superior work" when their innocent victims died.[111]

The US government involved 54 countries in its torture program. The rendition program sent detainees to other countries where they were tortured in secret "black sites."[112]

Obama tortures also.[113]

Those Americans who committed crimes as horrific as any in history have been given a pass by Obama.

No accountability for their crimes.[114]

This finishes off the rule of law in America, which was already on life support.[115]

CIA Torture Report Sparks Worldwide Condemnation: Even Nations That Participated Were Shocked How Far It Went.[116]

Here's a history of the CIA's torture program.[117]

Former president of Poland admits that Poland hosted a CIA torture prison:[118]

CIA destroyed evidence of its crimes.[119]

Instead of apologizing for the CIA's destruction of our country's reputation, CIA director John Brennan defended the policy and claimed it helped to protect us from terrorists. The CIA fought for months to block even the release of the truncated and redacted report that made it to the public. Have a look at Brennan.[120] He looks like and is more dangerous than a Nazi.

Just google CIA torture report and you will find much to read, including justifications of the torture program by neoconservatives, Republican members of the House and Senate, Dick Cheney, the presstitute media, and a large number of others.

Here's my two cents: *One purpose of the torture program was to produce self-incriminated "terrorists" to justify and feed the hoax "war on terror." The "war on terror" was public cover for secret agendas that the American people would have rejected. This is disturbing enough. Even more disturbing, the torture program shows that no one in the US and European governments who knew of the program and participated in torture has an ounce of humanity, integrity, compassion, and morality. They are evil people, and the ones who inflicted the torture enjoyed the pain and suffering that they inflicted on others.*

NEOCONSERVATIVES HAVE US ON THE BRINK OF WAR AND ECONOMIC COLLAPSE

December 12, 2014

On occasion a reader will ask if I can give readers some good news. The answer is: not unless I lie to you like "your" government and the mainstream media do. If you want faked "good news," you need to retreat into The Matrix. In exchange for less stress and worry, you will be led unknowingly into financial ruin and nuclear Armageddon.

The neoconservatives, a small group of warmongers strongly allied with the military/industrial complex and Israel, gave us Granada and the Contras affair in Nicaragua. President Reagan fired them, and they were prosecuted, but subsequently pardoned by Reagan's successor, George H.W. Bush.

Ensconced in think tanks and protected by Israeli and military/ security complex money, the neoconservatives reemerged in the Clinton administration and engineered the breakup of Yugoslavia, the war against Serbia, and the expansion of NATO to Russia's borders.

Neoconservatives dominated the George W. Bush regime. They controlled the Pentagon, the National Security Council, the Office of the Vice President, and much else. Neoconservatives gave us 9/11 and its cover-up, the invasions of Afghanistan and Iraq, the beginning of the destabilizations of Pakistan and Yemen, the U.S. Africa Command, the invasion of South Ossetia by Georgia, the demise of the ABM Treaty, unconstitutional and illegal spying on American citizens without warrants, loss of constitutional protections, torture, and the unaccountability of the executive branch to law, Congress, and the judiciary.

In short, the neoconservatives laid the foundation for dictatorship and for WW III.

The Obama regime held no one accountable for the crimes of the Bush regime, thus creating the precedent that the executive branch is above the law. Instead, the Obama regime prosecuted whistleblowers who told the truth about government crimes.

Neoconservatives remain very influential in the Obama regime. As examples, Obama appointed neoconservative Susan Rice as his National Security Advisor. Obama appointed neoconservative Samantha Power as U.S. Ambassador to the United Nations. Obama appointed neoconservative Victoria Nuland as Assistant Secretary of State. Nuland's office, working with the CIA and Washington-financed NGOs, organized the U.S. coup in Ukraine.

Neoconservatism is the only extant political ideology. The ideology is "America uber alles."

Neoconservatives believe that History has chosen the United States to exercise hegemony over the world, thereby making the U.S. "exceptional" and "indispensable." Obama himself has declared as much. This ideology gives neoconservatives tremendous confidence and drive, just as Karl Marx's conclusion that history had chosen the workers to be the ruling class gave early communists confidence and drive.

This confidence and drive makes the neoconservatives reckless.

To advance their agenda neoconservatives propagandize the populations of the U.S. and Washington's vassal states. The presstitutes deliver the neoconservatives' lies to the unsuspecting public: Russia has invaded and annexed Ukrainian provinces; Putin intends to reconstitute the Soviet Empire; Russia is a gangster state without democracy; Russia is a threat to the Baltics, Poland, and all of Europe, necessitating a U.S./ NATO military buildup on Russia's borders; China, a Russian ally, must be militarily contained with new U.S. naval and air bases surrounding China and controlling Chinese sea lanes.

The neoconservatives and President Obama have made it completely clear that the U.S. will not accept Russia and China as sovereign countries with economic and foreign policies independent of the interests of Washington. Russia and China are acceptable only as vassal states, like the UK, Europe, Japan, Canada, and Australia.

Clearly, the neoconservative formula is a formula for the final war.

All of humanity is endangered by a handful of evil men and women ensconced in positions of power in Washington.

Anti-Russia propaganda has gone into high gear. Putin is the "new Hitler."

Daniel Zubov reports on a joint conference held by three U.S. think tanks.

The conference blamed Russia for the failures of Washington's foreign policy. Sputnicknews.com unpacks how neoconservatives operate in order to control the explanations.[121] Even Henry Kissinger is under attack for stating the obvious truth that Russia has a legitimate interest in Ukraine, a land long part of Russia and located in Russia's legitimate sphere of influence.

Since the Clinton regime, Washington has been acting against Russian interests. In his forthcoming book, *The Globalization of War: America's Long War against Humanity*, Professor Michel Chossudovsky presents a realistic appraisal of how close Washington has brought the world to its demise in nuclear war.

This passage is from the Preface:

> The 'globalization of war' is a hegemonic project. Major military and covert intelligence operations are being undertaken simultaneously in the Middle East, Eastern Europe, sub-Saharan Africa, Central Asia and the Far East. The US military agenda combines both major theater operations as well as covert actions geared towards destabilizing sovereign states.
>
> Under a global military agenda, the actions undertaken by the Western military alliance (US-NATO-Israel) in Afghanistan, Pakistan, Palestine, Ukraine, Syria and Iraq are coordinated at the highest levels of the military hierarchy. We are not dealing with piecemeal military and intelligence operations. The July-August 2014 attack on Gaza by Israeli forces was undertaken in close consultation with the United States and NATO. In turn, the actions in Ukraine and their timing coincided with the onslaught of the attack on Gaza.
>
> In turn, military undertakings are closely coordinated with a process of economic warfare which consists not only in imposing sanctions on sovereign countries but also in deliberate acts of destabilization of financial and currency markets, with a view to undermining the enemies' national economies.
>
> The United States and its allies have launched a military adventure which threatens the future of humanity. As we go to press, US and NATO forces have been deployed in Eastern Europe. US military intervention under a humanitarian mandate is proceeding in sub-Saharan Africa. The US and its allies are threatening China under President Obama's 'Pivot to Asia'.
>
> In turn, military maneuvers are being conducted at Russia's doorstep which could lead to escalation.
>
> The US airstrikes initiated in September 2014 directed against Iraq and Syria under the pretext of going after the

Islamic State are part of a scenario of military escalation extending from North Africa and the Eastern Mediterranean to Central and South Asia.

The Western military alliance is in an advanced state of readiness.

As I have often remarked, Americans are an insouciant people. They are simply unaware. Suppose they were aware, suppose that the entire population understood the peril, could anything be done, or have the insouciant Americans fallen under the control of the police state that Washington has created?

I don't think there is much hope from the American people. The American people cannot tell genuine from fake leadership, and the ruling private elites will not permit real leaders to emerge. Moreover, there is no organized movement in opposition to the neoconservatives.

The hope comes from outside the political system. The hope is that the House of Cards and rigged markets erected by policymakers for the benefit of the One Percent collapses.

THE OUTLOOK
FOR THE
NEW YEAR

December 29, 2014

The Russian government no longer has any illusion that Europe is capable of an independent foreign policy. Russian President Vladimir Putin has stated publicly that Russia has learned that diplomacy with Europe is pointless, because European politicians represent Washington's interest, not Europe's. Foreign Minister Sergey Lavrov recently acknowledged that Europe's Captive Nation status has made it clear to Russia that Russian goodwill gestures are unable to produce diplomatic results.

With Moscow's delusion that diplomacy with the West can produce peaceful solutions shattered, reality has set in, reinforced by the demonization of Vladimir Putin by Washington and its vassal states. Hillary Clinton called Putin the new Hitler. While Washington incorporates former constituent parts of the Russian and Soviet empires into its own empire and bombs seven countries, Washington claims that Putin is militarily aggressive and intends to reconstitute the Soviet empire. Washington arms the neo-Nazi regime Obama established in Ukraine, while erroneously claiming that Putin has invaded and annexed Ukrainian provinces. All of these blatant lies are echoed repeatedly by the Western presstitutes. Not even Hitler had such a compliant media as Washington has.

Every diplomatic effort by Russia has been blocked by Washington and has come to naught. So now Russia has been forced by reality to update its military doctrine. The new doctrine approved on December 26 states that the US and NATO comprise a major military threat to the existence of Russia as a sovereign independent country.

The Russian document cites Washington's war doctrine of pre-emptive nuclear attack, deployment of anti-ballistic missiles, buildup of NATO forces, and intent to deploy weapons in space as clear indications that Washington is preparing to attack Russia.

Washington is also conducting economic and political warfare against Russia, attempting to destabilize the economy with economic sanctions and attacks on the ruble. The Russian document acknowledges that Russia faces Western threats of regime change achieved through "actions aimed at violent change of the Russian constitutional order, destabilization of the political and social environment, and disorganization of the functioning of governmental bodies, crucial civilian and military facilities and informational infrastructure of Russia." Foreign financed NGOs and foreign owned Russian media are tools in Washington's hands for destabilizing Russia.

Washington's reckless aggressive policy against Russia has resurrected the nuclear arms race. Russia is developing two new ICBM systems and in 2016 will deploy a weapons system designed to negate the US anti-ballistic missile system. In short, the evil warmongers that rule in Washington have set the world on the path to nuclear Armageddon.

The Russian and Chinese governments both understand that their existence is threatened by Washington's hegemonic ambitions. Larchmonter reports that in order to defeat Washington's plans to marginalize both countries, the Russian and Chinese governments have decided to unify their economies into one and to conjoin their military commands. Henceforth, Russia and China move together on the economic and military fronts. I recommend that you read this 27-page well-documented article.[122]

The unity of the Bear and the Dragon reduces the crazed neoconservatives' dream of "an American century" to dangerous nonsense. As Larchmonter puts it, "The US and NATO would need Michael the Archangel to defeat China-Russia, and from all signs Michael the Archangel is aligned with the Bear and its Orthodox culture. There is no weapon, no strategy, no tactic conceivable in the near future to damage either of these rising economies now that they are 'base pairs.'"

Larchmonter sees hope in the new geopolitics created by the conjoining of Russia and China. I don't dispute this, but if the arrogant neoconservatives realize that their hegemonic policy has created a foe over which Washington cannot prevail, they will push for a pre-emptive nuclear strike before the Russian-Chinese unified command is fully operational.

The US economy—indeed the entire Western orientated economy from Japan to Europe—is a house of cards. Since the economic downturn began seven years ago, the entirety of Western economic policy has been diverted to the support of a few over-sized banks, sovereign debt, and the US dollar. Consequently, the economies themselves and the ability of populations to cope have deteriorated.

The financial markets are based on manipulation, not on fundamentals. The manipulation is untenable.

With debt exploding, negative real interest rates make no sense. With real consumer incomes, real consumer credit, and real retail sales stagnant or falling, the stock market is a bubble. With Russia, China, and other countries moving away from the use of the dollar to settle international accounts, with Russia developing an alternative to the SWIFT financial network, the BRICS developing alternatives to the IMF and World Bank, and with other parts of the world developing their own credit card and Internet systems, the US dollar, along with the Japanese and European currencies that are being printed in order to support the dollar's exchange value, could experience a dramatic drop in exchange value, which would make the import-dependent Western world dysfunctional.

It took the Russians and Chinese a long time to comprehend the evil that has control in Washington. Therefore, both countries risk nuclear attack prior to the full operational capability of their conjoined defense. As the Western economy is a house of cards, Russia and China could focus on collapsing the house of cards before the neoconservatives can drive the world to war.

For example, what would happen to the thinly capitalized EU banks if Russia announced that the sanctions have hurt the Russian economy and deprived Russia of the ability to repay loans to the European banks? What would happen to Europe if Russia announced the termination of gas supplies to Europe as a result of Europe's hostile actions against Russia?

Washington doesn't hold all the cards. Russia and China also hold cards.

Larchmonter possibly is correct. 2015 could be a very good year, but pre-emptive economic moves by Moscow and Beijing could be required. Putin's current plan seems to be to turn away from the West, ignore the provocations, and mesh Russia's strategic and economic interests with those of Asia. This is a humane and reasonable course of action, but it leaves the West untroubled and undistracted by its economic vulnerabilities. An untroubled West remains a grave danger not only to Russia and China but also to Americans and the entire world.

CHARLIE HEBDO AND TSARNAEV'S TRIAL: CUI BONO?

January 8, 2015

Well known writers Thierry Meyssan and Kevin Barrett see the "terrorist" attack on Charlie Hebdo *as a false flag attack.*[123]

According to news reports, one of the accused in the attack on Charlie Hebdo *when hearing that he was being sought for the crime turned himself in to police with an ironclad alibi.*[124]

According to other news reports, police found the ID of Said Kouachi at the scene of the Charlie Hebdo *shooting. Does this sound familiar? Remember, authorities claimed to have found the undamaged passport of one of the alleged 9/11 hijackers among the massive pulverized ruins of the twin towers. Once the authorities discover that the stupid Western peoples will believe any transparent lie, the authorities use the lie again and again. The police claim to have discovered a dropped ID is a sure indication that the attack on* Charlie Hebdo *was an inside job and that people identified by NSA as hostile to the Western wars against Muslims are going to be framed for an inside job designed to pull France firmly back under Washington's thumb.*

There are two ways to look at the alleged terrorist attack on the French satirical magazine *Charlie Hebdo*.

One is that in the English speaking world, or much of it, the satire would have been regarded as "hate speech," and the satirists arrested. But in France Muslims are excluded from the privileged category, took offense at the satire, and retaliated.

Why would Muslims bother? By now Muslims must be accustomed to Western hypocrisy and double standards. Little doubt that Muslims are angry that they do not enjoy the protections other minorities receive, but why retaliate for satire but not for France's participation in Washington's wars against Muslims in which hundreds of thousands have died? Isn't being killed more serious than being satirized?

Another way of seeing the attack is as an attack designed to shore up France's vassal status to Washington. The suspects can be both guilty and patsies. Just remember all the terrorist plots created by the FBI that served to make the terrorism threat real to Americans.[125]

France is suffering from the Washington-imposed sanctions against Russia. Shipyards are impacted from being unable to deliver Russian orders due to France's vassalage status to Washington, and other aspects of the French economy are being adversely impacted by sanctions that Washington forced its NATO puppet states to apply to Russia.

This week the French president said that the sanctions against Russia should end (so did the German vice-chancellor).

This is too much foreign policy independence on France's part for Washington. Has Washington resurrected "Operation Gladio," which consisted of CIA bombing attacks against Europeans during the post-WW II era that Washington blamed on communists and used to destroy communist influence in European elections? Just as the world was led to believe that communists were behind Operation Gladio's terrorist attacks, Muslims are blamed for the attacks on the French satirical magazine.

The Roman question is always: Who benefits? The answer is: Not France, not Muslims, but US world hegemony. US hegemony over the world is what the CIA supports. US world hegemony is the neoconservative-imposed foreign policy of the US.

According to National Public Radio, *Charlie Hebdo* is about free speech. The US has free speech, claim NPR's pundits, but terrorists have taken it away from the French.

Just how does the US have free speech when *New York Times* reporter James Risen was psychologically put on the rack to force him to reveal his source, despite the fact that Risen and his source are protected by the US Constitution and whistleblower protections? Clearly, in the US, "national security" has trumped everything else.

"National security" has nothing to do with national security. It has only to do with protecting the criminals in the US government from accountability for their crimes. Every time you hear Washington invoke "national security," you know for a 100% fact that the government has committed yet another crime.

National security is the cloak for Washington's criminal operations. "National security" prevents the government's crimes from coming to light and thereby protects government from accountability.

One wonders what role "national security" will play in the trial of alleged Boston Marathon Bomber Dzhokhar Tsarnaev. Tsarnaev has been in custody since April 2013 and under indictment since April 22, 2013. Yet jury selection is only now beginning in January 2015. Why this long delay? The guarantee of a speedy trial no longer means anything, but with all sorts of charges in addition to the bombing for which the government claims eye witnesses and confessions and with the Tsarnaev brothers already convicted in the media, the long delay is a puzzle. Yet, we have not heard from Dzhokhar Tsarnaev himself. It is difficult to push away the thought that Dzhokhar's trial has been delayed in order to complete his conditioning and acceptance of his guilt and in order for the many questions raised by alternative media to be forgotten.

The print and TV media have dished up the government's explanation without investigation. However, the alternative media have taken great exception to every aspect of the case. As the US government has taught us since the Clinton regime, the safest assumption is that everything the government says is a lie.

The most suspicious aspect of the event was the speed with which an army of 10,000 heavily armed troops consisting of police from various jurisdictions and National Guard soldiers outfitted in military gear and provided with tanks or armored personnel carriers were on the streets of Boston. Never before has such a massive force equipped with military heavy equipment been employed in a manhunt, much less for one wounded, unarmed, 19-year old kid.

For such a force to be assembled and deployed so quickly suggests pre-planning. What was presented as a manhunt for one badly wounded suspect looks more like a test case and precedent for locking down one of America's largest cities. Squads of troops evicted US citizens from their homes at gunpoint and conducted indiscriminate searches of houses that contributed nothing to apprehending the alleged suspect.

The chances are zero that any household would have harbored a badly wounded unarmed fugitive dying from the lack of medical care.

Not only was Boston and its suburbs locked down, the Federal Aviation Administration restricted airspace over Boston and issued a "ground stop" for Logan airport. Why?

Several other cities in Massachusetts and even some other states put their police forces on alert. Why?

On the scene were the FBI, the Bureau of Alcohol, Tobacco, Firearms, and Explosives, the CIA, the Drug Enforcement Administration, and the National Counterterrorism Center. The US Attorney General committed the full resources of the US Department of Justice.

Why?

The only plausible answer is to raise the fear level in order to gain the public's acceptance of the lockdown of Boston and police invasions of citizens' homes. It makes no sense that danger from a badly wounded unarmed 19 year-old could possibly justify such expense and trampling of constitutional rights of citizens.

A non-gullible person must wonder if the bombing was an orchestrated event for the purpose of coordinating state, local, and federal governments in the lockdown of a major city. A poll of Bostonians last July found that 42 percent harbored doubts about the official version of events.[126]

The gullible always say that if a conspiracy existed someone would have talked. But people do talk. It just doesn't do any good. For example, during George W. Bush's first term a NSA whistleblower leaked to *The New York Times* that the NSA was bypassing the FISA Court and spying on American citizens without warrants. Under US law, NSA was in a conspiracy with the Bush regime to commit serious felonies (possibly for the purpose of blackmail), but *The New York Times* spiked the story for one year until George W. Bush was re-elected and the regime had time to ex post facto legalize the felonies.

Operation Gladio was a conspiracy kept secret for decades until a President of Italy revealed it.

The Northwoods Project was kept secret until years afterward when the second Kennedy Commission revealed it.

More than one hundred first responder police and firemen report hearing and personally experiencing multiple explosions floor by floor and even in the sub-basements of the World Trade Center twin towers, and these testimonies had no effect whatsoever.

It only took one high school physics professor to shoot down NIST's account of the collapse of WTC 7.

The fact that it has been conclusively proven that this building was brought down by controlled demolition has had no effect on the official story.

The co-chairmen and legal counsel of the 9/11 Commission published books in which they say that information was withheld from the Commission, that the US Military lied to the Commission, and that the Commission "was set up to fail." Neither Congress, the media, nor the US public had any interest in investigating why information was withheld, why the military lied, and why the Commission was set up to fail. These extraordinary statements by the leaders of the official investigation had no impact whatsoever.

Even today a majority of the US population believes Washington's propaganda that Russia invaded Ukraine and annexed some provinces. Neither judgment nor intelligence are strong points of the American public and juries.

Government tells Americans whatever story the government puts together and sits and laughs at the gullibility of the public.

Today the US public is divided between those who rely on the "mainstream media" and those who rely on the alternative Internet media. Only the latter have any clue as to what is really happening.

The official stories of *Charlie Hebdo* and the Tsarnaev brothers will be based not on facts but on the interests of government. As in the past, the government's interest will prevail.

CHARLIE
HEBDO

January 13, 2015

The *Charlie Hebdo* affair has many of the characteristics of a false flag operation. The attack on the cartoonists' office was a disciplined professional attack of the kind associated with highly trained special forces, yet the suspects who were later corralled and killed seemed bumbling and unprofessional. It is as if there were two different sets of people.

Usually Muslim terrorists are prepared to die in the attack, yet the two professionals who hit *Charlie Hebdo* were determined to escape and succeeded, an amazing feat. It is a plausible inference that the ID left behind in the getaway car was the ID of the two Kouachi brothers, convenient patsies, later killed by police, and from whom we will never hear anything, and not the ID of the professionals who attacked *Charlie Hebdo*.

An important fact that supports this inference is the report that the third suspect in the attack, Hamyd Mourad, the alleged driver of the getaway car, when seeing his name circulating on social media as a suspect realized the danger he was in and quickly turned himself into the police for protection against being murdered by security forces as a terrorist.

Hamyd Mourad says he has an iron-clad alibi. If so, this makes him the despoiler of a false flag attack.

Authorities will have to say that despite being wrong about Mourad, they were right about the Kouachi brothers.[127]

The American and European media have ignored the fact that Mourad turned himself in for protection from being killed as a terrorist as he has an alibi. I googled Hamid Mourad and all I found (January 12) was US and European media reporting that the third suspect had turned himself in. The reason for his surrender was left out of the reports. The news was reported in a way that gave credence to the accusation that the suspect who turned himself in was part of the attack on *Charlie Hebdo*. Not a single US mainstream media source reported that the alleged suspect turned himself in because he has an ironclad alibi.

308

Some media merely reported Mourad's surrender in a headline with no coverage in the report. The list that I googled includes the *Washington Post* (January 7 by Griff Witte and Anthony Faiola); *Die Welt* (Germany) "One suspect has turned himself in to police in connection with Wednesday's massacre at the offices of Parisian satirical magazine, *Charlie Hebdo*"; ABC News (January 7) "Youngest suspect in *Charlie Hebdo* attack turns himself in"; CNN (January 8) "Citing sources, the Agence France Presse news agency reported that an 18-year-old suspect in the attack had surrendered to police."

Another puzzle in the official story that remains unreported by the presstitute media is the alleged suicide of a high ranking member of the French Judicial Police who had an important role in the *Charlie Hebdo* investigation. For unknown reasons, Helric Fredou, a police official involved in this most important investigation of his lifetime, decided to kill himself in his police office on January 7 or January 8 (both dates are reported in the foreign media) in the middle of the night while writing his report on his investigation. A google search as of 6pm EST January 13 turns up no mainstream US media report of this event. The alternative media reports it, as do some UK newspapers, but without suspicion or mention whether his report has disappeared. The official story is that Fredou was suffering from "depression" and "burnout," but no evidence is provided. Depression and burnout are the standard explanations of mysterious deaths that have unsettling implications.

Once again we see the US print and TV media serving as a ministry of propaganda for Washington. In place of investigation, the media repeats the government's implausible story.

It behooves us all to think. Why would Muslims be more outraged by cartoons in a Paris magazine than by hundreds of thousands of Muslims killed by Washington and its French and NATO vassals in seven countries during the past 14 years?

If Muslims are responsible for the attack on *Charlie Hebdo*, what Muslim goal did they achieve? None whatsoever. Indeed, the attack attributed to Muslims has ended French and European sympathy and support for Palestine and European opposition to more US wars against Muslims. Just recently France had voted in the UN with Palestine against the US-Israeli position. This assertion of an independent French foreign policy was reinforced by the recent statement by the President of France that the economic sanctions against Russia should be terminated.

Clearly, France was showing too much foreign policy independence. The attack on *Charlie Hebdo* serves to cow France and place France back under Washington's thumb.

Some will contend that some Muslims are sufficiently stupid to shoot themselves in the head in this way.

But how do we reconcile such alleged stupidity with the alleged Muslim 9/11 and *Charlie Hebdo* professional attacks?

If we believe the official story, the 9/11 attack on the US shows that 19 Muslims, largely Saudis, without any government or intelligence service support, outwitted not only all 16 US intelligence agencies, the National Security Council, Dick Cheney and all the neoconservatives in high positions throughout the US government, and airport security, but also the intelligence services of NATO and Israel's Mossad. How can such intelligent and capable people, who delivered the most humiliating blow in world history to an alleged Superpower with no difficulty whatsoever despite giving every indication of their intentions, possibly be so stupid as to shoot themselves in the head?

Some who think that they are experts will say that a false flag attack in France would be impossible without the cooperation of French intelligence. To this I say that it is practically a certainty that the CIA has more control over French intelligence than does the President of France. Operation Gladio proves this. The largest part of the government of Italy was ignorant of the bombings conducted by the CIA and Italian Intelligence against European women and children and blamed on communists in order to diminish the communist vote in elections.

Americans are a pitifully misinformed people. All of history is a history of false flag operations. Yet Americans dismiss such proven operations as "conspiracy theories," which merely proves that government has successfully brainwashed insouciant Americans and deprived them of the ability to recognize the truth.

Americans are the foremost among the captive nations.

Who will liberate them?

RUIN
IS OUR
FUTURE

January 16, 2015

Neoconservatives arrayed in their Washington offices are congratulating themselves on their success in using the *Charlie Hebdo* affair to reunite Europe with Washington's foreign policy. No more French votes with the Palestinians against the Washington-Israeli position. No more growing European sympathy with the Palestinians. No more growing European opposition to launching new wars in the Middle East. No more calls from the French president to end the sanctions against Russia.

Do the neoconservatives also understand that they have united Europeans with the right-wing anti-immigration political parties? The wave of support for the *Charlie Hebdo* cartoonists is the wave of Marine Le Pen's National Front, Nigel Farage's UK Independence Party, and Germany's PEGIDA sweeping over Europe. These parties are empowered by the anti-immigration fervor that was orchestrated in order to reunite Europeans with Washington and Israel.

Once again the arrogant and insolent neoconservatives have blundered. *Charlie Hebdo*'s empowerment of the anti-immigration parties has the potential to revolutionize European politics and destroy Washington's empire.[128]

Russia, tired of Ukraine's theft of the natural gas that passes through the country on its way to delivery to Europe, has made a decision to route the gas to Turkey, thus bypassing Ukraine.

The Russian energy minister has confirmed this decision and added that if European countries wish to avail themselves of this gas supply, they must put in place the infrastructure or pipeline to bring the gas into their countries.

In other words, there is a potential for a cutoff in the future, but no cutoff at the present.

These two events—*Charlie Hebdo* and the Russian decision to cease delivering gas to Europe via Ukraine—should remind us that the potential for black swans, and unintended consequences of official decisions that can produce black swans, always exist. Not even the American "superpower" is immune from black swans.

Yesterday there was a black swan event, an event that could yet unleash other black swan events.[129]

The Swiss central bank announced an end to its pegging of the Swiss franc to the euro and US dollar.[130]

Three years ago flight from euros and dollars into Swiss francs pushed the exchange value of the franc so high that it threatened the existence of the Swiss export industries. Switzerland announced that any further inflows of foreign currencies into francs would be met by creating new francs to absorb the inflows so as not to drive up the exchange rate further. In other words, the Swiss pegged the franc.

Yesterday the Swiss central bank announced that the peg was off. The franc instantly rose in value. Stocks of Swiss export companies fell, and hedge funds wrongly positioned incurred major hits to their solvency.

Why did the Swiss remove the peg? It was not a costless action. It cost the central bank and Swiss export industries substantially.

The answer is that the EU attorney general ruled that it was permissible for the EU central bank to initiate Quantitative Easing—that is, the printing of new euros—in order to bail out the mistakes of the private bankers. This decision means that Switzerland expects to be confronted with massive flight from the euro and that the Swiss central bank is unwilling to print enough new Swiss francs to maintain the peg. The Swiss central bank believes that it would have to run the printing press so hard that the basis of the Swiss money supply would explode, far exceeding the GDP of Switzerland.

The money printing policy of the US, Japan, and apparently now the EU has forced other countries to inflate their own currencies in order to prevent the rise in the exchange value of their currencies that would curtail their ability to export and earn foreign currencies with which to pay for their imports. Thus Washington has forced the world into printing money.

The Swiss have backed out of this system. Will others follow, or will the rest of the world follow the Russians and Chinese governments into new monetary arrangements and simply turn their backs on the corrupt and irredeemable West?

The level of corruption and manipulation that characterizes US economic and foreign policy today was impossible in earlier times when Washington's ambition was constrained by the Soviet Union. The greed for hegemonic power has made Washington the most corrupt government on earth.

The consequence of this corruption is ruin.

"Leadership passes into empire. Empire begets insolence. Insolence brings ruin."

Ruin is America's future.

CHARLIE HEBDO, A FREE PRESS, AND SOCIAL SECURITY

January 24, 2015

Puzzled by the title? It will all become clear.

Europeans have written to me with more information that raises questions about the *Charlie Hebdo* affair.

Some point out the strange emptiness of the street on which the professional killers depart. Others point out the film has hallmarks of orchestration or staging. Still others point out the size and described physical attributes of the killers do not correspond with the accused brothers and that the getaway car turns away from the scene differently from the official description. Another puzzle is that the video of the police assault on the deli repeatedly shows police moving in front of other police who are firing their weapons, yet despite the pointblank range are not hit. And there are other matters.

All I can say is that clearly at least some Europeans notice and on the basis of what they have seen have a lot of suspicion. I cannot evaluate the information sent to me. I do not know the neighborhood in Paris or traffic patterns. I know nothing about film making. Those who know enough about these matters for their suspicions to be aroused are the ones who need to address these issues. Possibly some of these suspicions are contrived red herrings designed to redirect the focus of suspicion down dead ends and discredit skeptics.

In my articles I raised a question about the official story, which was so completely at the ready as to appear pre-packaged. I said that the official story had many of the characteristics of a false flag operation.

I did not say it was one. My intent is for the media to make some effort to verify the story and not simply repeat the script handed to them. I made it clear that I thought it unlikely the story would be examined by the print and TV media. As Patrick Smith makes clear in CounterPunch, an embedded media is not a media. Journalism is absent along with truth.

My column was used both by neoconservatives and the leftwing People for the American Way to attack or to try to embarrass Ron Paul.

I learned of this when an email arrived from a *Washington Post* reporter asking if I had considered the possible effect on Rand Paul's presidential prospects before writing the article for a Ron Paul website. Apparently, the reporter had in mind a story: "Roberts Derails Rand Paul's Presidential Hopes." I suppose the story was going to be that by publishing the conspiracy kook Roberts, Ron Paul had destroyed his son's chance to become President.

At the time I had no idea what the *Washington Post* reporter was asking about. I replied that I write for my website and that, once I post, many other websites from locations around the world pick up the column and repost it and that it is beyond my powers to consider what implications my columns might have for all the known and unknown websites that might choose to republish it.

Next I learned from readers that some non-entity named Luke Brinker, who doesn't even rate a Wikipedia entry, had attacked Ron Paul on the tabloid site Salon: "Ron Paul defends insane *Charlie Hebdo* conspiracy theory," and in the process called me a "paleoconservative crank and notorious 9/11 truther."

What was this all about? It turned out that the notorious neoconservative William Kristol had started it. Kristol's way of defending the official story was to try to bring embarrassment to Ron Paul, with the result that libertarians would line up with the official story in defense of Ron Paul.

Misrepresentation of my article was essential to the plot. My statement that the *Charlie Hebdo* affair has characteristics of a false flag event was turned into an accusation that it was a false flag event. Of course, we don't have proof one way or the other. On one side we have an official narrative that relies entirely on belief in the veracity of officials and their embedded media, which after Iraq, Libya, Syria, Iran, and Ukraine is not very high. On the other hand we have the suspicious aspects that many have pointed out.

When Ron Paul was deposed on People for the American Way's RightWing Watch, he stated the obvious.

He said that I had not said it was a false flag event but had pointed out reasons that suspicions needed to be investigated and answered for the sake of the credibility of the official account. Ron Paul said that he supports that sound approach and that it was important for people to think and not simply blindly accept government explanations.

That should have been the end of it. But no, libertarians responded not quite like Kristol had hoped but partially. Dale Steinreich wrote on LewRockwell.com that he "doesn't buy Roberts' posited theory," thus perpetuating the misrepresentation as I have no theory, only suspicions. Steinreich then takes issue with the various neoconservative and leftwing obscurantists who are out to get Ron Paul.

I think that Steinreich is unnecessarily defensive. Ron Paul needs no defense from proven warmongers and ideological jerks. Nevertheless, Steinreich took the bait. Part of his defense of Ron Paul is to write: "For clarity, Paul Craig Roberts is not a libertarian. . . . he is a supporter of federal programs such as Social Security and Medicare." As hardly anything could be worse than that, not even conspiracy suspicions, Steinreich concludes that "far more left progressives share the totality of [Roberts'] current views than libertarians."

So here we have again the view about which I have written so often that the great mass of people cannot evaluate what is said or written without first classifying it into a prevailing ideological box. If what is said fits their box, it is correct. If not, it is wrong. According to this way of thinking, if you support Social Security and Medicare you are a leftwing progressive. Therefore the leftwing freaks attacking Ron Paul are really attacking their own Paul Craig Roberts.

Steinreich certainly turns the tables on the feeble-minded who tried to attack Ron Paul through me.

This brings me now to the last part of my title, my real interest in this affair. Possibly on one occasion during his life William Kristol told the truth about something. I just don't know what it was. As for Salon and RightWing Watch, they have no following among thinking people. Essentially they serve as gatekeepers and propagandists for Washington and private interest groups. Everyone knows that William Kristol and the *Weekly Standard* want more war, especially with Israel's enemies, and that leftwing progressives hate people like Ron Paul, who believe in limited government and distrust the left progressives' god, which is government.

What interests me is Steinreich's opinion that I am a suspect supporter of freedom and liberty because I support Social Security and Medicare. Clearly, Steinreich knows little about my positions or the history of Social Security privatization, a debate I started with my *Business Week* column back in the 1980s.

During the 1980s and into the 1990s I supported Social Security privatization, or perhaps more precisely, looking at it closely. In one of my *Business Week* columns I wrote about the Chilean government minister who succeeded in privatizing the social security system in Chile. I do not know the current condition of Chile's social security system, but when I wrote the system had proved to be a success, and many Chileans had become share owners in Chile's economy.

The Chilean minister thanked me profusely for making him world famous. He travelled around the world explaining how he went about the task that he accomplished, and he ended up at the Cato Institute in Washington, at that time a libertarian think tank at which I spent several years before being evicted for being an independent thinker.

Back at the time I was advocating thought about Social Security privatization the Dow Jones was around 1,000. The subsequent rise in the market would have made privatization feasible. More importantly, perhaps, if Social Security had been privatized, it is unlikely Congress would have deregulated the financial system. It is one thing if gamblers wish to risk their money in a casino. It is another if it is the money of Social Security retirees.

Once the financial system was deregulated—a libertarian objective—it became impossible to privatize Social Security other than for insincere reasons of letting Wall Street rob retirees. The lack of accountability, which followed the last financial crash, and the declaration of financial institutions being too big to fail, and thus are carried on the nation's budget or the Federal Reserve's balance sheet, also make clear that it is impossible to trust old age security to an unaccountable financial system.

Therefore, being practical and not a libertarian ideologue, I understand that Social Security privatization is no longer possible on the basis of a sound and sincere case. It might still happen as part of the normal corruption that now engulfs the US government.

Neoconservatives have an ideology of US world hegemony and an agenda to achieve it. Everything that they do and say relates to their agenda.

The leftwing progressives and neoliberals have their agendas, and, like the neocons, admissible thought is agenda-specific.

Libertarians have an agenda, an honorable one but largely not practical. In the libertarian mind, it is government that misuses power. The remedy is to place power in private sector hands. Yet as all of history shows, private interests also misuse power.

The solution to the dilemma is countervailing power. Labor unions to offset capitalist monopolies and company stores. Private interests that government must both accommodate and regulate. The division of government power into executive, legislative and judicial, a distribution of power between federal, state, and local governments, and accountability of all to law and the Constitution.

Perfect results would not be forthcoming, but there would be more liberty and more justice than if one power rules us all. The goal is to keep Sauron off the throne.

Being impractical, libertarians have jeopardized a better outcome, and advanced a worse one, as much as have other groups. The rise of jobs off-shoring, misinterpreted by libertarians as free trade, destroyed the countervailing power of labor unions. As this domino fell, it knocked over another—the Democratic Party. The decline in union financial support sent Democrats to the same influence purchasers as patronized by Republicans, with the consequence that the same interest groups now control both parties.

Conservatives worshiping presidential power have supported the accumulation of undue power in the executive branch, power that has over-ridden the Constitution.

America is now a closed-mind country. Minds are closed by ideological agendas, by narrow private interests, and by the view that only conspiracy kooks dissent from official explanations. Dissent and protest are gradually being criminalized. The government does not succeed all at once, but gradually step by step.

Before too long we will have to believe the most fantastic stories or be arrested. That is the path that both government and ideologues have us on.

Peter Koenig has a clear vision of *Charlie Hebdo* and where it is taking us. His case is certainly logically superior to the official case supported by William Kristol and Luke Brinker that defending free speech means shutting down dissenting opinion. (According to my French correspondents, Koenig failed to apply his skepticism of the *Charlie Hebdo* affair to the reports that vastly over-sized the demonstrations.)[131]

FREEDOM, WHERE ARE YOU?

January 25, 2015

When the former Goldman Sachs executive who runs the European Central Bank (ECB) announced that he was going to print 720 billion euros annually with which to purchase bad debts from the politically connected big banks, the euro sank and the stock market and Swiss franc shot up. As in the US, quantitative easing (QE) serves to enrich the already rich. It has no other purpose.

The well-heeled financial institutions that bought up the troubled sovereign debt of Greece, Italy, Portugal, and Spain at low prices will now sell the bonds to the ECB for high prices. And despite depression level unemployment in most of Europe and austerity imposed on citizens, the stock market rose in anticipation that much of the 60 billion new euros that will be created each month will find its way into equity prices. Liquidity fuels the stock market.

Where else can the money go? Some will go into Swiss francs and some into gold while gold is still available, but for the most part the ECB is running the printing press in order to boost the wealth of the stock-owning One Percent. The Federal Reserve and the ECB have taken the West back to the days when a handful of aristocrats owned everything.

The stock markets are bubbles blown by central bank money creation. On the basis of traditional reasoning there is no sound reason to be in equities, and sound investors have avoided them.

But there is no return anywhere else, and as the central banks are run by the rich for the rich, sound reasoning has proved to be a mistake for the past six years. This shows that corruption can prevail for an indeterminable period over fundamentals.

As I demonstrated in my book, *The Failure of Laissez Faire Capitalism*, first Goldman Sachs deceived lenders into over-lending to the Greek government. Then Goldman Sachs former executives took over

Greece's financial affairs and forced austerity upon the population in order to prevent losses to the foreign lenders.

This established a new principle in Europe, one that the IMF has relentlessly applied to Latin American and Third World debtors. The principle is that when foreign lenders make mistakes and over-lend to foreign governments, loading them up with debt, the bankers' mistakes are rectified by robbing the poor populations. Pensions, social services, and public employment are cut, valuable resources are sold off to foreigners for pennies on the dollar, and the government is forced to support US foreign policy. John Perkins' *Confessions of an Economic Hit Man* describes the process perfectly. If you haven't read Perkins book, you have little idea how corrupt and vicious the United States is. Indeed, Perkins shows that over-lending is intentional in order to set up the country for looting.

This is what Goldman Sachs did to Greece, intentionally or unintentionally.

It took the Greeks a long time to realize it. Apparently, 36.5 percent of the population was awoken by rising poverty, unemployment, and suicide rates. That figure, a little over one-third of the vote, was enough to put Syriza in power in the January 25 Greek election, throwing out the corrupt New Democracy party that has consistently sold out the Greek people to the foreign banks. Nevertheless, 27.7 percent of the Greeks, if the vote reporting is correct, voted for the party that has sacrificed the Greek people to the banksters. Even in Greece, a country accustomed to outpourings of people into the streets, a significant percentage of the population is sufficiently brainwashed to vote against their own interests.

Can Syriza do anything? It remains to be seen, but probably not. If the political party had received 55% or 65% or 75% of the vote, yes. But merely securing the largest vote at 36.5% does not show a unified country aware of its plight and its looting at the hands of rich banksters. The vote shows that a significant percentage of the Greek population is unconcerned with foreign looting of Greece.

Moreover, Syriza is up against the heavies: the German and Netherlands banks who hold Greece's loans and the governments that back the banks; the European Union which is using the sovereign debt crisis to destroy the sovereignty of the individual countries that comprise the European Union; and Washington which backs EU sovereign power over the individual countries as it is easier to control one government than a couple of dozen.

Already the Western financial presstitutes are warning Syriza not to endanger its membership in the common currency by diverting from the austerity model imposed from abroad on Greek citizens with the complicity of New Democracy.

Apparently, there is a lack of formal means of exiting the EU and the euro, but nevertheless Greece can be threatened with being thrown out. Greece should welcome being thrown out.

Exiting the EU and the euro is the best thing that can happen to Greece. A country without its own currency is not a sovereign country. It is a vassal state of another power. A country without its own currency cannot finance its own needs. Although the UK is a member of the EU, the UK kept its own currency and is not subject to control by the ECB. A country without its own money is powerless. It is a non-entity.

If the US did not have its own dollar, the US would be of no consequence whatsoever on the world scene.

The EU and the euro were deception and trickery. Countries lost their sovereignty. So much for Western "self-rule," "freedom," "democracy," all slogans without content. In the entire West there is nothing but the looting of people by the One Percent who control the governments.

In America, the looting does not rely on indebtedness, because the US dollar is the reserve currency and the US can print all the money needed in order to pay its bills and redeem its debt. In America the looting of labor has been through jobs off-shoring.

American corporations discovered, and if they did not they were informed by Wall Street to move offshore or be taken over, that they could raise profits by moving their manufacturing operations abroad.

The lower labor cost resulted in higher profits, higher share prices, huge managerial bonuses based on "performance," and shareholder capital gains. Off-shoring greatly increased the inequality in income and wealth in the US. Capital succeeded in looting labor.

The displaced well-paid manufacturing workers, if they were able to find replacement jobs, worked part-time minimum wage jobs at Walmart and Home Depot.

Economists, if they are entitled to the designation, such as Michael Porter and Matthew Slaughter, promised Americans that the fictional "New Economy" would produce better, higher-paying, and cleaner jobs for Americans than the "dirty fingernail" jobs that we were fortunate our corporations were moving offshore.

Years later, as I have proven conclusively, there is no sign of these "New Economy" jobs. What we have instead is a sharp decline in the labor force participation rate as the unemployed cannot find jobs. The replacement jobs for the manufacturing jobs are mainly part-time domestic service jobs.

People have to hold 2 or 3 of these jobs to make ends meet. These part time jobs offer no medical or pension benefits.

Now that this fact, once controversial believe it or not, has proven completely true, the same bought-and-paid-for spokespersons for robbing labor and destroying unions claim, without a shred of evidence, that the off-shored jobs are coming home.

According to these propagandists, we now have what is called "reshoring." A "reshoring" propagandist claims that the growth of "reshoring" over the past four years is 1,775 percent, an 18 times increase.[132]

There is no sign whatsoever of these alleged "reshoring" jobs in the monthly BLS payroll jobs statistics. What reshoring is all about is propaganda to counteract the belated realization that "free trade" agreements and job off-shoring were not beneficial to the American economy or its work force, but were beneficial only to the super-rich.

Like people throughout history, the American people are being turned into serfs and slaves because the fools believe the lies that are fed to them. They sit in front of Fox News, CNN, and whatever. They read *The New York Times*. If you want to learn how badly Americans have been served by the so-called media, read Howard Zinn's *A People's History of the United States* and Oliver Stone and Peter Kuznick's *The Untold History of the United States*.

The media helps the government, and the private interests that profit from their control of government, control the brainwashed public. We have to invade Afghanistan because a faction there fighting for political control of the country is protecting Osama bin Laden, whom the US accuses without any proof of embarrassing the mighty US with the 9/11 attack. We have to invade Iraq because Saddam has "weapons of mass destruction" that he surely has despite the reports to the contrary by the weapons inspectors. We have to overthrow Gaddafi because of a slate of lies that have best been forgotten. We have to overthrow Assad because he used chemical weapons even though all evidence is to the contrary. Russia is responsible for Ukraine problems, not because the US overthrew the elected democratic government but because Russia accepted a 97.6% vote of Crimeans to rejoin Russia where the province had resided for hundreds of years before a Ukrainian Soviet leader, Khrushchev, stuck Crimea into Ukraine, at the time a part of the Soviet Union along with Russia.

War, War, War, that is all Washington wants. It enriches the military/security complex, the largest component of the US GNP and the largest contributor, along with Wall Street and the Israel Lobby, to US political campaigns.

Anyone or any organization that offers truth to the lies is demonized. Last week the new chief of the US Broadcasting Board of Governors, Andrew Lack, likened the Russian TV Internet service Russia Today to Boko Haram and the Islamic State terrorist groups. This absurd accusation is a prelude to closing down RT in the US just as Washington's puppet UK government closed down Iran's Press TV.[133]

Anglo-Americans are not permitted any different news than what is served to them by "their" governments.

That is the state of "freedom" in the West today.

IT IS TIME FOR IRAN
TO TELL THE WEST
'GOODBYE'

January 26, 2015

From all appearances, the Obama regime's negotiations with Iran, overseen by Russia, were on the verge of ending the contrived nuclear issue. An end to the confrontation is unacceptable to the Zionist Israeli government and to their neocon agents in America. The Republicans, a political party owned lock, stock, and barrel by the Israel Lobby, hastily invited Netanyahu, the crazed ruler of both Israel and America, to quickly come to tell the Republican Congress, which the insouciant American voters put in place, how to prohibit any accommodation with Iran.

Observing the Israeli-controlled Republican Congress, a collection of warmongers, taking steps to prevent any peaceful resolution of a fabricated issue, Iran's leader, Seyyed Ali Khamenei sent a letter to Western youth advising the youth of the Western world of the mischaracterization of Islam by Western propagandists.[134]

I respect Khamenei's effort to reach out to Western youth in order to help them differentiate the reality of Islam from the demonized portrait painted of Islam by Western politicians and media.

The question is: How much impact can Khamenei have? Khamenei's voice is important, but it is small in comparison to the Western liars and propagandists. Even an important representative, such as Khamenei, of a demonized country and a demonized religion, can hardly be heard over the din of propaganda against Iran and Islam.

Moreover, secret Western black op organizations can conduct terrorist operations in the name of Islam, such as possibly occurred with 9/11, the Boston Marathon Bombing, and *Charlie Hebdo*. The world is told that Islam is behind these attacks, but experts note that no real evidence is ever supplied. Just official assertions, such as those that proved incorrect about weapons of mass destruction in Iraq, Assad's use of chemical weapons in Syria, the false accusations against Gaddafi in Libya, and the false accusations against Russia in Ukraine. The makers of this propaganda have many voices, and their trumpets overwhelm the voice of Iran's leader.

Instead of appealing to the West, Iran needs to turn away from the West. The historical time of the West has passed.

The West has devolved into a police state in which government is no longer accountable to law or to the people. There are no jobs for young people, and no income security for the elderly. The West is actually in the process of looting itself. Just look at what is happening in Greece. In order to guarantee the profits of the private banks from outside Greece, the Greek people have had their pensions cut, their employment cut, their social services cut, and they have had to sell their valuable public properties at low prices to private purchasers from outside their country. The same looting is now going on in Ukraine, and Italy, Spain, and Portugal face the identical fate.

In America the entire economic policy of the country is conducted only for the benefit of the super-rich One Percent.

If we use J.R.R. Tolkien's *Lord of the Rings* as a metaphor for the West, the West is Mordor and Washington is Sauron.

It is pointless for Iran to negotiate with the West in hopes of gaining acceptance. Iran is on the same list as Saddam Hussein, Gaddafi, and Assad. The only way Iran can be accepted by the West is to consent to being an American puppet state. Suspicion about Iran's nuclear energy program is a contrived issue. If it were not the nuclear issue, it would be some other contrived issue, such as weapons of mass destruction, use of chemical weapons, terrorism, and so forth. Iran's leaders should understand that the real problem is Iran's independence of Washington's foreign and economic policies. Washington cannot say that the US wants regime change in Iran because Washington wants a puppet state, so Washington pretends that Iran represents a threat that must be overcome.

If Iran so much admires the decadent and corrupt West that it is willing to be a servile vassal in order to enjoy Western acceptance, all Iran needs to do is to capitulate and align with Washington's hegemonic policies.

If Iran, one of the two oldest civilizations and cultures on the planet, wishes to continue its existence without coming under the rule of the "exceptional" Americans, Iran must turn its back to the West, ally with Russia, China, India, and the other BRICS countries, and have nothing whatsoever to do with the Western criminals. It is beyond explanation why a civilization as old as the Iranian one would see anything in the West worthy of being associated with.

Above all, Iran should stop fighting other Muslims, even extreme ones who betray the Prophet Muhammad and soil Islam. Iran should not accept the role of being Washington's mercenary in the fight against the Islamic State. Iran should never help Washington kill Muslims, even misguided ones who betray the Prophet. Instead, Iran should understand that the Islamic State, even if it should be a creation of Washington, is enjoying its success because Muslim peoples are tired of being ruled by the West, which uses the antagonism between Sunni and Shi'ite to rule them both.

If the Islamic State is a Western creation, the Muslims who support it are not. The Islamic state is supported by Muslims because the Muslim people are tired of being ruled and ruined by America, Great Britain, and the French.

Khamenei should forget about America, where evil has taken hold and about which Khamenei can do nothing. Khamenei should try to unify the Muslim peoples and turn them in a new direction.

Islam is weak because it is not unified. For centuries Muslims, divided by ancient political claims, have permitted their religious differences to make them pawns of other powers. It requires leadership to repair a sectarian split, and that is the leadership Iran should attempt to provide. Iran cannot provide leadership by imposing its view. A unifying compromise among Muslims must be made. Fighting on the side of the Americans against the Islamic State perpetuates the split and seals the fate of Muslim peoples as colonies of the West.

The problems that Muslims face might be too large for leadership to rectify. Not only are Muslims afflicted by their internal split, Muslim populations in the West are now positioned by propaganda such that their leaders are compelled to support war against the Islamic State and Iran in order to protect Muslim communities from pogroms. Have history and propaganda made Muslims forever a colonized people?

RUSSIA
IN THE
CROSS HAIRS

January 26, 2015

Washington's attack on Russia has moved beyond the boundary of the absurd into the realm of insanity.

The New Chief of the US Broadcasting Board of Governors, Andrew Lack, has declared the Russian news service, RT, which broadcasts in multiple languages, to be a terrorist organization equivalent to Boko Haram and the Islamic State, and Standard and Poor's just downgraded Russia's credit rating to junk status.

Today RT International interviewed me about these insane developments.

In prior days when America was still a sane country, Lack's charge would have led to him being laughed out of office. He would have had to resign and disappear from public life. Today in the make-believe world that Western propaganda has created, Lack's statement is taken seriously. Yet another terrorist threat has been identified–RT. (Although both Boko Haram and the Islamic State employ terror, strictly speaking they are political organizations seeking to rule, not terror organizations, but this distinction would be over Lack's head. Yes, I know. There is a good joke that could be made here about what Lack lacks. Appropriately named and all that.)

Nevertheless, whatever Lack might lack, I doubt he believes his nonsensical statement that RT is a terrorist organization. So what is his game?

The answer is that the Western presstitute media, by becoming a Ministry of Propaganda for Washington, has created large markets for RT, Press TV, and Al Jazeera. As more and more of the peoples of the world turn to these more honest news sources, Washington's ability to fabricate self-serving explanations has declined.

RT in particular has a large Western audience. The contrast between RT's truthful reporting and the lies spewed by US media is undermining Washington's control of the explanation. This is no longer acceptable.

Lack has sent a message to RT. The message is: pull in your horns; stop reporting differently from our line; stop contesting the facts as Washington states them and the presstitutes report them; get on board or else.

In other words, the "free speech" that Washington and its EU, Canadian, and Australian puppet states tout means: free speech for Washington's propaganda and lies, but not for any truth. Truth is terrorism, because truth is the major threat to Washington.

Washington would prefer to avoid the embarrassment of actually shutting down RT as its UK vassal did to Iran's Press TV. Washington simply wants to shut up RT. Lack's message to RT is: self-censure.

In my opinion, RT already understates in its coverage and reporting as does Al Jazeera. Both news organizations understand that they cannot be too forthright, at least not too often or on too many occasions.

I have often wondered why the Russian government allows 20 percent of the Russian media to function as Washington's fifth column inside Russia. I suspect the reason is that by tolerating Washington's blatant propaganda inside Russia, the Russian government hopes that some factual news can be reported in the US via RT and other Russian news organizations.

These hopes, like other Russian hopes about the West, are likely to be disappointed in the end. If RT is closed down or assimilated into the Western presstitute media, nothing will be said about it, but if the Russian government closes down Washington's agents, blatant liars all, in the Russian media, we will hear forever about the evil Russians suppressing "free speech." Remember, the only allowable "free speech" is Washington's propaganda.

Only time will tell whether RT decides to be closed down for telling the truth or whether it adds its voice to Washington's propaganda.

The other item in the interview was the downgrading of Russian credit to junk status.

Standard and Poor's downgrade is, without any doubt, a political act. It proves what we already know, and that is that the American rating firms are corrupt political operations. Remember the Investment Grade rating the American rating agencies gave to obvious subprime junk? These rating agencies are paid by Wall Street, and like Wall Street they serve the US government and vice versa.

A look at the facts serves to establish the political nature of the ruling. Don't expect the corrupt US financial press to look at the facts, but I will.

Indeed, I will put the facts in context with the US debt situation.

According to the debt clocks available online, the Russian national debt as a percentage of Russian GDP is 11 percent. The American national debt as a percentage of US GDP is 105 percent, about ten times higher. My coauthors, Dave Kranzler, John Williams, and I have shown that when measured correctly, the US debt as a percent of GDP is much higher than the official figure, putting it about 18 times higher than the Russian ratio of national debt to GDP.

The Russian national debt per capita is $1,645. The US national debt per capita is $56,952.

The size of Russia's national debt is $235 billion, less than one quarter of a trillion. The size of the US national debt is $18 *trillion*, 76.6 times larger than the Russian debt.

Putting this in perspective: according to the debt clocks, US GDP is $17.3 trillion and Russian GDP is $2.1 trillion. So, US GDP is 8 times greater than Russian GDP, but US national debt is 76.6 times greater than Russia's debt.

Clearly, it is the US credit rating that should have been downgraded to junk status. But this cannot happen. Any US credit rating agency that told the truth would be closed and prosecuted. It wouldn't matter what the absurd charges are. The rating agencies would be guilty of being anti-american, terrorist organizations like RT, etc. and so on, and they know it. Never expect any truth from any Wall Street denizen. They lie for a living.

One website claims that the US owes Russia as of January 2013 $162.9 billion.[135] As the Russian national debt is $235 billion, 69 percent of the Russian national debt is covered by US debt obligations to Russia.

If this is a Russian Crisis, I am Alexander the Great.

As Russia has enough US dollar holdings to redeem its entire national debt and have a couple hundred billion dollars left, what is Russia's problem?

One of Russia's problems is its central bank. For the most part, Russian economists are the same neoliberal incompetents that exist in the Western world. The Russian economists are enamored of their contacts with the "superior" West and with the prestige that they imagine these contacts give them. As long as the Russian economists agree with the Western ones, they get invited to conferences abroad.

These Russian economists are de facto American agents whether they realize it or not.

Currently, the Russian central bank is squandering the large Russian holdings of foreign reserves in response to the Western attack on the ruble. This is a fools' game that no central bank should play. The Russian central bank should remember, or learn if it does not know, Soros' attack on the Bank of England.

Russian foreign reserves should be used to retire the outstanding national debt, thus making Russia the only country in the world without a national debt. The remaining dollars should be dumped in coordinated actions with China to destroy the dollar, the power basis of American Imperialism.

Alternatively, the Russian government should announce that its reply to the economic warfare being conducted against Russia by the government in Washington and Wall Street rating agencies is default on its loans to Western creditors. Russia has nothing to lose as Russia is already cut off from Western credit by US sanctions. Russian default would cause consternation and crisis in the European banking system, which is exactly what Russia wants in order to break up Europe's support of US sanctions.

In my opinion, the neoliberal economists who control Russian economic policy are a much greater threat to the sovereignty of Russia than economic sanctions and US missile bases. To survive Washington, Russia desperately needs people who are not romantic about the West.

Russia understands the devastation of war better than any other country. Therefore, the government relies on diplomacy rather than threats and is cautious about responding to provocations. Nevertheless, maintaining Russia's independence involves risks.

Indeed, the Russian government faces risks inside itself. The Atlanticist Integrationists inside the Russian government want victory for the West, not for Russia. Westernized Russians are more fearful of Russian Christian nationalism than they are of the West's machinations. A country afflicted with treason inside the government itself has reduced chance against Washington, a determined player.

Another fifth column operating against Russia from within is the US and German funded NGOs. These American agents masquerade as "human rights organizations," as "women's rights organizations," as "democracy organizations," and whatever other cant titles that serve in a politically correct age and are unchallengeable.

Yet another threat to Russia comes from the percentage of the Russian youth who lust for the depraved culture of the West. Sexual license, pornography, drugs, self-absorption. These are the West's cultural offerings. And, of course, killing Muslims.

If Russians want to kill people for the fun of it and to solidify US hegemony over themselves and the world, they should support "Atlanticist integration" and turn their backs on Russian nationalism. Why be Russian if you can be American serfs?

What better result for the American neoconservatives than to have Russia support Washington's hegemony over the world? That is what the neoliberal Russian economists and the "European Integrationists" support. These Russians are willing to be American serfs in order to be part of the West and to be paid well for their treason.

As I was interviewed about these developments by RT, the news anchor kept trying to confront Washington's charges with the facts. It is astonishing that the Russian journalists do not understand that facts have nothing to do with it. The Russian journalists, those independent of American bribes, think that facts matter in the disputes about Russian actions. They think that the assaults on civilians by the American supported Ukrainian Nazis is a fact. But, of course no such fact exists in the Western media. In the Western media the Russians, and only the Russians, are responsible for violence in Ukraine.

Washington's story line is that it is the evil Putin's intent on restoring the Soviet Empire that is the cause of the conflict. This media line in the West has no relationship to any facts.

In my opinion, Russia is in grave danger. Russians are relying on facts, and Washington is relying on propaganda. For Washington, facts are not relevant. Russian voices are small compared to Western voices.

The lack of a Russian voice is due to Russia itself. Russia accepted living in a world controlled by US financial and legal institutions and telecommunication services. Living in this world means that the only voice is Washington's.

Why Russia agreed to this strategic disadvantage is a mystery. But as a result of this strategic mistake, Russia is at a disadvantage.

Considering the inroads that Washington has into the Russian government itself, the economically powerful oligarchs and state employees with Western connections, as well as into the Russian media and Russian youth, with the hundreds of American and German financed NGOs that can put Russians into the streets to protest any defense of Russia, Russia's future as a sovereign country is in doubt.

The American neoconservatives are relentless. Their Russian opponent is weakened by the success inside Russia of Western cold war propaganda that portrays the US as the savior and future of mankind.

The darkness from Sauron America continues to spread over the world.

Note: On May 25, 2015, Russia's President Putin signed a law passed by both houses of the Russian Duma. The law authorizes the designation of foreign and foreign-funded non-profit as well as for-profit NGOs as "undesirables" on grounds of national security. After 20 years of being undermined by Western financed NGOs, the Russian government has finally put a halt to it.[136]

THE COWARDLY AND DESPICABLE AMERICAN PRESSTITUTES

February 5, 2015

There is a brouhaha underway about an American journalist who told a story about being in a helicopter in a war zone. The helicopter was hit and had to land. Which war zone and when I don't know. The US has created so many war zones that it is difficult to keep up with them all, and as you will see, I am not interested in the story for its own sake.

It turns out that the journalist has remembered incorrectly. He was in a helicopter in a war zone, but it wasn't hit and didn't have to land. The journalist has been accused of lying in order to make himself seem to be "a more seasoned war correspondent than he is."

The journalist's presstitute colleagues are all over him with accusations. He has even had to apologize to the troops. Which troops and why is unclear. The American requirement that everyone apologize for every word reminds me of the old Soviet practice, real or alleged by anti-communists, that required Soviet citizens to self-criticize and endlessly apologize.

National Public Radio (Feb. 5, 2015) thought this story of the American journalist was so important that the program played a recording of the journalist telling his story. It sounded like a good story to me. The audience enjoyed it and was laughing. The journalist telling the story did not claim any heroism on his part or any failure on the part of the helicopter crew. It is normal for helicopters to take hits in war zones.

Having established that the journalist had actually stated that the helicopter was hit when in fact it wasn't, NPR brought on the program a psychologist at the University of California, Irvine, an expert on "false memory." The psychologist explained various reasons a person might have false memories, making the point that it is far from uncommon and that the journalist is most likely just another example. But the NPR presstitute

332

still wanted to know if the journalist had intentionally lied in order to make himself look good. It was never explained why it made a journalist look good to be in a helicopter forced to land. But few presstitutes get to this depth of inquiry.

Now to get to the real point. I was listening to this while driving as it was less depressing to listen to NPR's propaganda than to listen to the Christian-Zionist preachers. In the previous hour NPR had presented listeners with three reports about civilian deaths in the break-away provinces in eastern and southern Ukraine. The first time I heard the report, the NPR presstitute recounted how explosives had hit a hospital killing 5 people in the break-away Donetsk Republic. The presstitute did not report that this was done by Ukrainian forces, instead suggesting that it could have been done by the "Russian-supported rebels." He didn't offer any explanation why the rebels would attack their own hospital. The impression left for that small percentage of informed Americans capable of thought is that presstitutes are not allowed to say that the Washington-backed Ukrainians attacked a hospital.

In all three reports, Secretary of State John Kerry was broadcast saying that the US wanted a diplomatic, peaceful solution, but that the Russians were blocking a peaceful solution by sending tank columns and troops into Ukraine. On my return trip, I twice more heard Kerry over NPR repeating the unsupported claim that Russian tanks and troops are pouring into Ukraine. Obviously, NPR was serving as a propaganda voice that Russia was invading Ukraine.

Think about this for a minute. We have been hearing from high US government officials, including the president himself, for months and months about Russian tank columns and troops entering Ukraine. The Russian government denies this steadfastly, but, of course, we cannot trust the now-demonized Russians.

We are not allowed to believe them, because they are positioned as the Enemy, and good patriotic Americans never believe the Enemy.

But how can we help but believe the Russians? If all these Russian tank columns and troops that have allegedly been pouring into Ukraine were real, Washington's puppet government in Kiev would have fallen sometime last year, and the conflict would be over. Anyone with a brain knows this.

So, we arrive at my point. A journalist told a harmless story and has been roasted alive and forced to apologize to the troops for lying. In the middle of this brouhaha, the US Secretary of State, the President of the United States, innumerable senators, executive branch officials, and presstitutes have repeatedly reported month after month Russian tank columns and troops entering Ukraine. Yet, despite all these Russian forces, the civilians in the break-away provinces of eastern and southern Ukraine are still being slaughtered by Washington's puppet state in Kiev.

If Russian tanks and troops are this ineffective, why are NATO commanders and neoconservative warmongers warning of the dire danger that Russia poses to the Baltics, Poland, and Eastern Europe?

It doesn't make any sense, does it?

So the question is: Why are the presstitutes all over some hapless journalist rather than holding accountable the Great Liars, John Kerry and Barack Obama?

The answer is: It is costless to the presstitutes to try to destroy, for totally insignificant reasons—perhaps just for the pleasure of it, like "American Sniper" killing people for fun—one of their own, but they would be fired if they hold Kerry and Obama accountable, and they know it. But they have to get someone, so they eat their own.

A democracy without an honest media cannot exist. In America democracy is a facade behind which operates every evil inclination of mankind. During the past 14 years the American people have supported governments that have invaded, bombed, or droned seven countries, killing, maiming, and displacing millions of people for no reason other than profit and hegemonic power. There is scant sign that this has caused very many Americans sleepless nights or a bad conscience.

When Washington is not bombing and killing, it is plotting to overthrow reformist governments, such as the Honduran government Obama overthrew, and the Venezuelan, Bolivian, Ecuadoran, and Argentine governments that the Obama regime is current trying to overthrow. And, also, of course the democratically elected government in Ukraine that has been supplanted by Washington's coup.

The new Greek government is in the crosshairs, and so is Putin himself.

Washington and its fawning presstitutes branded the elected Ukrainian government that was a victim of Washington's coup, "a corrupt dictatorship." The replacement government consists of a combination of Washington puppets and neo-Nazis with their own military forces sporting Nazi insignias. The American presstitutes have been careful not to notice the Nazi insignias.

Ask yourself why a journalist's false memory episode of an insignificant event is so important to the American presstitutes, while John Kerry and Barack Obama's extraordinary, blatant, blockbuster, and dangerous lies are ignored.

In the event you have forgotten the efficiency of the Russian military, remember the fate of the American and Israeli trained and equipped Georgian Army that Washington sicced on South Ossetia. The Georgian invasion of South Ossetia resulted in the deaths of Russian peace-keeping soldiers and Russian citizens.

The Russian military intervened, and the American and Israeli trained and equipped Georgian Army collapsed in five hours. All of Georgia was back in Russian hands, but the Russians withdrew and left the former province of Russia independent, despite the lies from Washington that Putin intends to restore the Soviet Empire.

The only correct conclusion that any American can make is that every statement of the US government and its presstitute media is a blatant lie designed to serve a secret agenda that the American people would not support if they knew of its existence.

Whenever Washington and its whore media speak, they lie.

IS PEACE
OR WAR
AT HAND?

February 9, 2015

At this time we do not know the outcome of the meeting in Moscow between Merkel, Hollande, and Putin.

The meeting with Putin was initiated by Merkel and Hollande, because they are disturbed by the aggressive position that Washington has taken toward Russia and are fearful that Washington is pushing Europe into a conflict that Europe does not want. However, Merkel and Hollande cannot resolve the NATO/EU/Ukraine situation unless Merkel and Hollande are willing to break with Washington's foreign policy and assert their right as sovereign states to conduct their own foreign policy.

Unless Washington's war-lust has finally driven Europeans to take control over their own fate, the most likely outcome of the Putin-Merkel-Hollande meeting will be more meetings that go nowhere. If Merkel and Hollande are not negotiating from a position of independence, one likely outcome after more meetings will be that Merkel and Hollande will say, in order to appease Washington, that they tried to reason with Putin but that Putin was unreasonable.

Based on Lavrov's meeting in Munich with the Europeans, the hope for any sign of intelligence and independence in Europe seems misplaced. Russian diplomacy relied on European independence, but as Putin has acknowledged Europe has shown no independence from Washington. Putin has said that negotiating with vassals is pointless. Yet, Putin continues to negotiate with vassals.

Perhaps Putin's patience is finally paying off. There are reports that Germany and France oppose Washington's plan to send weapons to Ukraine. French president Hollande now supports autonomy for the break-away republics in Ukraine. His predecessor, Sarkozy, said that Crimea chose Russia and we cannot blame them, and that the interests of Americans and Europeans diverge when it comes to Russia.

Germany's foreign minister says that Washington's plan to arm Ukraine is risky and reckless. And on top of it all, Cyprus has offered Russia an air base.

We will see how Washington responds to the French statements that European interests with regard to Russia diverge from Washington's. Washington does not recognize any valid interest except its own.

Therefore, it has been fruitless for Russia to negotiate with Washington and Washington's EU vassals. To come to an agreement with Washington has required Russia's surrender to Washington's terms. Russia must hand over Crimea and Russia's warm water port, and Moscow must stand aside while the Russian people in eastern and southern Ukraine, the "break-away" provinces, are slaughtered. Russia must support the hostile regime in Kiev with loans, grants, and low gas prices.

That is the only deal Russia has been able to get from Washington, because the EU has supported Washington's line. With French presidents reportedly now saying, "We are part of a common civilization with Russia," Europe is on the road to independence.

Can Europe stay on this road, or can Washington bring Germany and France back in line? A false flag attack could do it. Washington is a control freak, and the neoconservative ideology of US hegemony has made Washington even more of a control freak. Europe with an independent foreign policy means a great loss of control by Washington.

Alternatively, Russia can forget about the West and integrate with China and the East. Considering Washington's hegemonic posture, there is no counter-party for Russia's diplomacy. Predictions are difficult, because policies can have unintended consequences and produce black swan events. For example, the Islamic State is the unintended consequence of Washington's wars in the Muslim world. The Islamic State was created out of the Islamist forces that Washington assembled against Gaddafi in Libya. These forces were then sent to overthrow Assad in Syria. As Muslims flocked to ISIS's banner and its military prowess grew, ISIS realized that it was a new and independent force consisting of radicalized Muslims.

Radicalized Muslims are tired of Western domination and control of Muslim lands. Out of ISIS's self-awareness, a new state has been created, redrawing the Middle Eastern boundaries created by the British and French.

It is curious that Iran and Russia regard the Islamic State as a more dangerous enemy than Washington and are supporting Washington's moves against the Islamic State. As the Islamic State is capable of disrupting Washington's policy in the Middle East, Iran and Russia have an incentive to finance and arm the Islamic State. It is in Washington, not in the Islamic State, where Sauron resides and is gathering up the rings in order to control them all.

In their attempts to negotiate with Europeans, Putin and Lavrov should notice the total unwillingness of the EU to negotiate with its own members. Right in front of our eyes we see Merkel and Hollande driving their fellow Greek EU compatriots into the ground.

The EU has told the new Greek government that the EU doesn't care a whit about Greece and its people.

The Europeans only care that they don't get stuck with the cost of the bad loans the German and Dutch banks made to Greek governments in the past.

As I described in my book, *The Failure of Laissez Faire Capitalism*, one purpose of the "sovereign debt crisis" is to establish the principle that private lenders are not responsible for their bad judgment. Instead, the peoples of the country who were not parties to the loans are responsible. The EU is using the crisis not only to protect powerful private interests, but also to establish that over-indebted countries lose control of their fiscal affairs to the EU. In other words, the EU is using the crisis to centralize authority in order to destroy country sovereignty.

As Washington and the EU do not respect the sovereignty of Greece, one of its own, why does the Russian government think that Washington and the EU respect the sovereignty of Russia or Ukraine? Or of India, Brazil and other South American countries, or China? Currently Washington is trying to overthrow the governments of Cuba, Venezuela, Ecuador, Bolivia, and Argentina.

Washington respects no one. Thus, talking to Washington is a waste of time. Is this a game Russia wants to play?

THE MINSK
PEACE DEAL:
FARCE OR SELLOUT?

February 12, 2015

Judging by the report on RT[137] I conclude that the Ukraine peace deal worked out in Minsk by Putin, Merkel, Hollande, and Poroshenko has little chance of success.

As Washington is not a partner to the Minsk peace deal, how can there be peace when Washington has made policy decisions to escalate the conflict and to use the conflict as a proxy war between the US and Russia?

The Minsk agreement makes no reference to the announcement by Lt. Gen. Ben Hodges, commander of US Army Europe, that Washington is sending a battalion of US troops to Ukraine to train Ukrainian forces how to fight against Russian and rebel forces. The training is scheduled to begin in March, about two weeks from now. Gen. Hodges says that it is very important to recognize that the Donetsk and Luhansk forces "are not separatists, these are proxies for President Putin."

How is there a peace deal when Washington has plans underway to send arms and training to the US puppet government in Kiev?

Looking at the deal itself, it is set up to fail. The only parties to the deal who had to sign it are the leaders of the Donetsk and Lugansk break-away republics. The other signers to the Minsk deal are an OSCE representative which is the European group that is supposed to monitor the withdrawal of heavy weapons by both sides, a former Ukrainian president Viktor Kuchma, and the Russian ambassador in Kiev. Neither the German chancellor nor the French, Ukrainian, and Russian presidents who brokered the deal had to sign it.

In other words, the governments of Germany, France, Ukraine, and Russia do not appear to be empowered or required to enforce the agreement. According to RT, "the declaration was not meant to be signed by the leaders, German foreign minister Frank-Walter Steinmeier said."[138]

The terms of the agreement depend on actions of the Ukrainian parliament and prime minister, neither of which are under Poroshenko's control, and Poroshenko himself is a figurehead under Washington's control.

339

Moreover, the Ukrainian military does not control the Nazi militias. As Washington and the rightwing elements in Ukraine want conflict with Russia, peace cannot be forthcoming.

The agreement is nothing but a list of expectations that have no chance of occurring.

One expectation is that Ukraine and the republics will negotiate terms for future local elections in the provinces that will bring them back under Ukraine's legal control. The day after the local elections, but prior to the constitutional reform that provides the regions with autonomy, Kiev takes control of the borders with Ukraine and between the provinces. I read this as the total sell-out of the Donetsk and Lugansk republics. Apparently, that is the way the leaders of the republics see it as well, as Putin had to twist their arms in order to get their signatures to the agreement.

Another expectation is that Ukraine will adopt legislation on self-governance that would be acceptable to the republics and declare a general amnesty for the republics' leaders and military forces.

Negotiations between Kiev and the autonomous areas are to take place that restore Kiev's taxation of the autonomous areas and the provision of social payments and banking services to the autonomous areas.

After a comprehensive constitutional reform in Ukraine guaranteeing acceptable (and undefined) autonomy to the republics, Kiev will take control over the provinces' borders with Russia.

By the end of 2015 Kiev will implement comprehensive constitutional reform that decentralizes the Ukrainian political system and provides privileges of autonomy to the Donetsk and Lugansk regions.

Both Putin and Poroshenko are reported as stating that the main thing achieved is a ceasefire starting on February 15.

The ceasefire is of no benefit to the Donetsk and Lugansk republics as they are prevailing in the conflict.

Moreover, the deal requires the republics' forces to give up territory and to pull back to the borders of last September and to eject fighters from France and other countries who have come to the aid of the breakaway republics. In other words, the agreement erases all of Kiev's losses from the conflict that Kiev initiated.

All of the risks of the agreement are imposed on the break-away republics and on Putin. The provinces are required to give up all their gains while Washington trains and arms Ukrainian forces to attack the provinces. The republics have to give up their security and trust Kiev long before Kiev votes, assuming it ever does, on autonomy for the republics.

Moreover, if the one-sided terms of the Minsk agreement result in failure, Putin and the republics will be blamed.

Why would Putin make such a deal and force it on the republics?

If the deal becomes a Russian sell-out of the republics, it will hurt Putin's nationalist support within Russia and make it easier for Washington to weaken Putin and perhaps achieve regime change. It looks more like a surrender than a fair deal.

Perhaps Putin's strategy is to give away every advantage in the expectation that the deal will fail, and the Russian government can say "we gave away the store and the deal still failed."

Washington's coup in Kiev and the attack on the Russian-speaking Ukrainians in the east and south is part of Washington's strategy to reassert its uni-power position. Russia's independent foreign policy and Russia's growing economic and political relationships with Europe became problems for Washington.

Washington is using Ukraine to attack and to demonize Russia and its leader and to break-up Russia's economic and political relations with Europe. That is what the sanctions are about. A peace deal in Ukraine on any terms other than Washington's is unacceptable to Washington. The only acceptable deal is a deal that is a defeat for Russia.

It is difficult to avoid the conclusion that the Russian government made a strategic mistake when it did not accept the requests of the break-away provinces to be united with Russia. The people in the Donetsk and Lugansk provinces favored unification with the same massive majorities that the people in Crimea showed. If the provinces had been united with Russia, it would have been the end of the conflict. Neither Ukraine nor Washington is going to attack Russian territory.

By failing to end the conflict by unification, Putin set himself up as the punching bag for Western propaganda. The consequence is that over the many months during which the conflict has been needlessly drawn out, Putin has had his image and reputation in the West destroyed. He is the "new Hitler." He is "scheming to restore the Soviet Empire." "Russia ranks with ebola and the Islamist State as the three greatest threats." "RT is a terrorist organization like Boco Haram and the Islamist State." And so on and on. This CNN interview with Obama conducted by Washington's presstitute Fareed Zakaria shows the image of Putin based entirely on lies that rules in the West.[139]

Putin could be no more demonized even if the Russian military had invaded Ukraine, conquered it, and reincorporated Ukraine in Russia of which Ukraine was part for centuries prior to the Soviet collapse and Ukraine's separation from Russia at Washington's insistence.

The Russian government might want to carefully consider whether Moscow is helping Washington to achieve another victory in Ukraine.

WASHINGTON HAS RESURRECTED THE THREAT OF NUCLEAR WAR

February 24, 2015

Foreign Affairs is the publication of the elitist Council on Foreign Relations, a collection of former and current government officials, academics, and corporate and financial executives who regard themselves as the custodian and formulator of US foreign policy. The publication of the council carries the heavy weight of authority. One doesn't expect to find humor in it, but I found myself roaring with laughter while reading an article in the February 5 online issue by Alexander J. Motyl, "Goodbye, Putin: Why the President's Days Are Numbered."

I assumed I was reading a clever parody of Washington's anti-Putin propaganda. Absurd statement followed absurd statement. It was better than Colbert. I couldn't stop laughing.

To my dismay I discovered that the absolute gibberish wasn't a parody of Washington's propaganda. Motyl, an ardent Ukrainian nationalist, is a professor at Rugers University and was not joking when he wrote that Putin had stolen $45 billion, that Putin was resurrecting the Soviet Empire, that Putin had troops and tanks in Ukraine and had started the war in Ukraine, that Putin is an authoritarian whose regime is "exceedingly brittle" and subject to being overthrown at any time by the people Putin has bought off with revenues from the former high oil price, or by "an Orange Revolution in Moscow" in which Putin is overthrown by Washington orchestrated demonstrations by US financed NGOs as in Ukraine, or by a coup d'état by Putin's Praetorial guards. And if none of this sends Putin goodbye, the North Caucasus, Chechnya, Ingushetia, Dagestan, and the Crimean Tarters are spinning out of control and will do Washington's will by unseating Putin. Only the West's friendly relationship with Ukraine, Belarus and Kazakhstan can shield "the rest of the world from Putin's disastrous legacy of ruin."

When confronted with this level of ignorant nonsense in what is alleged to be a respectable publication, we experience the degradation of the Western political and media elite. To argue with nonsense is pointless.

What we see here with Motyl is the purest expression of the blatant propagandistic lies that flow continually from the likes of Fox "News," Sean Hannity, the neocon warmongers, the White House and executive branch, and congressional personnel beholden to the military/security complex.

The lies are too much even for Henry Kissinger.

As Stephen Lendman, who documents the ever growing anti-Russian propaganda, honestly states: "America's war on the world rages. Humanity's greatest challenge is stopping this monster before it destroys everyone."

The absurdity of it all! Even a moron knows that if Russia is going to put tanks and troops into Ukraine, Russia will put in enough to do the job. The war would be over in a few days if not in a few hours. As Putin himself said some months ago, if the Russian military enters Ukraine, the news will not be the fate of Donetsk or Mauriupol, but the fall of Kiev and Lviv.

Former US Ambassador to the Soviet Union (1987-91) Jack Matlock cautioned against the crazed propagandistic attack against Russia in his speech at the National Press Club on February 11. Matlock is astonished by the dismissal of Russia as merely "a regional power" of little consequence to the powerful US military. No country, Matlock says, armed with numerous, accurate, and mobile ICBMs is limited to regional power. This is the kind of hubristic miscalculation that ends in world destruction.

Matlock also notes that the entirety of Ukraine, like Crimea, has been part of Russia for centuries and that Washington and NATO have no business being in Ukraine.

He also points out the violations of promises made to Russia not to expand NATO eastward and how this and other acts of US aggression toward Russia have recreated the lack of trust between the two powers that Reagan worked successfully to overcome.

Reagan's politeness toward the Soviet leadership and refusal to personalize differences created an era of cooperation that the morons who are Reagan's successors have thrown away, thus renewing the threat of nuclear war that Reagan and Gorbachev had ended.

Washington's foreign policy, Matlock says, is autistic, which he defines as impaired social interaction, failed communication, and restricted and repetitive behavior.

Don't bother with the utter fool Motyl.[140]

DESTRUCTION OF TRUST BETWEEN NUCLEAR POWERS: CRIME OF THE CENTURY

February 25, 2015

Ambassador Jack Matlock made an important speech at the National Press Club on February 11. Matlock served as US ambassador to the Soviet Union during 1987-91. In his speech he describes how President Reagan won the trust of the Soviet leadership in order to bring to an end the Cold War and its risk of nuclear Armageddon. Reagan's meeting with Gorbachev did not rely on position papers written by staff.

It relied on a hand-written memo by Reagan himself that stressed respect for the Soviet leadership and a clear realization that negotiation must not expect the Soviet leaders to do something that is not in the true interest of their country. The way to end the conflict, Reagan wrote, is to cooperate toward a common goal. Matlock said that Reagan refused to personalize disagreements or to speak derogatorily of any Soviet leader.

Matlock made the point that Reagan's successors have done a thorough job of destroying this trust. In the last two years the destruction of trust has been total.

How can the Russian government trust Washington when Washington violates the word of President George H.W. Bush and takes NATO into Eastern Europe and places military bases on Russia's border?

How can the Russian government trust Washington when Washington pulls out of the Anti-Ballistic Missile Treaty and places Anti-Ballistic Missiles on Russia's border?

How can the Russian government trust Washington when Washington overthrows in a coup the elected government of Ukraine and installs a puppet regime that immediately expresses hostility toward Russia and the Russian-speaking population in Ukraine and destroys Soviet war memorials commemorating the Red Army's liberation of Ukraine from Nazi Germany?

How can the Russian government trust Washington when the President of Russia is called every name in the book, including "the new Hitler," and gratuitously accused of every sort of crime and personal failing?

Washington and its neoconservative monsters have destroyed trust with demonization and blame of Russia for violence in Ukraine for which Washington is responsible.

Washington has forced Europe to impose economic sanctions on Russia that are based entirely on lies and false accusations. The Russians know this. They recognize the blatant hostility, the blatant lies, the never-ending crude propaganda, the hypocritical double-standards, the push toward war.

Simultaneously China is experiencing hostile encirclement with Washington's "pivot to Asia."

By destroying trust, Washington has resurrected the threat of nuclear Armageddon. Washington's destruction of trust between nuclear powers is the crime of the century.

On February 24, I held accountable Alexander J. Motyl and the Council on Foreign Relations for publishing on February 5 a large collection of blatant lies in order to create a false reality with which to demonize the Russian government.[141] I observed that the publication of ignorant nonsense in what is supposed to be a respectable foreign policy journal indicated the degradation of the Western political and media elite.

I did not think things could get any worse, but one day later I came across Andrew S. Weiss' article in the *Wall Street Journal*.[142]

Weiss' article is the most amazing collection of misrepresentations imaginable. It is impossible to believe that the vice president for studies at the Carnegie Endowment could possible be so totally misinformed.

The false reality that Weiss creates precludes any diplomatic resolution of the conflict that Washington has created with Russia.

What is the explanation for Weiss' misrepresentations of Putin, the origin of the conflict and the cause of its continuation?

Recalling the confession of Udo Ulfkotte, an editor at the *Frankfurter Allgemeine Zeitung*, that he published under his name articles handed to him by the CIA and that the entire European press does the same: was Weiss handed the disinformation by the CIA, or by Victoria Nuland, or is the answer simply that Weiss worked on Russian, Ukrainian and Eurasian affairs at the National Security Council, the State Department and the Defense Department and is one of Washington's propaganda operatives currently operating out of a think-tank?

The more important question is: What is the purpose behind Washington's cause and misrepresentation of the conflict? Was the destruction of trust between nuclear powers intentional or a consequence of other purposes? Is Washington simply using its ability to control explanations in order to cover up its involvement in the overthrow of a democratically elected government, an outcome that has gone bad? Or is the answer merely that Washington is peeved that it failed to get its hands on Russia's Black Sea naval base in Crimea and has had to give up, at least for now, on getting Russia out of the Mediterranean and out of the Russian naval base at Tartus, Syria?

As I explained today to an international conference hosted by institutes of the Russian Academy of Sciences and Moscow State Institute of International Relations, the neoconservative ideology of US world hegemony requires the prevention of "the re-emergence of a new rival, either on the territory of the former Soviet Union or elsewhere" with sufficient resources and power to be able to serve as a check on unilateral action by Washington.

When Russian diplomacy blocked Washington's planned invasion of Syria and planned bombing of Iran, the neoconservatives realized that they had failed in their "first objective" and were now faced with a check on unilateral action. The attack on Russia instantly began. The $5 billion Washington had spent funding NGOs in Ukraine and cultivating Ukrainian politicians produced the overthrow of the elected Ukrainian government. Washington imposed a puppet government that instantly employed violent words and deeds against the Russian population, resulting in the secession of Crimea and the formation of other break-away provinces.

With English as the world language and the compliant media or presstitutes in Washington's service, Washington has been able to control the explanation, blame Putin for the crisis, and force Europe to breakup its economic and political relations with Russia by imposing economic sanctions.

In a vain and failed attempt to keep the US as the Uni-power capable of dictating to the world, the neoconservatives have recklessly and irresponsibly resurrected the threat of nuclear Armageddon. The neoconservative dominance of US foreign policy makes impossible any restoration of trust. Washington's propaganda is driving the situation toward war. As neither Washington nor the Russian/Chinese alliance can afford to lose the war, the war will be nuclear. Any survivors will be doomed by nuclear winter.

The entire world must quickly become aware of the danger and confront the evil regime that the neoconservatives—the Sauron of our world—have created in Washington. To do otherwise is to risk life on earth.

THE NEOCONSERVATIVE THREAT TO WORLD ORDER

February 26, 2015

This week I was invited to address an important conference of the Russian Academy of Sciences in Moscow. Scholars from Russia and from around the world, Russian government officials, and the Russian people seek an answer as to why Washington destroyed during the past year the friendly relations between America and Russia that President Reagan and President Gorbachev succeeded in establishing.

All of Russia is distressed that Washington alone has destroyed the trust between the two major nuclear powers that had been created during the Reagan-Gorbachev era, trust that had removed the threat of nuclear Armageddon. Russians at every level are astonished at the virulent propaganda and lies constantly issuing from Washington and the Western media. Washington's gratuitous demonization of the Russian president, Vladimir Putin, has rallied the Russian people behind him. Putin has the highest approval rating ever achieved by any leader in my lifetime.

Washington's reckless and irresponsible destruction of the trust achieved by Reagan and Gorbachev has resurrected the possibility of nuclear war from the grave in which Reagan and Gorbachev buried it.

Again, as during the Cold War the specter of nuclear Armageddon stalks the earth.

Why did Washington revive the threat of world annihilation? Why is this threat to all of humanity supported by the majority of the US Congress, by the entirety of the presstitute media, and by academics and think-tank inhabitants in the US, such as Motyl and Weiss, about whom I wrote recently?

It was my task to answer this question for the conference. But first you should understand what nuclear war means, elucidated by thebulletin. org.[143]

The Threat Posed to International Relations by the Neoconservative Ideology of American Hegemony

Address to the 70th Anniversary of the Yalta Conference,
Hosted by Institutes of the Russian Academy of Sciences and Moscow State Institute of International Relations,
Moscow, February 25, 2015

Colleagues,

What I propose to you is that the current difficulties in the international order are unrelated to Yalta and its consequences, but have their origin in the rise of the neoconservative ideology in the post-Soviet era and its influence on Washington's foreign policy.

The collapse of the Soviet Union removed the only constraint on Washington's power to act unilaterally abroad. At that time China's rise was estimated to require a half century. Suddenly the United States found itself to be the Uni-power, the "world's only superpower." Neoconservatives proclaimed "the end of history."

By the "end of history" neoconservatives mean that the competition between socio-economic-political systems is at an end. History has chosen "American Democratic-Capitalism." It is Washington's responsibility to exercise the hegemony over the world given to Washington by History and to bring the world in line with History's choice of American democratic-capitalism.

In other words, Marx has been proven wrong. The future does not belong to the proletariat but to Washington.

The neoconservative ideology raises the United States to the unique status of being "the exceptional country," and the American people acquire exalted status as "the indispensable people."

If a country is "the exceptional country," it means that all other countries are unexceptional. If a people are "indispensable," it means other peoples are dispensable. We have seen this attitude at work in Washington's 14 years of wars of aggression in the Middle East. These wars have left countries destroyed and millions of people dead, maimed, and displaced. Yet Washington continues to speak of its commitment to protect smaller countries from the aggression of larger countries. The explanation for this hypocrisy is that Washington does not regard Washington's aggression as aggression, but as History's purpose.

We have also seen this attitude at work in Washington's disdain for Russia's national interests and in Washington's propagandistic response to Russian diplomacy.

The neoconservative ideology requires that Washington maintain its Uni-power status, because this status is necessary for Washington's hegemony and History's purpose.

The neoconservative doctrine of US world supremacy is most clearly and concisely stated by Paul Wolfowitz, a leading neoconservative who has held many high positions: Deputy Assistant Secretary of Defense, Director of Policy Planning US Department of State, Assistant Secretary of State, Ambassador to Indonesia, Undersecretary of Defense for Policy, Deputy Secretary of Defense, President of the World Bank.

In 1992 Paul Wolfowitz stated the neoconservative doctrine of American world supremacy:

> Our first objective is to prevent the re-emergence of a
> new rival, either on the territory of the former Soviet
> Union or elsewhere, that poses a threat on the order of that
> posed formerly by the Soviet Union. This is a dominant
> consideration underlying the new regional defense strategy
> and requires that we endeavor to prevent any hostile power
> from dominating a region whose resources would, under
> consolidated control, be sufficient to generate global power.

For clarification, a "hostile power" is a country with an independent policy (Russia, China, Iran, and formerly Saddam Hussein, Gaddafi, Assad).

This bold statement struck the traditional American foreign policy establishment as a declaration of American Imperialism. The document was rewritten in order to soften and disguise the blatant assertion of supremacy without changing the intent. These documents are available online, and you can examine them at your convenience.

Softening the language allowed the neoconservatives to rise to foreign policy dominance. The neoconservatives are responsible for the Clinton regime's attacks on Yugoslavia and Serbia.

Neoconservatives, especially Paul Wolfowitz, are responsible for the George W. Bush regime's invasion of Iraq. The neoconservatives are responsible for the overthrow and murder of Gaddafi in Libya, the assault on Syria, the propaganda against Iran, the drone attacks on Pakistan and Yemen, the color revolutions in former Soviet Republics, the attempted "Green Revolution" in Iran, the coup in Ukraine, and the demonization of Vladimir Putin.

A number of thoughtful Americans suspect that the neoconservatives are responsible for 9/11, as that event gave the neoconservatives the "New Pearl Harbor" that their position papers said was necessary in order to launch their wars for hegemony in the Middle East. 9/11 led directly and instantly to the invasion of Afghanistan, where Washington has been fighting since

2001. Neoconservatives controlled all the important government positions necessary for a "false flag" attack.

Neoconservative Assistant Secretary of State Victoria Nuland, who is married to another neoconservative, Robert Kagan, implemented and oversaw Washington's coup in Ukraine and chose the new government.

The neoconservatives are highly organized and networked, well-financed, supported by the print and TV media, and backed by the US military/security complex and the Israel Lobby. There is no countervailing power to their influence on US foreign policy.

The neoconservative doctrine goes beyond the Brzezinski doctrine, which dissented from Detente and provocatively supported dissidents inside the Soviet empire. Despite its provocative character, the Brzezinski doctrine remained a doctrine of Great Power politics and containment. It is not a doctrine of US world hegemony.

While the neoconservatives were preoccupied for a decade with their wars in the Middle East, creating a US Africa Command, organizing color revolutions, exiting disarmament treaties, surrounding Russia with military bases, and "pivoting to Asia" to surround China with new air and naval bases, Vladimir Putin led Russia back to economic and military competence and successfully asserted an independent Russian foreign policy.

When Russian diplomacy blocked Washington's planned invasion of Syria and Washington's planned bombing of Iran, the neoconservatives realized that they had failed the "first objective" of the Wolfowitz Doctrine and had allowed "the re-emergence of a new rival . . . on the territory of the former Soviet Union" with the power to block unilateral action by Washington.

The attack on Russia began. Washington had spent $5 billion over a decade creating non-governmental organizations (NGOs) in Ukraine and cultivating Ukrainian politicians. The NGOs were called into the streets. The extreme nationalists or Nazi elements were used to introduce violence, and the elected democratic government was overthrown. The intercepted conversation between Victoria Nuland and the US ambassador in Kiev, in which the two Washington operatives chose the members of the new Ukrainian government, is well known.

If the information that has recently come to me from Armenia and Kyrgyzstan is correct, Washington has financed NGOs and is cultivating politicians in Armenia and the former Soviet Central Asian Republics.

If the information is correct, Russia can expect more "color revolutions" or coups in other former territories of the Soviet Union. Perhaps China faces a similar threat in Uyghurstan.

The conflict in Ukraine is often called a "civil war." This is incorrect. A civil war is when two sides fight for the control of the government. The break-away republics in eastern and southern Ukraine are fighting a war of secession.

Washington would have been happy to use its coup in Ukraine to evict Russia from its Black Sea naval base as this would have been a strategic military achievement. However, Washington is pleased that the "Ukraine crisis" that Washington orchestrated has resulted in the demonization of Vladimir Putin, thus permitting economic sanctions that have disrupted Russia's economic and political relations with Europe.

The sanctions have kept Europe in Washington's orbit.

Washington has no interest in resolving the Ukrainian situation. The situation can be resolved diplomatically only if Europe can achieve sufficient sovereignty over its foreign policy to act in Europe's interest instead of Washington's interest.

The neoconservative doctrine of US world hegemony is a threat to the sovereignty of every country. The doctrine requires subservience to Washington's leadership and to Washington's purposes. Independent governments are targeted for destabilization. The Obama regime overthrew the reformist government in Honduras and currently is at work destabilizing Venezuela, Bolivia, Ecuador, and Argentina, and most likely also Armenia and the former Central Asian Soviet Republics.

Yalta and its consequences have to do with Great Power rivalries. But in the neoconservative doctrine, there is only one Great Power—the Unipower. There are no others, and no others are to be permitted.

Therefore, unless a sensible foreign policy arises in Washington and displaces the neoconservatives, the future is one of conflict.

It would be a strategic error to dismiss the neoconservative ideology as unrealistic. The doctrine is unrealistic, but it is also the guiding force of US foreign policy and is capable of producing a world war.

In their conflict with Washington's hegemony, Russia and China are disadvantaged. The success of American propaganda during the Cold War, the large differences between living standards in the US and those in communist lands, overt communist political oppression, at times brutal, and the Soviet collapse created in the minds of many people nonexistent virtues for the United States. As English is the world language and the Western media is cooperative, Washington is able to control explanations regardless of the facts. The ability of Washington to be the aggressor and to blame the victim encourages Washington's march to more aggression.

This concludes my remarks. Tomorrow I will address whether there are domestic political restraints or economic restraints on the neoconservative ideology.

Address to the 70th Anniversary of the Yalta Conference,
Moscow, February 26, 2015

Colleagues,

At the plenary session yesterday I addressed the threat that the neoconservative ideology poses to international relations. In this closing session I address whether there are any internal restraints on this policy from the US population and whether there are economic restraints.

Just as 9/11 served to launch Washington's wars for hegemony in the Middle East, 9/11 served to create the American police state. The Constitution and the civil liberties it protects quickly fell to the accumulation of power in the executive branch that a state of war permitted.

New laws, some clearly pre-prepared such as the PATRIOT Act, executive orders, presidential directives, and Department of Justice memos, created an executive authority unaccountable to the US Constitution and to domestic and international law.

Suddenly Americans could be detained indefinitely without cause presented to a court. Habeas corpus, a constitutional protection which prohibits any such detention, has been set aside.

Suddenly people could be tortured into confessions in violation of the right against self-incrimination and in violation of domestic and international laws against torture.

Suddenly Americans and Washington's closest allies could be spied on indiscriminately without the need of warrants demonstrating cause.

The Obama regime added to the Bush regime's transgressions the assertion of the right of the executive branch to assassinate US citizens without due process of law.

The police state was organized under a massive new Department of Homeland Security. Almost immediately whistleblower protections, freedom of the press and speech, and protest rights were attacked and reduced.

It was not long before the director of Homeland Security declared that the department's focus has shifted from Muslim terrorists to "domestic extremists," an undefined category. Anyone can be swept into this category. Homes of war protesters were raided and grand juries were convened to investigate the protesters. Americans of Arab descent who donated to charities—even charities on the State Department's approved list—that aided Palestinian children were arrested and sentenced to prison for "providing material support to terrorism."

All of this and more, including police brutality, has had a chilling effect on protests against the wars and the loss of civil liberty. The rising protests from the American population and from soldiers themselves that eventually forced Washington to end the Vietnam War have been prevented in the 21st century by the erosion of rights, intimidation, loss of mobility (no-fly list), job dismissal, and other heavy-handed actions inconsistent with a government accountable to law and to the people.

In an important sense, the US has emerged from the "war on terror" as an executive branch dictatorship unconstrained by the media and barely, if at all, constrained by Congress and the federal courts. The lawlessness of the executive branch has spread into governments of Washington's vassal states and into the Federal Reserve, the International Monetary Fund, and the European Central Bank, all of which violate their charters and operate outside their legal powers.

Jobs off-shoring destroyed the American industrial and manufacturing unions. Their demise and the current attack on the public employee unions has left the Democratic Party financially dependent on the same organized private interest groups as the Republicans. Both parties now report to the same interest groups. Wall Street, the military/security complex, the Israel Lobby, agribusiness, and the extractive industries (oil, mining, timber) control the government regardless of the party in power. These powerful interests all have a stake in American hegemony.

The message is that the constellation of forces preclude internal political change.

Hegemony's Archilles heel is the US economy. The fairy tale of American economic recovery supports America's image as the safe haven, an image that keeps the dollar's value up, the stock market up, and interest rates down. However, there is no economic information that supports this fairy tale.

Real median household income has not grown for years and is below the levels of the early 1970s. There has been no growth in real retail sales for six years. The labor force is shrinking. The labor force participation rate has declined since 2007 as has the civilian employment to population ratio. The 5.7 percent reported unemployment rate is achieved by not counting discouraged workers as part of the work force. (A discouraged worker is a person who is unable to find a job and has given up looking.)

A second official unemployment rate, which counts short-term (less than one year) discouraged workers and is seldom reported, stands at 11.2 percent. The US government stopped including long-term discouraged workers (discouraged for more than one year) in 1994. If the long-term discouraged are counted, the current unemployment rate in the US stands at 23.2 percent.

The off-shoring of American manufacturing and professional service jobs such as software engineering and Information Technology has decimated the middle class. The middle class has not found jobs with incomes comparable to those moved abroad. The labor cost savings from off-shoring the jobs to Asia has boosted corporate profits, the performance bonuses of executives and capital gains of shareholders. Thus all income and wealth gains are concentrated in a few hands at the top of the income distribution. The number of billionaires grows as destitution reaches from the lower economic class into the middle class.

American university graduates, unable to find jobs, return to their childhood rooms in their parents' homes and work as waitresses and bartenders in part-time jobs that will not support an independent existence.

With a large percentage of the young economically unable to form households, residential construction, home furnishings, and home appliances suffer economic weakness. Cars can still be sold only because the purchaser can obtain 100 percent financing in a six-year loan. The lenders sell the loans, which are securitized and sold to gullible investors, just as were the mortgage-backed financial instruments that precipitated the 2007 US financial crash.

None of the problems that created the 2008 recession, and that were created by the 2008 recession, have been addressed. Instead, policymakers have used an expansion of debt and money to paper over the problems. Money and debt have grown much more than US GDP, which raises questions about the value of the US dollar and the credit worthiness of the US government. On July 8, 2014, my colleagues and I pointed out that when correctly measured, US national debt stands at 185 percent of GDP.[144]

This raises the question: Why was the credit rating of Russia, a country with an extremely low ratio of debt to GDP, downgraded and not that of the US? The answer is that the downgrading of Russian credit worthiness was a political act directed against Russia in behalf of US hegemony.

How long can fairy tales and political acts keep the US house of cards standing? A rigged stock market. A rigged interest rate. A rigged dollar exchange value, a rigged and suppressed gold price. The current Western financial system rests on world support for the US dollar and on nothing more.

The problem with neoliberal economics, which pervades all countries, even Russia and China, is that neoliberal economics is a tool of American economic imperialism, as is Globalism. As long as countries targeted by Washington for destabilization support and cling to the American doctrines that enable the destabilization, the targets are defenseless.

If Russia, China, and the BRICS Bank were willing to finance Greece, Italy, and Spain, perhaps those countries could be separated from the EU and NATO. The unraveling of Washington's empire would begin.

TRUTH
IS OUR
COUNTRY

March 15, 2015

Last week in Mexico at the annual awards conference of the Club De Periodistas De Mexico I was given the International Award for Excellence in Journalism. In my speech I emphasized that Truth is the country of real journalists. Unlike presstitutes, the loyalty of real journalists is to Truth, not to a government or corporate advertiser. Once a journalist sacrifices Truth to loyalty to a government, he ceases to be a journalist and becomes a propagandist.

Club De Periodistas De Mexico,
Mexico City, March 12, 2015

Colleagues,

Thank you for this recognition, for this honor. As Jesus told the people of Nazareth, a prophet is without honor in his own country. In the United States, this is also true of journalists.

In the United States journalists receive awards for lying for the government and for the corporations.

Anyone who tells the truth, whether journalist or whistleblower, is fired or prosecuted or has to hide out in the Ecuadoran Embassy in London, like Julian Assange, or in Moscow, like Edward Snowden, or is tortured and imprisoned, like Bradley Manning.

Mexican journalists pay an even higher price. Those who report on government corruption and on the drug cartels pay with their lives. The Internet encyclopedia, Wikipedia, has as an entry a list by name of journalists murdered in Mexico. This is the List of Honor. Wikipedia reports than more than 100 Mexican journalists have been killed or disappeared in the 21st century.

Despite intimidation the Mexican press has not abandoned its job. Because of your courage, I regard this award bestowed on me as the greatest of honors.

In the United States real journalists are scarce and are becoming more scarce. Journalists have morphed into a new creature. Gerald Celente calls US journalists "presstitutes," a word formed from press prostitute. In other words, journalists in the United States are whores for the government and for the corporations.

The few real journalists that remain are resigning. Last year Sharyl Attkisson, a 21-year veteran reporter with CBS resigned on the grounds that it had become too much of a fight to get truth reported. She was frustrated that CBS saw its purpose to be a protector of the powerful, not a critic.

Recently Peter Osborne, the UK *Telegraph*'s chief political commentator, explained why he resigned. His stories about the wrongdoings of the banking giant, HSBC, were spiked, because HSBC is an important advertiser for the *Telegraph*. Osborne says: "The coverage of HSBC in Britain's *Telegraph* is a fraud on its readers. If major newspapers allow corporations to influence their content for fear of losing advertising revenue, democracy itself is in peril."[145]

Last summer former *New York Times* editor Jill Abramson, in a speech at the Chautauqua Institution, said that *The New York Times* withheld information at the request of the White House. She said that for a number of years the press in general did not publish any stories that upset the White House. She justified this complete failure of journalism on the grounds that "journalists are Americans, too. I consider myself to be a patriot."

So in the United States journalists lie for the government because they are patriotic, and their readers and listeners believe the lies because they are patriotic.

Our view differs from the view of the *New York Times* editor. The view of those of us here today is that our country is not the United States, it is not Mexico, our country is Truth. Once a journalist sacrifices Truth to loyalty to a government, he ceases to be a journalist and becomes a propagandist.

Recently, Brian Williams, the television news anchor at NBC, destroyed his career because he misremembered an episode of more than a decade ago when he was covering the Iraq War. He told his audience that a helicopter in which he was with troops in a war zone as a war correspondent was hit by ground fire and had to land.

But the helicopter had not been hit by ground fire. His fellow journalists turned on him, accusing him of lying in order to enhance his status as a war correspondent.

On February 10, NBC suspended Brian Williams for 6 months from his job as Managing Editor and Anchor of NBC Nightly News.

Think about this for a moment. It makes no difference whatsoever whether the helicopter had to land because it had been hit by gun fire or for some other reason or whether it had to land at all. If it was an intentional lie, it was one of no consequence. If it was a mistake, an episode of "false memory," why the excessive reaction? Psychologists say that false memories are common.

The same NBC that suspended Brian Williams and the journalists who accused him of lying are all guilty of telling massive lies for the entirety of the 21st century that have had vast consequences. The United States government has been, and still is, invading, bombing, and droning seven or eight countries on the basis of lies told by Washington and endlessly repeated by the media. Millions of people have been killed, maimed, and displaced by violence based entirely on lies spewing out of the mouths of Washington and its presstitutes.

We know what these lies are: Saddam Hussein's weapons of mass destruction. Assad of Syria's use of chemical weapons. Iranian nukes. Pakistani and Yemeni terrorists. Terrorists in Somalia. The endless lies about Gaddafi in Libya, about the Taliban in Afghanistan. And now the alleged Russian invasion and annexation of Ukraine.

All of these transparent lies are repeated endlessly, and no one is held accountable. But one journalist misremembers one insignificant detail about a helicopter ride and his career is destroyed.

We can safely conclude that the only honest journalism that exists in the United States is provided by alternative media on the Internet.

Consequently, the Internet is now under US government attack. "Truth is the enemy of the state," and Washington intends to shut down truth everywhere.

Washington has appointed Andrew Lack, the former president of NBC News, to be the chief executive of the Broadcasting Board of Governors. His first official statement compared RT, Russia Today, the Russian-based news agency, with the Islamic State and Boko Haram. In other words, Mr. Lack brands RT as a terrorist organization.

The purpose of Andrew Lack's absurd comparison is to strike fear at RT that the news organization will be expelled from US media markets. Andrew Lack's message to RT is: "lie for us or we are going to expel you from our air waves."

The British already did this to Iran's Press TV.

In the United States the attack on Internet independent media is proceeding on several fronts. One is known as the issue of "net neutrality." There is an effort by Washington, joined by Internet providers, to charge sites for speedy access. Bandwidth would be sold for fees. Large media corporations, such as CNN and *The New York Times*, would be able to pay the prices for a quickly opening website. Smaller independent sites such as mine would be hampered with the slowness of the old "dial-up" type bandwidth. Click on CNN and the site immediately opens. Click on paulcraigroberts.org and wait five minutes.

You get the picture. This is Washington's plan and the corporations' plan for the Internet.

But it gets worse. The Electronic Frontier Foundation, which attempts to defend our digital rights, reports that so-called "free trade agreements," such as the Trans Pacific Partnership (and the Trans Atlantic Partnership) impose prison sentences, massive fines, and property seizures on Internet users who innocently violate vague language in the so-called trade agreements.

Recently, a young American, Barrett Brown, was sentenced to 5 years in prison and a fine of $890,000 for linking to allegedly hacked documents posted on the Internet. Barrett Brown did not hack the documents.

He merely linked to an Internet posting, and he has no prospect of earning $890,000 over the course of his life.

The purpose of the US government's prosecution, indeed, persecution, of this young person is to establish the precedent that anyone who uses Internet information in ways that Washington disapproves, or for purposes that Washington disapproves, is a criminal whose life will be ruined. The purpose of Barrett Brown's show trial is to intimidate. It is Washington's equivalent to the murder of Mexican journalists.

But this is prologue. Now we turn to the challenge that Washington presents to the entire world.

It is the nature of government and of technology to establish control. People everywhere face the threat of control by government and technology. But the threat from Washington is much greater. Washington is not content with only controlling the citizens of the United States. Washington intends to control the world.

Michael Gorbachev is correct when he says that the collapse of the Soviet Union was the worst thing that has happened to humanity, because the Soviet collapse removed the only constraint on Washington's power.

The Soviet collapse released a terrible evil upon the world. The neoconservatives in Washington concluded that the failure of communism meant that History has chosen American "democratic capitalism," which is neither democratic nor capitalist, to rule the world. The Soviet collapse signaled "the End of History," by which is meant the end of competition between social, political and economic systems.

The choice made by History elevated the United States to the pre-eminent position of being the "indispensable and exceptional" country, a claim of superiority. If the United States is "indispensable," then others are dispensable. If the United States is exceptional, then others are unexceptional.

We have seen the consequences of Washington's ideology in Washington's destruction of life and stability in the Middle East.

Washington's drive for World Hegemony, based as it is on a lie, makes necessary the obliteration of Truth.

As Washington's agenda of supremacy is all encompassing, Washington regards truth as a greater enemy than Russians, Muslim terrorists, and the Islamic State.

As truth is Washington's worst enemy, everyone associated with the truth is Washington's enemy.

Latin America can have no illusions about Washington. The first act of the Obama Regime was to overthrow the democratic reformist government of Honduras. Currently, the Obama Regime is trying to overthrow the governments of Venezuela, Ecuador, Bolivia, and Argentina.

As Mexicans know, in the 19th century Washington stole half of Mexico. Today Washington is stealing the rest of Mexico. The United States is stealing Mexico via financial imperialism, by subordinating Mexican agriculture and self-sustaining peasant agricultural communities to foreign-owned monoculture, by infecting Mexico with Monsanto's GMO's, genetically modified organisms, seeds that do not reproduce, chemicals that destroy the soil and nature's nutrients, seeds that leave Mexico dependent on Monsanto for food crops with reduced nutritional value.

It is easy for governments to sell out their countries to Washington and the North American corporations. Washington and US corporations pay high prices for subservience to their control. It is difficult for countries, small in economic and political influence, to stand against such power. All sorts of masks are used behind which Washington hides US exploitation—globalism, free trade treaties . . .

But the world is changing. Putin has revived Russia, and Russia has proved its ability to stand up to Washington.

On a purchasing power basis, China now has the largest economy in the world.

As China and Russia are now strategic allies, Washington cannot act against one without acting against the other. The two combined exceed Washington's capabilities.

The United States government has proven to the entire world that it is lawless. A country that flaunts its disrespect of law cannot provide trusted leadership.

My conclusion is that Washington's power has peaked.

Another reason Washington's power has peaked is that Washington has used its power to serve only itself and US corporations. The Rest of the World is dispensable and has been left out.

Washington's power grew out of World War II. All other economies and currencies were devastated. This allowed Washington to seize the world reserve currency role from Great Britain.

The advantage of being the world reserve currency is that you can pay your bills by printing money. In other words, you can't go broke as long as other countries are willing to hold your fiat currency as their reserves.

But if other countries were to decide not to hold US currency as reserves, the US could go broke suddenly.

Since 2008 the supply of US dollars has increased dramatically in relation to the ability of the real economy to produce goods and services. Whenever the growth of money outpaces the growth of real output, trouble lies ahead. Moreover, Washington's policy of imposing sanctions in an effort to force other countries to do its will is causing a large part of the world known as the BRICS to develop an alternative international payments system.

Washington's arrogance and hubris have caused Washington to ignore the interests of other countries, including those of its allies. Even Washington's European vassal states show signs of developing an independent foreign policy in their approach to Russia and Ukraine. Opportunities will arise for governments to escape from Washington's control and to pursue the interests of their own peoples.

The US media has never performed the function assigned to it by the Founding Fathers. The media is supposed to be diverse and independent. It is supposed to confront both government and private interest groups with the facts and the truth. At times the US media partially fulfilled this role, but not since the final years of the Clinton regime when the government allowed six mega-media companies to consolidate 90% of the media in their hands.

The mega-media companies that control the US media are GE, News Corp, Disney, Viacom, Time Warner, and CBS. (GE owns NBC, formerly an independent network. News Corp owns Fox News, the *Wall Street Journal*, and British newspapers. Disney owns ABC. Time Warner owns CNN.)

The US media is no longer run by journalists. It is run by former government officials and corporate advertising executives. The values of the mega-media companies depend on their federal broadcast licenses. If the companies go against the government, the companies take a risk that their licenses will not be renewed and, thus, the multi-billion dollar values of the companies fall to zero. If media organizations investigate wrongful activities by corporations, they risk the loss of advertising revenues and become less viable.

Ninety percent control of the media gives government a Ministry of Propaganda, and that is what exists in the United States. Nothing reported in the print or TV media can be trusted.

Today there is a massive propaganda campaign against the Russian government. The incessant flow of disinformation from Washington and the media has destroyed the trust between nuclear powers that President Reagan and President Gorbachev worked so hard to create. According to polls, 62% of the US population now regards Russia as the main threat.

I conclude my remarks with the observation that there can be no greater media failure than to bring back the specter of nuclear war. And that is what the US media has achieved.

HOW THE US GOVERNMENT AND MILITARY BECAME MURDER, INC.

March 24, 2015

Andrew Cockburn has written a must-read book. The title is *Kill Chain: The Rise of the High-Tech Assassins.* The title could just as well be: How the US Government and US Military Became Murder, Inc.

The US military no longer does war. It does assassinations, usually of the wrong people. The main victims of the US assassination policy are women, children, village elders, weddings, funerals, and occasionally US soldiers mistaken for Taliban by US surveillance operating with the visual acuity of the definition of legal blindness.

Cockburn tells the story of how the human element has been displaced by remote control killing guided by misinterpretation of unclear images on screens collected by surveillance drones and sensors thousands of miles away. Cockburn shows that the "all-seeing" drone surveillance system is an operational failure but is supported by defense contractors because of its high profitability and by the military brass because general officers, with the exception of General Paul Van Riper, are brainwashed in the belief that the revolution in military affairs means that high-tech devices replace the human element. Cockburn demonstrates that this belief is immune to all evidence to the contrary. The US military has now reached the point that Secretary of Defense Hagel deactivated both the A-10 close support fighter and the U-2 spy plane in favor of the operationally failed unmanned Global Hawk System. With the A-10 and U-2 went the last platforms for providing a human eye on what is happening on the ground.

The surveillance/sensor technology cannot see human footprints in the snow. Consequently, the drone technology concluded that a mountain top was free of enemy and sent a detachment of unsuspecting SEALS to be shot up. Still insisting no enemy present, a second group of SEALS were sent to be shot up, and then a detachment of Army Rangers. Finally, an A-10 pilot flew over the scene and reported the enemy's presence in force.

By 2012 even the US Air Force, which had been blindly committed to the unmanned drone system, had experienced more failure than could any longer be explained away. The Air Force admitted that the 50-year old U-2 could fly higher and in bad weather and take better pictures than the expensive Global Hawk System and declared the Global Hawk system scrapped.

The decision was supported by the 2011 report from the Pentagon's test office that the drone system was "not operationally effective." Among its numerous drawbacks was its inability to carry out assigned missions 75% of the time. The Chairman of the Joint Chiefs of Staff told Congress that in addition to the system's unacceptable failure rate, the drone system "has fundamentally priced itself out of our ability to afford it."

As Cockburn reports: "It made no difference. Congress, led by House Armed Services Committee Chairman Buck McKeon and Democratic Congressman Jim Moran (whose northern Virginia district hosts the headquarters of both Northrop and Raytheon) effortlessly brushed aside these pleas, forcing the Air Force to keep buying the unwanted drone."

Cockburn provides numerous examples of the utter failure of the unmanned revolution ushered in by unrealistic dreamers, such as Andrew Marshall, John Foster, William Perry, and David Deptula, who have done much harm to the US military and American taxpayers. The failure stories are legion and sad.

Almost always the victims are the innocent going about their everyday affairs.

The book opens with the story of three vehicles crammed with people from the same village heading to Kabul. Some were students returning to school in Kabul, some were shopkeepers heading to the capital to buy supplies, others were unemployed men on their way to Iran seeking work, and some were women bringing gifts for relatives. This collection of ordinary people, represented on screens by vague images, was willfully mistaken, as the reproduced conversations between drone operators and assassins show, for a senior Taliban commander leading forces to attack a US Special Forces patrol. The innocent civilians were blown to smithereens.

The second chapter tells of the So Tri, an indigenous people in the remote wilderness of southeastern Laos who were bombed for nine years because the stupid American military sowed their environment with sensors that called down bombs when human presence was detected. High-tech warfare misidentified the villagers with Viet Cong moving through jungle routes.

One heartbreaking story follows another. If surveillance suspects the presence of a High Value Target in a restaurant, regardless of nominal restrictions on the number of innocents who can be murdered as the "collateral damage" part of the strike, the entire restaurant and all within are destroyed by a hellfire missile. Remember that the Israelis denounce terrorists for exploding suicide vests inside Israeli restaurants. What the US military does is even worse.

On other occasions the US assassinates an underling of a High Value Target on the assumption that the Target will attend the funeral which is obliterated from the air whether the Target is present or not.

As the murders are indiscriminate, the US military defines all males killed to be valid targets. Generally, the US will not admit the deaths of non-Targets, and some US officials have declared there to be no such deaths. Blatant and obvious lies issue without shame in order to protect the "operationally ineffective" and very expensive high-tech production runs that mean billions of taxpayer dollars for the military/security complex and comfortable 7-figure employment salaries with contractors after retirement for the military brass.

When you read this book you will weep for your country, ruled as it is by completely immoral and inhumane monsters. But Cockburn's book is not without humor. He tells the story of Marine Lt. General Paul Van Riper, the scourge of the Unmanned Revolution in Military affairs, who repeatedly expressed contempt for the scientifically unsupported theories of unmanned war. To humiliate Gen. Riper with a defeat in a massive war game as leader of the enemy Red force against the high-tech American Blue force, he was called out of retirement to participate in a war game stacked against him.

The Blue force armored with a massive database (Operational Net Assessment) and overflowing with acronyms was almost instantly wiped out by General Riper. He sank the entire aircraft carrier fleet and the entire Blue force army went down with it. The war was over. The 21st century US high-tech, effects-based military was locked into a preset vision and was beaten hands down by a maverick Marine general with inferior forces.

The Joint Forces Command turned purple with rage. Gen. Riper was informed that the outcome of the war game was unacceptable and would not stand. The sunken fleet magically re-floated, the dead army was resurrected, and the war was again on, only this time restriction after restriction was placed on the Red force. Riper was not allowed to shoot down the Blue force's troop transports. Riper was ordered to turn on all of the Red force's radars so that the Red forces could be easily located and destroyed. Umpires ruled, despite the facts, that all of Riper's missile strikes were intercepted. Victory was declared for high-tech war. Riper's report on the total defeat of the Blue force, its unwarranted resurrection, and the rigged outcome was promptly classified so that no one could read it.

The highly profitable Revolution in Military Affairs had to be protected at all costs along with the reputations of the incompetent generals that comprise today's high command.

The infantile behavior of the US military compelled to create a victory for its high-tech, but legally blind, surveillance warfare demonstrates how far removed from the ability to conduct real warfare the US military is. What the US military has done in Afghanistan and Iraq is to create far more enemies than it has killed. Every time high-tech killing murders a village gathering, a wedding or funeral, or villagers on the way to the capital, which is often, the US creates hundreds more enemies. This is why after 14 years of killing in Afghanistan, the Taliban now controls most of the country. This is why Islamist warriors have carved a new country out of Syria and Iraq despite eight years of American sacrifice in Iraq estimated by Joseph Stiglitz and Linda Bilmes to have cost Americans a minimum of $3 trillion. The total failure of the American way of war is obvious to all, but the system rolls on autonomously.

The Revolution in Military Affairs has decapitated the US military, which no longer has the knowledge or ability or human tools to conduct war. If the crazed Russophobic US generals get their way and end up in confrontation with Russia, the American forces will be destroyed. The humiliation of this defeat will cause Washington to take the war nuclear.

Check out Stanislav Mishin's view of what awaits the foolish West:[146]

CAN EVIL
BE DEFEATED?

April 3, 2015

John W. Whitehead is a constitutional attorney. As head of the Rutherford Institute he is actively involved in defending our civil liberties. Being actively involved in legal cases, he experiences first hand the transformation of law from a shield of the American people into a weapon in the hands of the government.

American civil liberty was seriously eroded prior to 9/11, and the rise of the police/warfare state is a story I tell in *How America Was Lost*. Lawrence Stratton and I documented the loss of law as a shield of the American people in our book, *The Tyranny of Good Intentions* (2000, 2008). Whitehead in his book, *A Government of Wolves* (2013) and in his just released *Battlefield America* (2015) shows how quickly and thoroughly the police state has taken root.

We live in an electronic concentration camp. We are addicted to images on screens that disinform and propagandize us to accept and even welcome the police state activities that have destroyed our autonomy, privacy, and independence.

I write many columns on this subject. The advantage of a book is that it all comes together under one cover, and that is what Whitehead has done in *Battlefield America*.

The outlook for civil liberties grows bleaker by the day, from the government's embrace of indefinite detention for US citizens and armed surveillance drones flying overhead to warrantless surveillance of phone, email and Internet communications, and prosecutions of government whistle-blowers. The homeland is ruled by a police-industrial complex, an extension of the American military empire. Everything that our founding fathers warned against is now the new norm. The government has trained its sights on the American people. We have become the enemy. All the while, the American people remain largely oblivious.

Whitehead gives it to us straight. We are continually abused in the name of protecting us. Ordinary Americans are subject to far worst abuse from government than they ever could be from criminals and terrorists, both of which are bogymen used to justify the government's terrorism of the citizenry.

Four-year old children are handcuffed by police. Ninety-five year old citizens with walkers are body-slammed with their neck broken by police. War veterans without legs and wheelchair bound are shot and murdered by police. The police always justify their abuse and criminal acts by claiming they felt threatened. What kind of heavily armed police, usually together in gangs, is threatened by a four-year old, a 95-year old, a double amputee? The fact that police get away with this brutality shows their total lack of humanity and the total transformation of the purpose of police. Today a paranoid police protect not the public but the police state and themselves from an imaginary threatening public. We pay them to abuse and murder us.

On September 6, 7, and 8, 2014, the *Washington Post* reported that state and local police had become bandits, as in Mexico, who stop drivers in order to rob them. In "Stop and Seize," the *Washington Post* reported that "aggressive police take hundreds of millions of dollars from motorists not charged with crimes."

There are now training courses in which police are trained in the art of highway robbery. September 11, 2001, was used to create an industry that trains police in the aggressive techniques of highway interdiction. It is now routine for a traffic stop, whether justified or not, to result in the confiscation of your cash, other possessions, and your car itself. You can be robbed by police on the basis of their assumptions without being ticketed or charged with a crime.

Whitehead reports that in fiscal year 2012 the federal government alone seized $4.2 billion in assets despite the fact that in 80 percent of the cases no charge was issued.

Did you know that the school security industry is a $4.9 billion annual business that instills in youth acceptance of tyranny and punishments for infractions that are simply the normal behavior of youth?

Did you know that in 2006 a Halliburton subsidary, Dick Cheney's firm, was awarded a $385 million federal contract to build concentration camps in the US?

Did you know that Republicans have privatized the prison system and turned it into a $70 billion per year industry that demands ever more incarceration of citizens in order to drive profits? Consequently, 2.7 million American children now have at least one parent in prison, often on charges that would not constitute crimes in a civilized country.

US prison labor is now the cheapest form of labor available with prisoners paid between 93 cents and $4.73 per day. Prisoners make office furniture, work in call centers, fabricate body armor, take hotel reservations, work in slaughterhouses, manufacture textiles, shoes, and clothing, process agricultural products like milk and beef, package Starbucks coffee, shrink wrap software for Microsoft, sew lingerie for Victoria's Secret, produce the military's helmets, shirts, pants, tents, bags, canteens, and a variety of other equipment, make circuit boards for IBM, Texas Instruments and Dell, sew McDonald's uniforms, and perform labor services for Boeing, Motorola, Compaq, Revlon and Kmart.

Even the "mainstream" presstitute media has reported the US military drills in South Florida where military teams working with local police practiced rounding up American citizens for detention. The media has also reported the upcoming military occupations in Texas and Utah. There are protests but not on the level that a people conscious of the threat to their liberty would mount.

It seems clear that these are federal troops practicing control of the population which is being stripped of the constitutional right to hold government accountable. The pointless lockdown of Boston and its suburbs and the gratuitous house to house searches, a martial law exercise clearly prepared prior to the Boston Marathon Bombing, used fear created by the bombing, possibly a false flag operation, to teach the population compliance with, and acceptance of, martial law. The insouciant American population went along with it. If someone points out how they were manipulated, the fools scream "conspiracy theorist."

The official explanation of the military exercises practicing population control in South Florida, Texas and Utah is that the military is practicing for overseas actions. Why then are local police involved? More likely we are witnessing drills described in the US Army's 2010 publication, "Internment and Resettlement Operations."

It is now routine for police to amuse themselves by carrying out strip searches and vaginal searches of women. Police go out of their way to provoke resistance so that they can beat, taser, and murder. If they can't provoke it, they beat, taser, and murder anyway and claim their victim resisted arrest or threatened them. Have you noticed how the police find everyone threatening?

Whitehead shows that the educational system, entertainment, and television serve to indoctrinate and teach compliance. Television can do more than form public opinion. It is used to alter the worldview of the population. Our cars, household appliances, and smart homes are becoming devices designed to spy on us and report noncompliance. A society is being created in which there can be no autonomy and no freedom.

The technology that permits the electronic concentration camp is produced by thoughtless people who have no concern for liberty. How, Whitehead asks, do we maintain our humanity in the face of technologies designed to dehumanize us?

America now has preemptive prosecution. Whitehead reports that 95 percent of those convicted of terrorism between 2001 and 2010 were prosecuted not for deeds, but for beliefs, ideology, or religious affiliations.

The two most engaging chapters in *Battlefield America* are "The Matrix" and "The Posthuman Era," together a mere 17 pages. The fusion of machines with humans to which trans-humanists are committed will destroy human sensibility, memory, and morality, and probably humans themselves.

Corporate America is in it for the money. Whitehead tells us: "With every smartphone we buy, every GPS device we install, and every Twitter, Facebook, and Google account we open, we're helping Corporate America build a dossier for its government counterparts on who we know, what we think, how we spend our money, and how we spend our time."

Whitehead quotes Bill Joy, a cofounder of Sun Microsystems: "I think it is no exaggeration to say we are on the cusp of the further perfection of evil." Jim Edwards says, "We humans are now data bits."

In the penultimate chapter, Whitehead tells us what we can do, a question that I am forever asked by readers. Whitehead says that armed revolt is not an option. He believes that the tens of millions, perhaps 100 million, Americans who have pistols, rifles, and shotguns are not only unorganized, but outgunned.

The 21st century has been used to militarize state and local police forces and to brutalize their attitude toward the American public. Even police in small towns now have helicopters, armored personnel carriers, tanks, machine guns, rocket-propelled grenades, drones, night vision, heat sensors, sensors that can see through the walls of houses and into cars.

If this is not enough, in comes the National Guard or federal troops, Army Rangers, Navy Seals. Or simply the release of germs. Washington can deal with its citizens the same way it dealt with the indigenous peoples we call Indians. Washington has retained in its hands live smallpox, a deadly killer, and there now have been several generations of Americans who have not had smallpox vaccination, because the disease was eliminated by vaccination. All the government has to do is to release smallpox on resistant populations, and, of course, the government has numerous other such means.

How did it come to this?

In my opinion, as I so often write, Americans are distracted by sex, entertainment, the difficulty of providing for themselves and for families. They are locked into the disinformation that sustains the American Matrix, blinded by their patriotism and the 4th of July speeches and by their indoctrination that Americans are "exceptional and indispensable." And, of course, by their ignorance and arrogance.

Americans simply have no clue.

The purpose of the evil that masquerades as a government in Washington is to prevent those few Americans who do have a clue from informing the rest of the population. Whistleblowers are arrested and falsely prosecuted and imprisoned. Journalists have been intimidated into silence.

Now, to Whitehead's answer to what can we do. He says that we can mount "militant nonviolent resistance." This worked for Christians in the decomposing Roman Empire.

It worked for Mahatma Gandhi in India against the British colonialists. It was working for Martin Luther King in America before he was assassinated, most likely by the FBI.

Whitehead says that the mass of the citizenry cannot be assassinated. If citizens simply stop cooperating by listening to the lies on TV, by purchasing the devices used to control them, by amusing themselves in front of propaganda screens, by learning again how to think, how to be human, how to be moral, the American police state can be defeated.

It worked in the past, and possibly it can work again. If not, Washington will remain the home of Sauron, a threat to every American citizen and to the entire world.

THE IRAN NUCLEAR ENERGY AGREEMENT: FORCE AGAIN PREVAILS OVER LAW

April 7, 2015

The Israel Lobby and its associated neocon war criminals will block if they can the nuclear energy agreement, worked out by Putin, Iran, and Obama, which has the promise of bringing to an end the US orchestrated crisis over Iran's development of nuclear energy.

As a signatory to the nuclear weapons non-proliferation treaty, which Israel is not, Iran has the right under the treaty to develop nuclear energy. Iran, alone of all the signatories to the treaty, has had its rights under the treaty cancelled by economic sanctions imposed by the US and by the threat of a US military attack.

Neither US intelligence nor the International Atomic Energy Agency, which inspects Iran's enrichment sites, has reported any sign of an Iranian nuclear weapons program for the past decade. Despite the absence of any evidence of an Iranian nuclear weapons program, the crazed Israeli government and its neoconservative agents, who represent Israel's interests, not America's, have almost driven the US to war with Iran over nuclear weapons as non-existent as Saddam Hussein's weapons of mass destruction.

The nuclear energy agreement that has been reached eliminates any possibility of Iran diverting enriched uranium to a weapons program. Nevertheless Washington warmongers and the Israel Lobby are attempting to block the agreement with the argument that "Iran's leaders cannot be trusted."

The real question, however, is on what basis can Iran possibly trust Washington?

Iran should ask former Soviet president Gorbachev what Washington's word is worth. In exchange for Gorbachev's agreement to the reunification of Germany, Washington promised Gorbachev that NATO would not move one inch to the East and promptly took NATO to Russia's border and is now working to incorporate former parts of the Russian empire into NATO.

Iran should ask current Russian president Putin what Washington's word is worth. Sensing Russian strategic weakness, the George W. Bush regime broke the Anti-Ballistic Missile Treaty that Washington had signed with Moscow. Pulling out of the treaty, Washington announced anti-ballistic missile bases on Russia's borders, hoping to degrade Russia's strategic missile forces that serve as a guardian against Washington's pre-emptive first strike, a policy now permissible under Washington's revised war doctrine.

Iran should ask Germany, which was coerced into the Versailles Treaty in violation of every promise President Woodrow Wilson made to Germany in exchange for ending World War I. The extensive loss of Germany territory and crippling reparations greedily and thoughtlessly imposed on Germany, whose government most certainly did not start the war, led directly to World War II, also blamed on Germany despite the fact that the war began with Britain's and France's declaration of war on Germany.

Iran should ask the American Indians—the Iroquois, the Cherokee, the Sioux, Cheyenne, Comanche, the Nez Perce, and every other indigenous American people how many treaties Washington kept. In case you don't know the answer, it is zero. Washington did *not keep a single treaty* it made with Indian tribes. To fully comprehend the total worthlessness of Washington's word, read Ralph K. Andrist's book, *The Long Death: The Last Days of the Plains Indian*. No one who reads this book would sign any agreement with Washington.

An agreement with Washington is a prelude to treachery. It puts the signer at ease while Washington prepares the signer's doom. This is the way Washington operates.

Washington is now in the process of going back on the Medicare and Social Security promises Washington made to the American people. Washington has "borrowed" the earmarked payroll taxes that finance these programs, putting in their place non-marketable, and thereby worthless, IOUs and spending the money on its wars and handouts to the elites who don't need Medicare or Social Security. As Washington has robbed Social Security and Medicare of its earmarked revenues, Washington has begun the process of abolishing health and old age security for the American population. The world has never experienced robber capitalism as unleashed as it is today.

Washington already has put in place age limits on forms of health care, and Washington has robbed retirees of their cost-of-living adjustments by concocting a fraudulent measure of the consumer price index. Washington's goal is to privatize the programs, thus producing profits for its financial supporters and prohibitive costs for the elderly, disposable people whom Washington is throwing away.

No one can trust Washington. Least of all the American people.

Throughout history Washington has proven conclusively that its word is not worth the paper it is written on.

Everyone who ever trusted Washington has been betrayed. Possibly there is an exception somewhere, but the betrayals are vast and are sufficient in number to define Washington as the least trusted entity on earth. No extant entity has broken more agreements than Washington.

Iran should put no trust in an agreement with a government that has never kept its word.

Moreover, in order to get the agreement, Iran had to give up many of its rights that are granted to Iran by the Non-Proliferation Treaty. Alone among the signatories, Iran is discriminated against. Iran had to agree to this humiliation in order to avoid military attack and in order to have economic sanctions removed.

The real importance of the nuclear energy agreement is that Washington was able successfully to use coercion to force Iran to forego its treaty rights in order to avoid military and economic assault.

In other words, the agreement is yet another example of the world accepting Washington's use of force to require sovereign countries to give up their rights. Washington's hegemony has again prevailed.

Judging from the real outcome, the Iran nuclear energy agreement is another defeat for mankind.

WILL WASHINGTON KILL US ALL?

April 15, 2015

Did you know that Washington keeps 450 nuclear ICBMs on "hair-trigger alert"? Washington thinks that this makes us "safe." The reasoning, if it can be called reason, is that by being able to launch in a few minutes, no one will try to attack the US with nuclear weapons. US missiles are able to get on their way before the enemy's missiles can reach the US to destroy ours.

If this makes you feel safe, you need to read Eric Schlosser's book, *Command and Control*. The trouble with hair-triggers is that they make mistaken, accidental, and unauthorized launch more likely. Schlosser provides a history of almost launches that would have brought Armageddon to the world.

In *Catalyst*, a publication of the Union of Concerned Scientists, Elliott Negin tells the story of Soviet Lt. Col. Stanislav Petrov. Just after midnight in 1983 the Soviet Union's early warning satellite system set off the alarm that 5 US ICBMs were headed for the Soviet Union.

Col. Petrov was supposed to inform the Soviet leader, who would have 8 to 10 minutes to decide whether to launch in retaliation. Who knows what he would have decided. Instead Col. Petrov used his judgment. There was no reason for the US to be attacking the Soviet Union. Moreover, Petrov reasoned that an American attack would involve hundreds of ICBMs, possibly thousands.

He checked whether Soviet ground-based radar had detected incoming ICBMs, and it had not.

Petrov decided it was a false alarm, and sat on it.

It turned out that the early warning system had mistaken a pattern of sunlight reflection on clouds as missiles. This was a close call, but Negin reports that "a failed computer chip, and an improperly installed circuit card are some of the culprits" that could initiate nuclear war. In other words, the sources of false alarms are numerous.

Fast forward to today. Imagine an American officer monitoring the US early warning system.

This officer has been listening to 15 years of war propaganda accompanied by US invasions and bombings of 7 countries. Terrorist warnings and security alerts abound, as do calls from American and Israeli politicians for nuking Iran. The media has convinced him that Russia has invaded Ukraine and is on the verge of invading the Baltics and Poland. American troops and tanks have been rushed to the Russian border. There is talk of arming Ukraine. Putin is dangerous and is threatening nuclear war, running his strategic bombers close to our borders and holding nuclear drills. The American officer has just heard a Fox News general again call for "killing Russians." The Republicans have convinced him that Obama is selling out America to Iran, with Senator Tom Cotton warning of nuclear war as a consequence. We will all be killed because there is a Muslim in the White House.

Why isn't anyone standing up for America, the patriotic American officer wonders, just as the alarm goes off: Incoming ICBMs. Are they Russian or Iranian? Was Israel right after all? A hidden Iranian nuclear weapons program? Or has Putin decided that the US is in the way of his reconstruction of the Soviet Empire, which the American media affirms is Putin's goal? There is no room for judgment in the American officer's mind. It has been set on hair-trigger by the incessant propaganda that Americans call news. He passes on the warning.

Obama's Russophobic neocon National Security Advisor is screaming: "You can't let Putin get away with this!" "It might be a false alarm," replies the nervous and agitated president. "You liberal pussy! Don't you know that Putin is dangerous!? Push the button!"

And there goes the world.

Consider the extreme Russophobia being created among Americans by the Ministry of Propaganda, the demonization of Vladimir Putin—the "new Hitler," Vlad the Impaler—the propagandistic creation of "the Russian threat," the crazed neocon desire for US world hegemony, the hatred of Russia and China as rising rivals capable of exercising independent power, the loss of American Uni-power status and unconstrained unilateral action. In the midst of these emotions and minds swayed not by facts but by propaganda, hubris, and ideology, there is a great chance that Washington's response to a false alarm will bring the end of life on earth.

How much confidence do you have in Washington? How many times has Washington—especially the crazed neocons—been wrong?

Remember the 3-week "cakewalk" Iraq war that would cost $70 billion and be paid out of Iraqi oil revenues? Now the cost is $3,000 billion and rising, and after 12 years the radical Islamic State controls half of the country. To pay for the wars the Republicans want to "privatize," that is, take away, Social Security and Medicare.

Remember "Mission Accomplished" in Afghanistan? Twelve years later the Taliban again control the countryside and Washington, after murdering women, children, funerals, weddings, village elders, and kids' soccer games, has been driven out by a few thousand lightly armed Taliban.

The frustrations of these defeats have mounted in Washington and in the military. The myth is that we lost because we didn't use our full force. We were intimidated by world opinion or by those damn student protesters, or blocked from victory by some gutless president, a liberal pussy who wouldn't use all of our power. For the right-wing, rage is a way of life.

The neocons believe fervently that History has chosen America to rule the world, and here we are defeated by Vietnamese guerrillas, by Afghan tribesmen, by Islamist fundamentalists, and now Putin has sent his missiles to finish the job.

Whoever the White House fool is, he will push the button.

The situation is deteriorating, not improving. The Russians, hoping for some sign of intelligence in Europe, contradict Washington's anti-Russian lies. Washington calls truthful contradiction of its own propaganda to be Russian propaganda. Washington has ordered the Broadcasting Board of Governors, a US government agency, headed by Andrew Lack, a former chairman of NBC news, to counteract an alleged, but non-existent, "Kremlin Troll Army" that is outshouting the Western prostitutes and "perpetuating a pro-Russian dialogue" on the Internet. In case you don't remember, Lack is the idiot who declared RT to be a "terrorist organization." In other words, in Lack's opinion, one that he can enforce, a truth-teller is a terrorist.

Lack epitomizes well Washington's view of truthful reporting: If it doesn't serve Washington's propaganda, it is not true. It is terrorism.

Lack hopes to control RT with intimidation: In effect, he has told RT to shut up and say what we want or we will close you down as a terrorist organization. We might even arrest your American employees as aiders and abettors of terrorism.

To counteract a Revanchist Russia and its Internet Troll Army, the Obama regime is handing $15,400,000 to the insane Lack to use to discredit every truthful statement that emerges from the English language versions of Russian media. This amount, of course, will rise dramatically. Soon it will be in the billions of dollars, while Americans are evicted from their homes and sent to prison for their debts.

In his budget request, Lack, who seems to lack every aspect of humanity, including intelligence, integrity, and morality, justified his request, which will be granted, for the hard-earned money of Americans, whose standard of living is falling, with the wild assertion that Russia "threatens Russia's neighbors and, by extension, the United States and its Western allies."

Lack promises to do even more: "The US international media is now set forth to refute Russian propaganda and influence the minds of Russians and Russian-speakers in the former Soviet Union, Europe and around the world." Lack is going to propagandize against Russia inside Russia.

Of course, the National Endowment for Democracy and Radio Free Europe/Radio Liberty will be enriched by this anti-Russian propaganda campaign and will support it wholeheartedly.

Therefore, the Union of Concerned Scientists' call for cooperation with Russia to take ICBMs off hair-trigger status is unlikely to occur. How can nuclear tensions be reduced when Washington is building tensions as fast as it possibly can? Washington's Ministry of Propaganda has reconstructed Putin as Osama bin Laden, as Saddam Hussein, demonized figures, bogymen who evoke fear from the brainwashed American sheeple. Russia is transformed into al Qaeda lusting for another attack on the World Trade Center and for the Red Army (many Americans think Russia is still communist) to roll across Europe.

Gorbachev was a trick. He deceived the old movie actor. The deceived Americans are sitting ducks, and here come the ICBMs. The crazed views of the American politicians, military, and people are unable to comprehend truth or to recognize reality.

The propagandistic American "media" and the crazed neoconservatives have set humanity on the path to destruction.

The Union of Concerned Scientists, of which I am a member, need to come to their senses. It is impossible to work out a reduction in nuclear threat as long as one side is going all out to demonize the other. The demonization of Russia and its leader by *The New York Times*, *Washington Post*, CNN, Fox News, and the rest of the American Propaganda Ministry, by almost the entirety of the House and Senate, and by the White House makes reducing the threat of nuclear war impossible.

The American people and the entire world need to understand that the threat to life on earth resides in Washington and that until Washington is fundamentally and totally changed, this threat will remain as the worse threat to life on earth. Global Warming can disappear instantly in Nuclear Winter.

TRUTH IS WASHINGTON'S ENEMY

April 21, 2014

US Representative Ed Royce (R, CA) is busy at work destroying the possibility of truth being spoken in the US. On April 15 at a hearing before the House Committee on Foreign Affairs of which Royce is chairman, Royce made use of two minor presstitutes to help him redefine all who take exception to Washington's lies as "threats" who belong to a deranged pro-Russian propaganda cult.[147]

Washington's problem is that whereas Washington controls the print and TV media in the US and its vassal states in Europe, Canada, Australia, Ukraine, and Japan, Washington does not control Internet sites, such as this one, or media, such as RT, of non-vassal states. Consequently, Washington's lies are subject to challenge, and as people lose confidence in Western print and TV media because of the propaganda content, Washington's agendas, which depend on lies, are experiencing rougher sledding.

Truth is bubbling up through Washington's propaganda. Confronted with the possibility of a loss of control over every explanation, Hillary Clinton, Ed Royce, and the rest are suddenly complaining that Washington is "losing the information war." Huge sums of taxpayers' hard earned money will now be used to combat the truth with lies.

What to do? How to suppress truth with lies in order to remain in control? The answer says Andrew Lack, Royce, *et alia*, is to redefine a truth-teller as a terrorist. Thus, the comparison of RT and "dissident" Internet bloggers to the Islamic State and the designated terror group, Boko Haram.

Royce expanded the definition of truth-teller to include dissident bloggers, such as Chris Hedges, John Pilger, Glenn Greenwald and the rest of us, who object to the false reality that Washington creates in order to serve undeclared agendas. For example, if Washington wants to pour profits into the military/security complex in exchange for political campaign contributions, the politicians cannot say that. Instead, they claim to protect America from a dangerous enemy or from weapons of mass destruction by starting a war. If politicians want to advance American financial or energy imperialism, they have to do so in the name of "bringing freedom and democracy." If the politicians want to prevent the rise of other countries, such as Russia, President Obama has to depict Russia as a threat comparable to the Ebola virus and the Islamic State.

Noam Chomsky summed it up when he said that Washington regards any information that does not repeat Washington's propaganda to be intolerable.

Washington's assault on truth as a threat helps to make sense of the gigantic National Security Agency spy system exposed by William Binney and Edward Snowden. One of the purposes of the spy network is to identify all "dissidents" who challenge Big Brother's "Truth."

There is, or will be, a dossier on every "dissident" with all of the dissident's emails, Internet searches, websites visited, phone calls, purchases, travels. The vast amount of information on each dissident can be combed for whatever can be taken out of context to make a case against him or her, if a case is even needed. Washington has already successfully asserted its power over the Constitution to indefinitely detain without charges and to torture and to murder US citizens.

It was a couple of years ago that Janet Napolitano, head of Homeland Security, said that the department's focus had shifted from terrorists to domestic extremists. Lumped into the category of domestic extremists are environmental activists, animal rights activists, anti-war activists which includes disillusioned war veterans, and people who believe in states' rights, limited government and accountable government. Consequently, many dissidents, America's best citizens, will qualify as domestic extremists on several accounts. Chris Hedges, for example, is an advocate for animals[148] as well as concerned about the environment and Washington's never-ending wars.

The spying and the coming crackdown on "dissidents" might also explain the $385 million federal contract awarded to a subsidiary of Dick Cheney's firm, Halliburton, to build detention camps in the US. Few seem to be concerned with who the camps are to detain. There is no media or congressional investigation. It seems unlikely that the camps are for hurricane or forest fire evacuees. Concentration camps are usually for people regarded as unreliable. And as Lack, Royce, et alia, have made clear, unreliable people are those who do not support Washington's lies.

A perceived need by Washington, and the private power structure that Washington serves, to protect themselves from truth could also be the reason for the very strange military exercises in various of the states to infiltrate, occupy, and round-up "threats" among the civilian population.[149] Even the presstitute CNN reported that the National Guard troops sent to Ferguson, Missouri, were programmed to view the civilian protesters as "enemy forces" and "adversaries," and we know that the state and local militarized police are trained to view US citizens as threats.

As far as I can discern, not many Americans, whether Democrat or Republican, liberal, conservative, or super-patriot, educated or not, understand that Washington with the cooperation of its presstitute media *has defined truth as a threat.* In Washington's opinion, truth is a greater threat than Ebola, Russia, China, terrorism, and the Islamic State combined.

A government that cannot survive truth and must resort to stamping out truth is not a government that any country wants. But such an undesirable government is the government that Clinton-Bush-Cheney-Obama-Hillary-Lack-Royce have given us.

Does it satisfy you? Are you content that in your name and with taxes on your hard-earned and increasingly scarce earnings, Washington in the 21st century has murdered, maimed, and displaced millions of peoples in eight countries, has set America on the path to war with Russia and China, and has declared truth to be an enemy of the state?

THE CHOICE
BEFORE EUROPE

May 5, 2015

Washington continues to drive Europe toward one or the other of the two most likely outcomes of the orchestrated conflict with Russia. Either Europe or some European Union member government will break from Washington over the issue of Russian sanctions, thereby forcing the EU off of the path of conflict with Russia, or Europe will be pushed into military conflict with Russia.

In June the Russian sanctions expire unless each member government of the EU votes to continue the sanctions. Several governments have spoken against a continuation. For example, the governments of the Czech Republic and Greece have expressed dissatisfaction with the sanctions.

US Secretary of State John Kerry acknowledged growing opposition to the sanctions among some European governments.

Employing the three tools of US foreign policy—threats, bribery, and coercion—he warned Europe to renew the sanctions or there would be retribution. We will see in June if Washington's threat has quelled the rebellion.

Europe has to consider the strength of Washington's threat of retribution against the cost of a continuing and worsening conflict with Russia. This conflict is not in Europe's economic or political interest, and the conflict has the risk of breaking out into war that would destroy Europe.

Since the end of World War II Europeans have been accustomed to following Washington's lead. For awhile France went her own way, and there were some political parties in Germany and Italy that considered Washington to be as much of a threat to European independence as the Soviet Union. Over time, using money and false flag operations, such as Operation Gladio, Washington marginalized politicians and political parties that did not follow Washington's lead.

The specter of a military conflict with Russia that Washington is creating could erode Washington's hold over Europe. By hyping a "Russian threat," Washington is hoping to keep Europe under Washington's protective wing. However, the "threat" is being over-hyped to the point that some Europeans have understood that Europe is being driven down a path toward war.

Belligerent talk from the Chairman of the Joint Chiefs of Staff, from John McCain, from the neoconservatives, and from NATO commander Philip Breedlove is unnerving Europeans. In a recent love-fest between Breedlove and the Senate Armed Services Committee, chaired by John McCain, Breedlove supported arming the Ukrainian military, the backbone of which appears to be the Nazi militias, with heavy US weapons in order to change "the decision calculus on the ground" and bring an end to the break-away republics that oppose Washington's puppet government in Kiev.

Breedlove told the Senate committee that his forces were insufficient to withstand Russian aggression and that he needed more forces on Russia's borders in order to "reassure allies."

Europeans have to decide whether the threat is Russia or Washington. The European press, which Udo Ulfkotte reports in his book, *Bought Journalists*, consists of CIA assets, has been working hard to convince Europeans that there is a "revanchist Russia" on the prowl that seeks to recover the Soviet Empire.

Washington's coup in Ukraine has disappeared. In its place Washington has substituted a "Russian invasion," hyped as Putin's first step in restoring the Soviet empire.

Just as there is no evidence of the Russian military in Ukraine, there is no evidence of Russian forces threatening Europe or any discussion or advocacy of restoring the Soviet empire among Russian political and military leaders.

In contrast Washington has the Wolfowitz Doctrine, which is explicitly directed at Russia, and now the Council on Foreign Relations has added China as a target of the Wolfowitz doctrine.[150]

The CFR report says that China is a rising power and thereby a threat to US world hegemony. China's rise must be contained so that Washington can remain the boss in the Asian Pacific. What it comes down to is this: China is a threat because China will not prevent its own rise. This makes China a threat to "the International Order." "The International Order," of course, is the order determined by Washington. In other words, just as there must be no Russian sphere of influence, there must be no Chinese sphere of influence. The CFR report calls this keeping the world "free of hegemonic control" except by the US.

Just as General Breedlove demands more military spending in order to counter "the Russian threat," the CFR wants more military spending in order to counter "the Chinese threat." The report concludes: "Congress should remove sequestration caps and substantially increase the U.S. defense budget."

Clearly, Washington has no intention of moderating its position as the sole imperial power. In defense of this power, Washington will take the world to nuclear war. Europe can prevent this war by asserting its independence and departing the empire.

the New World Have Threat to World Order

Clearly, Washington has no intention of moderating its position as the sole superpower. In defiance of this power, Washington will take the world to nuclear war. Europe can prevent this war by asserting its independence and departing the...

A PRESCRIPTION FOR PEACE AND PROSPERITY

Trends Journal, **Spring 2015**

The question is often asked: "What can we do?" Here is a prescription for peace and prosperity.

We will begin with prosperity, because prosperity can contribute to peace. Sometimes governments begin wars in order to distract from unpromising economic prospects, and internal political stability can also be dependent on prosperity.

The Road to Prosperity

For the United States to return to a prosperous road, the middle class must be restored and the ladders of upward mobility put back in place. The middle class served domestic political stability by being a buffer between rich and poor. Ladders of upward mobility are a relief valve that permit determined folk to rise from poverty to success. Rising incomes throughout society provide the consumer demand that drives an economy.

When it worked, this is the way the US economy worked in the post-WWII period.

To reestablish the middle class the off-shored jobs have to be brought home, monopolies broken up, regulation restored, and the central bank put under accountable control or abolished.

Jobs off-shoring enriched owners and managers of capital at the expense of the middle class. Well paid manufacturing and industrial workers lost their livelihoods as did university graduates trained for tradable professional service jobs such as software engineering and information technology. No comparable wages and salaries could be found in the economy where the remaining jobs consist of domestic service employment, such as retail clerks, hospital orderlies, waitresses and bartenders. The current income loss is compounded by the loss of medical benefits and private pensions that supplemented Social Security retirement. Thus, jobs off-shoring reduced both current and future consumer income.

America's middle class jobs can be brought home by changing the way corporations are taxed. Corporate income could be taxed on the basis of whether corporations add value to their product sold in US markets domestically or offshore. Domestic production would have a lower tax rate. Off-shored production would be taxed at a higher rate. The tax rate could be set to cancel out the cost savings of producing offshore.

Under long-term attack by free market economists, the Sherman Antitrust Act has become a dead-letter law. Free market economists argue that markets are self-correcting and that anti-monopoly legislation is unnecessary and serves mainly to protect inefficiency. No doubt that a law passed in 1890 needs to be updated and aligned with today's conditions. A large array of traditionally small business activities have been monopolized by franchises and "big box" stores. Family owned auto parts stores, hardware stores, restaurants, men's clothing stores, and dress shops, have been crowded out by franchises and "big box" stores. Walmart's destructive impact on Main Street businesses is legendary. National corporations have pushed local businesses into the trash bin.

Monopoly has more than economic effect. When six mega-media companies have control of 90 percent of the American media, a dispersed and independent press no longer exists. Yet, democracy itself relies on media helping to hold government to account. The purpose of the First Amendment is to control the government, but today media serves as a propaganda ministry for government.

Americans received better and less expensive communication services when AT&T was a regulated monopoly. Free trade in communications has resulted in the creation of many unregulated local monopolies with poor service and high charges. AT&T's stability made the stock a "blue-chip" ideal for "widow and orphan" trust funds, pensions, and wealth preservation. No such risk free stock exists today.

Monopoly was given a huge boost by financial deregulation. Federal Reserve chairman Alan Greenspan's claim that "markets are self-regulating" and that government regulation is harmful was blown to pieces by the financial crisis of 2007-2008.

Deregulation not only allowed banks to escape from prudent behavior but also allowed such concentration that America now has "banks too big to fail." One of capitalism's virtues and justifications is that inefficient enterprises fail and go out of business.

Instead, we have banks that must be kept afloat with public or Federal Reserve subsidies. Clearly, one result of financial deregulation has been to protect the large banks from the operation of capitalism. The irony that freeing banks from regulation resulted in the destruction of capitalism is lost on free market economists.

The cost of the Federal Reserve's support for the banks too big to fail with zero and negative real interest rates has been devastating for savers and retirees. Americans have received no interest on their savings for 6.5 years. To make ends meet, they have had to consume their savings. Moreover, the Federal Reserve's policy has artificially driven up the stock market with the liquidity that the Federal Reserve has created and also caused a similar bubble in the bond market. The high prices of bonds are inconsistent with the buildup in debt and the money printed in order to keep the debt afloat. The dollar's value itself depends on quantitative easing in Japan and the EU.

In order to restore financial stability, an obvious precondition for prosperity, the large banks must be broken up and the distinction between investment and commercial banks restored.

Since the Clinton regime, the majority of the Treasury secretaries have been top executives of the troubled large banks, and they have used their public position to benefit their banks and not the US economy. Additionally, executives of the large banks comprise the board of the New York Fed, the principal operating arm of the Federal Reserve. Consequently, a few large banks control US financial policy. This conspiracy must be broken up and the Federal Reserve made accountable or abolished.

This requires getting money out of politics. The ability of a few powerful private interest groups to control election outcomes with their campaign contributions is anathema to democracy. A year ago the Republican Supreme Court ruled that the rich have a constitutional right to purchase the government with political campaign contributions in order to serve their selfish interests.

These are the same Republican justices who apparently see no constitutional right to habeas corpus and, thus, have not prohibited indefinite detention of US citizens. These are the same Republican justices who apparently see no constitutional prohibition against self-incrimination and, thus, have tolerated torture.

These are the same Republican justices who have abandoned due process and permit the US government to assassinate US citizens.

To remove the control of money over political life would likely require a revolution.

Unless prosperity is to be only for the One Percent, the Supreme Court's assault on democracy must be overturned.

The Road to Peace is Difficult

To regain peace is even more difficult than to regain prosperity. As prosperity can be a precondition for peace, peace requires both changes in the economy and in foreign policy.

To regain peace is especially challenging, not because Americans are threatened by Muslim terrorists, domestic extremists, and Russians. These "threats" are hoaxes orchestrated in behalf of special interests. "Security threats" provide more profit and more power for the military/security complex.

The fabricated "war on terror" has been underway for 14 years and has succeeded in creating even more "terror" that must be combated with enormous expenditures of money. Apparently, Republicans intend that monies paid in Social Security and Medicare payroll taxes be redirected to the military/security complex.

The promised three-week "cakewalk" in Iraq has become a 14 year defeat with the radical Islamic State controlling half of Iraq and Syria. Islamist resistance to Western domination has spread into Africa and Yemen, and Saudi Arabia, Jordan, and the oil emirates are ripe fruit ready to fall.

Having let the genie out of the bottle in the Middle East, Washington has turned to conflict with Russia and by extension to China. This is a big bite for a government that has not been able to defeat the Taliban in Afghanistan after 14 years.

Russia is not a country accustomed to defeat. Moreover, Russia has massive nuclear forces and massive territory into which to absorb any US/NATO invasion. Picking a fight with a well-armed country with by far the largest land mass of any country shows a lack of elementary strategic sense. But that is what Washington is doing.

Washington is picking a fight with Russia, because Washington is committed to the neoconservative doctrine that History has chosen Washington to exercise hegemony over the world. The US is the "exceptional and indispensable" country, the Uni-power chosen to impose Washington's will on the world.

This ideology governs US foreign policy and requires war in its defense. In the 1990s Paul Wolfowitz enshrined the Wolfowitz Doctrine into US military and foreign policy. In its most bold form, the Doctrine states:

> Our first objective is to prevent the re-emergence of a new rival, either on the territory of the former Soviet Union or elsewhere, that poses a threat on the order of that posed formerly by the Soviet Union. This is a dominant consideration underlying the new regional defense strategy and requires that we endeavor to prevent any hostile power from dominating a region whose resources would, under consolidated control, be sufficient to generate global power.

As a former member of the original Cold War Committee on the Present Danger, I can explain what these words mean. The "threat posed formerly by the Soviet Union" was the ability of the Soviet Union to block unilateral US action in some parts of the world.

The Soviet Union was a constraint on US unilateral action, not everywhere but in some places. This constraint on Washington's will is regarded as a threat.

A "hostile power" is a country with an independent foreign policy, such as the BRICS (Brazil, Russia, India, China, and South Africa) have proclaimed. Iran, Bolivia, Ecuador, Venezuela, Argentina, Cuba, and North Korea have also proclaimed an independent foreign policy.

This is too much independence for Washington to stomach. As Russian President Vladimir Putin recently stated, "Washington doesn't want partners. Washington wants vassals."

The Wolfowitz doctrine requires Washington to dispense with governments that do not acquiesce to Washington's will. It is a *"first objective."*

The collapse of the Soviet Union resulted in Boris Yeltsin becoming president of a dismembered Russia. Yeltsin was a compliant US puppet. Washington became accustomed to its new vassal and absorbed itself in its Middle Eastern wars, expecting Vladimir Putin to continue Russia's vassalage.

However at the 43rd Munich Conference on Security Policy, Putin said: "I consider that the unipolar model is not only unacceptable but also impossible in today's world."

Putin went on to say: "We are seeing a greater and greater disdain for the basic principles of international law. And independent legal norms are, as a matter of fact, coming increasingly closer to one state's legal system. One state and, of course, first and foremost the United States, has overstepped its national borders in every way. This is visible in the economic, political, cultural and educational policies it imposes on other nations. Well, who likes this? Who is happy about this?"

When Putin issued this fundamental challenge to US Uni-power, Washington was preoccupied with its lack of success with its invasions of Afghanistan and Iraq. Mission was not accomplished.

By 2014 it had entered the thick skulls of our rulers in Washington that while Washington was blowing up weddings, funerals, village elders, and children's soccer games in the Middle East, Russia had achieved independence from Washington's control and presented itself as a formidable challenge to Washington's Uni-power. Putin and Russia have had enough of Washington's arrogance.

The unmistakable rise of Russia refocused Washington from the

Middle East to Russia's vulnerabilities. Ukraine, long a constituent part of Russia and subsequently the Soviet Union, was split off from Russia in the wake of the Soviet collapse by Washington's maneuvering. In 2004 Washington had tried to capture Ukraine in the Orange Revolution, which failed to deliver Ukraine into Washington's hands.

Consequently, according to Assistant Secretary of State Victoria Nuland, Washington spent $5 billion over the following decade developing NGOs that could be called into the streets of Kiev and in developing political leaders who represented Washington's interests.

Washington launched its coup in February 2014 with orchestrated "demonstrations" that with the addition of violence resulted in the overthrow and flight of the elected democratic government of Victor Yanukovych. In other words, Washington destroyed democracy in a new country with a coup before democracy could take root.

Ukrainian democracy meant nothing to Washington intent on seizing Ukraine in order to present Russia with a security problem and also to justify sanctions against "Russian aggression" in order to break up Russia's growing economic and political relationships with Europe.

Having launched on this reckless and irresponsible attack on a nuclear power, can Washington eat crow and back off? Would the neoconservative-controlled mass media permit that? The Russian government, backed 89% by the Russian people, have made it clear that Russia rejects vassalage status as the price of being part of the West. The implication of the Wolfowitz Doctrine is that Russia must be destroyed.

This implies our own destruction.

What can be done to restore peace? Obviously, the EU must abandon NATO and declare that Washington is a greater threat than Russia. Without NATO Washington has no cover for its aggression and no military bases with which to surround Russia.

It is Washington, not Russia, that has an ideology of "uber alles." Obama endorsed the neoconservative claim that "America is the exceptional country." Putin has made no such claim for Russia. Putin's response to Obama's claim is that "God created us equal."

In order to restore peace, the neoconservatives must be removed from foreign policy positions in the government and media. This means that Victoria Nuland must be removed as Assistant Secretary of State, that Susan Rice must be removed as National Security Adviser, that Samantha Power must be removed as US UN ambassador.

The warmonger neoconservatives must be removed from Fox 'News,' CNN, *The New York Times*, *Washington Post*, and *Wall Street Journal*, and in their places independent voices must replace propagandists for war.

Clearly, none of this is going to happen, but it must if we are to escape Armageddon.

The prescription for peace and prosperity is sound. The question is: Can we implement it?

PENTAGON
BEATS THE
DRUMS OF WAR

July 10, 2015

The fabrication of "the Russian security threat" has moved into high gear. At his confirmation hearing on July 9 as the nominee as Chairman of the Joint Chiefs of Staff, General Joseph Dunford told the US Senate that Russia presents an "alarming" threat to US national security. The previous day Air Force Secretary Deborah James declared "Russia to be the biggest threat."

The "alarming" and "worrisome" Russian behavior evoked by these two representatives of the military-security complex is part of the hoax created in order to keep the massive US military/security complex funded. To support the armaments corporations that supply political campaign donations and high-paying jobs for retired generals and pentagon officials as consultants and lobbyists, Washington needs a foe more powerful than a few Muslim terrorists.

The fact that "the Russian threat" is a hoax does not mean that a real threat is not present. Washington's demonization of Russia is so intense and so outrageous in its audacious lies that the groundwork is being laid for a military confrontation. General Dunford and Secretary James might be directing their rhetoric at the 24 NATO countries that have not met Washington's call to increase their arms purchases to 2% of GDP, but the irresponsible accusations have destroyed trust among the largest nuclear-armed powers. Today neither the Russian nor Chinese governments trust Washington. Indeed, by words and deeds Washington has forced Russia and China to build up their strategic forces in expectation of an American attack.

The situation is more dangerous than the risks associated with marketing a "threat" in order to fund the military-security complex. The neoconservatives have convinced the politicians and the military that countries with independent foreign policies are threats because of their sovereignty. The just-released "National Military Strategy of the United States of America 2015"[151] defines countries that have independent foreign policies as "revisionist states" that fail to act "in accordance with international norms." International norms are decided by Washington. A failure to act in accordance with international norms means to act independently of Washington's will. Countries who act this way are defined as national security threats. The Pentagon's report defines the foremost threats as Russia, China, Iran, and North Korea.

Russia is particularly singled out. Washington's view toward Russia is the same as Cato the Elder's view toward Carthage. Cato the Elder finished his every speech on any subject in the Roman Senate with the statement: "Carthage must be destroyed." Carthage was a check on Roman unilateralism just as Russia is a check on Washington's unilateralism.

The Pentagon report tells us that unless Russia becomes compliant with US hegemony and becomes a vassal like Europe, Canada, Australia, and Japan, war with Russia is our future.

By resurrecting distrust leading to conflict between nuclear powers, neoconservatives with their ideology of American supremacy have become the greatest threat to world order and to life itself.

ENDNOTES

1. http://www.informationclearinghouse.info/ article37599.htm
2. http://www.globalresearch.ca/are-the-iranian-protests-another-us-orchestrated-color-revolution/14040
3. http://www.informationclearinghouse.info/article37635.htm
4. See for example: http://www.huffingtonpost. com/2014/02/12/us-press-freedom-index-2014_n_4773101.html
5. http:// www.informationclearinghouse.info/article37599.htm
6. http://www.usatoday.com/ story/news/world/2014/02/16/ukraine-government-protests/5435315/
7. http://www.aljazeera.com/news/europe/2014/02/eu-report-corruption-wid espread-bloc-20142313322401478.html
8. http://data.worldbank.org/country/ukraine
9. http://www.sott.net/article/273602- US-Assistant-Secretaryof-State-Victoria-Nuland-says-Washington-has-spent-5-billion-trying-to-subvert-Ukraine
10. http://www.rt.com/news/ukraine-kiev-firearms-weaponspolice-934 /
11. http://www.informationclearinghouse.info/article37700.htm
12. Sources:
    http://rt.com/news/ukraine-right-sector-militants-210/
    http://rt.com/news/war-monument-toppled-ukraine-351/
    http://rt.com/news/ukraine-acting-president-yanukovich-339/
    http://rt.com/news/ukraine-opposition-yanukovich-coup-273/
    http://www.themoscowtimes.com/news/article/russia-pledges-to-fight-for-crimea-if-ukraine-splits/
    495034.html
    http://www.bbc.co.uk/news/world-europe-26312008
    http://www.channel4.com/news/kiev-svoboda-far-right-protests-right-sector-riot-police
    Russian General: "We Are At War": http://www.globalresearch.ca/russian-general-we-are-at-war/5370348
    February 24 statements by the Russian Foreign Ministry: http://rt.com/news/russia-ukraine-dictatorial-terror-486/
    Russian response to Susan Rice: http://rt.com/news/russia-usa-rice-advice-450
13. http://www.youtube.com/ watch?v=Jg8h526sB7w&feature=youtu.be
14. http://www.informationclearinghouse.info/ article37752.htm
15. http://rt.com/news/radicalopposition-intimidating-techniques-882/
16. http://www.youtube.com/ watch?v=MSxaa-67yGM&feature=player_embedded
17. http://rt.com/news/putin-drill-combat-army-864/
18. http://www.kommersant.ua/doc/2424454
19. http://www.informationclearinghouse.info/article37889.htm
20. http://rt.com/op-edge/ukraine-west-international-law-966/
21. http://www.globalresearch.ca/ukraine-us-launches-a-fascist-government-and-world-war-three/5372945
22. http://www.globalresearch.ca/whos-who-in-ukraines-new-semi-fascist-government-meet-thepeople-the-u-s-and-eu-are-supporting/5372422
23. http://www.whitehouse.gov/the-press-office/2014/03/06/executive-order-blocking-

property-certain-persons-contributing-situation
24. http://www.bbc.com/news/ world-europe-26606097
25. http://rt.com/news/tymoshenko-calls-destroy-russia-917/
26. http://rt.com/news/pro-russian-picket-ukraine-397/
27. http://on.rt.com/sbzj4o
28. http://news.antiwar.com/2014/03/26/obama-wants-more-nato-troops-in-eastern-europe/
29. http://news.antiwar.com/2014/03/26/us-presses-eu-nations-to-hike-military-spending-to-confront-russia/
30. Barnes, pp. 691-692
31. http://www.globalresearch.ca/regime-change-in-ukraine-and-the-imfs-bitter-economic-medicine/5374877
32. http:// rt.com/news/us-europensa-snowden-549/
33. http://www.zerohedge.com/news/2014-04-04/us-threatens-russia-sanctions-over-petrodollar-busting-deal
34. http://rt.com/news/lavrov-ukraine-nato-convention-069/
35. http://rt.com/news/eastern-ukraine-violence-threats-405/
36. http://www.truth-out.org/buzzflash/commentary/retiring-obama-administration-prosecutor-says-the-sec-is-corrupt/18585-retiring-obama-administration-prosecutor-says-the-sec-is-corrupt
37. http:// rt.com/news/cuba-usaid-senate-zunzuneo-241/
38. https://www.youtube.com/watch?v=gETF0_SOXcg
39. http://www.counterpunch.org/2014/04/09/65578/
40. http://rt.com/news/lavrov-kerry-ukraine-talks-200/ See also: http://www.information-clearinghouse. info/article38196.htm
41. http://rt.com/news/ukraine-russia-operation-criminal-288 /
42. http:// www.informationclearinghouse.info/article38202.htm
43. http://www.cnbc.com/id/101576080
44. http://www.informationclearinghouse.info/article38253.htm
45. http://www.informationclearinghouse.info/article38254.htm
46. http://www.usatoday.com/story/news/world/2014/04/17/jews-ordered-to-register-in-east-ukraine/7816951/ See also: http://rt.com/news/fake-news-ukraine-russia-364/
47. http://www.claritypress.com/LendmanIII.html
48. https://www.bostonglobe.com/news/politics/2014/05/20/david-barron-author-con-troversial-drone-memo-looks-likely-for-confirmation-appeals-court-democrats-say/sC0PW4fmoaN9qgaWWxHUTL/story.html
49. http://cnsnews.com/news/article/patrick-goodenough/and-country-posing-greatest-threat-peace-2013-ends
50. http://www.paulcraigroberts.org/2014/05/30/lethality-nuclearweapons/
51. http://www.globalresearch.ca/us-plans-first-strike-attack-on-russia-or-china/5384799
52. http://www.globalresearch.ca/70-years-ago-december-1941-turning-point-of-world-war-ii/28059
53. http://www.latimes.com/business/la-fi-oil-20140521-story.html
54. http://www.csun.edu/~vcmth00m/iraqkuwait.html
55. See among other sources: http://www.freerepublic.com/focus/f-news/1102395/posts
56. http://www.opednews.com/populum/printer_friendly.php?content=a&id=180039
57. https://www.foreignaffairs.com/articles/united-states/2006-03-01/rise-us-nuclear-primacy
58. http://www.paulcraigroberts.org/2014/05/30/lethality-nuclear-weapons/
59. http://climate.envsci.rutgers.edu/pdf/ToonRobockTurcoPhysicsToday.pdf
60. http://www.rt.com/news/166132-nuclear-weapons-report-obama/
61. https://www.youtube.com/watch?v=BfvMlyCnjDs If you are impatient, listen to the 7 minute marker to the 9:35 marker.
62. http://www.russianmission.eu/en/news/new-edition-white-book-human-rights-violations-ukraine

63. http://rt.com/news/173644-photos-plane-malaysia-crash/
64. http://rt.com/news/173672-malaysia-plane-crash-putin/
65. http://www.bloomberg.com/bw/articles/2014-07-17/the-malaysia-airlines-shootdown-spells-disaster-for-putin
66. http://www.globalresearch.ca/mh-17-crash-in-ukraine-official-statement-from-russian-defense-ministry/5392000
67. https://www.washingtonpost.com/world/national-security/malaysia-flight-17-prosecution-faces-major-evidentiary-and-legal-obstacles/2014/07/22/a8c7ebe4-11db-11e4-98ee-daea85133bc9_story.html
68. https://beta.congress.gov/113/bills/s2277/BILLS-113s2277is.pdf
69. http://www.globalresearch.ca/collapse-of-ukraine-government-prime-minister-yatsenyuk-resigns-amidst-pressures-exerted-by-the-imf/5393168
70. http://rt.com/news/175292-nato-poland-supplybase/
71. http://www.commondreams.org/news/2014/07/25/gen-dempsey-were-pulling-out-our-cold-war-military-plans-over-ukraine
72. http://rt.com/news/176120-fake-ukraine-images-defence/
73. http://www.paulcraigroberts.org/2014/07/27/another-state-department-hoax-paul-craig-roberts/
74. http://rt.com/news/176040-lavrov-russia-ukraine-plane
75. https://www.youtube.com/watch?v=NePChnsuMNs
76. See: http://www.thedailybeast.com/articles/2014/07/28/as-israel-enforces-its-buffer-zone-gaza-shrinks-by-40-per-cent.html, http://www.informationclearinghouse.info/article39255.htm, and http://news.antiwar.com/2014/07/28/senateleader-israel-may-need-more-us-aid-for-war/print/
77. http://rt.com/news/175852-gaza-ceasefire-deathtollthousand/
78. http://rt.com/news/175860-london-gaza-protest-march/
79. http://rt.com/uk/174920-david-ward-israel-tweet/
80. http://freebeacon.com/national-security/russian-strategic-bombers-conduct-more-than-16-incursions-of-u-s-air-defense-zones/
81. http://freebeacon.com/national-security/russian-strategic-bombersconduct-more-than-16-incursions-of-u-s-air-defense-zones/
82. http://financearmageddon.blogspot.co.uk/2014/07/official-warning-u-s-to-hit-russia-with.html
83. http://www.unz.com/article/the-ukraine-corrupted-journalism-and-the-atlanticist-faith/
84. http://www.atimes.com/atimes/Central_Asia/CEN-01-080814.html
85. http://www.unz.com/article/the-ukraine-corrupted-journalism-and-the-atlanticistfaith/
86. http://www.unz.com/runz/american-pravda-who-shot-down-flight-mh17-in-ukraine/
87. http:// www.globalresearch.ca/weve-opened-the-gates-of-hell-fukushima-spews-radiation-world-wide/5395912
88. http://rt.com/news/180268-putin-russia-mobilize-confrontation/
89. http://sputnikipogrom.com/europe/germany/18213/russian-appeal/
90. http://rt.com/news/180844-ukraine-recognizes-russia-humanitarian-aid/
91. http://vineyardsaker.blogspot.com/2014/08/watershed-press-conference-by-top.html
92. https://www.youtube.com/watch?v=yH35raTPVu8
93. http://www.informationclearinghouse.info/article39547.htm
94. V.I. Lenin, "A Contribution to the History of the Question of the Dictatorship," October 20, 1920, in *Collected Works*, 4th Russian edition, p. 326.
95. http://www.americanthinker.com/2014/08/how_to_solve_the_putin_problem.html
96. http://www.zerohedge.com/news/2014-09-01/ex-nsa-director-us-intelligence-veterans-write-open-letter-merkel-avoid-all-out-ukra
97. https://www.youtube.com/watch?v=-wSMhGE_Mpk
98. https://www.youtube.com/watch?v=3Zbv2SvBEec#t=23
99. http://www.washingtonsblog.com/2015/04/head-fbis-anthrax-investigation-calls-b-s.html

100.   See also: http://www.globalresearch.ca/no-airliner-black-boxes-found-at-the-world-trade-center-seniorofficials-dispute-official-911-claim/5400891

101.   http://slavyangrad.org/2014/09/12/we-will-not-allow-for-russia-to-be-ripped-asunder-and-ruined/

102.   http://vineyardsaker.blogspot.ca/2014/09/strelkov-from-swimming-with-piranhas-to.html

103.   http://slavyangrad.org/2014/09/13/the-new-round-of-sanctions-the-pre-war-period/#more-3665

104.   http://russia-insider.com/en/germany_politics_media_watch/2014/11/06/01-08-03pm/our_exclusive_interview_german_editor_turned_cia

105.   http://eng.news.kremlin.ru/news/23137

106.   http://fas.org/man/smedley.htm

107.   https://theintercept.com/2014/11/14/despite-cynicism-genuine-excitement-hillary-clinton-candidacy/

108.   http://wallstreetonparade.com/2014/10/hillary-clintons-continuity-government-versus-elizabeth-warrens-voice-for-change/

109.   http://news.antiwar.com/2014/12/11/cia-chief-slams-release-of-torture-report-summary/print/ and http://news.antiwar.com/2014/12/11/congress-passes-bill-to-sanction-venezuela/

110.   http://www.informationclearinghouse.info/article40428.htm

111.   http://www.informationclearinghouse.info/article40431.htm

112.   http://www.informationclearinghouse.info/article40435.htm

113.   http://www.informationclearinghouse.info/article40430.htm

114.   http://news.antiwar.com/2014/12/10/justice-dept-spurns-calls-to-prosecute-cia-torturers/

115.   http://www.informationclearinghouse.info/article40434.htm

116.   http://news.antiwar.com/2014/12/10/cia-torture-report-sparks-worldwide-condemnation/

117.   http://www.nytimes.com/interactive/2014/12/09/world/timeline-of-cias-secret-interrogation-program.html?_r=0

118.   http://news.antiwar.com/2014/12/10/former-polish-president-admits-to-cia-torture-site/

119.   http://www.freep.com/story/news/local/2014/12/10/levin-interrogation-cia-tapes-torture/20207577/

120.   http://rt.com/usa/213663-brennan-cia-torture-report/

121.   http://sputniknews.com/columnists/20141205/1015538604.html

122.   http://vineyardsaker.blogspot.ca/2014/12/vineyard-of-saker-white-paper-china.html

123.   See http://www.voltairenet.org/article186441.html and http://presstv.com/Detail/2015/01/10/392426/Planted-ID-card-exposes-Paris-false-flag

124.   https://www.intellihub.com/18-year-old-charlie-hebdo-suspect-surrenders-police-claims-alibi/

125.   http://reason.com/blog/2014/07/22/human-rights-watch-all-of-the-high-profi

126.   http://www.globalresearch.ca/four-in-ten-bostonians-skeptical-of-official-marathon-bombing-account/5390848

127.   https://www.intellihub.com/18-year-old-charlie-hebdo-suspect-surrenders-police-claims-alibi/

128.   See my weekend interview with King World News for my thoughts on this potential game-changer. http://kingworldnews.com/paul-craig-roberts-new-crisis-worse-russia-unleashing-black-swans-west/

129.   http://www.zerohedge.com/news/2015-01-16/largest-retail-fx-broker-stock-crashes-90-swiss-contagion-spreads

130.   http://www.zerohedge.com/news/2015-01-15/its-tsunami-swiss-franc-soars-most-ever-after-snb-abandons-eurchf-floor-macro-hedge-

131.   http://www.informationclearinghouse.info/article40797.htm

132.   http://www.manufacturingnews.com/news/2015/A.T.Kearny-No-Data-Supporting-

Reshoring-0112151.html
133. http://rt.com/usa/225819-rt-isis-point-view-competition/
134. See https://www.youtube.com/watch?v=wywwMEnUc40 and https://en.wikipedia.org/wiki/To_the_Youth_in_Europe_and_North_America
135. http://people.howstuffworks.com/5-united-states-debt-holders.htm#page=4
136. http://www.globalresearch.ca/putin-signs-undesirable-ngos-bill-into-law-on-the-grounds-of-russias-national-security/5451655
137. http://rt.com/news/231667-minsk-ceasefire-deal-breakup/
138. http://rt.com/news/231571-putin-minsk-ukraine-deal/
139. https://www.youtube.com/watch?v=Duu6IwW3sbw
140. http://www.foreignaffairs.com/articles/142840/alexander-j-motyl/goodbye-putin
141. http://www.paulcraigroberts.org/2015/02/24/washington-resurrected-threat-nuclear-war-paul-craig-roberts/
142. http://www.wsj.com/articles/putin-the-improviser-1424473405
143. http://thebulletin.org/what-would-happen-if-800-kiloton-nuclear-warhead-detonated-above-midtown-manhattan8023
144. http://www.paulcraigroberts.org/2014/07/08/deteriorating-economic-outlook/
145. http://www.globalresearch.ca/why-i-have-resigned-from-thetelegraph/5432659
146. http://russia-insider.com/en/2015/03/22/4790
147. http://www.prisonplanet.com/bloggers-compared-to-isis-during-congressional-hearing.html
148. http://www.opednews.com/articles/Choosing-Life-by-Chris-Hedges-Animals_Cattle_Corporate_Dairy-150420-878.html
149. http://www.zerohedge.com/news/2015-04-16/signs-elites-are-feverishly-preparing-something-big
150. http://carnegieendowment.org/files/Tellis_Blackwill.pdf
151. http://news.usni.org/2015/07/02/document-2015-u-s-national-military-strategy

INDEX